THE CAPE COLOUR QUESTION:

A HISTORICAL SURVEY

DR. JOHN PHILIP

THE
CAPE COLOUR QUESTION
A Historical Survey

By W. M. MACMILLAN

Sometime Associate Member of
All Souls College, Oxford
Professor of History at
The University of the Witwatersrand, Johannesburg

FOREWORD

by C. W. de Kiewiet

C. HURST & CO.
LONDON
HUMANITIES PRESS
NEW YORK

TO

JOHN MACMILLAN

MISSIONARY AND TEACHER

IN PIAM MEMORIAM

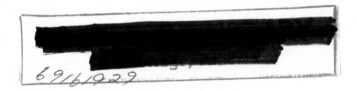

6 9/6/1929

FIRST PUBLISHED IN MCMXXVII
BY FABER & GWYER LIMITED
24 RUSSELL SQUARE LONDON W.C.1
MADE AND PRINTED IN GREAT BRITAIN
BY R. & R. CLARK LIMITED EDINBURGH
ALL RIGHTS RESERVED

Published in the United Kingdom by
C. Hurst & Co., 13 James Street, London, W.C.2
and in the United States of America by
Humanities Press Inc., 303 Park Avenue South,
New York, N.Y. 10010
PRINTED IN THE NETHERLANDS

FOREWORD

by C. W. de Kiewiet

Some books die almost in the act of their birth. Some flourish briefly, and then fall into a decline without issue or memorable consequence. From time to time a book appears which not merely endures in itself, but contains the fertile seed of other books and studies. Those which trace their ancestry back to the quiet appearance of the *Cape Colour Question* in 1927 are numerous.

Habent sua fata libelli-books have their own destined careers.

The *Cape Colour Question* was published forty-one years ago. The decision to republish it is far more than an antiquarian act. South Africa is making a very different effort to deal with the problem of the Cape Colour People than Professor Macmillan described or implicitly recommended in his book. For that single reason alone it is fitting to return to the pages of one who today is recognised as South Africa's first and still most thoughtful social historian.

The *Cape Colour Question* has the special qualities of an original historical document because it is the only book which draws fully on the Philip Papers, written by the only scholar who was able to study them completely and carefully before they were tragically destroyed by fire.

As Professor Macmillan's first serious publication the *Cape Colour Question* has three principal strengths. It was contemporary history in the best and most precise meaning of Benedetto Croce's famous phrase, which Professor Macmillan himself quotes in the book. It used and pioneered a methodology which was lacking in the writing of South African history up to that time. This methodology profoundly altered the writing of South African history, and indeed of much history with race relations as its theme. Finally it was prescient in a manner that not even the most favourable review in 1927 could have discerned or anticipated.

These three qualities grew and stood out more clearly in the studies that logically followed the *Cape Colour Question*. The very title *Bantu Boer and Briton*, and the order of its ethnic nouns, reveal Professor Macmillan moving from one part, one period,

v

one group, on to the whole of South African history, in all its parts, all its periods, and all its population. In *Complex South Africa* his ideas are more maturely expressed, also more bluntly and more ominously. It was here that he drew the clearest contemporary conclusions from the history of the Cape Colour People as he first began to understand it from his researches in documentary sources. Professor Macmillan's long subsequent residence outside South Africa must not obscure the fact that he wrote as a South African from within South Africa, and with a Scotsman's capacity for penetrating within the experience of Cape Colour People, of Bantu, Boer and Briton. He understood the themes of segregation and racial difference, of conflict and competition, but undertook to show that they should not mislead men into failing to recognise and to accept the fact that South Africa was the sum of all its peoples, of all their labour and would not finally prosper without all their co-operation.

The *Cape Colour Question* was the first major challenge of the ordering of priorities in the life and politics of South Africa. Exactly twenty-five years after the ending of the Boer War the attention of the country and of its government was still focussed upon the two white elements of the population. The phenomenon of the Poor Whites, in fact, painfully and dramatically reinforced the conviction that the issues that lay between Boer and Briton, and within the white population as a whole, were incontestably the first concern of the emerging nation. Professor Macmillan's position was not that these priorities were in themselves wrong, but that they were incomplete, their economics unconvincing, and their outcome profoundly to be feared. White South Africa should re-examine its fear of its non-white population, and especially re-examine its tendency to legislation based on ideas of difference and competition. He asked men to consider the record of the Cape Colour People.

The effort to keep them outside the bounds of the colony had not been successful. The indictment of vagrancy and shiftlessness had not prevented them from entering usefully into the economic life of the Cape Colony. The fear that their entry into the same legal and political community would endanger white civilisation had not been realised. These were lessons that a later generation should not ignore in dealing with similar problems, however greatly expanded and multiplied.

The voice of Professor Macmillan was heard in the land. General Smuts once twitted him on his views, saying that maybe a later generation would better understand his views and honour him. The twitting was also serious. In that most critical period between the two World Wars, South Africa's leaders left its priorities where they were.

Today Africanists are numbered in the thousands. They persuade the foundations to invest in cross fertilisation and interdisciplinary studies, and do so with all the enthusiasm of fresh discovery. Forty years ago Professor Macmillan, by himself, and at no cost to anybody, practised these virtues. He began, as an historian should, with the manuscript sources. He absorbed everything in the Philip collection of letters and documents till he had an archivist's familiarity with them. But then he infused into them a knowledge of anthropology and economics, well before pure historians had shed their doubts of these brash newer disciplines. He was his own geographer, travelling to the places whereof he spoke. He was his own statistician, collecting raw material, and making his own interpretations. He combated the typical South African conviction that its problems and its history were unique, and could only be understood by South Africans. He sought and found explanations of South African history in the rural economics of mediaeval Europe, in miscegenation in Latin America, and the enclosure movement of the English eighteenth century. Thus be undermined the narrow provincialism of his students and readers. Most emphatic was his insistence that the problems of South Africa were part of the problems of the African continent, and of the entire imperial and colonial world as it then still was.

To affirm that the *Cape Colour Question* and its literary successors were prescient could be met with a flat denial. In this very year of its reissue, the Cape Colour People are being ushered out of their legal and political community with the white population of the Cape. It was this community with men who had once been Hottentots, slaves and vagrants which Professor Macmillan regarded as the achievement of the nineteenth century, and the promise of the twentieth century. Instead of the greater Bantu population following, however laboriously and slowly, the destiny of the Cape Colour People, these have been thrust back again into a social, legal and political state which separates them from white and black alike. Professor Macmillan has had his wish fulfilled in one respect. There is no doubt today about the priority of problems of race and colour. But where Professor Macmillan envisaged a continuing search for compatibility and association, his proposed

vii

experiment has been replaced by an experiment based on difference and separateness.

His argument that statesmanship should co-operate with the processes of history that were weaving the races together has been contradicted. Yet his writing does not thereby forfeit its quality of prescience. When he was writing the *Cape Colour Question*, the advent of independence for Africa and Africans still seemed to lie beyond the horizon of the twentieth century, at a distance in time too great to cause anxiety in the minds of General Smuts, South Africans, Rhodesians and Kenyans. But surely his perspective on the timing and the rate of historical change was profoundly right. The *Cape Colour Question* has risen out of its obscurity to become the world Colour Question. It has thrust itself on the attention of the world at the highest levels. It has become the stuff of the most dangerous contention between great powers. The interpretation of the history of the centuries of colonisation and racial contact is no longer entirely in the hands of white men. The breaking of this monopoly will surely become one of the most important forces in shaping the politics and the diplomacy of international relations. Even the vast scholarship of American history is being recast by the insurgent American Negro. "Thought," once wrote Goethe, "is the thought of action and action is the action of thought." As the years pass it will become plainer that the advent of political independence which Professor Macmillan began to see in *Africa Emergent* was but the first incomplete step in a vast continuing readjustment in the former world of empires and colonies. Professor Macmillan was deeply worried about the isolation of South African thought and action. That there is still isolation in South African thought and action can hardly be denied. But there is a new isolation imposed on South Africa by much of the world. Of greater import, and not for South Africa alone, may be the growing trend of Africans and men of colour to make separatism their own weapon, and to seek to turn it against those from whom they learned it.

June, 1968.

Preface

IN South Africa, tradition, warped by sentiment, has been too strong for the spirit of History. The documentary evidence, moreover, has been only partially investigated. This book draws largely on a hitherto untapped source, the private papers of Dr. John Philip, the study of the documents being consistently checked by a parallel study of the present-day conditions which have developed out of historical circumstance.

The people of the Union, long disposed to ascribe their difficulties to uninformed 'interference' from outside, begin to find that even now, as masters of their own destiny, they are far from a 'solution' of their Colour Question. This book is the fruit of a conviction that a better understanding of the oldest phase of this question is an indispensable preliminary to any hopeful approach to the complex problems that remain. It does not seek to cover the whole field. It discusses part only of the story of the Philip papers, and does not attempt a complete account of Philip's own life and policy. Later, I hope to treat the origins and growth of the Bantu question; but the history of the Cape Coloured People comes first. In its fundamental principles, moreover, though not necessarily in details, the old Cape Colour Question is like a paradigm of the problem of contact that is now developing on the African Highlands, all along the backbone of the Continent, from the Union to Kenya. This African and World Race Problem, ever increasingly urgent in our day, is to be regarded as the culmination of centuries of development, and is not to be solved, in a flash, by passing Acts

ix

of Parliament, least of all by wild planning for the future, with an imperfect or erroneous understanding of the past.

The Coloured People of to-day, of all shades of colour, are very different from the aboriginal Hottentots. Very early the Hottentots mixed and blended with Negro and Malay elements, and they have acquired, above all, a strong dash of European blood. But too much stress must not be laid on the debt they owe to their white blood; there is evidence that, even in the eighteen-thirties, the so-called Hottentots, 'vagrant' and despised, had already become a mixed race, not very different in outward characteristics from the Coloured People of to-day. Their progress is therefore highly significant; and the conditions that produced this wholesale miscegenation give food for thought. Their history is, in fact, the story of how the descendants of the nomadic aborigines, a physically inferior stock, originally less well endowed than the Bantu, without even the rudiments of an agricultural tradition, have come to achieve a measure of civilisation deemed sufficient to entitle them to a full share in European privileges.

Yet the Bantu are dismissed by some as inherently 'inferior', and incapable of rising in the scale of civilisation; whereas the truth is that their best efforts are heavily weighted by the European land-hunger which has forced them into a position of economic dependence and impotence; at the same time, their rise, even now, is fast enough to inspire such panic legislation as the notorious 'Colour Bar' Act of 1926. In face of this, the history of the Cape suggests that in new Africa, as in old Europe, Freedom without compromise should be the touch-stone of policy. Those, for example, who advocate a mere vocational training, 'specially adapted to African needs', must not bar the way, even of the few, to true education. In like manner, plans for the 'separate development' of the Bantu— too often little more than an excuse for barring them from a share in the privileges of the dominant Europeans—cannot be forced upon them; for without freedom, the Bantu can have no true 'culture of their own'.

It remains to acknowledge many obligations : To Mr. A. D. Philip, who, at the suggestion of the Rev. G. P. Ferguson, entrusted me with the editing of his great-grandfather's papers; to Mr. J. W. Philip for the portrait of his grandfather, and for his helpful interest ; to the officials of the London Missionary Society for access to their Records, and especially to Mr. David Chamberlin for much and various help; to Mr. J. G. Gubbins, for the use of some MSS. and rare pamphlets; and to Professor G. E. Pearse and Mr. E. Tucker for the sketch map. Many senior students of the University of the Witwatersrand have helped me to sift the Philip MSS.; Miss L. S. Sutherland, M.A., now of Somerville College, and Miss Heather Moore, B.A., have helped me also by research in the Cape Town Archives, and Mr. C. W. de Kiewiet, M.A., by research both in Cape Town and at the Public Record Office. I have also to thank the Council of the University of the Witwatersrand for the leave of absence which made it possible to complete the book at this time.

Mr. Lionel Curtis was kind enough to spare time to read my first rough draft in MS., and his criticism was invaluable. To Professor E. A. Walker I owe several suggestions and corrections, as well as the privilege of consulting the proofs of his own *History of South Africa*. I should like also to acknowledge the free use I have made of Sir George Cory's researches, though sometimes I have been forced to differ from his conclusions. For proof-reading I am indebted to Dr. J. S. Marais and Miss M. L. Hodgson; also to Professor R. F. A. Hoernlé and to the Rev. C. F. Andrews, whose criticisms have been of great assistance.

Finally, I wish to thank the Warden and Fellows of All Souls for the great privilege of residence with them while completing the book. My wife has borne throughout the heaviest burden of all.

W. M. MACMILLAN.

ALL SOULS COLLEGE,
OXFORD, *January* 1927.

Contents

P A R T   I

The Setting of the Problem

P A R T   I I

From 'Hottentot' to 'Eurafrican'

Chapter XI

Chapter XII

Chapter XIII

Chapter XIV

Chapter XV

Chapter XVI

Chapter XVII

Chapter XVIII

Maps and Illustrations

Chronology

1819 Creation of neutral belt between Fish and Keiskamma Rivers; [*arrival of Dr. John Philip at the Cape*]

1820 ARRIVAL OF 5000 BRITISH SETTLERS IN ALBANY; Sir Rufane Donkin, Acting Governor

1821 Return of Lord Charles Somerset

1823 Arrival of Crown Commission of Inquiry

1824 Publication of the *Commercial Advertiser*, etc.

1825 Creation of Governor's Council of Advice

1826 General Bourke, Acting Governor

1827 Charter of Justice

1828 ORDINANCE 50; Sir Lowry Cole, Governor; Press freed from control of the Executive; Dr. Philip's *Researches in South Africa* (2 vols.)

1833 EMANCIPATION ACT; Colonel Wade, Acting Governor

1834 Sir B. D'Urban, Governor; Second Charter of Justice; Creation of nominated Legislative and official Executive Councils; Emancipation of Slaves at Cape: Sixth Kafir War (Dec.)

1836 Abandonment of 'Province of Queen Adelaide'; BEGINNING OF THE GREAT TREK; Ordinance permitting formation of Municipalities

1838 Sir George Napier, Governor; foundation of Republic of Natal by Emigrants

1842 Masters and Servants Ordinance, replacing Ordinance 50

1843 Natal proclaimed British Territory; Treaties with Adam Kok (Griqua) and Moshesh (Basuto)

1844 Sir Peregrine Maitland, Governor

1846 Seventh Kafir War

1847 Sir H. Pottinger, Governor, followed in Dec. by Sir H. Smith; Annexation of British Kaffraria

1848 British Sovereignty proclaimed over Orange River Territory

1848–9 Anti-Convict Agitation

1850 Eighth Kafir War (Dec.)

1851 Hottentot 'Rebellion'; [*Dr. Philip died*]

1852   Recognition of independence of Transvaal by Sand River Convention; Sir George Cathcart, Governor; end of Eighth Kafir War

1853   PROMULGATION OF CAPE CONSTITUTION

1854   Sir George Grey, Governor; Meeting of first Cape Parliament; Bloemfontein Convention and abandonment of Orange River Sovereignty

1872   'Responsible' Government

1873   Missionary Institutions Act

1910   UNION OF SOUTH AFRICA

1913   Natives' Land Act (restricting Bantu land-ownership)

1926   Mines and Works Amendment ('Colour Bar') Act

Some Abbreviations and References

'Cory': 'The Rise of South Africa', four volumes, by Sir George E. Cory, Longmans.

'Theal': 'The History of South Africa after 1795', five volumes, by Dr. Geo. McCall Theal.

'Theal's Records': 'Records of Cape Colony', 35 volumes, edited by Dr. Geo. McCall Theal.

Eybers' Documents: (illustrating South African Constitutional History), Routledge.

'Bird's Annals of Natal', two volumes (Pietermaritzburg).

Statements in the text of the book on modern Bantu and 'Poor White' questions are based on the author's published pamphlets and papers, viz.:

'The South African Agrarian Problem' (Johannesburg), 1919.

'The Land, the Native, and Unemployment' (Johannesburg), 1924.

Ten Articles on the Roots of the Native Question, *The Cape Times*, 12th April 1926, and days following.

Part I

THE SETTING OF THE PROBLEM

. . . truth, whose mother is history, the rival of time, the depository of great actions, the witness of what is past, the example and instruction to the present, and monitor to the future.

CERVANTES.

Chapter I

INTRODUCTORY

IN the learned world the equanimity of scientific historians
has latterly been disturbed. For a generation the critical
investigation of sources has been the goal and end of all
historical study. But Benedetto Croce's now famous saying
that "every true history is contemporary history" suggests
the danger of too great aloofness from common life, and is a
warning that, without an effort to 'think things together', the
historian will inevitably fall into a snare.

An inability to see the wood for the trees is a failing which
particularly besets the writers of a young country like South
Africa; incidents loom too large, distracting by reason of their
family interest or local romance. The traditional view of the
early struggles of white colonization in South Africa is wrapped
in a cloud of sentiment, which may do honour to our filial
feelings, but makes against real understanding. History has
commonly been interpreted in the light of Voortrekker and
colonial opinion. There is an impression that, had only
colonial views prevailed seventy or a hundred years ago, the
present Native difficulties of the Union might have been
avoided altogether. It is heresy to suggest that, where the
views of European colonists were opposed to those of the
British Government, or of the missionaries, the colonists were
often wrong. In the years when, by extending the area of
contact between the races, the Great Trek set in train the events
that have produced the perplexing Bantu problem of to-day,
a first Colour Question was being worked out in the Cape;
and the truth is that whereas for slaves and 'Hottentots' the
missionaries got at least some of their policy carried through,
on the other hand the colonists did have their own way with

3

the Bantu. The result is that while the 'Coloured People' now present little difficulty, the Native tribes are so congested on their 'Reserves', or so completely landless, as to be reduced to a state parlously like that of the 'Hottentots' of a century ago.

The full effects of early mistakes are only now beginning to be felt, and no policy should be hastily improvised in our day in ignorance or imperfect understanding of what has gone before. To-day, when the fortunes of many white colonists are adversely affected, and their hope of earning even a bare living seems to be directly threatened by Native competition, there is an almost impatient demand for effective 'handling' of the so-called Native Question. But the question admits of no impatient 'handling'; least of all by a community with little training or experience in hard political thinking. For a whole generation the minds of the South African people have been absorbed in the abstract rivalries of Empire and Republic, to the neglect of pressing social and economic readjustments; and these problems have so largely been left to solve themselves, that they are now beyond mere legislative expedients.

Less than a century ago, there was no Bantu population within the colonial boundaries, and the Bantu were a problem only of frontier defence and of police. In those days only the slaves and Hottentots raised a burning domestic question, and, thanks chiefly to missionary teaching and influence, their problem was set on the way to virtual 'solution' by the grant of at least potential legal and political equality. It seems worth while, therefore, to isolate for the moment the story of this earlier development in the Cape Colony; for the modern complexities of the second, or Bantu, Question have somewhat obscured its significance.

In the Union since 1910, the more liberal Cape tradition of native policy has hardly been able to hold its own against the oppressive weight of South African tradition. To-day, for example, the first step in a concerted series of measures for the solution of the latter-day Bantu problem is a flat contradiction of the lessons of experience. The 'Mines and Works Amendment' or 'Colour Bar' Act of 1926 gives the Government of the day the power to exclude the native Bantu from employment as skilled workers, or in effect, to erect a statutory barrier against the economic advance of the most intelligent and enlightened of the Bantu; and it is a safe prophecy that if it is allowed to stand, however carefully it may be administered, the far-reaching principle of this Act will give it historical notoriety long after most of the chief actors in the drama of the parliamentary session of 1926 are dead and forgotten.   The idea of this short and momentous Act, and the spirit that gave it birth as the first instalment of a 'new' policy, lie deep in South African history.   The last word has not been said on the policy of the early or middle nineteenth century, and until that policy is set in the clear light of history, South Africa will lay the blame for the present confusion on the wrong shoulders.

In the early days of acute friction, Dr. John Philip was from 1819 to 1851 the leading representative in South Africa of the unpopular policy of 'Exeter Hall'.   Even now, Dr. Philip's name is anathema.   In his later days, under Governor Maitland, his position was so strong that he does not seem to have felt any need to vindicate himself.   But in the seventy years after his death, first Philip's son, and then a grandson, worked at intervals at a 'Life', based on masses of his own documents, or those collected from his correspondents both at home and abroad.   But the work was never completed, and in 1920 the raw material was handed over to me for investigation.   Any detailed catalogue of the contents of two packing cases of almost entirely unsorted letters is impracticable.   The nature of the documents will appear from this book.   The letters include not only originals or duplicates of what must be a very large proportion of those of any importance written by Dr. Philip himself between 1818 and 1850 in the course of a strenuous career.[1]   There are also letters received from his own mission-aries, or from those of other Societies, especially French and American, all over South Africa; and his activity in public affairs brought him letters from prominent people at home and abroad, from 'Settlers' as well as from his own intimates like Pringle, Fairbairn, and Stockenstrom, while not a few letters that passed between such protagonists have found their way into the 'Philip' collection.   At times of excitement or crisis there was of course a particularly active correspondence, and among these documents there are not only important 'Memorials' to Governors (commonly known already from the Archives), but also special 'Reports' to the London Missionary Society, and to leaders of 'Exeter Hall' like T. Fowell Buxton—and what are almost more interesting—letters and replies from Buxton and others, including, for

[1] Gaps (which are few) I have filled in by an examination in London of the files preserved in the offices of the London Missionary Society.

example, an important, and hitherto unsuspected, series of personal 'notes' from Sir Benjamin D'Urban to Dr. Philip in 1834. The whole mass of these documents furnishes a most remarkable commentary on the events of fully thirty critical years. Their emergence necessitates a radical revision of the traditional and hitherto accepted interpretation of South African history.

Native troubles, as they are called, and missionary and humanitarian efforts on behalf of the Natives, have been at the root of perhaps most of the misunderstandings of South African history. Through the habit of treating the history of the Colony in a water-tight compartment, the struggle with the initial stages of the Native problem has never been viewed in its proper setting. It is on the general question of race-contact that the new material throws fresh light. The Philip MSS. reflect ideas and changes that were at work throughout the civilized world. Without some understanding of the origins of the movement that produced them, it is not possible to do justice to the work of the early Protestant missionaries, any more than it is to judge the early workings of British autocracy, and the subsequent political and constitutional development, at the Cape.

For example, the study of events of the second half of the nineteenth century makes it clear that those have done a disservice to historical understanding who have deprecated the fundamental importance of the abolition of slavery. Dr. Theal, and those who follow him in this matter, take too narrow a view of the far-reaching effects of the Emancipation movement. Though it may be that the 'Trekkers' said 'not a word in favour of slavery', they were certainly far from accepting the logical conclusions of emancipation by recognizing the rights of subject races. But long before the Act of 1833, a very effective British demand for the abolition of slavery produced the long series of legislative, judicial, and administrative measures that were making the position of the slave-owners untenable, so that emancipation itself came almost as a relief from continued interference. Not only slave Ordinances proper, but laws for the protection of Hottentots and other free persons of colour, like Ordinance 50 of 1828—Circuit Court cases in prosecution of masters for alleged ill-treatment of servants, either freemen or slaves—the veto on local Vagrancy Laws for the suppression of what seemed to the farmers to be 'unchecked vagabondage'—the unprecedented tenderness for Native rights manifested in the D'Urban-Glenelg settlement after the war of 1835—even the despairing policy of recognizing Native Treaty States, designed to put a stop to the hitherto almost automatic extension of the frontier of the Colony by the advance of small bands of pioneers—all these things were different manifestations of the same crusade against slavery. Long ago Bacon had urged (in vain) the need to 'use them justly'; the new movement centred at Exeter Hall did not rest content with mere emancipation of slaves, but, whatever its limitations, developed the idea of freedom, and pressed for an entirely new orientation of policy towards all the backward coloured races.

The war of principles thus staged led in North America to one of the greatest Civil Wars in history. In South Africa, from the nature of things it was not to be expected that a population of slave-owners would accept the views of the Emancipationists in their entirety; even with modifications their innovations provoked a good deal of strenuous opposition; and the inevitable troubles which attended the slow passing of slavery may explain a great deal of what has been read as a rooted antagonism between the British and Dutch peoples. The British Governors of that day were far from being open and avowed emancipationists. But the beginning of British rule synchronized with the most active period of the anti-Slavery Movement, and also with the maturing of problems of colour at the Cape. In those days too, the Governor's fiat was law. In so far, therefore, as the Governors accepted the humanitarian views represented by Dr. Philip, or were obliged by pressure from London to shape their policy somewhat in that direction, British rule itself came to incur some of the unpopularity of these new measures for the protection of the coloured races. At the time, it is true, Dutch and British colonists were united in hot opposition to the Philanthropists. Fairbairn's *Commercial Advertiser* was as bitterly assailed in the columns of the *Grahamstown Journal* as in those of *De Zuid Afrikaan*. Dr. Philip has left it on record that he was gravely threatened in several places, but actually mobbed only in the streets of Grahamstown, and the Settlers suffer his most severe strictures for their attitude to the rights or wrongs of the Natives.[1] The presentation of a Bible to old Johannes Uys by

[1] Dr. Philip writes to D. Gray, Aberdeen, in an undated letter of about 1820: 'Much is said in England against the Dutch inhabitants of Cape Town, but you may rest assured that they are not the worst part of the population.'
Writing later of Grahamstown he complains that 'evangelical

the citizens of Grahamstown[1] was no stray episode; and other leaders like Piet Retief himself, who had lived in Grahamstown as well as on his farm, or James Boshof,[2] knew that they were sure of a sympathetic hearing when they sent their manifesto of grievances to the Grahamstown paper.

It was only in later years that estrangement became antagonism. Isolated in their own republics, and embittered by recollection of the many hardships of their exodus, many of the Boers tended to remember that the head and front of offending against their prejudices was the British missionary party, and that the Government itself was sometimes the agent of the hated 'missionary' policy. They occasionally went further, and included in their condemnation all things and persons British. Yet in truth the men of two nations thus thrown together could hardly have had more in common than Dutch and British, or less to divide them. There is no religious feud, and all over the country the Dutch Reformed Church repaid the debt it owed to Scots like the Murrays, and has often ministered to Scots Presbyterians and to English Nonconformists. As the fires of the slavery agitation died out, and even in spite of them, friendly personal co-operation and intermarriage have been usual. By general consent, naturalized Englishmen or Scots were good and loyal burghers of the old Orange Free State, and men of both races contributed to make the old Cape Parliament one of the most successful and distinguished in the British Dominions. Mr. J. H. Hofmeyr met with little or no opposition when he asked for, and obtained, equal rights for the Dutch language in Parliament; and a few years later the same Dutch leader took an active part in the proceedings of the first Imperial Conference in 1887, showing himself there as an undoubted supporter of the British connection. Though occasions of sharp difference were not wanting, as in 1881, yet it is generally conceded that in spite of everything, the promise of the early 'nineties was that Dutch and English in South Africa would settle down in peace and concord.

But racial bitterness, sprung from the happenings of more

---

religion' may become a 'mere fashion' like any other. 'In the town in which the profession of religion is general and in which evangelical doctrines are popular, the spirit of bitterness against the freedom of the natives, and against those that have espoused the cause of the oppressed, has been manifested in a higher degree than in any other district of the Colony.'

[1] Cory, iii, p. 401.   [2] Bird's *Annals*, i, 504.

recent years, has added immeasurably to the difficulty of re-interpreting the story of the early days of British rule. In the calmer atmosphere of the 'nineties, the study of South African history, which might have made for peace and conciliation, was unduly neglected. But the Jameson Raid and the dour struggle of the Anglo-Boer War inevitably issued in an Afri-kander national feeling far more self-conscious than any that had existed before, and South African historical research has been far too much the child of the bitter feeling aroused by the memories of the years 1896 and 1899–1902. It has been con-cerned at times, not so much with impartial truth, as with the citation of grievances to prove the persistent malevolence of the ancient enemy.

Where historical judgment has been so strongly influenced by feeling or sentiment, the missionaries who, as friends of the natives, no doubt helped to provoke the Trek itself, have inevitably suffered detraction. In a debate in the Union House of Assembly on a Report of the affair of the Bondelswart Hottentots in 1923, the conflict of opinion was summarized as one of 'sentiment against sense', and 'missionary against colonist'. Now the original antagonism to the Missionary-Philanthropists was shown not only by the Dutch colonists, but by the general public opinion of the Colony. Sir George Cory is undoubtedly so far right. But it does not follow that because Philip's was a small party, therefore all truth was with the colonists. Indeed, the difficulty, whether of governing the native races or of understanding South African history, is greatly increased by the common assumption that all the sense is on one side and all the sentiment on the other. In the absence of direct representation of natives, and in face of their, as yet, limited capacity for self-expression, legislation cannot afford to be guided only by the 'sense' of white colonists. However imperfectly or distortedly, it can only be through the so-called 'missionary point of view' that statesmen can hope to gauge, what they dare not disregard, the attitude and feelings of the Natives for whom they legislate. In these matters truth is emphatically not all on the side of colonial sense or 'realism'. It may, and must, lie somewhere between that and missionary 'idealism'; and as, *pace* Piet Retief, the colonist is inevitably an interested party, the missionary is, if anything, likely to come nearer impartiality.

Finally, though in their hostility to the missionaries Dutch and British peoples, colonists both, were then in substantial agreement, the events of the years about 1836 remain something of a suppressed complex, Dutch-speaking South Africans still cherishing a sense of grievance, while their English-speaking fellows keep almost shamed silence. It is only in the light of fresh evidence, and by relating the events of this chequered and all too living past to the problems of the present day, that some of the darkness may be dispelled; for, as we know from the psychologists, misunderstanding arises not only from ignorance but also from avoidance of the facts.

Dr. Philip at least saw the South African question as a whole. He was conspicuously free from the persistent habit of thought that makes an abstraction of Colour, and treats South African history as the story of the fortunes only of its European pioneers. Educated natives speak, not without justification, of the European Question; and for right thinking about their own problems, modern South Africans have much to learn from the true history of the work of Dr. Philip and his colleagues. The fortunes of the white and coloured races are inseparably linked, and the two stories cannot be divorced.

Our new documents relate to a short period, 1819–1851; but in those years the issues were cleared, and the whole subsequent course of South African development decided. The problem thrashed out in the old Cape Colony is essentially a particular example of the World Race Problem, and the South African colour question of the present day is not isolated or 'without parallel in the rest of the world'.

Chapter II

HISTORICAL GEOGRAPHY, AND THE GENESIS OF THE BOER

THERE is in the English language no comprehensive word or phrase, like Economic Imperialism, which adequately describes the gradual subjugation of uncivilized native peoples and the absorption of their lands, not by exploiting capitalists, but by the remorseless advance of white agricultural colonization. Strictly, no doubt, this is 'colonization'; but the word has been so glossed over as to lose most of its real significance. European historians have written of the process with unction, as a distinguishing mark of national vigour and as proof of the prowess of their own civilization, salving occasional doubts with the doctrine of the 'white man's burden'. For writers in the colonies, on the other hand, it is almost impossible to treat with detachment what is so much a part of their everyday life. On the surface colonial life is calm enough, but there is disturbance beneath. The South African Native as he appears to-day, even if he has become a hewer of wood and drawer of water, is by no means miserable or downtrodden; but any show of independence or resentment by a Native—let alone an outbreak or even a strike—arouses such disproportionately heated antagonism and white 'solidarity' as to suggest that it springs from an inverted fear of the black man. Dingaan's Day, the festival of White Civilization, celebrates the overthrow of a Zulu despot, and the long series of Kafir Wars are mere stages in the triumph of the robust young colonial community over the forces of barbarism which hemmed it in.

The truth is that the South African Colour Question is only one phase of the World Problem which arises from the economic

competition of peoples with widely different standards, complicated by social distinctions, intensified by racial misunderstandings, and distorted by fear.

In its historical origin, however, the South African question
has special features of its own. The capitalistic exploitation of
the Tropics has had more attention and criticism than the
essentially different process that has been at work in South
Africa during the last hundred years. In North America and
in Australia the Red Indians and Blacks have so far died
out under the stress of the changes imposed upon them as to
constitute no special difficulty. In the Southern States of
North America the negro population was imported by the white
planters for their own ends, and their descendants make an
even more formidable demand upon the assimilative powers
of the older Anglo-Saxon community of the 'Melting Pot'
than does the mixture of tongues and races of later-comers
from Southern and Eastern Europe. In Natal the short-
sighted policy of sugar planters of the first generation has left a
similar small but thorny problem of Indians in South Africa.
But only in South Africa did rival streams of white and black
colonists come into collision and competition for possession of
an almost empty continent; here alone not only have the blacks
proved too hardy and powerful to be permanently ousted, but,
the days of slavery being over, they have persisted[1] as an ever-
present factor in the life of what the dominant whites would
fain see develop as a 'White Man's Country'. The little
understood Kafir Wars of the early days are properly to be
regarded as the struggle between streams of colonizers for the
possession of valuable *land*.

In this long-drawn struggle with the colonial power, the
blacks, in this matter of land, have been almost more trenchantly
dealt with than if their fate had been determined by an Economic
Imperialism. The great Chartered Companies have not usually

[1] The accepted theory is that the South African Natives are
increasing more rapidly than the Europeans. The mortality among
Natives is so colossal that, with the enforced celibacy of labour conditions, it seems doubtful whether the effective rate of increase, if it
is very great, can long continue. Moreover, the early Native population is probably underestimated; the 'depopulation' caused by the
Chaka Wars is matter of tradition only and has never yet been closely
investigated. Dr. Theal once (V, p. 255) states that the '*rate* of
increase' in the Transkei may be inferred from the fact that in
1904 the population *was* 817,867. On the other hand, the gradual
improvement in the efficiency of the census would seem to make it
likely that the progressive increase of the Native population is somewhat magnified.

lacked keen and powerful critics, watchful and jealous of the privileges exercised by a small group of capitalists. There has been little in their support to equal the solid political pressure which can always be exercised by a united colonial community both upon its own immediate rulers and upon the responsible powers at Home. However absolute the Governor, he lives the active social life of the colony, hears its views, and comes to share also some of its prejudices. He can hardly remain deaf to a cry that the life and safety of his community depend upon pushing the black peril yet farther into the interior, and he is hardly in a position to make a nice distinction between demands that are genuinely military and defensive, and those that are born of a land hunger as insatiable with white colonists as with black. By the advance of colonization the Native may learn a great deal and reap material benefits; but he commonly buys his own advance in civilization at the price of his status on the land, or even of the land itself.

No doubt the white South African farmer, even the less efficient, makes better use of the land than did the Kafir before him. Certainly also the Great Trek appreciably speeded up the development of the interior, and even served to rescue the country, and in some instances Natives themselves, from a cruel and savage barbarism. The experience of Liberia and Abyssinia also suggests that white guidance is all but indispensable to the progress of purely Native communities, and in the vast spaces of South Africa there is happily even yet the possibility of sustenance for far greater numbers of members of both races. But because huge distances and lack of transport made pastoralism the only practicable resource either of the early white settlers, or of the Natives before them, an acute land-hunger has been a marked feature of all South African life and history. The agriculture of South Africa is still a matter of 'vast possibilities' and of a 'great future', rather than of positive achievement. The Great Trek itself fatally postponed the inevitable day when shortage of land should compel the white colonists rather to concentrate their energies upon the intensive development of a more restricted area than spread themselves in still further expansion.[1] The habits and conditions inherited from the days of unlimited space die hard. To-day the

[1] Experience seems to show that where closer settlement is being tried to-day, there are white men almost starving on fifteen acres of land who would probably be more successful if they could learn to concentrate on four or five. See pamphlet, *S.A. Agrarian Problem*, Johannesburg, 1919; and for Native conditions see also *note, Intro.*, p. xvi.

European agricultural problem is to check the exodus, from rural areas, of whites who cannot readily adapt themselves to life on the smaller farms, which are all that the pressure of population has left them.

As for the Natives, all too closely herded as they are in most of the Territories that remain to them—originally constrained by the calculated pressure of taxation, which has been almost the one consistent item of Native policy—they are now compelled to push out in ever greater numbers into competition with their white masters in the industrial labour market. The fatal lure of the town may have increasing attractions for their young men; but ultimately stern economic necessity, rather than free choice, makes the Native of to-day the white man's competitor in the economic sphere, as his fathers were on the field of battle. The failure of the so-called 'Poor Whites' to maintain themselves on the land, and the economic pressure which drives Natives into competition with the Poor Whites in the unskilled labour market, are the outcome of events that happened and of a policy that took shape as early as the 'thirties and 'forties.

There is a certain inevitability about the process which precludes the invidiousness of apportioning blame. But the history of South Africa is rightly to be regarded as one long episode of colonization in the stricter sense we have suggested—the military and economic subjection by the expanding white races of blacks who, though barbarian, were once free. Even for the white colonists difficulties are sufficiently serious. How far the uneasy and fearful freedom of barbarism may be replaced for the blacks by the freedom of Christianity and civilization is still one of the world's mighty problems.

In the beginning, the first faint shadow of the Colour Problem fell across van Riebeeck's path, when in the years following 1652 he set about his allotted task of establishing a refreshing station for the Dutch East India Company's ships on the shores of Table Bay. His policy, and that of his successors, was (ultimately in vain) to reduce to a minimum the contact between the company's servants (or after 1657 the Free Burghers) and the Hottentots, the original inhabitants. Van Riebeeck even built a stockade across the sandy narrows of the Cape Peninsula to separate the infant settlement from the Hottentots' '*Holland*' in the mountains beyond. And all but two hundred years later, Earl Grey, not by any means a 'Little

Englander', harassed by Kafir Wars and their attendant Boer troubles, writes in this vein . . .

You are aware that apart from the very limited extent of territory required for the security of the Cape of Good Hope as a naval station the British commonwealth and nation have no interest whatever in maintaining any territorial dominion.[1]

The development of the port of call into a great colony was only very indirectly due to the East India Company, to whom the Cape was indeed little more than an 'obstruction on the way to the Indies'. And the Company for its part, though not before blood had been shed, formally 'bought' its port from the Hottentots. The baubles it paid may have represented not so inaccurately its value to its former owners; and one reads less and less, as time went on, of any payment whatever for the vast tracts of African land later absorbed by Europeans. But if it provokes a smile to read of van Riebeeck's boundary fence, it is only because the process of colonization was so inevitable a sequel once the contact was begun between civilized and backward races. For all its variety and huge spaces, South Africa has little in the way of natural geographical boundaries; the interior depends on but a few inconvenient artificial harbours, and the whole is an economic unit. For perhaps a hundred years, so sparse was the population—white or coloured— that a few thousands, more or less, made little real difference. The pioneer work fell to families and to individuals, and the long, slow process developed a highly individual type, the Boer. The Government was distant, almost an abstraction, and it was not till long afterwards that increasing numbers, and the economic pressure which resulted, left later generations, and their governments, to tear their hair over the thorny 'problems' which racial contact had brought to birth.

It was only natural for the Company and its settlers to seek to find what lay beyond Table Bay. The Company itself was not uninterested in hopes of gain suggested by old legends of Monomotapa, but it very soon set its face against all new responsibilities. The well-known and active Governor, Simon van der Stel, himself pushed out north-west, braving the lion, and actually suffering a charge by a rhinoceros, but beyond verifying the existence of a 'Copper Mountain' in the Namaqualand desert he found nothing to encourage hopes of riches like those of Mexico or Peru. The future, however, lay east rather than north-west, and not with the Company and its

[1] P.R.O., Grey to Cathcart, 11.1.1852.

servants, but with the Free Burghers to whom it looked to provide fresh meat and vegetables needed for the passing fleets. The Company was orthodox in believing that private enterprise should take all the risks of farming; yet so straitly did it control the prices paid for farm products that its own restrictive policy, reinforcing the influences of geography, contributed not a little to the over-speedy and excessive dispersal of the farmers over the interior, whither they pressed forward to escape the Company's interference and control. Even by the end of the seventeenth century burghers were thinly spread over the vine-growing Western Province, past Stellenbosch and Drakenstein to Waveren (Tulbagh). Thence they followed the Breede River valley, and (the Company bowing to the inevitable) by 1746 Swellendam, more than a hundred and fifty miles from the Cape Town base, had its local government official, or *Landdrost*, and had become the centre for farmers scattered still farther away towards Mossel Bay.

Beyond Swellendam the pioneers soon passed out of the narrow zone of regular winter rains, with little or no frost, and almost unfailing mountain streams, which make the Western Province unusually suitable for regular agriculture. In this original western belt, if anywhere, the Cape might have grown into a strong, settled, and therefore perhaps more ordinary, agricultural colony. And how far, in spite of everything, this desirable result was achieved, many famous old Dutch farmhouses still stand to bear witness. Had this area been an island, or anything but the fringe of a vast continent; had even the way into the interior been more effectively barred by mountains, or had the feeble Hottentots been replaced by the Kafirs as far west as, say, the Breede River valley, South African history might have been more like that of the old North America east of the Alleghanies. But with no obstacle to force the early settlers to consolidate their position before they ventured farther afield, South Africa was reserved for a more difficult but less humdrum future. Slow but sure, the ox-waggon was very early a fitting national emblem.

To understand the course of South African colonization, it is important to know something of its historical geography, of which the modern political map gives a poor, or even a false, conception. The main lines of railway date only from the late nineteenth century, and their routes were determined, not by the natural progressive development of the country's resources, but by a sudden dash to secure to each of the leading ports its share of the trade and wealth of the newly-discovered mines of

Kimberley and the Rand. And our concern is with the early formative days when the golden Rand was undreamt of.

The greater part of the Union of South Africa is a vast inland plateau, broken in parts by *kopjes* and relatively low ridges of hill, indiscriminately known as *bergen*, or mountains, though only occasionally deserving the more dignified title, as in the great ridge of the Drakensberg. At no great distance from the coast—fifty or a hundred miles—is the escarpment, the 'edge of the berg'; and though from many parts of the coast belt this escarpment looks formidable, the barrier is mountain usually on the sea side, but mere hill beyond. Thus from almost any point on the coast, a journey of about one hundred miles brings the traveller, by way of one or two 'terraces', roughly 1000 and 2000 feet above the sea, on to the 3000- or 4000-foot level, which stretches far away into the interior, rising very gradually to as much as 5000 or even 6000 feet in the south central Transvaal, and then dropping rather suddenly to the unhealthy, semi-tropical, but attractive, Low Veld of the far north-east. In spite of its latitude, this high plateau is dry and very healthy, the heat of the summer normally tempered by heavy thunderstorms and cool nights, the winter cool, even frosty, and bracing. The dry atmosphere, which makes it so healthy, is also its most serious drawback, and it is subject to devastating droughts; so that, with soil and accessibility, water-supply and rainfall have determined the course and character of its colonization.

In the seventeenth and eighteenth centuries, when both colonists and indigenous Hottentots were few in numbers, it was natural for expansion to flow eastwards, along the base of the Karoo escarpment, for the most part along the first or 1000-foot level, rather avoiding both the coast itself and the droughty interior. The Orange or Great River was first crossed by a European in 1760, and named only in 1779. The Dutch colonists never completely lost their ancestral love of the sea, and almost every little village from Stellenbosch onwards had its own particular 'Strand', or summer holiday resort. But the 'Strandveld', as they call it, is for the most part poor, sandy and difficult, so for their farms they chose rather the better soil of the slightly higher levels, less sandy than the coast, and less dry than the interior because tempered by the influence of the sea-breezes. Expansion, therefore, followed the Swellendam line, and beyond it, the Long Kloof, rather than the exceptionally well-watered and beautiful coastal forest strip of George and Knysna. The farmers would no doubt

c

have pushed on across the Fish River into the Adelaide, King William's Town belt, and thence into the Transkei, but that about 1778, the date of the 'first' Kafir War, the Boer colonists for the first time met with a serious and dangerous check when they came face to face in the neighbourhood of the Fish River with the advancing Bantu. To the rule that early expansion followed the terrace only one remove from the coast there is, therefore, one significant and little-noted exception. In the ordinary course the next *landdrostdy* to Swellendam ought to have been in the direction of Uitenhage, which was founded only in 1802. Actually it was Graaff-Reinet, 1786, at last on the Karoo. The site of the village happened to be fertile and, for the small population of those early days, well-watered; but there can be little doubt that here for the first time the natural line of advance was deflected by the menacing opposition of the Kafirs. But for this Kafir difficulty the development of the great plateau, which is to-day almost the essential South Africa, might have been still further delayed.[1]

For the other great factor in South African development— the dependable winter rainfall is confined to a small area, the Western Province, near Cape Town. The summer fall is most reliable along the south-east coast and in the east, where the moisture from the Indian Ocean seems to be stopped and distributed by the great mountain barrier of the Drakensberg. When, therefore, the Western Province was left behind, and all through the eighteenth century, the advancing colonists found themselves in the central area where they could never be quite sure either of their winter or summer rains. It was in this dry zone that Boer character and habits were really moulded. North and north-west of Cape Town the country is dry and almost desert, and to the east, for a long distance, even the coastal rains are less certain; inland, the dry scrubby 'Karoo'[2]—glorious after its occasional rains and, in parts,

[1] In the event, the plateau was first extensively colonized to the north and east, in the Republics. On the Western Karoo, comparatively near Cape Town and Tulbagh, the earliest township is Beaufort West, suggesting in its name the date of its origin, the time of Lord Charles Somerset, son of the Duke of Beaufort, and Governor as late as 1814–26. Other Karoo names are equally significant of their nineteenth-century origin: Victoria West and Prince Albert, Aberdeen and Carnarvon, Sutherland, Fraserburg and Murraysburg, the last three names after well-known Scots recruits to the ministry of the Dutch Reformed Church. In the two republics most older place names are of obviously unmixed Dutch origin, bestowed by the Voortrekkers after 1836.
[2] Hottentot word for a 'dry place'.

fertile under irrigation—held out no great inducement or possibilities to would-be settlers. Farther on, however, the country gradually changes and improves. North and east of a line somewhere beyond the Fish River the scrubby Karoo bush gives place to 'grass veld', and, under the influence of the Drakensberg aforesaid, the summer rainfall becomes a good deal more reliable. Droughts of course there often are, and little or no running water; the rivers, for the most part, are little more than storm-water courses; but, as a rule, in summer the plains of the great 'High Veld' plateau (as distinguished from the 'Karoo') are covered with long green grass. Though the higher altitudes are cold in winter, the veld is sufficiently nutritious, in favoured parts at least, to tide the cattle over till the next rains. There was, indeed, a temptation for settlers in this area to escape the winter by trekking to the warmer Low Veld for a few months; and still the enormous difficulty of transport made agriculture take second place to pastoralism. To the north-west of the 'High Veld' the rainfall gradually decreases, and the country slopes away at last to the almost rainless Kalahari.

It was thus in the peculiar circumstances of the eighteenth century, with the dry or droughty climate, the inevitable concentration on cattle-rearing rather than on agriculture, and not least, the absence of any formidable and organized enemy like the Kafirs, that the distinctive character of the South African Boer was evolved. The Trekkers of the nineteenth century were quite distinct from their own forebears, whether Dutch, Huguenot, or Lutheran, going where and when they pleased, unused to the restraints of government, contemptuous and regardless of Native adversaries, as of Native rights.

The influence of geographical conditions was emphasized rather than counteracted by the rule of the Company of Merchants. The first blow to hopes for a real agricultural colony at the Cape fell as early as 1658, when van Riebeeck imported the first shipload of slaves to remedy the shortage of labour. The result was that hard manual toil was soon left to slaves. Early in the next century the better sort of official was complaining that too much of the agriculture was similarly left, while the farmers amused themselves shooting.[1] This

---

[1] Cf. the Reports of de Chavonnes and van Imhoff, Cape Town, 1918 (van Riebeeck Society); and for the shooting, Simon v. d. Stel in 1681. Later, and yet quite early in history, I have found stray references, *e.g.* by Robert Moffat in 1823, to the practice of farmers allowing coloured people to 'plough' (to grow a crop) for the Boer

was very largely the fault of the Company itself. Since its first and only concern was the victualling of its own ships, it severely cut the prices it paid for farm produce; but its control was too weak to prevent officials like Willem A. van der Stel from monopolizing what scanty outlet there was for supplies. Agriculture, therefore, gave such poor returns that there were strong motives for getting away from the control of Cape Town. But the farther the farmers went from the base the more impossible were conditions of transport, and the greater the inducement to concentrate on the rearing of animals that would carry themselves to market on their own legs. This, with the less regular rainfall, soon made them almost totally dependent on cattle-rearing and hunting rather than on the more strenuous pursuit of agriculture. It also demanded more and more space for ever - increasing flocks and herds. As a further incentive to the dispersal of the population, the Hottentots, themselves unorganized, pastoral and nomadic, and decimated by the ravages of smallpox, could offer no effective resistance, and were never dangerous neighbours even to isolated families of Boers. It is little wonder that before the eighteenth century was out, the semi-nomadic Trek-Boer was the characteristic South African colonist.

The Boer type was hardy and venturesome enough. The Hottentots, and the fierce but still scantier Bushmen who once possessed the land, had few terrors even for the solitary pioneer. He was thus little used to depending on his distant government, but owed his continued links with civilization chiefly to the services of the Dutch Reformed Church. It was not till the end of the eighteenth century, or even later, when contact was made with the main body of the Bantu tribes, that conditions began to demand more serious thought and organization; and later Governments found the Boer not a little intractable in his independence, when it came to imposing legal restraints on his dealings with the coloured races as a condition of the protection which came to be necessary to his continued safety on the borders of Kafirland. With it all, a sturdy tradition of civilization survived the physical hardships of earlier days. Nurtured by their Church, but schooled chiefly by rough human experience, the Boers are a friendly, patient, frugal, enduring, good-looking people; they have produced many shrewd and able leaders, of whom Paul Kruger is only the best

---

landowner. This practice, usually on the 'shares' system, the famous Natives Land Act 1913 sought to suppress.

known. Liberal views were hardly to be looked for, least of all in their attitude towards the Native races. But some allowance may be made for natural anxiety in face of the dangers of the unknown, and for their actual sufferings at Native hands; for it was with no idea of organized conquest that the Boers penetrated ever farther into the interior. The Boers, like the Kafirs, if not also the Hottentot aboriginals, were driven forward by the imperative needs of their ordinary everyday life as pastoralists. They must push on, or lose their stock and starve. And for a long time there was land, and to spare.

At our time of day it is hard to picture what the everyday life of the pioneers must have been. If they had meal for bread, there were no facilities on trek for anything but rough and primitive cooking,[1] with little fruit and no vegetables, meat three times a day, and the fat of the tailed native sheep as the only variant to the lean of the buck they shot. In the hard dry winters of the interior, or on trek, milk was often scarce or unobtainable; and if the Boers are still great coffee drinkers, the development of the taste was natural, coffee being the ingredient most likely to drown the taste of the muddy water, drawn from stagnant pools and dams, where the water was often enough shared with the trampling cattle. The name of the Witwatersrand (Ridge of *White* Waters) seems to bear witness to the pleasure of the Trekkers—after their long experience of the turgid *fonteine* and 'water-holes' of Karoo and High Veld —at meeting the (not pellucid) running streams flowing from this Rand. The plight of the pioneer Boers in times of sickness —without shops or doctors, or medical or any other comforts— suggests something of what they owed to their women. Altogether the Boers developed as a notably solid, steady and abstemious race.

On the other hand, the scattered and isolated life they led had its disabilities and has left its mark. The Boer capacity for co-operation in social and political life is not strong. With John Brand's Free State as a shining exception to prove the rule, the history of their own republics, from the earliest days of the Trek, is full of deplorable faction and schism. There is also a social danger in the contact of higher and lower races in the physically hard yet morally easy-going life of the Frontier. Except for the occasional excitement of a Native War or rising, the life of the pioneer is one long round of tending flocks, hunting, or wandering slowly in search of new pasture. It is a

[1] *E.g.* dough broiled in fat (*vet koekjes*), or in an expressive vulgarism of Boer War days, 'maag bomme' (stomach bombs!).

monotonous existence into which sustained effort hardly enters. In South Africa, as apparently also in the Southern States of North America, mere isolation has had a demoralizing effect upon the character of a fraction of the population, and, combined with the traditions of slavery, it has left an evil legacy. The ' Poor White ' problem is not all due to dependence and reliance on the Natives; nor yet is it *caused* by Native competition and undercutting of wages.

Many other factors help to explain the existence even of a 'submerged twentieth '.[1] Some who are loosely damned as 'Poor Whites' are victims of the causes which have accentuated poverty in every Western society. Still more have been crowded off the land by an economic revolution. As the population has increased, land has become too scarce and too valuable for the wasteful superficial methods which sufficed in the more spacious days; but these methods are the settled habit and the only resource of some of the older population, who are abnormally slow to see the possibility of any alternative. Moreover, neither agricultural organization nor the land laws have kept pace with the changed conditions. By the operation of the Roman-Dutch law of intestacy, and by its tradition of equal division among heirs, farms are often absurdly subdivided, the portions becoming untenable. A comparatively new landless class of shares-tenants, or *bijwoners*, has therefore arisen, for whom, as tenants at will, the law affords no adequate protection. Bad marketing methods, credit operations, land speculations, faulty finance, and other causes multiply the misfortunes, not only of these tenants, but even of landowners, and swell the ranks of the broken men whose exodus from the country into villages and towns makes the 'Poor White' problem. These things, with the effects of drought, are enough in themselves to explain the almost general *malaise* of South African agriculture, as well as the 1921 census returns, which show that in most of the central districts of the Union the rural population is declining.[2]

The modern agrarian trouble has arisen in the natural course of historical evolution, and has little to do with the Natives— though of course Native competition is now a serious complication of the difficulty of finding employment for these landless Europeans. The human stock is for the most part sound enough. It is thrifty, even to a fault, and capable of enduring great hardships; long ago Dr. Philip wrote of farmers who

[1] *The S.A. Agrarian Problem*, Johannesburg, 1919.
[2] *Official Year Book*, No. vi, p. 145, map.

'have the art of *keeping* money, not of *making* it'. Barter and shop credit still take the place of cash transactions, and many quite well-to-do farmers tend to deal in kind, and hardly know the use or value of money. They will more readily part with a sheep than with a shilling. They submit to an unhealthily low standard of living rather than spend even on things they ought to spend on. A *predikant* tells of a substantial Northern Transvaal farmer who, having had an extra good season, announced that he was going to treat himself to a new house, 'even if it cost him *a hundred pounds*'. Outside the old Western Province the standard of comfort is very low, and in the far North it descends to the mere *hartebeest huis*, of wattle and daub—to the great increase of the danger from malarial fever. As in the mid-eighteenth century, when there were lusty protests from Swellendam to Cape Town, at opposite ends of the settlement, against a suggestion for promoting immigration,[1] they are still nervous of closer settlement. But means must be found to establish a denser and more intensively occupied farming population. This, more than anything else, would better economic conditions and make for the elimination of the 'Poor Whites'. As they are, many of them are endowed with the characteristic pioneer virtues of daring and hardihood, and have shown themselves able to rise to competence on the railways, in the police, or in industry.

There is, however, a residue of almost utter degenerates whose downfall must be ascribed chiefly to their traditional habit, developed in the old isolated days, of leaving all the hard work to the Native. The Boers, indeed, with all their qualities and virtues, carried Puritan manners and traditions into the nineteenth century, and applied the Old Testament as their standard of conduct towards the coloured races. The curse of Ham was taken as gospel. Or again, the dark races were Amalekites and Canaanites, to be smitten hip and thigh, and, wherever possible, driven out; but there was always a reservation in favour of sufficient *Gibeonites* to be hewers of wood and drawers of water.

Some such theory is widely held, and it makes Colour prejudice most virulent among those whose white skins are their chief or only claim to racial superiority. An antipathy to 'Kafir work' persists, especially perhaps in the remoter districts—on the Cape-Kafir frontier, among the trek-Boers of the far North-West, and on the edge of the low country of the Transvaal, which is still a hunters' Paradise. The danger of

---

[1] Reports of de Chavonnes and van Imhoff.

such utter demoralization must have been infinitely greater had colonial expansion continued to be, as in the eighteenth century, a matter of unregulated individualism and of peaceful penetration by isolated pioneers. Paradoxical as it seems, it may well be that the more peaceful the expansion of the colony the greater the danger to the moral stamina of the colonists. To some extent instinctive and born of contempt, white prejudice against the black has unfortunately grown with the complexity of South African life; it was greatly embittered by the wars and conflicts of the last century, and threatens to reach a climax under the stress of the even more acute economic competition of to-day.

By the very fact of their existence the coloured races have given South African history its distinctive character. The opposition of the Bantu to the advance of European colonization makes Native wars loom large in the past. Reduced to impotence, the coloured races have ceased to be a military menace; but the very completeness of their military subjection has left them a minimum of land of their own, and they can no longer be a separate self-contained community. They must, therefore, continue to be the distinctive factor in the economic life of to-day as in the colonizing process of yesterday.

Colour prejudice is very far from being a monopoly of the Dutch population. The Dutch Church produced, in its turn, a strong New Testament missionary wing; and now that the country is self-governing and, it may be, released from any conscience-numbing possibility of intervention by 'Downing Street', the leaders of the Dutch South Africans show an ever keener sense of responsibility towards the dark races. The Natives, who are now an inseparable part of the South African whole, must either continue, as now, to be a race of low-grade servants—a drag on the general prosperity—or they must be set by the white people on the road to efficiency and progress, even if only on grounds of European self-interest. It has always been hard for the average South African to believe that the laughing, toiling black is not a person to be envied; in fact, that he is not in every way very 'well off'. When the European comes to realize that black poverty, ignorance and degradation are as lowering to white society as his own slums, then salvation may be nearer. It is often said—it may begin to be believed—that either the Native must be raised up, or he will drag down White Civilization itself to a lower level. The fear that is now so rampant is based on an old economic fallacy. The progress of the coloured section of the community is thought to threaten the well-being of the Whites; whereas it is the very degradation and poverty of the blacks that now make their competition so formidable.

The devil of fear must be exorcised. To this end perhaps nothing can be so efficacious as a more enlightened under-standing of history. The Bantu are held to be a finer stock than the old Hottentots. Proportionately they outnumber the Europeans by little more than did Hottentots and other coloured races the Cape Colonists of a century ago. But by a slow and devious process the old Cape Colony raised even its despised Hottentots to become useful citizens, and, in the eyes of Union law, members of civilized society.

Chapter *III*

THE COLOURED RACES—PRIMITIVE CUSTOM AND CIVILIZED LAW—THE POSITION OF THE HOTTENTOTS IN 1795 [1]

ALMOST all the political complications in South African history have been the result of conflicting views on how to govern the native Bushmen, Hottentots, or Bantu. The position of the Hottentots was thrashed out in the earlier nineteenth century; the Bantu have been an ever-changing perplexity from the eighteen-thirties to the present day. Of the unlucky Bushmen there is little for history to say. The eighteenth century all but completed their extinction, at the hands of white and coloured foes indiscriminately. Their weapons and paintings remain in caves from end to end of the country, and are rather of ethnological than of historical interest. Their living influence can hardly now be traced, unless in the Boer commando system, famous in later times, which had its origin in the largely voluntary combination of Boer farmers for purposes of defence and offence against the real and imagined depredations of this wild and primitive people. Their resistance to colonial encroachment took the form of 'thieving', and was at one time almost formidable. The great commando of 1774 pursued the Bushmen for 300 miles with something like war, and according to Theal, 503 Bushmen were killed and 239 taken prisoners and bound to the service of the farmers. Little attempt was made to under-

---

[1] G. W. Stow's *Native Races of South Africa*, London, 1905, is still the most useful authority, for Bushmen especially. Cape slaves were drawn, in uncertain proportions, some of them from the Malay Peninsula, the remainder from East and West Central Africa.

26

stand their strange mentality, and none to provide them with
'reserves', where they might be free to follow their own bent.
Their veld lore made them useful herds, and stray individuals
or families were sufficiently 'tame' to be employed in Boer
families, as to this day. It is true that neither benevolent
employers nor missionaries found them quick to respond to
civilizing influences. The well-established colonial tradition
came to be that the Bushman is a wild animal to be shot at sight;
and unhappily it was on this inadequate theory that the Bushman of earlier days was usually dealt with, and destroyed. As a
factor in later history the Bushmen are negligible.

Apart from the slaves, who were all imported, the Hottentots, a pastoral and nomadic people whom van Riebeeck encountered in the beginning, are the first group of real historical
importance. In those days they had vague possessory rights
over the land from the shores of Table Bay to the Fish River,
and perhaps beyond. Their numbers it is hardly possible to
estimate, but they can never have been a dense population.
Like the Boers after them, they seem to have avoided the
inland plateau, till pressure drove them there. The area they
inhabited was limited, and their method of life so rude that
even on the coastal belt they can hardly have been more than
three to the square mile. They were a stage higher than the
Bushmen—whose blood it is possible they inherited—in that
they had domesticated cattle, and hairy, fat-tailed sheep; but
unlike the more formidable 'Kafirs', they were quite ignorant
of agriculture. While the Bushman social organization seems
never to have got beyond the family stage, the Hottentots had
tribal 'captains', who, for their part, had nothing like the
authority and organization of the Kafir chiefs. Hottentot
resistance, therefore, to the advance of the Dutch settlers was
hardly even as vigorous as that of the more primitive Bushmen,
so that by the beginning of the nineteenth century free Hottentot captaincies had all but completely disappeared. Legal
ownership of land was denied them; the policy of native
reserves was not yet invented; and the mass of the remnant
of this people had been reduced to the absolute economic
dependence which belonged to the status of the 'free person
of colour'. Degrees of dependence there may have been. For
example, some of the Hottentots escaped beyond the shifting
borders of the Colony. There they mixed with runaway slaves,
or more remote Korannas, as well as with a sprinkling of pioneer
or refugee whites; the offspring formed the wandering bands
of Griquas or 'Bastards' who in the early nineteenth century

followed a nomadic and often, no doubt, a plundering existence in the neighbourhood of the Orange River. Others, captured by commandos in raids on or in the colony itself, were 'indentured' to the service of frontier farmers, and reduced, in effect, to the status of serfs. Only a small remnant of the Hottentots retained a semblance of freedom under their own captains within the colonial boundaries, such "kraals" as survived in this way tending to become mission stations. About 1803 the Batavian Government authorized the London missionary van der Kemp to found the first of the purely missionary 'Institutions', a farm settlement for the protection of Hottentots, at Bethelsdorp, and in 1813, by the good offices of Sir John Cradock, a migration from Bethelsdorp founded Theopolis. Meantime other institutions had grown up, and in 1822 Lord Charles Somerset recognized a distinction between those which were the property of the London Missionary Society, and others, like Pacaltsdorp and Genadendal, over which the Government claimed a special jurisdiction as survivals of older Hottentot captaincies, and 'belonging' in some sense to the Hottentot inhabitants. The great mass of the Hottentots, however, were scattered about the country as dependants in the service of individual Boers; and it was this class who constituted the really formidable problem of government.

The Hottentots were beyond doubt deplorably backward. Nothing whatever had been done to adapt them to the changed conditions brought about by the advent of the white man. In the spirit of the 'Nordic Legend', with wearisome iteration, the text-books dismiss the race with the epithets 'dirty, thieving, and lazy'. But scores of passages might be quoted in which the missionaries describe our own ancestors in just the same terms. To give one at random; these are the words used of St. Walock's fifth-century converts,[1] the forebears of the solid and efficient rural stock of Aberdeenshire:

> But the race whom he preferred to convert to the faith of Christ, and whom actually by his preaching and exhortation he did convert, no one would hesitate to describe as fierce, untamed, void of decency of manners and virtue, and incapable of easily listening to the word of truth, whose conversation was rather that of the brutes that perish than of men. For they had neither altar nor temple, nor any oratory in which they might return thanks to their Creator, but like brute beasts were given to eating, sleeping, and gorging.

The influence and fate of the Hottentots, so generally

[1] Aberdeen Breviary, quoted by J. G. Michie in the *History of Logie Coldstone and the Braes of Cromar.*

ranked by South African tradition as among the lowest of the
low, have been curiously and strikingly different from that of
the Bushmen.   Except in distant parts of South-West Africa,
the pure-blooded Hottentot is now almost as rare as the real
Bushman; but his extinction has been of a very different
order.   He has shown a power of amalgamation and adapta-
bility above the average.   Conquered by the Bantu, and submerged by the European, his type yet persists, suggesting that
he had distinctive qualities of his own.   West of the Kei, and
in the North-West (Bechuanaland), the Bantu met and mixed
freely with them, and Hottentot influence survives in place-
names like Keiskama ('Clear Water').   According to local
tradition there is one mountain of 'the Hottentot', which
is said to commemorate a Kafir chief known by that name.
Still more significant, it appears to be from Hottentot associations that the South African Bantu acquired the famous clicks
which are superficially the most distinctive feature of their
language.   Many so-called Kafirs betray unmistakably Hottentot features.   Also, in the dry interior, the Hottentots, with
the addition of a dash of European blood, are the principal
constituent of the small mixed race known as Griquas, who
played a not unimportant part in the history of the interior,
and produced in Andries Waterboer, and the later Adam Kok,
chieftains of some character and ability.   But, above all, the
Hottentots are very much with us yet, being by far the most
distinct element in the great mixed mass, descended from
Hottentots, slaves, and Europeans, but forming now one
distinct class, whom we describe as 'Cape Coloured'.

The charge of 'thieving', indiscriminately hurled alike at
Hottentots, Bushmen, and Kafirs, suggests comment.   It is an
old saying that it is unsafe to bring an indictment against a
nation; but the complaints of the European against primitive
peoples like the South African natives are so widespread as
to demand some investigation.   Almost certainly there is one
explanation, striking deep down to the core of the problem.
It is convenient and proper that in civilized communities the
law against theft should be so firmly established as to appear to
be grounded in fundamental and axiomatic moral principle.
Yet in truth the details of our law of property are highly
conventional, and very largely depend on accidents of history
and individual point of view.   They are neither fundamental
nor immutable, and the sacred rights of personal property or
individual ownership of land, which were the most fruitful
matter of friction with the African natives, are in truth the

privilege of the 'ruling classes', and of recent growth—the product largely of the commercialization of Europe since the close of the Middle Ages.[1]   They show extreme tenderness for the privileges of individuals.   Even in feudalism there were land*lords* in plenty, but only one land*owner*—the representative of the nation, the King.   The right of the village community to share the land, the pasture, the waste, and the water, was communal, not individual, and entrenched against the lord's encroachment by old custom, which had some of the force of law.   Similarly, the Kafir chief controlled the land, in trust for his tribe—though no doubt, also, Kafir chief, like feudal lord, might on occasion override his dependants by brute force. Had the meeting of European and African occurred in the Middle Ages rather than after the Reformation, it is possible that the contact might have been easier and more natural.   As it is, the scrappy survivals of Kafir tribal custom throw a good deal of light on the customs relating to land and property among the Anglo-Saxons or Germans, on the interpretation of which European scholarship has long been divided.   In Kafir custom, though he may have certain rights, even in property, the individual is always strictly subordinate to the community. It may even be that the extreme individualism of the Western European, with its late-born emphasis on property, explains the violence of the antipathy displayed toward the aboriginals by their conquerors of the great 'Nordic' race.   The Protestant, individualist, commercialized Germanic races have been less inclined to mix with dark peoples than their Catholic, social, agriculturist cousins of the Latin South.   Not that the Northern commoners submitted without a struggle when their own masters began to force upon them newer views of the sacred rights to property in land, and in everything on that land.   To believe the men who framed the Forest laws of the Norman conquerors, the early English must have been as incorrigible 'thieves' as ever were Hottentots or Bushmen; and the provisions of the latest Stock Theft Act [2] of the Union of South

[1] *The Acquisitive Society*, by R. H. Tawney (Bell, 1922): 'For the definition of a privilege is a right to which no corresponding function is attached'.

[2] Act No. 26 of 1923.   At an Albany Farmers' Congress, held in Grahamstown on 1st April 1925, Colonel Kirkpatrick, Deputy Commissioner of Police, replied to complaints about stock-thieving, that 'the cost of living had enormously increased, but the native was not receiving remuneration commensurate with that increase. It was the considered opinion of every police officer that the food of the farm servant wanted looking into. . . . If farm hands were

Africa, which makes the theft of a sheep by a starving and underpaid Native herd an offence comparable with manslaughter, may be set against the spring-guns and man-traps for trespassers which were defended in the British House of Commons as lately as the nineteenth century.[1]

Our laws against theft—the Ark of the Covenant of civilization—are scarcely an ultimate standard, to be ruthlessly applied to peoples of varying circumstances and mentality. The so-called savage, like the poorest of our own poor, readily shares his last bite with his fellows—in that way, it may be, more truly a man than his 'betters'. But at the same time, if he 'owns' not so much as one sheep, he regards the nearest 'fountain', and the beasts that share it with him, as in some indefinable way 'his'. If the trekking Boer, with his developed sense of individual property, chooses, as he must, to water his cattle at the Bushman's fountain, then the Bushman who lives by his skill in the chase, and to whom beef is more palatable than mutton, justifies his action of 'theft' by immemorial custom, which gave him a 'right' to animals using his own water-hole.

The 'Kafirs', too, are bitterly blamed for their 'thieving propensities';[2] yet they were a comparatively advanced people, and their own tribal law and custom made considerable provision for the compassing of thieves. Here, even more clearly, much of the difficulty can be explained by the post-mediæval development of European ideas of property; for English Edgar's tenth-century Ordinance of the Hundred might very well stand as a description of the modern Bantu custom known as 'spoor-law'.[3] The basis of Bantu law is still communal, but their attachment to the site of the graves of their chiefs shows them to be more than nomadic in their attitude to land. Though scholarship is only just beginning to throw light on the ways of primitive thought, it is clear that this strange and late development, the European idea of private ownership in land

better treated and it could be proved that there was no necessity to steal, heavier sentences would be imposed.' He also called attention to the failure of farmers to protect their cattle by a proper system of branding (*The Star*, 1st April 1925). Judges of the Eastern Districts Circuit have made similar comments from the Bench.

[1] A. V. Dicey, *Law and Opinion in England.*
[2] Cf. Cory, *History, passim.*
[3] Stubbs' Select Charters, and Sections 2, 4, 5, 6, and 8 of the Ordinance. Possibly even the cryptic clause 8, 'An ox's bell, and a dog's collar, and a blast-horn' as an 'informer', would be intelligible to the Kafir.

and grazing, put a heavy burden on the Kafirs, for it commonly excluded them from the privilege of using land which they regarded as their own. In an immense country with no boundary fences, when people came together in search of grazing and water, there was nothing to prevent the mixing of their cattle. Abram and Lot, in similar circumstances, found room for a mutually agreed policy of 'segregation'; but, failing this, there was no law but that of might. And indeed the wholesale charges of thieving levelled against the Kafirs are a little disingenuous. A law against theft must apply to white and black alike, but the whites for their part had little or no regard for the communal rights of the natives. Dr. Philip, writing to Sir B. D'Urban in July 1834 on the troubles of the Kafir frontier, which he ascribed to the encroachments of white colonization, put the case bluntly, but not inaccurately:

> The migration of the Boers into the country of the Bushmen and other tribes is not less unjustifiable than the alleged inroads and robberies laid to the charge of the Caffres by the Colonists. The natives have just as much justice on their side when they seize the cattle of the Boers, as the Boers have in seizing their country. It is said they only take possession of these tracts of country at certain seasons, and afterwards return to their farms within the colony. But these seasons are seasons of scarcity to the natives as well as to the farmers and this makes their conduct doubly aggressive. Their flocks and herds consume the whole pasturage of the countries they invade and the natives are left in a state of utter destitution.

This the Colonial Government knew quite well. More than once Sir B. D'Urban, like earlier Governors, issued proclamations against emigration, even when protesting [1] that they were powerless to stop the outward flow of Boers, who often had no thought of return. There is little evidence that the Government ever made any serious attempt to enforce its pious proclamations.[2] The clash of war was the inevitable result of this policy of *laissez-faire*. The Kafirs' systematic cattle-stealing from the Colony was largely, therefore, a defensive act of war, and their only way of protecting their own rights to the land.

With their own keen sense of justice, the Bantu keep a

[1] Cf. opinion of Attorney-General Oliphant in September 1834, which was a result of these representations made by Dr. Philip in July.

[2] On the contrary, Major Dundas, Landdrost of Albany, on 11th April 1828 issued a qualified permission to evade the law; and on 13th September 1840 Capt. Rawstorne, in charge at Colesberg, complained that the Cape of Good Hope Punishment Act of 1836 was a dead letter.

peculiar balance between privilege and duty. If, to this day, even educated and trusted natives betray what to European minds seem strange vagaries with regard to domestic property or church finance—habitually, for instance, ranking courtesy above truthfulness—yet their social system is less selfish than much of our 'acquisitive' individualism. It may yet prove more of a curse than a blessing if Western ideas of property, severely on their trial as they are, go further in the breaking down of the older traditions of mutual help and assistance. These at least mitigate among the Bantu the extremes of wealth and poverty that disfigure our Western society—perhaps unfortunately disguising the truth by freeing the State from the trouble and expense of Native Poor Relief. Though it would be impossible for two races to maintain, in the same community, divergent codes, yet it is certainly unreasonable to look for the adaptation of the more backward people to a strange and new standpoint except in the course of generations.[1]

The Hottentot also in much of his offending was but fulfilling his own rule of life. In early British times his prime offence was vagrancy, which meant that he chose to live as a primitive nomad by 'thieving', rather than by service with the farmers. The definitions of an abortive Vagrant Law of 1834 indicate the connotation of the term 'thieving'. 'That the searching for and the digging for roots', it runs, 'or fruits, the natural produce of the earth, or wild honey, or the searching for, taking and killing any game, or any other wild animal, of what kind soever, on any ground not being the property of the person so doing', or 'not having previously obtained permission', shall not be deemed to be 'lawful

[1] On 1st September 1848, Rev. H. Dyke wrote from Thaba Bosigo to Dr. Philip, commenting as follows: 'It is apparent that affairs in this land will soon assume an aspect different to that which they have hitherto worn; the political position of the Bassouto is undergoing a great change, they are now brought into constant contact with the whites, and this cannot long be a peaceful contact unless the old customs of the natives are much modified or replaced by the laws of the new comers, for which laws I doubt if they (the natives) are prepared to give acceptance as yet. Probably the Governor during his journey in these parts, will be proposing plans which will in many respects affect the feeling of the people towards the British. I am fully aware it is impossible to satisfy the natives in every respect, but I trust His Excellency may be directed aright and patiently consider the claims of the different tribes before he makes any final decision; in his visit of January last, he was too sweeping in his arrangements, in a few years therefore the greatest mistakes may have arisen; it is indeed a time for those interested in the aborigines to lift up their prayer for South Africa.'

D

employment by which any person can *honestly* earn the means of subsistence'.   This accurately represents the white colonists' point of view; for in 1834 this measure actually passed the Legislative Council, in face of opposition from all the official members, being later disallowed.   The phrases quoted could hardly more accurately describe the original and natural life of the Hottentots.   This, indeed, was recognized by the officials, who justified their dissenting vote by minuting their opinion—that the Hottentots had been deprived of these means of natural subsistence, with no compensation in land; that they had received no systematic instruction of any kind to teach them a better way of living, and that they ought not to be 'punished' for living their own life until such other provision had been made for them.[1]   They had suffered revolution both in the mode of their life and in their ideas of property—their addiction to petty thieving arising from this lack of conformity with civilized convention.   They were primitive people, who had not yet learned the religion of work for work's sake; and when they tried to live on game, or even on roots, Nature's gift of food, they could find these fruits only on land which had become 'private property'.   They could satisfy their hunger, if not in service that was serfdom, then only by 'thieving', even on the open veld.

The Hottentots are further said to have been incurably lazy.   But laziness is a relative term.   No pastoral people need be as hard - working as a settled agricultural peasantry: nor could the Hottentots, under South African conditions, have been other than pastoralists.   But once they had lost their land, and, in consequence, the possibility of keeping cattle, they were almost compelled to 'steal'.   For in depriving them of their rights in the land the colonists had done nothing whatever to teach them a new mode of life.   Where the Europeans themselves were so destitute of educational facilities, the absence of Hottentot schools was pardonable.   But from the day, in 1658, when the first slaves were imported till the time of the abolition of the slave trade, in 1807, the utility of the Hottentots, even as producers, was never thought worth considering.   While many of them drifted into the service of the white colonists, chiefly with the outlying cattle farmers, the more settled agriculturists of the West trusted to imported slaves for their manual labour and despised the Hottentots too much even to set about curing their 'laziness' by teaching

[1] Draft Vagrant Law, with comments of officials, in *Grahamstown Journal*, 25th September and 2nd October 1834.

them and giving them some motive for work. Only when the slave supply stopped, after 1807, did the farmers begin to demand measures to compel the Hottentots to fill the gap. In truth, the fate of the Hottentots might have been kinder— could hardly have been worse—had the Company taken van Riebeeck's advice and allowed the aboriginals to be reduced definitely to the hard school of slavery. But, rejecting that logical alternative, the Company tried an impossible compromise. It refused to include the Hottentots in the Colony. Though they came to be an inseparable part of its economic system, they were yet outside the law, as if they were an independent and distinct people. It was not that the Company or its officials were willingly countenancing injustice. Often they punished white colonists for offences against Hottentots. Once, at least, they cancelled a grant of land on the ground of the prior occupational rights of one Wild-Schut, a Hottentot captain on the outskirts of Stellenbosch.[1] But without administrative machinery, and without police to make protection effective, it was the Rule of a Company rather than of a State; and the definition of the legal status of the Hottentots was left a thorny legacy to the Company's successors.

When, after 1795, the Government of the diverse peoples of South Africa passed for ever from the hands of a Company of Merchants to a responsible State Government, the issues left on one side by the Company were no longer to be evaded. The theory that the Hottentots were an independent people, outside the Colony and beyond its laws, could not suffice when the great majority of them were either the actual servants of the colonists, or else wanderers on colonial land. In either case they were within the Colony, but they had neither protection as servants, nor any legal right to the land. Significantly, it is at this point that these nomads began to be called 'Vagrants'. The nomad is indifferent to land rights; he owns cattle and grazes them where he will, with no one seriously disputing his right to come and go as he will. The vagrant can hardly own anything; and his wanderings are on land which definitely belongs to another. Many of the Boer farmers were themselves nomadic; but the Hottentots, having lost all effective right to the land, had also lost their cattle and become vagrants by fate, not by choice. They could not but become dependent on the stronger race who had dispossessed them. It may well be that it was chiefly the

---

[1] Governor van Plettenberg to Landdrost of Stellenbosch, 31st January 1772, in D. Moodie, *Authentic Record*.

servants among them who retained any relics of their old wealth in cattle; for the Boer farmer readily allows his friends and his servants to 'run' their cattle, and share with his own stock the barrenness of his own extensive grazing lands. But for those Hottentots who had lost their cattle there was nothing to induce them to serve, certainly no good wages; and the very poorest of them probably became vagrants indeed, living precariously on roots and wild honey, supplemented at times no doubt by game and other 'theft'.

Here, then, were two classes to engage the attention of the Government that was to succeed to the evil legacy left by the East India Company. The regular servants could not now be enslaved, but their relation to the ordinary law of the land must be defined. The other class was an even greater difficulty, and for more than a generation, it would seem, if the colonists' complaints are to be believed, the bulk of the Hottentots were idle vagrants. That there was a class who never rose above vagrancy the circumstances of their recent history made inevitable; nothing whatever had been done to give them any substitute for the degraded 'freedom' of which the coming of the Europeans had deprived them; the first permanent missionaries and teachers arrived only in the very last years of the eighteenth century. The colonists, however, were very partial judges of what constituted vagrancy. Just at this time the removal of the Company's heavy restraints on trade brought economic revival. Synchronizing as it did with one of the periodical war-time 'booms', due to the passing by, or to the actual presence in Cape Town, of unusually large and no doubt spendthrift bodies of troops, this created something of a shortage of labour. When, in addition to all this, in 1807 the slave-trade was abolished, the shortage became so acute that at last the Hottentots, hitherto despised and neglected, came to be regarded as the obvious source from which to replenish the labour supply. In these circumstances Hottentots, great and small, the aged and infirm, nursing mothers and young children, were regarded as potential servants; and all who did not conform to the demand were classed as idle vagrants. In the same way South Africans of the present day tend to forget that to provide the Rand alone with a labour force of some 200,000 able-bodied adult males there must be a residue, somewhere, of a still greater number of non-effectives. The self-same charges of 'idleness' are hurled, in much the same terms as a century ago, against modern native 'Reserves' that any investigation would show to be utterly denuded of their able-bodied male population. The number of Hottentot 'vagrants' was grossly and habitually exaggerated.

The snares for any Government which had to deal with this situation are obvious enough at this distance of time. On the one hand, as an outside authority, concerned first of all for peace and order, it was bound to legislate for the protection of the weaker race against any excessive or arbitrary claims by the stronger colonists. On the other, the claims of the colonists, who after all were habitual slave-owners, had far readier access to the ear of the Government, and were little likely to err on the side of moderation. As early as 1799 General Dundas attempted to protect the servant Hottentots by reducing the terms of their service to a formal contract. In 1802 the British Governor's adjutant wrote to the first of the London missionaries, the scholarly if eccentric van der Kemp, urging him to continue his exertions on behalf of the Hottentots of Graaff-Reinet, and promising strong representations to the 'future government' on behalf of the Hottentots generally.

But the full force of the inevitable clash between Government and colonists on the question of Hottentot rights was yet to come. The first British occupation was always regarded as temporary; the Batavian Republic was little more than two years in control; and it was some time before the second British occupation of 1806 was known and felt to be permanent. Yet under its enlightened chiefs, the Commissary de Mist and General Janssens, there were straws to show which way the wind was blowing with the Batavian Government. It was by the influence of Dr. van der Kemp with his old college acquaintance, General Janssens, that the Batavian Republic, and not the fussy philanthropy of any British Governor, gave its sanction to the foundation of the missionary institution of Bethelsdorp— the object in the next generation of such virulent colonial abuse. Its aim was religious and educational, but also merely protective; Bethelsdorp and other institutions soon became the refuge of the necessarily dependent classes, the infirm, the weak, and the aged (and the mere existence of such centres doubtless brought hangers-on who suggested vagrancy and idleness to farmers who were greedy for a cheap labour supply). In addition, as the years passed, the more intelligent of the Hottentots came to learn that only on mission stations had they any secure base for the carrying on of trades, or even for 'transport-riding'. On ordinary farms—even with the development, after 1809, of protective contracts of service—the operation of restrictive pass laws and of the system euphemistically known as 'apprenticeship', gave some warrant for allegations that the lot of 'free' Hottentots was worse than that of slaves.   A slave's person was an asset, and even his family and dependants were worth caring for as the natural means of conserving and increasing the owner's 'property'.   A Hottentot's person and dependants were entirely his own affair.   To his employer the family were a mere encumbrance, and even if the servant himself died he could easily be replaced—whereas a slave cost money.

In the very midst of these political changes the missionaries came, heralding the birth of a new attitude towards the child races, and demanding some attempt to straighten out this difficult problem.   The successive Governments undoubtedly wished and tried to defend and protect the Hottentots, and to better their position; but even the Government ideal came somewhat into collision with the aims and interests of the farmers who desired above all else to make sure of a plentiful supply of cheap farm labour, and to have it under their own control.   If there were bound to be differences of opinion between any self-respecting Government and the farmers, who were still unrepentant slave-owners, the clash was intensified by the coming of the van der Kemps and Reads, who were not only full of sympathy for the hardships of the Hottentots, but armed with more detailed knowledge than any earlier Europeans had possessed of how things actually were with their Hottentot followers.   Not unnaturally, the farmers showed resentment at the doubts that began to be cast on the benevolence of the despotism they exercised over their servants.   But if, in their championship of Hottentot rights, the missionaries might on occasion be one-sided advocates, the farmers were no less prone to one-sidedness and exaggeration from their own point of view.

It fell to the responsible officials of a British Government that had the ill fortune also to be an alien to most of the colonists to mediate between these almost irreconcilable antagonists. The day of slavery was nearly over, but the alternative was yet to seek.

Chapter IV

COLONIAL GOVERNMENT AT THE TIME
OF THE TORY REACTION

THERE is a tradition that the treatment by Great Britain of its colonial possessions has always been marked by the high degree of freedom allowed to its subjects. The independence of the United States of America was merely the ripe fruit of a long enjoyment of very slightly fettered self-government; and in later times, historians of the British Commonwealth can point, with just cause for satisfaction, to the free development of the great Dominions. The optimistic regard of Burke and his eighteenth-century contemporaries for the delicate mechanism of the British constitution has combined with the national pride of the great Whig historians in the constitutional progress of Parliament, and the complacency of late Victorian Imperialists, to stretch the measure of truth in this claim into an unduly wide generalization. The tradition is of the freedom that 'slowly broadens down from precedent to precedent'.

But what may be true for the early days of the American colonies, and does on the whole distinguish the *laissez-faire* and 'Little Englandism' of the middle or later nineteenth century,[1] does not hold for the early years of the same century. So far from the substitution of British for Dutch rule at the Cape involving constitutional progress towards freedom, the first

[1] 'But for the help of many of the men who have been called separatists and Little Englanders, the Imperialists, both Tory and Whig, in their blindness to the growing nationhood of the Dominions, and in their anxiety to build up an Imperial super-state, might have brought the Empire to the brink of dissolution' (Duncan Hall, *British Commonwealth of Nations*, pp. 51-53).

generation of British rule at the Cape of Good Hope is marked, if anything, by an actual increase in the autocratic power of the Governors. Minor reforms indeed there were bound to be. The fiscal oppressions of the Company were somewhat relieved, though the Colony could not escape the effect of currency disorders which followed the great wars. The severity of the penal code was mitigated by the abolition of torture. The year 1798 saw the institution of the first regular inland post, and in 1800 the Government *Gazette* first appeared, though this was far indeed from signifying freedom of publication. Sir George Yonge was personally responsible for attempts to introduce improvements in agriculture. In addition, the royal instructions to the first regular Governor provided for liberty of conscience (though the first Wesleyan in 1814 had to get special leave to preach in public); and while it was also ordered that inquiry be made into the educational needs of the Colony, it was the 'twenties before any effective steps were taken to supply the want of teachers.

On the whole, the early British authorities were tender of the susceptibilities of their new Dutch subjects, and carried on with very little change the institutions that were familiar. The old courts and Roman-Dutch common law, together with the Dutch language and Dutch officials, continued as before, with improvements allowing Landdrosts' courts somewhat wider jurisdiction in petty cases. It has indeed been suggested[1] that the Landdrosts under the new regime tended to be English-speaking half-pay officers—less of the people than in Dutch days; but men like Colonel Cuyler of Uitenhage were more closely allied in interest with the Dutch burghers than some Dutch officials—for example, in the days of the quarrel with van der Stel. One important reform, the institution in 1811 of a Circuit Court, did indeed, for special reasons, cause serious friction; but no accidental trouble can make it anything but a reform to have brought the scattered population of a huge colony into closer touch with the administration of justice.

But improvements like these do not in themselves go far to justify complacency about the innate superiority of British colonial government and institutions. On the very best showing, early British rule at the Cape was benevolent despotism. Even the benevolence is doubtful. Lord Durham's view[2] was that even in Canada, at this time, the Governor's executive authority was hampered by instructions from Home, and by

[1] Eybers, *Select Documents*, p. xxvii.
[2] *Durham Report*, ed. Lucas, vol. 2, pp. 101 *et seq.*

the need of referring everything to the Colonial Office in London. For example, where important decisions of Native or frontier policy were concerned, the Cape system failed to yield the benefits of prompt decision, which might have been some compensation for absolutism. The Cape, that is to say, suffered the full effect of that worst of polities, a weak despotism, in that while individuals might be made to feel the sharp sting of a Somerset's displeasure,[1] there is no instance of any large measure of reform or progress that was carried through by force of his personality or prerogative.

The essence of the matter, so far as the Cape is concerned, was expressed in the model instructions to Earl Macartney in 1796, which vested 'all the powers of government, as well Civil as Military, solely in you our Governor'.[2] Any such feeble local check on autocracy as the old time Fiscal's independent right of access to the authorities in Holland was swept aside; and when the issue was joined with Somerset in the eighteen-twenties, there clearly were cases where champions of colonial rights had difficulty in getting their complaints transmitted to Downing Street.[3] For the rest, the drafting of new laws and the interpretation of old, with the administration of either, the appointment and dismissal of judges, and in the last resort the presidency of the final court of appeal, were one and all 'vested solely in the Governor'. The judges of the old Dutch Court had at least held office for life, and some provision was made for complaints by the Burgher Council to be transmitted in extremity to Holland.[4] But here, in short, were legislative, executive and judicial power all finally reposing in one man—no academic 'division of powers', but the very type and pattern of autocracy. The autocrats at the Cape had their strict counterpart in Lord Charles Somerset's contemporary, Governor Lachlan MacQuarie of New South Wales,[5] and the system remained unchanged till after the fall of Somerset. The Cape, it may be said, was a colony peopled by aliens, newly acquired by right of conquest, and needing a firm rule to tide it over a period of transition; and the peculiar penal character of the Australian settlement did not lend itself

[1] See below, Chap. XIV., and for a possible exception, p. 72.
[2] Eybers, pp. 5 *et seq.*
[3] C. C. Records, cases of Edwards, etc. Here lay the effectiveness of missionaries like Dr. Philip, who, through "Exeter Hall", were able, in defiance of the Governor, to get the ear of the House of Commons and of Downing Street.
[4] Eybers, p. 25.
[5] M. Phillips, *A Colonial Autocracy*, P. S. King.

to constitutional experiments in freedom.   But neither at this time was British rule in the older colony of Canada running smoothly, nor according to the general will of its colonists; for there, says the Durham Report, 'the Colony has in every crisis of danger, and almost every detail of local management, felt the mischief of having its executive authority exercised on the other side of the Atlantic'.

The truth is that in the midst of greater distractions nearer Home, the Mother country took but little interest in the affairs of the Colonies.   The Colonies evoked in those days little but 'indifference tempered by uneasiness';[1] national pride in 'our Imperial heritage' is the product of a much later day. The loss of the American Colonies was long regarded by men of all parties as a portent of the inevitable end.   The orthodox economists, a powerful force, were apt to extend Adam Smith's condemnation of 'colonial monopoly' to colonies in themselves.   While the trade with free America was growing, in spite of independence, and the Navigation Laws, the pillar of the old colonial policy, were obviously passing away, the emphasis in colonial debates tended to be laid by Joseph Hume and later Radicals on the trouble and expense involved in maintaining any colonies at all.[2]   Even in the 'thirties and 'forties, when the efforts of Wakefield and his school had begun to bear fruit in experiments in systematic colonization, the House was more than once counted out on the occasion of a colonial debate;[3] and it was no less a person than Disraeli who spoke of these wretched colonies as 'a millstone about our necks'.   References to the colonies are few and far between in the speeches not only of Cobden, Bright, and Gladstone, but, before 1870, even of Disraeli.   So far as concerns the Cape, which never attracted even Gibbon Wakefield's attention, the *Annual Register*, the well-known chronicle of all events likely to be of any public interest, gave a short account of the Kafir War of 1835, but in 1836, the classic year of the Great Trek, it had no reference whatever to events at the Cape of Good Hope.

In the matter of colonial government there is some confusion about the effect of American independence; sometimes it may have tempted Governors to try the 'firm hand'; but after 1807 men so eminent as Canning showed much hesitation before going counter to the West Indian Parliaments in the

---

[1] Mills' *Colonization of Australia*, pp. 24-30.
[2] Smart, *Econ. Annals*, ii, pp. 224, 272.
[3] See reference in Mills, *op. cit.*, p. 23.

matter of slavery.[1]   Even in 1791 the older tradition of freedom
was sufficiently vigorous, not only to secure a parliamentary
constitution for the 'United Empire' Loyalists of Upper
Canada, but apparently to force the same doubtfully desired
benefit upon the comparatively lately conquered French of the
Province of Quebec. (*'C'est une machine anglaise pour nous
taxer'*, they are said to have complained.)   But no such boon
was thrust upon the Dutch at the Cape, nor even on the
English settlers in Australia, for many years to come.   The
dominant influence even in colonial policy, for the next generation, was reaction against the far more potent forces loosed
thirteen years later by the French Revolution.

Nor was there any real improvement till new influences
at Home began to bring about a fundamental change of colonial
policy, and the development of the principle of colonial self-
government.   In the early nineteenth century, therefore,
British Colonial policy was far removed from the tradition of
freedom, and fell inevitably under the influence of the dominant
Tory Reaction.   Governors carried out a policy either in
accord with their own personal whims, or by express direction
of their superiors in Downing Street.   Policy was largely in
the hands of individuals whose ideas or prejudices were
moulded by forces at work in Great Britain.   When colonial
opinion counted for so little, great issues depended on the
peculiar outlook and traditions of the great British governing
class, as it was in the days before 1832 and the Reform Act.

Now, it is the orthodox view that the reinforcement of the
more long-suffering, politically backward Dutch at the Cape
by the coming of the 1820 Settlers is almost, in itself, sufficient
explanation of the political agitation which marked the later
years of Governor Lord Charles Somerset.   The Governor,
we are told, on his return from England in 1821, was so
absorbed by 'anxiety and concern for his own personal and
family affairs' that he was 'precluded from realizing the
altered state of things which was called into existence by the
arrival of so many people from England, bringing with them
their large ideas of freedom of speech and action'.[2]   No
doubt the Settlers furnished individual leaders like Thomas
Pringle who were more formidable and experienced than the
older Dutch colonists; yet, in all its history, the 'Settlers'
City', Grahamstown, has never been conspicuous as a home

---

[1] On the Anti-Slavery Movement, see Coupland's *Wilberforce*
(Oxford, 1923), and Smart, *Economic Annals of the Nineteenth Century*
(Macmillan).   [2] Cory, ii, p. 245.

of Radicalism. For reasons of its own prestige, it may be, it opposed to the end the adoption of full Responsible Government; and the truth is that the Settlers themselves, drawn as they were from amongst the best and most venturesome of the distressed industrial classes, can have included but a small percentage either of enfranchised voters or of practised political agitators. The Reform Movement of that time was an affair of the manufacturers and of the middle classes, working class agitation belonging rather to a later day. Some of the Settlers may have witnessed scenes like the immortal election at Eatanswill, but any considerable practice of freedom of speech would certainly have cost them dear in the England they had left behind them.

On the other hand, that Somerset was obsessed by 'anxiety for personal and family affairs' is very probable. Such concern was, indeed, characteristic of the great English ruling family connections. Their zest for 'places' was nearly shameless. In the words of Lord Rosebery, the creed of the eighteenth-century Whigs—the exposition of the 'principles of the Glorious Revolution'—maintained 'a triple divine right: the divine right of (their) families to govern the Empire, to be maintained by the Empire, and to show their superiority by humbling and bullying the sovereign of the Empire'.[1] Not the least significant part of this indictment is the last clause, with its perfect counterpart in the theology current in the mid-eighteenth century, according to which the deistic Almighty left the world He had called into being to follow its own devices, without inconvenient divine intervention.[2] The God of Deism was typified in the conception of the Whig constitutional monarch, whose great merit, in the palmy days of Whiggism, before the innovations of the 'Patriot King', was to mind his own business, and to leave the great Whig families to manage the kingdom. The essentials of the system practised by the earlier Whigs continued, even when the distinction between Whig and Tory became blurred; the spoils of office were the perquisites of that small but brilliant ruling class, self-seeking, yet not wanting in public spirit, the English aristocracy.

The working of the British constitution in the eighteenth and early nineteenth centuries differed in important particulars of spirit, rather than of letter, from that noble fabric as we know it to-day. While seldom or never completely losing

[1] Quoted in Fortescue, *British Statesmen of the Great War*, p. 21.
[2] L. Stephen, *English Thought in the Eighteenth Century*.

touch with popular feeling, the constitution secured no continuous and effective popular control of British national policy; the country was governed, not like France, by a paid bureaucracy, centred in and wholly dependent on the Crown, but, with a total absence of administrative centralization, by the aristocracy and gentry.   This class not only dominated both Houses of Parliament,[1] but, without payment, monopolized and controlled the extensive machinery of local government.   There was 'the combination of an absolute centralization of legislative power, with an utter absence of administrative centralization'.[2]   The weakness of the central administration is the mark of the Revolution Settlement.   It was of set purpose that Parliament kept control in its own hands, or in that of its own members or adherents.   The carrying out of works by the Government would have necessitated a central body; and boards and committees involved patronage and 'places'. But the popularity of Place Acts was due, not to a conscientious objection to places in themselves, but to the fear that their 'gift' would pass to the Crown, and work to the elevation of the powers of King or Cabinet, at the expense of those of the aristocracy.

It must of course be said that this aristocratic government had its merits.   It was certainly not unpopular, and perhaps reflected with fair accuracy 'the will of the people'.   There is a modern South African parallel in the persistence with which the growing class of landless, rural Dutch send to represent them in Parliament the wealthiest landlords in their neighbourhood, and are scarcely even yet conscious that the interests of landlords and of landless *bijwoners* may be in sharp conflict.   Their wealthy and successful neighbours are their natural leaders, even as the peers and squires were the leaders of the rustics of England a hundred years ago, as they sometimes are still.   There was, in favoured spots, a good deal of vigour and even of popular participation in some of the old organs of Local Government.   The sound political instinct, which perhaps honourably distinguishes English life, owes not a little to the long discipline which obliged even a small class of ratepayers to take responsibility, and pay local rates, for supplying their own local needs.   No doubt much that was desirable was left undone; but there was less dependence on

---

[1] Of 513 members for England and Wales, 306 were returned by 160 persons: Anson, *Law and Custom*, p. 124; see also, Halévy, *England in 1815*.

[2] Leslie Stephen, *English Utilitarians*, i, p. 30.

appeals, *ad misericordiam*, to 'the Government', and less expenditure, it may be, on inspectors and on officials at the capital.   Though much of the burden of Government fell on men with the limitations of Squire Western, it seems to be the considered judgment of the leading modern authority that the trading and dishonest Justice of the Peace was the exception, and that the ruling classes of England gave honourably a good measure of voluntary unpaid service.[1]   The old system had one supreme merit.   It did in great measure avoid the fatal modern divorce between the possession of great riches and public responsibility or 'function'.   The right to property was comparatively easily tolerated, so long as it carried with it a corresponding duty to assume the onerous tasks of government.

On the other hand, if the rights of the aristocracy carried their corresponding duties, yet the duties, in their turn, were very widely conceived of as carrying with them the right to be suitably rewarded by perquisites and places.   Commissions in the army, seats in Parliament, patronage in the Church, were the personal property of the ruling classes.   Well might Paley suggest as the suitable text for a university sermon in honour of Pitt's visit to Cambridge: 'There is a lad here which hath five barley loaves and two small fishes, but what are they among so many?'

So far as the Colonies were concerned, there is little doubt that the 'loaves and fishes' were of particular interest to the Home Government.   At the height of the struggle with Napoleon, Grenville and Windham were conducting a 'lengthy correspondence of ceremonious acrimony' as to whether a certain auditorship at the Cape of Good Hope was in the 'gift' of the Treasury or of the Colonial Office.[2]   The worthy but by no means distinguished husband of Lady Anne Barnard owed his appointment to the good offices of Henry Dundas, the well-known Lord Melville.   The stay and support of Lord Charles Somerset was the great Beaufort connection, which, as he boasted against his critics, controlled a dozen or more seats in the House of Commons.   One after another, gentlemen whose chief qualification for office was that they had served with Wellington in the Peninsula, or in France, were sent to fill the post of Governor.   For the personal character of these Governors there may be nothing but respect, tempered perhaps by a remark on the tenderness of men like Somerset for the placing of their own dependants.   The

[1] S. and B. Webb, *English Local Government*, i, p. 372.
[2] Fortescue, *British Statesmen of the Great War*.

serious danger of the system was that these Governors might find themselves transplanted, with no training, and less equipment of ideas, to positions of virtual irresponsibility. At Home there were effective checks on tyrannical Government. Even the Tory reaction broke at last on the strength of public opinion, not wholly unexpressed even in a muzzled Press. Above and beyond the Press were the powers, occasionally asserted, and always to be feared, of an independent Bench, and the still more formidable independence of juries, which in that age, especially, were a wholesome check on the executive Government. In colonies of the Cape type, acquired by right of conquest, there was no such check. The Governor was at once legislature, executive, judiciary, and newspaper press (the Government *Gazette* being till 1824 the only semblance of a newspaper). His superior at Home was, till 1854, Secretary of State both for War and for the Colonies; after 1815 the portfolio of War was perhaps less absorbing; but, with rare exceptions, the Colonial Secretaryship was long regarded as a junior Cabinet post, to be filled by new or less distinguished members.[1] The Home direction of colonial policy, therefore, more especially perhaps between 1827 and 1839, when ministers were constantly changing, tended to pass into the hands of permanent officials. Several of these, as it happened, were men of considerable ability and eminence. The first Sir James Stephen (Gibbon Wakefield's *Mr. Over-Secretary Stephen*, or *Mr. Mother-Country*) was influential as early as 1825, and permanent head of the Department from 1836 to 1847; he was succeeded by the historian Merivale, 1847–1859, who was followed by Frederick Rogers, Lord Blachford, 1860–1871. It is by no means easy to estimate the influence of these great Civil Servants.

It remains that there was justification for James Mill's distrust of 'Colonies which make places, and wars that breed more places'. Colonial policy was, till at least 1867, a concern chiefly of the upper classes, and of these very often only for the sake of the spoils. No doubt the Reform agitation of the late 'twenties, and the passing of the Reform Act in 1832, made some difference, and mitigated the irresponsible autocracy practised by the earlier Governors; but liberal grants of self-government became the fashion only with the second generation of Whig reformers, after the Durham Report. This liberalism,

[1] The choice of the Colonial Secretaryship by a man of the political importance of Mr. Joseph Chamberlain in 1895 was regarded as something of a portent.

which contributed much to build up the best British colonial tradition, followed, if it was not produced by, *laissez-faire* economics. Self-government was a device for relieving the Mother Country of the expense and responsibility of colonies. The characteristic attitude of the middle years of the century was that which left South Africa to go very much its own way, as when the British Government recognized the independence of the two Dutch Republics in 1852 and 1854. Not till the basis of Government at Home was broadened by the enfranchisement of the working-classes was there much scope for the later 'imperial sentiment' which draws popular support from those whose children founded homes and discovered El Dorado in the Colonies.[1]

For the Cape, which even in the 'thirties and 'forties attracted far fewer of these emigrants than Canada or Australia, there was only one important English class to which its affairs were not matters of complete indifference; and the neglect, born of this indifference, was the opportunity which gave their place in Cape affairs to those who alone had any direct information about them—the Evangelical philanthropists and their active Colonial representatives, the Missionaries. At least once, in the memorable crisis of 1835, the Colonial Secretary of the day drew, with far-reaching consequences, upon this private source of information, to make good the deficiencies, as it seemed to him, of the despatches of the Colonial Governor.[2]

[1] Duncan Hall, *op. cit.*
[2] P.R.O.   Papers relating to Kafir War of 1835, C.O. 48, No. 165.

Chapter V

THE HUMANITARIAN AND MISSIONARY MOVEMENTS: 'EXETER HALL'

'And so the earth and the sea closed over one who was great as a poet, and greater still as a *philanthropist*.' [1]

THE name Philanthropist has long fallen into ill-repute. It may be that a pompous solemnity of bearing and lack of humour laid the nineteenth century Philanthropists open to ridicule. Years after Canning had made glorious fun of the *Needy Knife-Grinder and the Friend of Humanity*, they were still appealing to each other, in the same old phrase, as the 'friends of humanity'. But a good deal of their ill-repute must be set down to the unpopularity of their views, and to the unjust opprobrium that clings to those who have the courage to champion the cause of the weak and the oppressed. In South Africa they are commonly pilloried as 'the pseudo-philanthropic party'.

In England the champions of the 'oppressed natives of Africa' were 'Wilberforce of the Africans', Thomas Fowell Buxton, and their circle. The 'Wilberforce of Africa' was Dr. John Philip of the London Missionary Society. Though it is true to say that they were both phases of one great movement towards freedom, little direct connection can be traced between the ideas of this group and those of the French philosophers; and so far as the Cape is concerned, all the driving force behind British policy in the first half of the nineteenth century seems to have lain in the religious movement.

The Protestant Foreign Missionary Movement, which so profoundly influenced colonial history, was the typical product

[1] Mary Shelley, on the death of her husband (Dowden's *Life*).

of the Evangelical Revival of the eighteenth century. While
the Church of Rome never ceased its missionary activities, the
Churches of the Reformation almost wholly abandoned the
attempt to carry out the mission of the Church to all nations,
till their conscience was pricked by the Revival.[1] The later
Protestantism hardly lived up to the religious fervour from
which the Reformation sprang. The work of Calvinists and
Puritans in the Netherlands, in Scotland, and in England, made
greatly for political freedom; but in the long and bitter struggle
for existence they lost the gentler graces, and ultimately Protestantism sank into the languor from which it was revived only by
Wesley and the Evangelicals.

In the first generation the new movement made headway
chiefly amongst the humbler classes of the population. Society
looked askance at this outbreak of fervid, unreasoning religious
enthusiasm. It was only in the decade of the French Revolution, when the festival of reason was celebrated within the walls
of Notre Dame, that the spirit of the Methodist Revival at last
kindled a strong flame within the Established Church, which
had virtually driven John Wesley himself outside the pale. In
England the years of the greatest vigour of the French Revolution were the most active period of religious propaganda. Then
it was that William Wilberforce and his friends began to
'organize, to send into all lands, especially their own, the
witnesses of the Church'.[2] In 1804 they founded the British
and Foreign Bible Society. Another agent was the Religious
Tract Society (1799); and Wilberforce himself, besides forming
a Society for the Reformation of Manners, was responsible for
a characteristic contribution to the edification of the faithful
in his 'Practical view of the prevailing Religious System of
Professed Christians in the Higher and Middle Classes of this
Country contrasted with real Christianity', a title which reflects
faithfully the essentially non-popular character of the new
development. The Church and Rectory at Clapham were the
centres from which emanated a living stream for the fructifying
of the moral waste places of England. Patrons like Henry
Thornton did something to heal the breach between Christians,
conforming and non-conforming, by keeping open house, and
providing summer holidays for needy Congregationalist and

[1] The chief and honourable exception to the rule was the missionary work of the small band of Moravian Brethren. The Society for
the Propagation of the Gospel, 1714, gave some attention, it would
seem, to the religious needs chiefly of English settlers in the Colonies.
[2] Stephen, *Ecclesiastical Biography*, vol. ii.

Wesleyan preachers. Zacchary Macaulay, returned from practical philanthropy at Sierra Leone, presided over the *Christian Observer*,[1] and Hannah More was one of those who made it fashionable to 'work amongst the poor'.[2] Many of Dr. Philip's well-connected correspondents, such as Captain Vernon, son of an Archbishop of York, or Sir Jahleel Brenton, are full of concern for missions to seamen or for infant schools. The Sunday Schools were begun, some years earlier (1781), to provide the poorer classes with training in the three R's.

In spite of all this upper-class zeal and beneficence, it was the humble Methodists who kept the British working-class from drifting, like many continental socialists, into open antagonism to Christianity. These good and pious people, the Evangelicals of the Established Church, did but little to mitigate what has been described as 'the isolation of the poor' at that time.[3] Wilberforce, who often voted against his own Tory party, never failed to support authority when economic discontents were in question—the Combination Laws, the Six Acts, or the Suspension of Habeas Corpus. The friend of humanity and of African slaves, like others who had the clearest view of the economic defects of slave labour, always thought that British working men with grievances were over-anxious about 'the concerns of this world'.

The emphasis of recent historians has been on the social and economic accompaniments of the Industrial Revolution. The extraordinarily narrow and short-sighted attitude of Wilberforce and his friends to social and economic reform has therefore alienated thinkers, for example, in the Labour Movement, who seem to be the successors of Wilberforce and the missionaries as the most watchful defenders of the rights of the 'oppressed of Africa'; while the champions of the 'colonists' have been at no pains to analyse the views of the Evangelicals, and rend the missionaries with criticisms which, so far as they are just, would apply to the whole trend of eighteenth-century thought. The blindness of Wilberforce to the meaning of the struggles at his own door is, however, balanced by that of leaders on the other side, like Cobbett, who not only supported the slave trade by arguments from Scripture, but could see in the martyrdom of the missionary Smith of Demerara,

[1] A favourite contributor seems to have been the Rev. J. Bowdler, brother of Thomas, whose name has so doubtfully enriched the English language.
[2] Trevelyan's *Life of Macaulay*, p. 222.
[3] J. L. and B. Hammond, *Village Labourer*.

done to death by his sufferings at the hands of a colony of slave owners, nothing but the mad folly of 'this mischievous CANTER'.[1]

The Evangelical Revival from which the missionary movement sprang began in a reaction against the tyranny of reason, and its great achievement was to rediscover and emphasize the personal and emotional elements in religion which had been unduly repressed in the eighteenth century. But faith, born in the first exultant moment of conversion, may wither because, like Jonah's gourd, it has no roots. On the intellectual side Evangelicalism was weak. Unlike Puritanism, its far more robust forerunner, it produced no great literature, not even a school of apologists or theologians. Their faith seemed to the Evangelicals to need no defence; they were content, like Wilberforce himself, to accept 'received truth', leaving Christian apology to Broad Churchmen like Paley. Based as it was on the emotions, Evangelicalism was almost destitute of philosophic basis, repelling many, 'even thinkers grown up under its influence'.[2] It set little store by forms and organization, in Church or State—differing in this, fundamentally, from early Puritanism. But it is some measure of the influence of the Evangelicals that the moral standards of the squires and dowagers of Fielding or Smollett are so different from those of to-day. Their influence also, followed up and supplemented by that of the Tractarians, put an end to pluralities and absenteeism (the state of affairs existing in 1812, when of 10,000 incumbents of the Church of England nearly 6000 were non-resident),[3] and to the ascendancy of the 'two-bottle orthodox'. Though the Evangelicals, with their emotional piety, were often deficient in a sense of humour, and frowned upon much that we count harmless amusement or valuable recreation, in this they were not unlike the Utilitarians. In spite of this, Evangelicalism gained a firm hold on the opinions and sympathy of the lay mass of the nation, leaving its enduring mark in the attitude of mind commonly known as the 'Nonconformist conscience'.

The Evangelicals, indeed, were strong with the strength of the religious genius Luther rather than with that of the statesman and organizer Calvin; and, like Lutheranism, the enthusiasm was less enduring. Inevitably, when their own intellectual interests were so slight, the outlook of the Evangelicals on other than religious questions took its colour from

[1] Quoted in Smart, *Economic Annals*, ii, p. 179.
[2] An obviously autobiographical reference in Leslie Stephen's *English Thought in the Eighteenth Century*, ii, p. 425.
[3] J. L. and B. Hammond, *The Village Labourer*, ch. viii.

the prevailing currents of thought. In humanitarian activity, which honourably distinguishes this religious revival from Puritanism, stern opponents of worldliness made common cause with men who were direct products of the Age of Reason. Even the period of the great Tory reaction is marked, not only by repressive measures, but also by notable reforms—the first, though feeble, Factory Act, 1802; the Act for the Prohibition of the Slave Trade, 1807; the Abolition of the Whipping of Women, 1820; the earliest attempt to forbid cruelty to animals, 1822; the Prohibition of the use of spring-guns.[1] The difference between Puritanism and Evangelicalism is due in great measure to the influence of that very rationalism which the Evangelicals abhorred. In the words of Mr. G. M. Trevelyan, 'Religion had been to school with her rival, Reason. From Cromwell to Wilberforce, the road lay through Voltaire'.[2]

One other weakness (which in some sort turned to strength) Evangelicalism shared with the thought of its day. Like the French revolutionaries, who sought to begin all things new, and like Bentham, in his contempt for legal antiquarianism, the Evangelicals made light of the authority of the Church or of Tradition. They ignored religious growth or development, and merely set their faces against the early ventures in Biblical criticism of the Tübingen School of Baur, or of Strauss, or of Renan. In Scotland the battle for freedom was fought quite late, in the famous case of Robertson Smith, who was dismissed from his Aberdeen Chair in 1881 for 'heresy'. In all the thought of the time there is a singular absence of the spirit of historical criticism, the whole age tending to the view expressed by Shelley, when he condemned history as 'that record of crimes and miseries'. This contempt for history explains the facility with which Bentham could as readily think of framing a Code of Laws for Morocco as for England, and some of the South African missionaries may have shown a zeal more consistent than expedient; in their anxiety to break down social or racial barriers some of them married Hottentot wives. Till the growth of nationalism in the nineteenth century there was little historical criticism to lay stress on the marked differences between races, between higher and lower civilizations, even between civilization and barbarism. An academic equalitarianism made some of the missionaries under-rate the difficulties and tend to over-simplify the problem. This has afforded a target for abuse of missionaries and all their works; but it has

---

[1] Dicey, *Law and Opinion*, pp. 103 ff.
[2] *England under the Stuarts*, G. M. Trevelyan, p. 34.

been much exaggerated by extremists of another school, and was a weakness which they shared with many of the best thinkers of their day.

But, in words paraphrased from Professor Dicey—the historical research which brings into prominence dissimilarities between different classes, and especially different races, 'tends not indeed to remove reasonable grounds for securing an equality of rights, but to quench the confident enthusiasm necessary for carrying out even the most well-approved and the most beneficial among democratic innovations'. . . . 'Could the Abolitionists, either in England or in the United States, have fought with success their desperate battle against oppression, had they not been strengthened by an unswerving faith in the essential similarity of all human beings, whether blacks or whites'? [1]

That English interest in missions was emotional rather than intellectual or scientific, and that even the emotions were sometimes based on imperfect information about the sufferings of poor Africa, does not mean that the natives had no wrongs, that the colonists required no watching, or even that the agitation at Home was ineffective. The missionaries were criticized from the beginning for the undesirable political reactions likely to result from their activities. Sydney Smith, for example, feared that they would cause the loss 'of our settlements, and consequently, of the chance of that slow, solid and temperate introduction of Christianity which the superiority of the European character may ultimately effect in the Eastern world'. In Africa, in fact, whole districts have been 'added to the Empire', largely by missionary influence; but as for the 'superiority of the European character', the pioneers of Empire do not necessarily manifest the superiority of European culture amongst primitive peoples. If British humanity can claim most of the credit for the restriction of slavery, it was also British indifference, except to the profits, that made her, for a long time, the chief slave-trading nation. Nor did European and Protestant culture save the Redskins of North America from being debauched and destroyed; nor the Aborigines of Australia, nor the Bushmen of Africa, from virtual extermination. On the other hand, the protection afforded by the Roman Catholic Jesuit Fathers did much, even in the older days of colonization, to preserve the native Indian peoples of America, and to save them from such devastation as was wrought by the earlier *Conquistadores*. It is significant that the aboriginal

[1] Dicey, *op. cit.* p. 461, note.

races who, perhaps, suffered most severely at the hands of
European conquerors were the Caribbeans, who seem to have
been exterminated before the days of missionary protectors
like las Casas; while some of the natives in other lands, who
had to face the Protestant and Teutonic colonizers before the
days of Protestant Missions, fared little better. For the last
hundred years missionaries of all creeds have been the first
line of defence for backward subject races all over the world.

The effect of missionary propaganda on the less primitive
races of the East is difficult to estimate; but it is certain that
Western ideas, heavily in debt as they are to Christian teaching,
must sooner or later have made their influence felt; and it is not
unreasonable for Christianity to be presented by those who
believe in it, rather than casually, by those indifferent, if not
hostile, to its traditions. But for backward peoples, it is often
overlooked that Western civilization itself owes much of its
best to a Missionary Movement. The Church of the Dark
Ages transformed the barbarian Celts and Teutons into the
civilized nations of modern Europe. The Church in those
days was vastly more than a spiritual force; it was the preserver
and transmitter of the traditions of civilization and culture.
The clergy were not only teachers, but contributed more than
any other class to the moulding of the institutions of civilized
government. The responsibility of the missionary to the backward races of to-day is very similar. He stands to the Kafir
'kraal' as the representative, not only of a form of religion,
but also of the higher civilization from which he comes. Even
in temporal concerns the raw Native naturally looks to the
missionary to mediate between himself and the powerful
society of which the missionary is the representative. Of
necessity the modern missionary must be a 'politician'.

In their championship of native races the missionaries had
behind them the force of the English Evangelical Movement,
whose organization, together with the votes they commanded,
gave them weight and importance. In Evangelical religious
circles all over the country missionary and Bible Society meetings were the vogue. Once a year, in London, there was a
veritable gathering of the clans of missionary and humanitarian
societies for the 'May Meetings', held commonly in that
famous 'Exeter Hall', in the Strand, which has given its name
to the colonial policy they advocated. At these meetings [1]

[1] Rev. J. Campbell writes: 'The Tract Society has now two
annual meetings, one at 11 A.M. at Willis' Rooms, St. James's, for
the sake of nobility, M.P.'s, etc., and the other in the City of London

missionary ambassadors from the 'foreign field' itself were a superlative attraction; if they were not there themselves, their letters were sometimes read, as Mr. Buxton once read those of Dr. Philip, 'telling some of the good news you have told us', or, at other times, rousing indignation by tales of 'your horrid commandos', or of the ill-treatment and oppression of the coloured races. A letter from Mrs. Philip to her husband throws light on the doings at these May meetings, and incidentally on her own personality.

May 10th, 1828.

MY DEAR HUSBAND,

I received your kind and anxiously looked-for letter on the 7th and was I assure you very glad to see it. . . . I had a good deal to do last week, but as we had got reserved tickets to the Anti-Slavery Society and I felt exceedingly anxious to go, I went and thereby brought on a considerable degree of fever which I did not get free of till yesterday. At the same time I am very glad I went. I had the high gratification of hearing and seeing Mr. Brougham, Mr. Wilberforce, Mr. Denman, Sir James McIntosh and Mr. Buxton, besides a very neat speech from the Duke of Glouster—such an assemblage of great Men and eloquent speakers I never expect to see congregated together, and the bold manly yet tempered manner in which the sense of the meeting was expressed upon the conduct of the West India planters in refusing to comply with the Order in Council sent out to them, and their determination to procure petitions praying that Parliament might enforce their own regulation, showed more of the true freeborn spirit of Englishmen than I have ever had an opportunity of witnessing. His Royal Highness told them that it was only public opinion that could carry the measure into effect and he hoped he would have to present a petition as long as would extend from one end of the Parliament House to the other, and that it would be followed by thousands more, and that this was the just and lawful means which Englishmen had of obtaining what they desired from Government. Mr. Brougham's speech was too short in my opinion. Mr. Wilberforce was so low that I did not hear it all distinctly, but I was very pleased with Mr. Denman, Sir James McIntosh and Mr. Buxton. I like his, Mr. B.'s, face very much—(though I wish he would stir himself a little in behalf of the Hottentots). I was not able to go to hear the Bishop of Winchester preach, but I understand it was an excellent Sermon. Mary and Miss Foulger heard him. I am told by Mr. Millar that the Meeting of the Bible Society was exceedingly interesting, that three Bishops spoke *well*, several Noblemen and ministers of the Church of England, but that by far the best speech (he says the most eloquent and most applauded), was delivered by Mr. Orme. . . .

. . . I went yesterday morning with the Girls and Miss Foulger to the meeting of the British and Foreign School Society. Lord John Russell in the Chair. I had again the pleasure of hearing

---

Tavern, which meeting *at 6 A.M.* is too early an hour for the gentry.' (He himself was present at 11 A.M.)

Mr. Wilberforce distinctly and was much gratified with his speech and with Mr. Orme's who came down on the meeting in a strain of powerful commanding eloquence and was received with very great applause. Lord John Russell is not what you would call a good speaker though a very pleasing looking man—he hesitates and appears at a loss for words—and I should not feel anxious for him to take up your cause unless he was thoroughly master of the subject. I should think that from the success that has attended his late exertions he must speak better when he has studied the subject. On the whole the meeting was not nearly as interesting as the Anti-Slavery Society, the report was too long and many of the speakers prosing. I was quite tired of George Clayton with all his mannerisms, thanking the Ladies, and one poor man, a Mr. Wale, a clergyman, was literally coughed down. But we had a very great treat in the evening in hearing James of Birmingham preach—I think I may say the most splendid sermon I have heard; nor would I wish to convey to your mind the idea that it was all imagery—splendid imagery abounded throughout the whole but there was a great deal of truly excellent thought and practical application. His text was 'Other men have laboured and ye have entered into their labours'. It would be vain for me to attempt to give an outline of his sermon. It is perhaps sufficient to say that after sitting nearly six hours at the British & Foreign School Society, without Dinner or anything except tea, I looked to the clock when he had finished and found to my astonishment that he had preached rather more than an hour and fifty minutes. I think I could have enjoyed another hour. The congregation was immense, hundreds went away and the Collection was 107 pounds some odd shillings. I am going this evening to the Irish Evangelical. . . . I must now conclude by informing you that we are on the whole pretty well. Both Girls and boys send their kind love to you. I have had no letters from William since you left, and sent him a cake the other day. I begin to long very much for your return, pray mention in your next what time I may expect you.

I remain your affectionate wife,

JANE PHILIP.

May 13th.

Numerically the strongest element in the Evangelical Movement was probably the Nonconformist wing. Wilberforce and Buxton, themselves of the Established Church, were often principal speakers at the May Meetings of bodies like the London Missionary Society. Their common interests thus secured a far larger measure of co-operation between Church and Dissent than at any time since the Act of Uniformity, but there was no question of organic union or reunion. Now if the co-operation with Nonconformists was a source of weakness to the Evangelicals within the Church of England, the leadership of 'Churchmen' made all the difference between weakness and strength to 'Exeter Hall'. Had the movement relied solely on Nonconformist backing it would have made far less headway against the social prejudices which have always been

powerful in English public life.   The 'conversion' of Wilberforce, in 1785, began a new phase of the movement.   It was
no longer possible to point the finger of social scorn at a movement which had the whole-hearted countenance and support of
a man like William Wilberforce, an ornament of the highest
society, and the lifelong friend of Pitt himself.   Evangelicalism
was soon strong among the laity in the citadels of high society,
especially, as Dr. Philip's letters often show, among officers of
the Navy and Army, and among high officials of the Honourable
East India Company's service, whose support gave 'Exeter
Hall' that hall-mark of 'respectability' without which it must
have made little headway against the prejudices of the English
world of fashion.   In the House of Commons the so-called
'Clapham Sect', with its triumvirate, Wilberforce, T. F.
Buxton, and Dr. Lushington, held a position markedly detached from strict party divisions, but too influential to be
safely ignored by any Government.[1]   When questions were to
be asked, or resolutions moved, on the wrongs suffered by the
native protégés of the missionaries, the Clapham Sect were
often better informed than Ministers, and always ready to act
on the missionaries' behalf.   Thus when Dr. Philip diligently
fulfilled Buxton's request—expressed for example in a letter of
September 1834, 'Pray keep me well informed',[2]—Buxton
for his part used this information to maintain pressure on
Ministers ; as in September 1834, when he was not too well-
pleased with the attitude of his friend Mr. Spring Rice, and
wrote—'If he prove other than favourable to our views . . .
then to war with him we must go'.   Concern for the interests
of the native races helped to keep Mr. Buxton in Parliament
somewhat against his inclinations.   Even after he lost his seat
at Weymouth in 1837 he was anxious 'that natives may not be
cheated out of their land'; and Lord Glenelg,[3] on the 1st
February 1838, wrote offering to consider the heads of any Bill
Mr. Buxton might propose for securing in general the rights of
the aborigines.   This pressure, moreover, as exercised by
Wilberforce and Buxton, was not the distant influence of the

[1] Miss Buxton writes in 1833 of a sort of 'club' of men from
'all parties', who met nightly during the session at 9 P.M., drank
tea, and engaged in 'reading and prayer'.
[2] That Philip kept him 'well-informed' may be inferred from
Buxton's remark in 1834. 'Your last packet was charged £5.   I got
it reduced to £1.7.'   In future Philip is requested to save such
expense by posting under cover to Sir George Grey, Under-Secretary
for the Colonies.
[3] Letter in Records of Aborigines Protection Society, London.

Lobby, but the more intimate personal contact of London clubs or drawing-rooms.

Evangelical support of the weaker races had little definite connection with political radicalism. Organizations like the London Missionary Society took kindly and naturally to the patronage of the great.

Dr. Philip was in many ways typical of Evangelicalism, which may almost be regarded as the religious aspect of the middle-class movement of the day. As a young man of twenty-nine years, settling in his first 'charge' at Newbury, Berks, he noted with guileless satisfaction the strength of the Nonconformists of that town, attributing this to their having not fewer than 'three Ministers of character and *property*, a thing which added greatly to their influence in general society'. And in a fragment written probably forty years later, though referring to a still earlier date, he had not changed his attitude of respect for the socially great. He describes how, as a promising youth, he was 'taken up' by the local Parish Church minister, whose wife was a cousin of the great Lord Melville:

'I learnt then', he says, 'the effect of genuine religion in civilizing and improving the human race, from its tendency to bring the cultivated and humbler classes into friendly intercourse.'

On the other hand, in language now happily going out of fashion, he used to distinguish between the 'respectable' (a word which was the very motto of his party) and those whom one of his colleagues, in a notorious reference, described as 'Cockneys and pin-makers, who shrink from the bold gaze of a natural man'; these Dr. Philip himself sometimes referred to as 'common mechanics'. Mrs. Philip, similarly, was anxious to get Government officials to join the Temperance Society in 1832, as an example to 'the lower orders'.[1]

Yet Philip, at least, like many of the more vigorous of the English Evangelicals, was a Whig in politics. Wilberforce

---

[1] Philip's colleague Campbell has some characteristic comments. Of the patronage enjoyed by the L.M.S. and the Religious Tract Society from Lord Teignmouth, from Porteous, Bishop of London, and 'the late venerable Bishop of Durham', he writes in 1830: [These men] 'were the means of setting the Society in an elevated situation in public estimation. Respectability in Society is really a talent from God which, if properly used, may be of great service in the cause of truth'. Elsewhere he writes of 'the infidel tenets of Owen of Lanark' and Owen's 'concern for *this* world, not the next'. Moreover, 'systematic deism and infidelity was in former days confined to the philosophic ranks; now they spread to the *lower orders*'. He speaks also of 'the incredible spread of Socialism'.

and the Evangelical Churchmen were Tories. But the English Independents and Baptists retained so much of the older Puritan tradition as to be always suspicious of authority, and Whig in sympathy. The habit of mistrusting the State and State interference, originally in church matters, brought them easily into line with—perhaps helped to produce—the dominant thought of their age, the *laissez-faire* economics. The Nonconformist Whigs developed readily, as time went on, into constitutional Liberals, never having been revolutionaries. In South Africa Philip began with almost implicit faith in the goodwill of the Government. His earlier letters show that he 'enjoyed' access to 'great' men like the Governor. It was no love of opposition, but the compelling force of conscience, that made him a critic and a 'politician'; his unpopularity, indeed, was the result, not of the violence, but of the effectiveness of the blows he aimed at very weak spots in the armour of the colonial system. Dr. Philip, at least, was on guard against the danger that Nonconformist association with rank, wealth, and power might tend to impair the freshness and vigour of their independence. Writing to Dr. Philip in 1824, Dr. Thomas McCrie, a Scottish seceding divine, well known as the biographer of John Knox, passed strictures on dissenters who

despise politics as 'low and earthly', but *not* money-making. Many leading Whigs are notoriously infidel and irreligious; and 'Do no harm to religion by interfering with politics and political measures' is a very plausible and persuasive motion when seconded by a voice which whispers, 'Do thyself no harm by displeasing men of power and influence'.

Nor was the support Dr. Philip got from his friends at Home quite unaffected by this spirit of political caution. The publication of the *Researches* in 1828 was his appeal to public opinion against the Government; but it was also provoked by the failure of his attempts to goad the Directors of his Society into greater activity on behalf of the Hottentots. Tradition, indeed, has it that even on the main principle of Negro slavery they were not all equally staunch—some of them having "West Indian interests"; [1] and in 1843 Dr. Philip was driven to resign his office by way of protest against what he considered to be the half-heartedness of the Directors' support.

[1] In 1832, something like popular clamour forced the resignation, on account of his alleged West Indian interests, of Mr. W. A. Hankey, Treasurer of the L.M.S. from 1819 to 1832.

'Exeter Hall', therefore, is something of an abstraction. It comes to this, that the missionaries in the backward countries depended for material and moral support on the Old Country. Normally they were financed almost entirely from home; and in emergency (sometimes political emergency) additional help was obtainable.[1]   It was of real importance to the missionaries and their work that the adherence of Wilberforce and his friends made middle-class Evangelicalism 'respectable', if not fashionable; so that it often had influential support in high places and politics, even in Downing Street itself.[2] Moreover, since the Evangelicals had votes and organization, 'Exeter Hall' could not be entirely disregarded, if only because of its latent voting strength.

Yet the extent and nature of its influence, even in South African history, has been much exaggerated. So long as Buxton was in Parliament (only till 1837), he certainly made effective use of the information sent him by Dr. Philip. In the 'forties Philip's influence and knowledge still had some weight, and served at least to defer that abandonment of responsibilities which characterized the next decade of British policy in South Africa. Happily, also, this influence held long enough to secure the political freedom of all classes in the Cape Colony. But even in the 'forties, the Treaty States were a mere *pis aller*, the Home Government stolidly refusing to incur the expense of the policy urged upon it by Dr. Philip; what he wanted was the complete administrative control of the disputed territory. In the 'fifties there was no one to receive the mantle of John Philip; in the crisis of the Kafir War of 1851 the London Missionary Society itself refused to touch 'politics'; and, henceforth, humanitarian influences in British colonial policy prevailed with greater difficulty than ever against the considerations of economy or expense, strongly urged by Sir William Molesworth and the Radicals.

In the last resort, the real strength of 'Exeter Hall' was that, thanks largely to the influence of Evangelicalism, the interests of subject races made a strong appeal to the sympathy and

[1] For example, in 1830 Dr. Philip was relieved of the heavy burden of expense due to the Mackay libel case; and in 1837 James Cropper, a merchant of Liverpool, and others, helped to find a sum of money to enable Fairbairn to meet losses incurred in consequence of the attitude taken by the *Commercial Advertiser* on the question of the Kafir War.

[2] Mr. James Stephen, of the Colonial Office, like Lord Glenelg, was the son of a leading member of the 'Clapham Sect', and a nephew by marriage of Wilberforce.

imagination of the British people. This was perhaps also a source of weakness, so that the sentimental and uncritical emotions of Exeter Hall quite early began to shake confidence, and to make the name a byword, even among the elect.[1] Yet its hold on the public conscience was so strong that it sufficed to make British public opinion in the nineteenth century the most formidable court of appeal in the world for oppressed native peoples everywhere. In their own colonial policy British ministers have had to take some care not to incur the too violent criticism and displeasure, however latent it might seem, of 'Exeter Hall'.

[1] William Philip, missionary at Hankey, probably the ablest of Dr. Philip's sons, writes on 14th March 1843 to his younger brother Durant:
'You ask me why I can remain in the Colony preaching to a few while thousands of heathen exist beyond its boundary. Your intelligence on this subject is the result of all the fine declamatory speeches of Exeter Hall, where the figures of 'doors open', and 'waiting millions' are liberally employed to garnish a threadbare subject. But you will be better able to judge of the value of such rhetorical tropes when I tell you that one missionary among these Heathen rung his bell himself for seven years without anyone attending his worship beyond the members of his own family. And that in Caffreland of which so much has been spoken, twenty or thirty is a very good congregation, and that there are not perhaps so many members in all the churches together in Caffreland as in one church under my care.'

Part II

FROM 'HOTTENTOT' TO 'EURAFRICAN'

Figure to yourself a ship, in which the sailors are quarelling together about the pilotage—each of them thinking he has a right to steer the vessel, although up to that moment he has never studied the art. Do you not think that the pilot who is master of his craft, and devotes his attention to the year and its seasons, to the sky, and the stars, and the winds, is sure to be called by the mariners a useless star-gazing babbler?

PLATO'S REPUBLIC.

Chapter VI

SLAVERY AT THE CAPE OF GOOD HOPE

SOUTH AFRICAN History is the story of the colonizing
process by which a handful of European pioneers, set
in a country inhabited by relatively numerous backward
Natives, have become the founders of a modern State. Had
Dutch and English been thrown together in an empty continent,
differences of language and of tradition would hardly have
mattered; there would probably have been little to record
but the normal ups and downs of prosperity, and the almost
petty divisions and distractions of any young country. As
it is, its history is essentially different from that of any of its
sister Dominions; and parallels, suggested by concentrating,
as is usual, on the fortunes of the white colonists, are for the
most part fallacious. The fact that a vast majority of the
inhabitants are people of colour, far behind the dominant
Europeans in civilization, while enormously complicating its
political and constitutional development, makes South Africa
likely to remain, if not the happiest, at any rate one of the most
interesting countries in the world.

It is natural that the European colonists should dominate
the story, since it was their energy and their interests that made
the new State. But when Great Britain took the Cape in
1806, the Europeans were a mere handful, some 30,000 in all,
outnumbered, if anything, by the actual slaves, and at least
balanced by a number of 'free' Hottentots who were doubtfully better off even than the slaves. These scattered colonists
had, no doubt, an individuality of their own; but being
without political traditions, they submitted with little demur
to a government that was an almost unmitigated autocracy.
In the 'twenties the doings of quite a number of insignificant

people[1] crowd the pages of Cape history; protests that were obviously moved by personal interests and grievances rather than by large questions of principle, or by concern for the general good, were signs that in the growing complexity of colonial life the colonists were beginning to demand some voice in determming the general policy of their government. The agitation even bore fruit. The Advisory Council of 1825 was the first feeble check on the power of the Governor; and presently—what was of far greater moment—the Charter of Justice of 1827 secured to the Cape an independent Bench, without which, for example, a free Press was impossible. Yet no sooner was this first step gained than, in 1828, the country entered upon a period in which, for many years, the extension of the political and constitutional privileges of its white colonists had to take a second place because of the urgency of questions raised by the presence of slaves, Hottentots, and other coloured persons in the Colony itself (to say nothing of the untamed hosts of the Bantu on its borders). Further progress was impossible without some settlement of the conditions on which these white colonists could be entrusted with responsibility for the government of the backward races.

Apart even from the fundamental question of whether or not slavery was to continue, there were difficulties. To the white colonists, whose chief concern was to make sure of the services of the Hottentots as a substitute for the now prohibited import of slaves, the coloured people were primarily a labour problem. The Government, on the other hand, supported if not driven by the Humanitarians, sought guarantees for the satisfactory treatment of these Hottentot servants. Till the Hottentots' rights were secured, and so long as they were obviously unfit to share the responsibilities of government, the Home Government rightly hesitated to give them into the unfettered control of their employers and masters. How these questions were dealt with in the old Cape Colony is the principal theme of this book. The conditions, and the principles at stake, were much the same as those in the Union of South Africa to-day.

Of course, in earlier days, there was also a question of Frontiers, which now that the Bantu are a conquered race is at

[1] The almost meaningless wrangles of O'Halloran, Bishop Burnett, Cooke and Edwards, and a good many more, acquire some significance only if they are taken as evidence of the 'growing pains' of the Colony (Cory, ii, chaps. v and vi, *passim*; and below, chap. xiv).

most a matter of police. For more than a century after 1652, more and more land was appropriated by the younger generation of colonists, or by newcomers—with no effective restraint from the Government, and without serious opposition from any original owners. In time, however, as land hunger grew with what it fed on, there ceased to be enough land to go round, except at a cost both in money and in disorder and bloodshed. On the natural geographical line of their advance, the colonists encountered a formidable barrier in the 'Kafirs'; and even in the barren North, the desultory claims of pioneering colonists were met by counter-claims of earlier Griqua or 'Bastard' refugees from the colony itself. The 'Kafir Wars', in fact, were the struggle with the Natives for possession of the land itself. The Home Government, therefore, before trusting the Colony with any full measure of responsibility for the management of its own affairs, desired some limit to the expansion of a community whose appetite for land could only be satisfied by involving Great Britain in the heavy expenses of Kafir Wars.

Most of the significant events of South African history, and many of the trivial details, stand related, in some way, to one or other of three main threads running through the whole story. As in the other Dominions, there is the gradual growth of a self-governing State. But this is complicated, in a way that makes it unique, by the Colour Question, in one of its two aspects: first, while almost consistently unfavourable to any extension of their political rights, the white community has always been anxious to obtain the labour of the Natives or Coloured People on the easiest possible terms; second, in earlier times at least, political or constitutional progress was often interrupted by the physical struggle for possession of the land.

It was the opening of the seas and the discovery of the New World which began the modern phase in the history of slavery. In the days of Prince Henry, African slaves were sold in Portugal; it was, however, not in Europe, but on the plantations of America that economic needs led to the huge and distinctively modern growth of African slavery, which, after three centuries, became the great object of humanitarian attack. The labour problem in the new lands has always been supremely difficult, since though spices, coffee, sugar, cocoa, cotton, and latterly copra and rubber, are in themselves legitimate objects of European desire, yet in the warm climates, which can alone advantageously produce them, the attempt to supply sufficient to meet the European demand can only succeed with the help of native labour. This in turn involves a revolution in habits of life, and probably the loss of land, by the native inhabitants. With the experience of centuries behind us it is comparatively easy for benevolent people to point to the example of West Africa, where natives cultivating their own patches for themselves appear to have made considerable success. Slowly it may begin to sink into ordinary intelligences that the one effective way of inducing the habit of work in raw natives, whose needs are easily supplied by the roots of the forest and a girdle of palm leaves, is to raise their intelligence and their standard of life. The lash of the slave overseer is less effective than the creation of new wants which, for example, change a native love of finery into a habit of preferring European dress.

The problem, unfortunately, was first met with, not by benevolent people, but by rough, and often enough brutal, adventurers, eager, as Brougham said of the planters of his own more settled day, 'not to live, but to gain; not to enjoy, but to save; not to subsist in the colonies, but to prepare for shining in the mother country'. In the policy which governed tropical colonies the laws of economic necessity were but a threadbare cloak for common greed of gain. The crops desired were few in number, and, therefore, specialized; and this, coupled with the fact that the directing whites were but a handful, favoured an extensive plantation culture rather than intensive production by small holders. Possibly, with the best will in the world, the production of sugar or cotton crops demands a large proportion of low-grade, unskilled labour, rather than a small quantity of a highly intelligent kind. The medical science of the day was primitive, and the white men's power of resistance to the diseases of an enervating climate was very low; but even had health been equal to the strain, their numbers were too few to attempt closer settlement; and economically, tropical production could not afford to continue if based on labour earning wages sufficient to maintain a European standard of life. Dependence on black labour was therefore inevitable. But the tropical native has not even yet acquired the habit of continuous work. Having worked hard enough to satisfy his immediate wants, he seems to demand absolute rest. Amazing feats of endurance may be seen where a gang of Natives, with apparently imperturbable good humour, will gruel for hours at the loading of a violently rocking ship in an open roadstead. But though Natives may get through one laborious spell of work even more rapidly than a similar number of Europeans, yet they probably cannot maintain anything like the same steady average over any prolonged period. The truth is that in a state of nature the black man is a free man and therefore a casual worker, who will slave when he has an object—such as a wife to buy, or food or clothes—and appear to idle when his immediate needs are satisfied. It is almost impossible for Native mentality to grasp the elementary fine points of European business organization. Time being little object to him—'*Môre is ook 'n dag*' (to-morrow is also a day), as the Afrikander says— a native will not, without close supervision, push himself to fulfil an urgent European contract. He will not even realize the urgency of dealing with a crop just when it is ripe, if a village festival or beer dance happen to come in the way. Thus the undoubtedly demoralizing effect of lording it habitually over a subject and inferior race is not the only danger that besets the white masters of a tropical plantation. The distinguished Doctor Schweitzer has shown how the white supervisors in the tropics, being themselves responsible to absentee owners, and not, like the missionaries, the masters of their own time and actions, are in danger of becoming hard towards the Natives:

My wife and I were once very much delighted with a newly arrived trader, because in the conversations we had with him he was always insisting on kindness towards the natives, and would not allow the slightest ill-treatment of them by his foremen. The next spring, however, he had the following experience. Lying in a pond some sixty miles from here, he had a large quantity of mahogany, but he was summoned to Lambarene to clear off some urgent correspondence just as the water began to rise. He ordered his foremen and labourers to be sure to use the two or three days of high water to get all the timber, if possible, into the river. When the water had fallen, he went back to the place and found that nothing whatever had been done! They had smoked, and drunk, and danced; the timber which had already lain too long in the pond was almost completely ruined and he was responsible to his company for the loss. His men had been thoughtless and indifferent because they did not fear him enough. This experience changed him entirely, and now he laughs at those who think it is possible to do anything with the natives without employing relentless severity.

.   .   .   .

That it is so hard to keep oneself really humane, and so to be a standard-bearer of civilization, that is the tragic element in the problem of the relations between white and coloured men in Equatorial Africa.[1]

The fact that the supervision of Natives is a severe trial of patience accounts in some measure for the hard attitude

[1] Schweitzer, *On the Edge of the Primeval Forest*, ch. vii.

commonly acquired by Home-born settlers in the native-labour colonies. On the other hand, the temptation to mere exploitation and to get rich quickly—the short-sighted using up of the resources of the land itself by forced and inefficient labour— what the Germans expressively describe as *Raub-bau*—brings its own Nemesis. The forced labour of the tropics, and of slavery, is in the long run as inefficient as the English 'statute' labour on the roads, which died a natural death only in 1845.[1]

For the Natives themselves it is sometimes argued that slavery is a necessary stage in the development of child races; that, for their own good, they have to learn in the school of hard disciplined work. But this view gives undue credit to the aims and methods of the slave-owner as schoolmaster. The truth may very well be that there is an irreconcilable conflict between the motive of exploiting tropical products for European markets, and that of uplifting and civilizing the Native peoples. The commercial end is supposed to be best served by employing black labour under close supervision, indentured for as long a period as possible,[2] and collected in gangs as far removed as can be from the disturbing incidents of tribal or village life. But whether on great plantations or in mine compounds, this divorce from his natural life and surroundings is, in its effects, the worst treatment possible for Native morals and civilization. Barrack life is notoriously bad even for Europeans. The moral development of the Native can best be secured where he can live under the restraints of his own family and tribal life— engaged, as he progresses in civilization, more and more in small scale agriculture, or in native industries, at his own pace rather than at that imposed by the needs of the vast amount of capital invested in the exploitation of the tropics.

But in the old days, far removed from the common moral restraints of an old-established society, and with little or no effective supervision from Home for the protection of native interests, the earliest colonists were not favourably placed for a just solution of the problem. With little or no psychological or physiological knowledge of the native races, they had to buy their experience at some cost to themselves, and at a far heavier cost to the subject blacks. Slavery became general in the Colonies, and Central Africa was decimated to maintain the supply. At last the moral conscience of Europe was awakened,

[1] S. and B. Webb, *The King's Highway*.
[2] Rand mining experience seems to be finding that, in the long run, short-term contracts, of less than a year, give the best economic results.

and the humanitarians of the late eighteenth century, with Wilberforce and the Evangelicals in the van, led the attack on the slave-trade, and eventually on slavery itself.

The Cape Colour Question really began with the crusade against slavery. Hitherto European Governments had paid little or no attention to the condition of the subject races, and slavery was general throughout the Colonies. In its way, moreover, slavery was a straightforward, if immoral, solution of the difficulties arising out of the contact between white conquerors and subject races. The slave had no 'rights'; he must do as he was bid by the master to whom he belonged; at the same time, he had some value as property, and might hope, therefore, to be reasonably cared for by his owner. Now, however, the powerful body of opinion, that had put a virtual stop to the slave-trade, went on to urge that property in human beings was in itself intolerable and must be ended; and the issues raised by emancipation were far too complex to be settled finally by a single measure like the Emancipation Act of 1833. Slaves, by very reason of their past, were not fit to take their places, immediately, as complete citizens of a civilized community; and there were free subject peoples fully as backward as the slaves themselves. The problem now was to define the rights of the emancipated subject races, and their status in society, in face of the difficulty that a large proportion of the white colonists, lately the owners of the slaves, were still unconverted on the main issue of slavery, and utterly opposed to accepting their own servants as even potential fellow-citizens.

At the Cape of Good Hope the slaves were, indeed, the least part of the problem. In such a predominantly pastoral community the number of slaves was relatively small, and only a proportion of the subject population; it was not as in the West Indies, where, except for a handful of white planters and supervisors, virtually the whole of the inhabitants were slaves. One of the effects of the Prohibition of the Slave Trade in 1807 was, however, that the Cape Colonists, who did not share the anti-slavery scruples of their new rulers, began to demand that the aboriginal Hottentots should be set to work as servants, with pressure if necessary, to supplement the now restricted supply of slaves. The Hottentot was free, in theory, to give his services where he chose, on his own terms. In practice, however, he and his kind had no land, no home base, and no economic reserve, so that their choice lay between service with the farmers (on such terms as were suggested by slave-owning masters, or determined by their own abject helplessness), and, alternatively, 'vagrancy' (presently to be certified as a crime punishable by law).   The Humanitarians in South Africa, therefore, bent on attacking slavery in all its roots and branches, soon gave almost closer attention to the condition of the Hottentots than to the slaves, whose state was in some ways comparatively enviable.   The Cape Colonists thus found themselves attacked simultaneously on two fronts. For years they suffered what seemed to them fussy slave regulations, only to be threatened in the end with the total loss of their property in slaves; at the same time they were not allowed to have all their own way with the Hottentots, whom they looked upon, at best, as inferior substitutes for the slaves.

It was of course the new attitude to slavery that interfered with colonial designs upon the Hottentots; and it was when their minds were inflamed by the attack on slavery that the colonists were first compelled to face the more general question of the rights and status of those subject races who had never been slaves.   It was a shock to established ways of thinking to find slavery condemned as immoral; but it demanded a not less radical change of mind to accept the deduction that even Hottentots and 'Kafirs' are not chattels but persons. Logically, the history of slavery comes first in a treatment of this whole question, though in South Africa it was in itself a smaller issue, and though, in time, it overlaps the development of wider problems.

The very fact that, in the West Indies, Jamaica alone had nearly ten times as many slaves as the Cape, meant that Cape interests got little special attention; and this possibly added to the difficulties of the passing of Cape slavery.   The pressure of a policy directed, in the main, towards breaking the obstruction of the West Indian legislatures, bore hardly, there can be little doubt, on a community where colonial and slave-owning interests had no such means of defence.   For the Cape, it will be remembered, as a colony newly conquered, had its laws imposed by mere fiat of an irresponsible Governor; or else by Order in Council which did not require the sanction or approval even of the British Parliament.   For example, while Wilberforce began as early as 1815 to press for a registry of slaves, and succeeded in securing his end only by an Act of 1819, the Cape Governor had already acted on his own initiative in 1816.   By a proclamation of 26th April 1816, provision was made for keeping a complete record of property in slaves, and to prevent it receiving any addition except by birth.[1] Any slaves not registered, at latest by September 1817, were to be deemed to be manumitted.

In 1823, acting on orders, the Governor proceeded to deal with slave conditions by a proclamation, which incidentally throws light on some of the implications of slavery.

It prohibited forced slave labour on Sundays, required children from three to ten years of age in towns and villages to be sent to school at least three days a week; provided for the regular marriage of slaves; and forbade sales which separated husband and wife, or parents from children under eight years; hours of labour were restricted to twelve in summer, and ten in winter, and extra work, as in harvest time, was to be paid for. In addition, slaves were given rights to property, which might be used as they chose; and punishment was to be 'mild' and 'domestic', being restricted to twenty-five cuts with a 'rod or similar implement', and not to be repeated within twenty-four hours.

From 1826 onwards, changes and additions to the regulations, suggested very largely by West Indian rather than by Cape conditions, came thick and fast. Sunday labour was now to be paid for; it was made easier for slaves to claim manumission, or to enforce it, at a price to be fixed by valuators, and slave Protectors were appointed to see that the slave laws were strictly carried out. 'Practical' men at the Cape objected that 'a forfeiture of property in a slave by His Majesty's Government on account of ill-treatment is something very new and strange'.[2] A little later the Consolidating Order of 2nd February 1830, which applied to all the Crown Colonies, prescribed in detail the quantities of food and clothing to be allowed to slaves as well as their hours of labour. It also required every slave-owner to keep a 'Punishment Record Book', which was to be submitted twice a year to the Protector for inspection. This indeed proved unworkable, and on the 6th February 1832 masters living more than twenty miles from Cape Town or Grahamstown were excused from keeping record books. But, meantime, another order, in November 1831, caused a very climax of resentment in the minds of the Cape Colonists by prohibiting the employment of slaves

[1] For details of this and other regulations, see Theal, ii, pp. 67 ff.

[2] 'Memorial', quoted by Cory, iii, p. 33. In 1822, however, a Memorial by J. Thomas, Esq., complains of 'regulations with a manifold tendency to uphold slavery'. Thus: 'It is incumbent on everyone previously to the manumission of slaves to pay a sum of 50 rix-dollars for permission to do so, independently of providing security that he shall not become burdensome to the public, which is certainly all that is necessary to prevent abuse.'

between 6 P.M. and 6 A.M., and, in particular, by authorizing the Slave Protectors to enter upon estates, or into slave dwellings, at discretion.   To the Boer farmer, quite as much as to the Englishman, his home is his castle, and now his cup must have been full.   Public meetings of protest were held.   Under the influence, it seems, either of the Rev. A. Murray or of Captain Stockenstrom, Graaff-Reinet distinguished itself by putting forward the proposal to fix a date from which all female slave children should be declared free; more tentatively, and at a price, they would free the boys as well.   Other villages were less restrained.

The institution of the Punishment Book was the occasion, in April 1831, of a small 'riot' at Stellenbosch, and Mrs. Philip writes about the same time of the ostracism of a Dutch friend who at Paarl ventured to obey the law in this matter. The excitement was so great that in June 1832 Sir Lowry Cole found it necessary to publish a temporary ordinance [1] for the prevention and suppression of meetings likely to be a danger to peace and good order, and to call attention to the 'full and entire power lawfully vested in him to remove from the settlement any person whose continuance therein should be deemed by him to be prejudicial to the peace, good order, and security thereof'.

It is impossible to deny that the slave-owners had a case. Though the Cape slaves were comparatively few in number, their small numbers may have enhanced their value, which was estimated at nearly three million pounds.   The right to slaves as property was secured both by ordinary law and by the terms on which the Cape capitulated to Great Britain; while also, like any other property, many of the slaves were mortgaged to meet the needs of their owners' estates.   Owing to the humanitarian tendency to over-simplify the problem, there was no attempt to adapt policy to differing conditions in different colonies.   The regulations designed to reform slavery were framed to suit, not scattered South African farms, but the very different conditions prevailing on West Indian sugar plantations.   In addition, the process of enforcing the new order could hardly have been more vexatious.   The more constitutional obstruction in the West Indies hindered reform, the more frequent and numerous were the instructions from

[1] Theal, ii, 70.   Philip claims that Sir Lowry Cole acted in this matter under pressure exercised by Fairbairn's newspaper, and its exposure of a 'plot' to resist by force (Philip to Buxton, 25th July 1832).

London to the Colonies; and, in the end, the total abolition of slavery, even when it was seen to be the inevitable outcome of the struggle, was delayed, out of regard for the feelings of the same West Indian legislatures. If, where slavery is legally tolerated, the authority of the master is systematically weakened and undermined, endless difficulties must arise. For slavery is in its essence the rule of the master over the persons of slaves who are his property; it is the very negation of the rule of law where the State controls and governs the terms of a contract between master and servant, or employer and employee. Yet at the Cape nominal slavery was combined with regulated hours of labour, punishment record books, and the intrusion of slave protectors between the slave and the authority of his master —this, moreover, in a society where the State had few administrative officers of its own, and was bound to depend on slave-owning Landdrosts and field-cornets for the execution of the new laws. No doubt, therefore, the spate of new regulations, and the unsettlement caused by the apprehension of more changes to follow, caused stirrings of excitement, which spread to the easily disturbed minds of the slaves themselves. In 1825, indeed, several farmers were murdered by slaves near Worcester.

At the same time it has been usual to excuse the Cape Colonists too much. They may have suffered for the misdeeds of the West Indians, as well as for their own slave-owning; in the best of circumstances abolition must have entailed a difficult social transition, affecting details in the everyday life of the people; yet no civilized country now openly tolerates slavery, where human beings are mere objects of traffic and a source of cheap power. Sooner or later slavery had to be ended, and it is hard to see how the process of its overthrow could have failed to cause violent opposition, whenever and however the end had come. There is no clear evidence that Cape slavery differed in essence from the slavery which prevailed elsewhere; that it was no worse, does not make it better, or a venial offence against humanity. Strong local tradition still tells of the lawless doings of runaway slaves,[1] and even the slave rising of 1825 had at least one precedent, before the emancipation movement had fairly begun, in the more extended activities engineered by certain people called Hooper and Kelly in 1808.[2] There is no question of Cape slavery being 'such a little' thing that it was for that reason excusable. It was, in fact,

[1] There is a 'drostder's' cave, the refuge of such runaway slaves, near the top of Simonsberg, a 4600-feet mountain near Stellenbosch.
[2] Cory, iii, 19.

slavery. In Dr. Theal's own words, Cape slaves 'could be bought and sold like cattle, they were without legal family ties, they were subject to the caprice of anyone who happened to own them, a mother and her children could be widely separated'. Such things were inevitable, as were also 'occasional treatment with excessive rigour', and even 'crimes of violence perpetrated upon them'. [1]

Dr. Theal's evidence makes any appeal to that of Dr. Philip almost superfluous [especially as the slaves, unlike the Hottentots, were not his parishioners, and Dr. Philip left the anti-slavery agitation more to others]. On his first tour, however, in 1819, he wrote:

> The slave system as it is carried on in the Colony is injurious to morals, to industry, to wealth and comfort. Half a dozen of good English servants could do more work than twenty slaves. In the Lange Kloof you may find from twenty to fifty slaves and Hottentots on one farm and under one roof. From such a retinue of servants it might be expected that the farmer should cultivate much land. This is not however the case; he does not seem to think of more than is necessary to supply his family and servants with food and enable his wife and daughters to appear fine when they go to church. . . .

The treatment of slave families deserves illustration. In some 'Remarks on an Anonymous Letter in the *Cape Courant*, 23rd November 1822', Dr. Philip dealt with the alleged 'mildness' of Cape slavery: from the *Gazette* itself, of the previous 12th of October, he quoted an advertisement:

> There will also be sold a female slave, 54 years, with five children (13, 10, 9, 7, 5 years old), each to be put up separately.

And as to the practice: once when Dr. Philip went to a sale in the Long Kloof to buy a span of oxen, he found a woman and three children (two of them girls of 13 and 10), 'exhibited like cattle'; they were stood upon a table and 'sold separately, and to different purchasers'. The letter continues:

> The grief of the slaves and the marked insensibility and jocular countenances of the farmers are a striking commentary on the miseries of slavery and on its debasing effects on the hearts of its abettors. [2]

That Cape slavery, 'predial' or other, was particularly mild is mere assertion, and irrelevant; certainly neither Dr.

[1] Theal, ii, p. 63.

[2] Dr. Philip more than once remarks on the temptation to unscrupulous slave-owners to encourage such intercourse with female slaves as was calculated to 'improve' the 'breed' of slaves—children becoming the property of the slave mother's owner.

Philip nor his friends suggested that it was any worse than in the West Indies or elsewhere. Slaves who were skilled artizans may even have done particularly well in places like Cape Town.[1] The advantage or disadvantage of being a slave on a smaller estate, with the possibility of closer and more personal relations with the slave-owner, would depend on the character and disposition of the master.[2] When at last it came to emancipation, the protests from the Cape slave-masters were not very different from those elsewhere. The idea of keeping a Punishment Record Book provoked, as we saw, a 'riot' that must be unique in the annals of Stellenbosch. Excellent as were its motives, the Cape of Good Hope Philanthropic Society for helping slaves to purchase their freedom achieved but little; it got no real support from a public[3] that found more congenial occupation in organizing meetings of protest against the movement for bettering the slave status. Even the proposal to set free slave children is not so much philanthropy as good business when it includes the payment of compensation at £12 a head.[4] The Governor, recognizing, indeed, that the Order of 1830 (that requiring a Punishment Record to be kept) was impracticable, was obliged to write to Lord Goderich that if he must enforce obedience to the law as it stood, he would require a larger military force than was then in South Africa.

Yet the end seemed to be quiet enough. The Emancipation Act passed, and on the 1st of December 1834 took effect, with hardly a ripple of excitement in the calm of life at the Cape. Sir Benjamin D'Urban seems, indeed, to have been a little apprehensive, and to have made the coming of the 1st of December a reason for delaying his promised and expected visit to attempt a settlement of affairs on the Kafir frontier —a piece of procrastination that probably had fatal results.

[1] Cory, iii, p. 16.
[2] The songs and legends of the Negroes of the South seem to have little South African counterpart, probably because the Cape slaves were both few and relatively scattered.
[3] It is indeed often asserted that the colonists were prepared and preparing to abolish slavery by a gradual process of their own. How very feeble and gradual such efforts were is shown by the researches of Prof. A. F. Hattersley, who proves that the Cape of Good Hope Philanthropic Society was responsible, at a generous estimate, for the emancipation of only 102 slaves in the four years 1828–33, the slave population at that time amounting to some 39,000 (art. in *S.A. Quarterly*, June 1922).
[4] Theal, vol. ii, p. 66, . . . an 'admirable device', suggested apparently by Lord Charles Somerset.

Respectable historians have fogged the issues by giving countenance to the old theory that what the colonists resented at last was not the loss of their slaves, but the method of emancipation, and this in face of the almost unanimous testimony of the Trekkers themselves.   In the very considerable body of evidence they have left, giving their own account of the motives of the great exodus, the group of grievances on which all are at one is that which has to do with slave regulations and emancipation.[1]   Yet it is still almost universally assumed that their chief grievance was the inadequacy of the compensation.   Some of it, in fact, never reached the owners for the reason that claims were made payable in London, with the inevitable result that inexperienced Boer farmers were left to fall a prey to the wiles of commission or collecting agents. The complaint does less than justice to the wisdom and liberality of the British Parliament. Logically there was nothing to be said for paying compensation to those who lost their property in slaves, since their title to such property had been decreed immoral.   But it was a sound political instinct which made even stalwarts like Buxton and Philip agree to make the transition from slavery as easy as possible by supporting or even advocating the payment; and though perhaps certain to disappoint the expectations that had been aroused, the amount of £20,000,000, actually voted, was in itself a very large and even generous sum in days when the national expenditure was not counted in the globular millions to which a twentieth-century war has accustomed us.   In supporting this vote at all, Buxton and his colleagues in Parliament incurred no small measure of criticism from their own supporters.   Slaves, it was held, would still have to work for a living, and wages were likely to be little more than the previous cost of their keep.   On these and on moral grounds the opponents of compensation were uncompromising.   With more practical knowledge, Dr. Philip argued the case as follows:

I have always been an advocate for compensation. The following are the grounds on which I have pleaded for it:
(1) The land will ultimately gain in increase of value what the Planters may lose in a transition from slave to free labour, but as their estates, with few exceptions, are deeply mortgaged, the present proprietors, without compensation, would be ruined and would derive no advantage from the increased value of the land.

---

[1] Cf. Retief and others in Eybers' *Documents*; Retief, Celliers, Boshof, Pretorius, and Anna Steenkamp in Bird's *Annals of Natal*; Piet Uys in Theal's *Sketches*.

(2) A universal bankruptcy among the present proprietors would so far injure the colonies and create a defalcation in the revenues which might ultimately prove as great a loss to the nation as the money that may be advanced by way of compensation.

(3) I have always considered a reasonable compensation to the Planters as an act of humanity to the slaves themselves, as any plan that might create a universal bankruptcy among the present proprietors of slave establishments might throw a great proportion of the slaves out of actual employment and leave them without the means of subsistence. . . . This is a case in which I am better pleased with an excess of generosity, for the reasons stated, than I should have been with anything bordering on the other extreme.[1]

With regard to the waste and misdirection of money involved in collecting claims from London, though the results were often unfortunate, it should be recognized that the financial difficulties in the way of any other arrangement must have been almost insuperable. London was the natural money market, and had another plan been adopted we should probably have heard a good deal more about the utter disorganization of Cape currency and exchange which must have resulted. As it was, money transactions figured but little in the normal round of the Cape farmer's business, and this gave collecting agents their chance to take advantage of simplicity and inexperience.

But there is still another side to this question. The labour value of the slaves was unaffected; it may even have been enhanced by their improved status; and the compensation money was by no means dead loss. There is evidence that its circulation contributed to something like a boom of prosperity in the late 'thirties. Missionaries and others with fixed incomes complained bitterly of the high or enhanced cost of living at places like George, Uitenhage, and Grahamstown—the London Missionary Society, which had its own financial worries, being frequently asked for even temporary relief to supplement its small salaries.[2] The evidence of Sir Andries Stockenstrom is of indirect value:

'Is it not a fact', he writes to Dr. Philip in August 1842, 'that hitherto there has been no new war, no fire, no slaughter, though the system has been in operation for six years; that instead of being ruined, the clamorous themselves boast that what they bought for a

---

[1] Philip to T. F. Buxton, 1st September 1833. For Buxton's attitude and the criticism it met with from his own supporters, *vide* *Memoir of T. F. Buxton*.

[2] £75 per annum was a good average salary; missionary artizans seem to have received incredibly small amounts, £35 or even less. Yet in 1840 Robt. Steven, a Director, in reporting a drop in income, playfully wonders how the Society is to escape the bankruptcy court.

rix-dollar before, during and soon after the war, is now worth a pound? . . . (Mark, *en parenthese*, that I am myself a Frontier Boer.) I have been on or about my estate for the last two years. So much is the country improved . . . that I have often been absent, leaving my family (women and children) entirely in charge of blacks; and in spite of alarms, and rumours of wars, we have never felt ourselves more at ease anywhere. Property for which no one would have given three thousand pounds in 1836, I would not now take ten for, and my nearest neighbour has lately refused £3375 for land which in 1834 cost him six hundred."

Sir Andries' point was, of course, to vindicate the success of his own frontier policy. Whether or not his good opinion of the benefits of the frontier system was justified, his economic facts are supported by other evidence showing that the flow of compensation money was not without effect. Never in the history of the colony had there been such a liquidation of assets. Between November 1836 and June 1839 the slaves brought into the country over one million sterling in ready money.[1]

This is in no way to question the fact that a good many individuals and families were very hard hit. Where slaves were security for a mortgage no doubt some one suffered, not necessarily the slave-owner, who may sometimes have cut debts as well as losses even at the price of bankruptcy; and though but a small proportion of the compensation money went unclaimed, a good many hundreds of slave-owners got nothing, even if it was only that they might not feel 'deprived' of the luxury of 'a legitimate sense of grievance'[2] against the British Government. Some of those who thus refused all offers may have carried their grievance out of the Colony and cherished it long afterwards in the Trekker States. On the whole it is likely that some of the solid and respectable slave-owners, particularly in the more settled West, suffered real loss, and others temporary financial embarrassment; still another class, some of them no doubt 'new' men, diverted a fair share of the compensation money into their own pockets, taking full advantage, if Stockenstrom's evidence may be credited,[3] of the opportunities of cheap and profitable invest-

---

[1] The Compensation Commissioners in the colony valued the slaves at £3,041,290; apparently a scrutiny in London reduced the assessment to £2,824,224; the amount eventually awarded to the Cape was only £1,247,401. Of this sum only some £24,913 remained unpaid in June 1839 (Cory, iii, pp. 42 and 44).

[2] Adv. Cloete's phrase, quoted by Cory, iii. pp. 43 and 44, note.

[3] Frequent references in Stockenstrom's letters to Fairbairn, from 1837 onwards, in Mr. J. G. Gubbins' collection, and to Fairbairn and Dr. Philip in my own keeping.

ment offered by the abandoned Eastern farms of the Boer Trekkers. That the economic influences at work in the country were little recognized or understood would not lessen the general feelings of bitterness and discontent.

Tradition, therefore, is misleading as to the effect of emancipation. Nor can it have it both ways, that slavery had little or nothing to do with the Trek, and again, that not emancipation itself but the method of compensation was the cause of bitterness. If the Eastern farmers who actually trekked owned scarcely any slaves, neither were they seriously affected by compensation; and yet in the words of Mrs. Anna Steenkamp, written long afterwards when things could be viewed in perspective:

The reasons for which we abandoned our lands and homesteads, our country, and kindred, were the following:

(1) The continual depredations and robberies of the Kafirs . . . (with unfulfilled promises of compensation for stolen property).

(2) The shameful and unjust proceedings with reference to the freedom of our slaves; and yet it is not so much their freedom that drove us to such lengths, as their being placed on an equal footing with Christians, contrary to the laws of God, and the natural distinction of race and religion, so that it was intolerable for any decent Christian to bow down beneath such a yoke; wherefore we rather withdrew, in order thus to preserve our doctrines in purity.[1]

To make light of the evils of Cape slavery, and to try to view it except as one aspect of the wider colour question, is only to add to the difficulty of understanding the later South African attitude to Native policy. If 'there never was an attempt in South Africa to defend the system in theory',[2] this was obviously because it was taken for granted. To insist that at last emancipation was hailed rather as a relief from suspense is not to say that it was in itself any more welcome: the conventional attitude of the colonists, both to slaves, and later to the free people of colour, remained that of the slave-master. The Act of 1833, and even the passing of apprenticeship in 1838, did not at once, nor for a long time, radically alter the mental approach of South Africans to the problem of how to treat the black people in their midst. The Cape indeed, Dutch and British alike, accepted the new order. Those who did not, took refuge in the two republics, where the dominant point of view continued to be that of those who, like Mrs. Steenkamp, cherished an abiding belief in the literal application of the 'Curse of Ham'.

[1] From *Cape Monthly Magazine*, September 1876. Quoted in Bird's *Annals of Natal*, i, p. 459.   [2] Theal, ii, p. 63.

G

The crusade against slavery was not ended.   Dr. Philip was under no illusions on this subject.   On the passing of the Act of 1833 he wrote to Fowell Buxton:

> While I congratulate . . . allow me to remind you that your labours are not yet finished. . . . The nation must be kept alive to this subject . . . its eyes kept steadily fixed on our colonies and on the House of Commons till it is known that the law which abolishes slavery is not to become a dead letter in the hand of those to whom its execution is entrusted. . . .
> The spirit which has so long and furiously resisted the improvement and the emancipation of the Negro will employ all its unabated and malignant energies to render nugatory all that has been done in his favour.   If the Abolitionists fail to follow up the advances lately gained . . . those that come after us will have to fight all our battles over again . . . and destroy a species of colonial bondage which will arise out of the ashes of the monster which has now been destroyed.

After 1833 the question enters a new phase, which continues to our own day.   In South Africa, if the black is no longer a slave, what are his rights and his status, economic, social, political, in the society of which he has become a part?

The 'Native Problem' had only just begun.   It fell to be dealt with, from the very beginning, in an atmosphere charged with the excitement and prejudice that were evoked by the preliminary fight to put an end to slavery.   And though slavery as an institution died in 1834, its legacy is the element of *hubris* in the conventional South African attitude to coloured races, to this day.

Chapter VII

SOUTH AFRICA IN 1806—THE MISSIONARIES AND THE FIRST ROUND IN THE FIGHT FOR COLOURED RIGHTS

THE white colonists, whose views of the fitness of things were so violently disturbed by the attack on slavery, were a very small community, widely scattered over an immense area. Their position was determined (Chap. II) by geographical influences, by the unconcern or weakness of their East India Company rulers, and by the extraordinarily difficult conditions of colonization, with no better means of transport than the lumbering ox-waggon. In the Eastern States of America, (the great New England group were founded hardly more than thirty years earlier than the Cape of Good Hope,) a strong group of colonies had arisen along the seaboard, shut in by the line of the Alleghanies; and before there were even the beginnings of any 'crossing' to Kentucky, or any serious development of the West, American colonization had a solid base of operations behind it. Before the end of the eighteenth century the population of the original thirteen colonies was most of three millions, a hundred times the white population of the Cape in 1806, and nearly double the total reached by the white population of the whole Union of South Africa more than a century later.

The conditions of their eighteenth-century life determined the typical Boer character and outlook. The Boers had no close ties with Europe and no vestige of a humanistic centre of civilization or culture. Life, if by no means easy or comfortable, was monotonous and uneventful, and too lonely and isolated for political development. Economic progress was

83

slow. Except on a few of the older and more settled farms of the West, where the quality of the domestic architecture suggests some degree of stability and comfort, farming gave little more than bare subsistence. The normal tenure was the Leenings-Plaats, in effect a one-year lease (the size of the farm being about 6000 acres, its limits often roughly determined as the land within 'half-an-hour' of a given centre). In practice the tenure was secure enough, the lease being rarely, if ever, cancelled, except for failure to pay the annual fee of 24 rix-dollars, and the system was popular. But land was so easily procured that this loose tenure rather encouraged the already strong *Wander-Geist*. It was easy come, easy go. As the sons grew up, instead of developing their old home, they tended to move out to take up new leases of their own. Thorough and devoted labour was likely to be rare where there was so little settled attachment to one spot, or to any real 'home' less immense than all South Africa. Governor-General van Imhoff as early as 1743, seeing the weakness, proposed smaller farms, the conversion of leasehold into freehold, and a somewhat higher fee for the more valuable land. But nothing was ever done to encourage more intensive work. There was therefore little economic development and little of the change which makes exciting history. Like the patriarchs whom their life and manners call to mind, succeeding generations of Boers 'begat sons and daughters, and were gathered to their fathers'.

Yet there was warning that the government of this people might have its difficulties. In the very first year of the Free Burghers, 1658, van Riebeeck had to deal with a Remonstrance from a noble band of fourteen Boer farmers against the restrictions laid upon them by the Company. They protested, 'want zij gheen Compagnie's slaven willen wezen' . . . which is to say, freely rendered, that they were not going to be the slaves of the Company or of any one else. But the earliest hint of a more real political opposition by the burghers was roughly suppressed by the action of Governor Willem van der Stel against the Stellenbosch farmer Adam Tas, in 1706. Officials were turned farmers on such a scale that they were able, by privilege of their position, to monopolize the very limited Cape market for farm produce. The episode strikes the attention, if only because it is so isolated. For the first time, Dutch farmers made common cause with French Huguenots in asserting the rights of the governed to consideration as citizens; and thus combined, they proved troublesome enough to make the Company think it advisable to hasten the recall of the offending Governor.   But this made little real or permanent difference.   From first to last the interests of the Company, by the very law of its being, continued to be almost diametrically opposed to those of the colonists; and in any community less weak and scattered there must have been still more serious friction.   However much it might try to control its officials, the immense time and distance separating the Colony from Holland or from Batavia, on which the Cape was technically dependent, made effective supervision difficult.   Thus the elaborate instructions left behind him by Governor-General van Imhoff in 1743 are probably more enlightening as to the prevailing practices of officials in the matter of fees and perquisites, than effective at the time in stopping them; for in 1778, more than thirty years later, the colonists' agitation against van Plettenberg was in essentials the same as in 1706, demanding, in addition to the removal of vexatious restraints upon trade, that some check be put upon the peculations of the Company's officials.   As yet the relation of colonists to the backward races of the country had given rise to no radical difference of opinion between Government and governed, and therefore to no serious question of public policy in the matter.

Little love was lost between the colonists and their old Government.   Quite early a very pronounced cleavage arose in South African society between a section with urban and even overseas traditions, represented by official Cape Town, and those others, apt to regard themselves as the only true South Africans, whose spiritual home was Stellenbosch or, later, Pretoria or Bloemfontein.   Before ever the British took charge, the Government had come to be looked upon by the up-country people as an alien, to be evaded or opposed in every way possible. The Company, if it was a despot, was a weak despot.   Even its cherished monopoly was habitually infringed, by its own officials and by colonists alike.   An endless stream of Placaats in restraint of smuggling and of other illicit forms of trade is the measure of the failure of the Government, in spite of the increasing severity of the penalties it threatened, to enforce its restrictive policy, which was a constant irritant.   Even in the collection of taxes, if it saved itself the costs of administration, the Government was habitually fleeced by farmers who were left to make their own assessment of the "opgaaf" or tithe.

'This day,' writes Adam Tas, on 7th January 1706, 'Mr. van der Bijl presented his return; of wheat, 15 muids sowed, 90 reaped; rye, 5 sowed, 25 reaped; bestials, large and small, 135; sheep, 1000.

From this return I can perceive I have made mine own more than
the half too big.'

Leal love and loyalty could not be felt for this Government
of merchants ; the very instinct of loyalty to a State was
weakened, to be revived only in the last days of the Boer
Republics, a century later.

Inevitably in these circumstances there was singularly little
concrete political thought or action.   So far from serving even
a political apprenticeship, for the days when the country should
come to have a Government of its own, the Boers became
utterly intolerant of the give-and-take which is necessary in the
working of political institutions.   Who was not with them was
against them.   The mere differences of opinion, which in well-
ordered communities are held in check by loyalty to a common
State, came to be regarded as grounds for breaking away
altogether, and forming a separate little community of the
Elect—rather a Cave of Adullam.   Their own interests were
all.   In the eyes of the Boers it was not the function of a
Government to bind varying interests into a stronger whole;
its chief merit would seem to have been that of the Victorian
child, namely, that it should be seen and not heard.   So at
the time the Company came to grief in the decade of the French
Revolution, the Boers expressed their pent-up sense of grievance by hiving off in the first of their long series of short-lived
separatist 'republics', at Swellendam and Graaff-Reinet.
Mere shadows of republics as they were, with no effective
authority, they were significant as a piece of self-assertion,
showing that the farmers of the interior felt themselves distinct
and aloof from the 'parasites'[1]—mere officials, tradespeople,
lodging-house keepers and hangers-on of Government at the
Castle in Cape Town.   The outbreak of republics was a warning that any future Government, which claimed to be South
African, must follow, certainly not run seriously counter to, the
supposed interests of the Veld, or even 'Back Veld', on pain
of losing their allegiance altogether.   It is significant that even
in the seventeen-nineties there was, not one united farmers'
republic, but two, entirely separate and distinct.   It is true
there were, as well, the more solid Western farmers; but the
Boers were so far justified in their claim to be the backbone
of the infant community, since they were the typical product
of the country.   The seeds of disunion and disruption which
mark the course of nineteenth-century history in South Africa

[1] Term used by Dr. L. Fouché in pamphlet, *Die Evolutie van
die Trek Boer.*

were sown, not by its new British rulers, but in the Dutch eighteenth century.

To the Cape Colony, as it was between 1795 and 1806, the changes in its Government were almost less of a fundamental shock than the arrival at the same time of missionaries to the Hottentots. Nor is it for want of notice that the place of the missionaries in South African history is habitually misunderstood. All accounts agree in giving almost unstinted praise to the Moravian Brethren and the Wesleyan Methodists. The conventional praise of this group serves to point the blame and censure still levelled at what was in the early days the much more important London Missionary Society. The coming of the missionaries marked an epoch because it challenged the accepted views on the rights of the subject races.

In the first place, until the arrival of the missionaries there was no one at all to state the case for the coloured races. It takes two to make a quarrel; and since throughout the eighteenth century the aboriginal tribes were merely ignored, and themselves quite voiceless, there was no Colour 'Question'. The first lonely missionary, the Moravian George Schmidt, withstood the opposition he met for barely seven years, 1737 to 1744, though hostility was decently cloaked by the confessional difficulties that were raised by official Calvinists against a Moravian's administration of the sacraments; and it was all but half a century before Schmidt's successors arrived at the Cape in 1792. The new Moravians were quickly followed by representatives of the London Missionary Society —van der Kemp and Kicherer in 1798, James Read and William Anderson, pioneer in Griqualand, in 1800; and very soon, *et post hoc et propter hoc*, there are the beginnings of a Hottentot question.

Now if it was chiefly by missionary influence that the position of the backward races was first recognized to involve a question of political morality, the awakening of any sense of responsibility towards the Hottentots was in a peculiar degree the work of the London missionaries. When the contentiousness of the leaders of this Society is contrasted with the docility of the Wesleyans and others, it tends to be forgotten that there were reasons for their taking a more radical and independent attitude. The Moravians, a much smaller body, were disabled for conflict with the authorities by the fact that they were aliens. The Wesleyans again, originally more politically conservative, began work at the Cape only in 1816, and, great missionaries as they were, they were at first almost all in Kafirland; within the borders of the Colony itself their stations were few and unimportant. In addition, they were very closely associated with the white colonists; by far the strongest communion in the Settler districts, the Wesleyans no doubt appreciated or understood the colonists' point of view, but were naturally also more careful of antagonizing their white parishioners. On the other hand, the London Society of those days, though it had only a few representatives at important strategic points in Kafirland, and hardly any white colonial congregations, was by far the strongest missionary society within the Colony, and held in addition an almost continuous line of stations along the Northern border which was soon to be on the direct route of the trekking Boers.[1] Until the latest 'forties, moreover, the great Bantu peoples were a distant, or at least an external, problem. That the earlier phase of the South African Colour Question was in relation, not to the 'Kafirs', but to the Hottentots, most of whom were followers or dependants of the London Society, is in itself sufficient explanation of the apparently disproportionate 'political' activities of the early London missionaries. By coming at all, they hastened the day when the status of the Hottentots must inevitably become a live issue; and by their presence as the teachers of this people, they were also their leaders and spokesmen, drawn into the forefront of the struggle, against colonists or Government, as the case might be. By the time the Kafirs, many of them converts and disciples of the Wesleyan and other societies, became a serious part of the internal colonial problem of conduct and relationships, the London missionaries, in their fight for the Hottentots, had compelled colonial opinion to take the first step up and away from slavery. The earliest Bantu subjects of the Cape Colony had at least this advantage, that they were recognized from the beginning as human beings, and not mere slaves. This they owed, above all, to the hard blows given and received by the pioneer London missionaries on behalf of the Hottentots.

The first battle was very soon joined, though it was the middle 'twenties before the whole question of Hottentot status assumed the magnitude of a problem. The criticisms of van der Kemp and Read were directed chiefly against isolated and individual acts of ill-usage, and in this, at least, missionaries were on common ground with the Government; for in 1809 the Government itself began to legislate on Hottentot labour con-

[1] For list of these stations, see p. 105, *note* 3.

ditions,[1] administrative officials agreeing with the missionaries
in a desire to see the relations between colonial masters and
Hottentot servants governed, not merely by the will of the
master, but by the Rule of Law. Indirectly at least, the
Hottentots obtained some additional protection against personal
violence by the institution in 1811 of a Circuit Court for the
better administration of justice in outlying districts.

This would seem to be the firstfruits of missionary agitation;[2] and colonial opinion, though it had not yet begun to
feel the effects of the attempt to reform the system of slavery,
was soon in violent revolt. The first grievance was what was
felt to be the humiliation of the so-called 'Black Circuit' of
1812, when the Government ordered an investigation of charges
of cruelty alleged especially by Mr. James Read. The result
was a series of trials by the Circuit Court at Uitenhage and
elsewhere, and there was violent resentment at the charges of
violence that were laid, it seemed by missionary prompting, on
behalf of slaves and Hottentots, against members of respectable
colonial families. The charges were repudiated, then and later,
as false and malicious, emphasis being laid on the fact that
relatively few of the accused colonists were actually convicted.[3]
The point to be emphasized, however, is not the acquittals, but
the convictions. Most of the alleged offences had been committed years earlier, when no court of justice was available;
evidence must have been almost impossible to collect, since at
any time there are obvious disabilities in the way of a slave
arraigning his master—the difficulty being all the greater when
the chief witnesses were fellow-slaves or Hottentots, gathered
from scattered farms years after the event. In spite of all this,
at least eight colonists were convicted of crimes of violence
against their servants (none, it is true, of murder); several
were found to have withheld wages, and several more were
reserved for trial at a later session of the Court.[4]

[1] See Chap. XIII, below. (Dundas really began in 1799.)
[2] Sir George Cory, i, p. 210, is at pains to prove by an argument
based on the dates of letters written by the Rev. James Read, the
Cape Governor, and Lord Liverpool, that missionary protests had
nothing to do with the beginning of Circuit Courts. The truth would
seem to be that any decent State must have recognized the necessity
for making its courts of justice more accessible to all its subjects;
and to that extent the Cape Government needed little pressing. But
van der Kemp and Read were unquestionably the first to emphasize
that the Hottentots stood in need of such protection, and it seems
reasonable to judge from the evidence that their efforts hastened this
desirable reform.   [3] Theal, i, p. 202; Cory, i, pp. 211-218.
[4] See Cory, vol. i, in loc. cit.; also du Plessis, i, p. 133.

The question at issue was the just treatment of inferiors, in itself one of the most searching of character tests. With regard to the Boer colonists it must be said that, in general, they emerge from this test as well as English or any other masters placed, as they have been, in almost irresponsible control of a backward race of servants. Any adequate knowledge of the country and of its people will suggest countless instances of lifelong and devoted service by individual Natives, and by whole families, to Boer masters. The Boer at his best is perhaps the typical landlord aristocrat, with the aristocrat's virtues.[1] The law of the land, however, cannot rest content with a general rule, without providing a remedy in those particular cases where, however rarely, the privileges of a master race may be abused. To this day the Boer master almost prides himself upon being a stern disciplinarian; his benevolence and kindliness are conditional upon a marked degree of docility and obedience on the part of the servant, who is subject to strict and speedy visitation if he fails to 'know his place'. In those days, if the servant was not a slave, he was at best a 'free person of colour', not only closely hedged about by regulations enforceable by a Boer field-cornet, but at all times subject to the discipline of a master who, if only by reason of the distance from the seat of Government, was in most cases at once policeman and judge in his own cause. It may be true that travellers like Barrow, to say nothing of some of the missionaries, exaggerated or generalized what they saw or heard; a few fell into the error of drawing an indictment against the Boers as a nation, though in later years Dr. Philip at least was fully more severe in his strictures on English than on Boer colonists. But a certain wounded self-esteem on the part of Cape colonists has made them shut their eyes to the bare possibility that there were abuses, so that many fail even yet to recognize the true significance of the 'Black Circuit'. The volume of evidence that there were flagrant abuses was too great to be ignored, either by any self-respecting Government of that day, or by the modern historian.

Three years after the 'Black Circuit' came the unfortunate episode of Slagter's Nek.[2] Once again the long arm of the law

[1] Cf. Basil Williams on the old Cape Parliament, in the *Life of Cecil J. Rhodes*.
[2] For a full story of a miniature rebellion, see Cory, vol. i, pp. 323-368.
  Frederick Bezuidenhout, after repeated summons, failed to appear in court, and was ultimately killed in resisting arrest. There was a

reached out to the remote interior, this time in an attempt to enforce a warrant of arrest against one Bezuidenhout, who failed to answer a summons of court—with a tragic sequel. But however tragic this sequel, the immediate occasion of the crisis was the resentment, and all too characteristic petulance, of a Boer farmer and his friends at finding that the treatment or the discipline of a Hottentot servant should be questioned in a court of law. Now it may be that in 1812 missionary allegations of violence and ill-usage compelled the Government to extend the scope of the newly-constituted Circuit Court to the examination of respectable farmers (on charges which were proved to be not without foundation); so far as Slagter's Nek is concerned, however, the missionaries may have suggested to the Hottentots the possibility of seeking the protection of the courts, as they were entitled to do; but there missionary responsibility in this matter began and ended. This time it was the Government of the country which shouldered the duty of teaching reluctant colonists that not their own will but the law must be supreme. The traditions which have grown up round the 'Black Circuit' and 'Slagter's Nek' could hardly have attained the vigour they did except in a very independent community of slave-masters, little used to the most elementary restraints and formalities of the law. The farmer could not, in short, continue to be his own policeman as well as his own judge; and the chastisement of a servant, hitherto an unchallenged right of the master, was now to come under the review and control of the State and of its law courts. At the time this was almost a revolutionary innovation; and so deep was the resentment it caused that, even yet, colonial opinion is slow to recognize, either that legal intervention was inevitable, or that the attendant troubles were to be expected in the progress of civilized government in South Africa. This was actually the first round in the fight with the idea underlying slavery.

For the London Missionary Society the outcome of this preliminary storm was almost disastrous. Dr. van der Kemp, the earliest leader, died on the eve of the contest, in 1811. His successor, James Read, though active for full fifty years—

half-hearted rising among the farmers, who nearly came to blows with a force at Slagter's Nek. Johannes Bezuidenhout was killed while trying to escape. After trial by a special commission, five rebels were publicly hanged, fines or sentence of imprisonment or banishment being imposed on most of the others.

he died only in 1852—had not the personal qualities or mental equipment of a leader—least of all in a contest which would involve the championship of the rights of the Natives against the full force of colonial opinion.   Even in 1811 the internal affairs of the Society were far from happy.   As early as February 1811 the Directors had written urging van der Kemp to remove from Bethelsdorp to Cape Town, there to undertake the duties of Agent and Superintendent; this was held to be desirable for the better control of remote missionaries, and for better ordering the work of

instructing the children, both male and female, of promoting industry among the natives, bringing them forward in the knowledge of the useful arts, and laying among them the foundations of social order.

Late in the same year a formal resolution confirmed van der Kemp's appointment and, in case of his decease or departure, nominated the Rev. James Read as his successor; but Read seems never to have assumed the full responsibility of office.   The visit of the Rev. John Campbell, a prominent Director, between 1812 and 1814, produced little but an interesting book of *Travels*; and in practice Dr. George Thom, resident in Cape Town, seems to have undertaken as much of the business of the Society as James Read, who was far away in the interior.   Divided control soon brought dire chaos. Dissension arose between factions led by Read and Dr. Thom respectively, and matters came to a head at the meeting of a 'Synod', organized by Dr. Thom's party, at Cape Town in August 1817.

There was of course some substance in the complaints of the protesting missionaries.   The administrative regulations drawn up by Dr. van der Kemp evidently needed drastic revision.   Salaries, at that time only £35 to £45 per annum, and subject to violent fluctuations according to the state of the Cape Exchange, were grossly inadequate.   The state and the conduct of the 'Institutions', Bethelsdorp and others, needed careful consideration.   The policy of mixed marriages between missionaries and Hottentots was open to question; and there was obviously valid objection to ecclesiastical irregularities, even if distance was their chief occasion.[1]   There were baptisms by unordained men, and marriages of the unbaptized— this last being 'unscriptural', though it happened—'yes! at

[1] One missionary in Namaqualand seems to have solved the difficulty due to the distance of his station from any regular marriage officer by performing the ceremony of *his own* marriage with a Hottentot convert.

Bethelsdorp'. There was no competent local authority to deal with general administration or with personal irregularities, chief among them an alleged lapse into cardinal 'sin' by the Rev. James Read himself.[1] Yet so far from helping to solve these difficulties, the meeting in 1817 merely intensified party feeling by the dispute about control. Some, like the Rev. George Barker and Robert Moffat, recognizing the impediments of distance, were for a Resident Director and Superintendent. Thom, on the other hand, 'testified against one minister of the Gospel being placed over another', and, failing, one cannot but feel, his own appointment as Director, favoured the formation of a permanent 'Committee' of management. Read, in any case, was now impossible as Superintendent.

Yet what disturbed some of the Synod most of all was Read's 'imprudence' in falling foul of the Government, and his general attitude and policy towards the Hottentots. What was held to be the incapacity of the missionaries for the 'control' of their converts was the Government's warrant for taking steps, just after the 'Synod', to 'put down' the two Bushman stations, which were begun in 1814 when Read, so his critics alleged, sent missionaries beyond the frontier 'without Government sanction'. There was also trouble because Mr. Anderson, who had achieved the arduous task of settling some of the nomadic Griquas in a community at Klaarwater, had failed or refused to 'commandeer' the services of the Griquas, demanded for military purposes in the Colony. Even on the matter of slavery the Synod was half-hearted; Robert Moffat and others were definitely for the emancipation of slaves; one Seidenfaden, however, 'would leave it to the conscience of my wife'! The upshot was a compromise resolution to the effect that 'it is not proper for missionaries to *buy or sell* slaves'.[2] But whether it was to

---

[1] The case of Read presents some difficulties. The evidence of what is called his 'fall' was not enough to warrant the 1817 Synod reaching a decision and they left it to the Directors. Campbell, at one time inclined to believe the charge, seems to have been attracted by the personality of Read, his companion on a long tour in 1819–20. Philip at first was harder on him, and Read seems to have been suspended about that time, and to have served only as a supernumerary or artizan on various stations for over ten years. He was reinstated after full proof of 'penitence' only in 1830, when Dr. Philip allowed him to accept the 'call' of the Hottentots on the Kat River Settlement.

[2] Quotations are from 'Draft Record' of the 1817 'Synod' in the Records of the L.M.S., London. The Draft is 'for missionaries

heal the internal disorder of the Society, or for the guidance of public policy, the Synod made no real contribution; and such extreme caution as it displayed in its attitude to the authorities was little calculated to further the cause of Hottentot or any other freedom.   Before very long, indeed, Dr. Thom and Mr. Taylor abandoned the Society, and accepted from the Government appointments to local Dutch churches.   Evan Evans also seceded, and a fourth, Mr. Brownlee, 'had consented to occupy one of our stations, giving up his connection with the Society, and to receive a salary from Government'. Mr. Moffat, indeed, refused offers of a mission station which were pressed upon him by the authorities, and Mr. Brownlee returned to the Society in 1825.   After the storm of 1812–15 these happenings began a period of comparative calm, and for several years there was no fresh development in the Colour Question.

---

only'—and only for those who approved of the meeting.   It is signed by Evan Evans, L. Marquard, Robert Moffat, Johs. Seidenfaden, John Taylor, George Thom.

Chapter VIII

DR. JOHN PHILIP

AFTER the affair of Slagter's Nek and the temporary collapse of the London Missionary Society about 1817, and before the fight for Hottentot rights was renewed, there were two all-important changes at the Cape. In 1820 came the British Settlers, and with them new personalities and an entirely new political situation. But a year before this the Government itself demanded an inquiry into the affairs of the L.M.S.

At home complaints against the missionaries and the workings of the missionary system were made by the home Government to the Board of Directors of the London Society. But these complaints became so frequent and of such a nature that the only method the Directors could fall upon, at last to pacify Lord Bathurst, was to promise to send out a Deputation to Africa to investigate the grounds of these complaints and to find out a remedy for the evils complained of.[1]

Thereupon in 1819 the missionaries acquired in Dr. John Philip a leader of vigorous intellect and personality, who was soon to get an entirely new grasp of the position with regard to the backward races, and for thirty critical years to stand as their doughty advocate and champion.

The theme of this book was evolved from the study of Dr. Philip's private papers (see Chap. I). The very bitterness with which his memory is still commonly regarded bears testimony to the force of character and far-reaching influence of this one man. The generally received view of Philip's work sorely needs restatement, for it is still that of his colonial

---

[1] Memorandum of Philip's—undated, probably late.

95

contemporaries and opponents.   Even historians have accepted,
endorsed, and enlarged the categorical charge of his opponents,
that Philip was 'more a *politician* than a missionary'.[1]   In a
note of Sir George Cory's,[2] any more favourable view of his
character is assumed to depend on the condition that 'all
despatches of governors, statements of judges and officials are
unworthy of credit'.   The general retort to charges of this
kind is sufficiently obvious.   For many years Dr. Philip conducted a lone fight, at first without even newspaper support,
against the Somerset regime; later, when he had the *Commercial Advertiser* with him, he was still the leader of the
opposition to the Native policy and system of the very 'governors, judges, and officials' to whom Sir George Cory appeals.
These men had no critics to face in a popular Parliament, but
they were officials fighting for life and reputation in defence of
their own policy against a trenchant and formidable critic, so
that their statements are the *ex parte* pronouncements of one
side to a controversy.

It is commonly cited to prove that Philip was at best a
'political meddler' that he compares unfavourably with the
Moravian and Wesleyan missionaries.   To assess the comparative success of missions, and make sweeping estimates of
spiritual values, is difficult; and to take as the test of efficiency
the greater or less degree of friction with the civil Government
is certainly to beg the question.   Philip was driven to politics
by what he regarded as the sins of the Government against
missionary interests, and his rivals, as he himself pointed out,
'meddled' when it suited them, even 'taking the part of the
oppressor against the oppressed'.   'Nothing is *politics* with
them', he continues, 'but the advocacy of the civil rights of
the oppressed.'   When the Wesleyans and others publicly
expressed their approval of Sir Benjamin D'Urban's policy
towards the Kaffirs,[3] they no doubt acted in complete good
faith—as did the London missionaries in opposing it.   One side
was as 'political' as the other.

In his day Dr. Philip was one of the very small circle of
educated and public-spirited citizens of the Cape Colony,
bound to have attracted attention if he took any part at all in
public affairs.   It was a small community where class distinctions counted for little, and one man was as good as his
neighbour; just for this reason the white colonists were acutely

---

[1] 'Philip is, it is to be feared, more a *politician* than a missionary.'
Sir Lowry Cole to Secretary of State, 25th October 1830.
[2] Cory, ii, p. 426.   [3] Theal, ii, p. 118.

class-conscious in their attitude to the coloured people in their midst. There was likely to be violent disapproval of any one who dared to take an independent and unpopular stand against accepted social prejudices, and Dr. Philip's views being as unpalatable as they were, his prominence easily became notoriety. The Philip papers, only now available, are an indispensable corrective to the hitherto undisputed official and colonial views of the influence of 'Exeter Hall' in South Africa.

As to Philip's person, the time has gone by, even were the material available, for an intimate biography. In 1922 apparently no one in Cape Town, and not the oldest living inhabitant of his own beloved Bethelsdorp, remembered seeing him in person.[1] Of his personal traits there is little or no surviving family tradition—except perhaps of his singularly keen and piercing eyes. He was born of a family of weavers at Kirkcaldy in the year 1775. This is the correct account; his father was not a schoolmaster.[2] But the weaver does not go dressed in ragged trousers (any more than John Bunyan's *tinker* father), with an almost equally ragged mind. Since Sir James Barrie has immortalized the Society of *Thrums*, it should be easy to reconstruct the surroundings in which John Philip grew up. The weavers of Fife, working in their own homes before the days of great factory cities, were an intelligent, proud, and independent stock, of whom Dr. Chalmers and Mr. M'Culloch noted that, in the worst days of the old Poor Law, 'coming on the rates' was almost unknown. Though Philip began work at the early age of eleven, he grew up with an inherited taste for books. In an autobiographical fragment he noted that amongst his father's treasures were writings of Bacon, Swift, Dr. Johnson, and Newton. At the age of fifteen, like Zacchary Macaulay and James Stephen the elder, older contemporaries who became prominent in the crusade against slavery, he seems to have contemplated a West Indian clerkship. Deferring to a 'dream', he abandoned this idea, and continued to work at his trade in Fife. At the age of twenty he became works manager in a 'power' mill in Dundee, but left his employment after

[1] At Hankey in 1924 there was a very old coloured woman who could describe the opening of the irrigation tunnel in 1845. She remembered Dr. Philip as *'n dikke* (stout), and Mrs. Philip was still to her, *Juffrouw* (Madam).

[2] See Cory, ii, 404 *note*, 'Some say his father was a weaver'. The facts in the text are drawn from fragments of autobiography and from the text of an incomplete 'Life' compiled by a son and a grandson, Revs. T. D. and Fred. Philip.

H

only six months for the reason that he would not 'sanction or
be privy to' the conditions of labour to which children were
subjected.   Finally, he became an independent 'master' and
'in six months was doing well'.

At this point, however, his life prospects underwent a
complete change, when he yielded to a feeling which drew him
to the ministry.   Of any sudden conversion there is no evidence.
Even in his 'teens he seems to have been a speaker at missionary
meetings, his first public speech having been to make suggestions for reform of procedure at some such meeting.   He was
caught up in a strong wave of the Evangelical Revival, which
spread through Scotland in the seventeen-nineties.   In his
youth he doubtless knew the sectional differences which long
agitated 'Thrums'.   While   his   parents   adhered   to   the
Established Church of Scotland, his uncles were 'Glassites'.
John Philip himself came under the influence of the Haldanes,
the founders of Scottish Congregationalism; on their advice he
betook himself in 1799 to the Hoxton Academy of the English
Independents, and, unlike the Haldanes themselves, to Congregationalism he ever afterwards adhered.   His three years' college
course at Hoxton was much distracted, after the fashion at such
seminaries, by teaching and preaching, first in workhouses and
Sunday schools in London, then in town and country round
about.   In after life accordingly, his earlier schooling having
been negligible, Philip shows himself very little a finished or
exact scholar.   His culture was that of the largely self-taught
man, showing wide but rather discursive reading.   His writing, to the considerable distress of would-be biographers, lacks
the finish and precision which more severe scholastic discipline
might have given.   Yet he learned some balance and judgment,
and knowing his own mind, was not driven about by every new
wind of doctrine.   Of the spiritual restlessness of James Haldane,
whose 'New Light' disturbed the harmony of his Aberdeen
congregation, he could write: 'He seemed to feel as if the Bible
had for the first time been brought to light, and that nobody
seemed to have understood it till then': and of the two Haldanes,
he quotes with approval from his friend the Rev. Mr. Cowie
of Huntly, that he feared they 'had gone to sea without a chart
or compass and thought every island a discovery of their own;
but they would find that former navigators were neither all
fools nor bad men'.

With three 'calls' to choose from, Philip passed in 1802
from Hoxton to Newbury, Berks.   While there his Sunday
evening 'lectures' had some qualified success.   One of his

audience was a curate fresh from Oxford, who told him that he had liked 'as much of the lecture as he could understand', with the consequence that Philip set himself, apparently with success, to correct and subdue his Scots accent. In 1804, with a little hesitation it would seem, he decided to accept a call to the charge of the first Congregational Church (George Street) in Aberdeen. His doubts were overcome by the thought that the position offered was 'respectable', and the new charge likely, according to his friend Cowie, to be 'a strong centre of the missionary interest in the North—there being many experienced Christians in the country'. The London Missionary Society and the kindred Bible and Tract Societies continued to be his chief interests throughout his stay in Aberdeen, and several of his congregation, including one future rival, Dr. Thom, volunteered for missionary work. The fact therefore that Philip was asked to go as one of a deputation, and remain as the fully accredited Resident Director of his Society at the Cape, was manifestly a tribute to his activities on behalf of missions in the North of Scotland, and to the success of his work in Aberdeen. He was, in fact, a Person in missionary circles at home even before, in 1819 or 1820, he was armed with 'some diploma', the doctor's degree of Columbia University.[1]

[1] An entertaining letter from an Aberdeen parishioner, one Jas. Bisset, shows that the degree was 'in the air' in 1818. . . . 'Dec. 28, This day I have sent off to Liverpool one Journal and two Chronicles, and addressed them to the Revd. *Dr.* Philip; the Gew-Gaw of a Degree makes not the smallest alteration in me, nor will it in you. If you had got it according to merit, or the Rule of proportion you ought to have had it before *I ever saw you*. It will be a long time before they make Mr. Doig (*i.e.* a 'candidate' for the Church in Aberdeen) a Dr.—poor man! between seeking out another wife, the darkness of the East Church, and the dimness of his eyesight *now*, he has much to do,—O *that* Reading Preachers, or Preaching Readers, they cut a sorry figure in the end; the Candles are lighted up in the East Church at the beginning of the service just now, it is all the urim and thumim that such preachers want! Yet after all I must confess that I am not a little proud of the Degree, it may do good.'
Bisset adds: '13 Feb. 1819. The clergy of all denominations seems to take things very easy since you left Aberdeen. I suppose they think they are weel quit of you, being delivered now from the whip and the spur.'
It seems likely that the descendants of the English Puritans maintained some touch with their cousins in North America during the time that British Universities were almost closed to 'Nonconformists'.
I am indebted to Mr. Geo. W. Lyon for making inquiries which show that John Philip was actually admitted to the doctor's degree of

It is scarcely too much to say that almost every action in Dr. Philip's career has been somewhat misrepresented. It is not true that in his Aberdeen congregation about 1818 'har-

---

Columbia University only in 1819, and of Princeton College in 1820. The library of Princeton Theological Seminary contains reports on Africa made by him at least as late as 1833.

Extract from the Minutes of the Trustees of Columbia College, June 7, 1819

The following letter was presented and read.

To the Chairman of the Trustees of Col. College.

Monday, 7 June 1819.

Sir,

Being necessarily hindered from attending the Board of Trustees this morning, I beg leave to submit the enclosed to their consideration, and to express a hope that it will receive their favourable notice. I need not state to the board the difficulties which embarrass the attainment of academical honors in the British Universities, by persons not attached to either of the established churches. I shall only add that the gentlemen whose signatures recommend the application for Mr. Philip, are personally known to me, and occupy an honorable standing at home.

Very respectfully
Sir
your obt. hble. servt.
(signed) I. M. MASON.

The following certificate was enclosed in the above letter, viz.

LONDON, *Jan.* 7, 1819.

We whose names are underwritten take the liberty of certifying to the president and members of the Senatus Academicus of Columbia College New-York that the Revnd John Philip, lately of Aberdeen, now of Cape Town, South Africa, was regularly educated in the old College or Academy of Protestant Dissenters at Hoxton near London —that he possesses very respectable talents; and has made distinguished progress in Literature, Science, and Divinity. That his religious and moral character hath placed him high in the scale of public estimation while his usefulness hath been extensive as the sphere in which he moved. That we conceive it to be right that some public mark of esteem and honour should, by those who are clothed with legitimate authority to confer such a mark, be bestowed on our excellent friend; and as we trust that such a mark of merited esteem may eventually conduce to the success of his ministerial labours, we humbly and earnestly request this college to confer on him the degree of Doctor in Divinity.

A. WAUGH, D.D. Minr. of the Scots Church in Well Street, Mary le Bone.

J. PYE SMITH, D.D. Pastor and Prof. Theol. in the Acad. Prot. Diss. at Homerton.

WILLIAM NICOL, D.D. Minr. of the Scots Church Swallow Street, St. James's.

mony was disturbed';[1] nor even quite correct that he 'offered his services to the London Missionary Society'.[2] As minister of the George Street Congregational Church from 1804 he had refused a good many urgent invitations to move from Aberdeen.[3] On the 10th October 1817, Rev. G. Burder, Secretary to the Society, sent out an official circular, stating the need for someone to undertake the management of affairs at Cape Town, and asking the recipients to suggest any 'minister or other person in the compass of your acquaintance' with the requisite qualifications for this task. A note enclosed in Philip's copy, addressed to 'Dear Brother', gives more details about the state of South Africa, beginning bluntly, 'Can you go?' The Directors soon came to a decision.

OLD JEWRY, LONDON,
11 *Novr.* 1817.
Dear Brother,

You are already apprized of the intention of the Directors of the Missionary Society to send a Deputation of their brethren to South Africa, to set in order the affairs of the Missions in that country; and the occasions of such a measure you also know. The Directors, aware the very great importance of sending out persons duly qualified for such an undertaking, have earnestly implored the direction of the only wise God. . . .

Our dear Brother Campbell, who, a few years ago, paid a visit to South Africa, for a similar purpose, has signified his readiness to comply with the wishes of the Directors . . . Mr. Campbell however intends, after effecting with the brother who shall accompany him whatever is practicable for the Settlement of the Society's affairs, to return to England. But it appears to the Directors necessary that another Brother should accompany Mr. Campbell, to assist him in the arrangement of the affairs that relate to the several stations, and when he has accomplished that work to abide at or near Cape Town, as the Agent, or Superintending Director, on behalf of the Board of Directors at home; to inspect all the affairs and proceedings of the Missionaries; to see that the Regulations agreed upon are observed; to afford them his advice in cases of difficulty, and to transact any

---

ROBT. WINTER, D.D., Pastor of the Prot. Diss. Church in New Court Carey Str., London.

WM. MANUEL, D.D., Minr. of the Scots Church, London Wall, London.

WM. ALERS HANKEY, Treasurer of the London Missionary Society.

GEO. BURDER, Secretary of the London Missionary Society.

Whereupon Resolved that Mr. Philip be considered as nominated for the degree of Doctor of Divinity.

[1] Cory, vol. ii, p. 404.
[2] du Plessis, *Christian Missions in South Africa*, p. 142.
[3] There are at least four ' calls ' or letters of invitation preserved among Philip's papers.

negotiations that may be necessary between the Missionaries, or the Directors, and the Colonial Government at the Cape.

The Directors, Sir, having looked around them among the various ministers of the Gospel in England and Scotland, who have evinced their zeal for the cause of Missions, have directed their eyes to you, as being, in every point of view, in their judgment, a fit and proper person to be their Representative in these momentous concerns; and they have, after solemn prayer and mature consideration, unanimously, and most cordially Resolved, and do hereby communicate to you that resolution, that you be earnestly requested to undertake for them, or rather for our dear and common Lord and Master, this labour of love, and go forth in His name, to promote His blessed cause in South Africa. . . .

The Directors will address a letter expressive of their Sympathy to the people of your pastoral regard, and requesting them to resign you to the Lord for this greater work, to which we apprehend that He is now calling you. . . . We shall hope, that if it be His holy will to employ you in this great work, the heart of your dear spouse, and the hearts of your people will be inclined to comply with a request, thus presented to you in a most cordial and affectionate manner by your brethren the Directors.

> Signed in their name, and by their order by,
> (Signed) W. ALERS HANKEY, (Treasurer)
> GEO. BURDER, (Secretary)

To Rev. John Philip.   Aberdeen.

In the letter to the congregation in Aberdeen the Directors write:

In so weighty a concern we dare not look to a man of ordinary make, and we trust you will readily see the importance of having placed at the Head of our operations in Africa, a man of solid learning, Scriptural piety, ardent missionary zeal, prudent deportment, and gentle manners.

This appeal was, however, by no means decisive. Mr. Philip hesitated long. His congregation steadily obstructed. On the 28th February 1818 Burder writes: 'We are sorely unwilling to give you up. We hear of nothing so satisfactory as your own going.' In April, though pressure on Philip was maintained, there seems to have been some thought of getting a Mr. Dewar. By July the George Street congregation got so far as to think of releasing Philip for two years—a period regarded by the Directors as too short for the purpose. At last, only on the 8th of September 1818, Philip definitely accepted the invitation—the church reluctantly agreeing. It is no small tribute to his popularity that letters from members of his congregation show that as late as February 1819 the deacons contemplated keeping his church vacant in case Philip should decide to return to them within the two years.

The deputation sailed at last by the 600-ton *Westmoreland*
in November. Early in December they were driven back to
Liverpool, the ship having been dismasted in a heavy storm.
Even after sighting Table Mountain they were driven off by a
storm, and delayed another three weeks, landing only on the
26th February 1819.

It was in Aberdeen that Philip met, and in 1809 married,
one Jane Ross, the daughter of a well-to-do citizen, the de-
signer of Union Bridge which spans the Denburn—its wide
granite arch being unique in its day. Mrs. Philip was a woman
of character and ability, and, till her death in 1847, not only was
she her husband's adviser in chief, but she took entire charge
of the financial affairs of the Society in South Africa. It is a
tribute to her capable management, and to the integrity of both
of them, that for years the Philips were put on no regular
salary, but were left to help themselves from the funds according to their needs.[1] It appears that Mrs. Philip kept a tight
hold on the family purse, for the interesting reason that her
husband's generosity made him fair game for all the beggars,
and if he had money in his pocket, he was sure to return from
a walk down town with them emptied by his benefactions and
almsgiving. His wife further helped to determine the length
and scope of Philip's journeys, and in his long absences from
Cape Town she managed the affairs both of their own and of
the French Missionary Society. A few 'love' letters survive
from 1809, and are full of discussions of religious doubts and
difficulties. Others are more human. 'Pray remember',
she writes to London in 1836, 'I am still flesh, and not all
spirit'.

The range of his correspondence shows that Dr. Philip had
a faculty for forming friendships with people of intellectual
quality and ability, and not least with those who were likely to
help him to get things done. Among his correspondents who
write as friends, in the rather ponderous style then customary,
to 'My dear friend', and 'My very dear Sir', etc., etc., there
were, in Aberdeen, Principal Tulloch of King's College, Drs.
Dewar, Principal, and Ewing, Principal-elect, of Marischal
College. Elsewhere there are Dr. McCrie and many leading
Humanitarians, Captains Owen, Vernon, and (later General
Sir) James Alexander, Sir Jahleel Brenton of the Admiralty,
and other fairly prominent naval and military officers, or
judges and officials of the East India Company's Service,

---

[1] From a lawyer's letter, extant, it appears that Philip left estate
valued in all at £2300.

recuperating at the Cape. At least one Cape Town resident of European reputation, the astronomer Sir John Herschel, and Lady Herschel, were for years regular family correspondents. The outstanding example was, however, the English Evangelical leader, Thomas Fowell Buxton, who after 1826 was the chief agent of Philip's influence with the British Government. Even if Philip's friendships show his respect for 'position', yet obviously they were for no possible profit for himself. The Buxton relationship was an intimate family friendship, begun during Philip's visit to England from 1826 to 1829, and continued without a break to the end of his life. Several of his best letters are written to Miss Buxton.

His circle was of all denominations, and Philip himself was a broad-minded ecclesiastical statesman. Many examples show a marked detachment of mind in his handling of Biblical and theological questions. He recognizes, though not advising, the 'dignity' for woman in taking the veil. He gives short shrift to Mr. William Parker, the anti-papal champion, who expects him to give evidence that Colonel Bird was a Roman Catholic: 'You must be aware that I have invariably protested against your conduct in mixing personalities against individuals with your own grievances. . . .' But where a principle was involved, or the rights of the native races, he was the stern and obstinate fighter, difficult even with his own friends. Philip was the dour, sometimes humourless Scot. Of an incident of the voyage to England in 1826 he could write:

We had a providential escape being drowned this time. In a moonless and dark night, a large vessel crossing our course passed immediately under our stern. There appeared to have been no lights on either ship, and she was not seen by the watch on deck till her midship was on a line with that of the 'Coromandel'. Under such circumstances, the hearts of those who are ordinarily inattentive to Providence pray to Heaven, and my first feelings were gratitude to God that the cause of the coloured population of South Africa was not buried with me in the deep.

This note of somewhat exaggerated importance, without the saving grace of humour, laid Philip open to the misunderstanding and abuse that have outlasted his own day. Unnecessary animosity marks the differences he had with his own colleagues, for example with Robert Moffat, though most of his disagreements were sooner or later mended, and friendly relations resumed, as with the Rev. Andrew Murray, Colonel Bird, Sir John Wylde, or the Rev. William Shaw. Philip's opinions

may have been strong and hard.[1] When he arrived in South
Africa he was forty-four years of age, and his mind and habits
must have been set; but a mere adaptable youth would have
made little of the task that confronted the missionaries of that
day. For full thirty years Philip directed the affairs of all the
distant and scattered stations of his Society in South Africa.
Usually at least every second year, till he was an old man of
seventy, he went on long ox-waggon treks as far afield from
his base at Cape Town as Kafirland, Philippolis, and Kuruman. In 1842 he visited Moshesh at Thaba Bosigo; and if
he shows some impatience with his missionary colleagues, it
is not surprising, in view of the independence of Independency
—of all forms of Church government the most impatient of
control.

Few even of the Government officials had better opportunities of judging the problems of the country as a whole.
Not only was Philip a constant traveller himself, but all the
time he was getting official reports and semi-private communications from all the scattered stations, from French and American missionaries as well as his own.[2] It is often forgotten that
the mission stations then under the control of the London
Society spread over an area almost equal to that of the present
Union of South Africa, and were even more extensive and
important than those of the great Wesleyan Society.[3] More-

---

[1] Cf. Fairbairn's comment: ' What sort of a man is Chase ?
The Doctor declaims against him, but I receive his opinions of individuals with caution. He is a strongminded man with principles
sound and liberal, but he is sometimes wrong-headed and hard-
mouthed.' To Pringle, 2 Dec. 1825.
On the striking letter of 1 Sept. 1833, twice quoted above, pp. 78
and 82, Mr. Buxton has written the comment: ' Unreserved, *and
too full of private feeling to be made public*.'
[2] Philip had partial supervision of these missions.
[3] The mission stations under Philip's control included Cape
Town, Stellenbosch (early left to the Rhenish mission), Paarl, Tulbagh,
Caledon, Zuurbraak (Swellendam), Pacaltsdorp (George), Dyssels-
dorp (near Oudtshoorn), Hankey, Uitenhage, Bethelsdorp, Port
Elizabeth, Grahamstown, Theopolis, Kat River, Keiskama Station,
King William's Town, Blinkwater (Fort Beaufort), Somerset East,
Graaff-Reinet, Colesberg, Philippolis, Bethulie (later French), Griquatown, Taungs, Kuruman (these three with numerous sub-stations),
besides a number in Namaqualand.
This list, by no means complete, is compiled from letters in my
possession. Some of these stations were transferred to other societies
in Philip's lifetime, and of set purpose and policy the great majority
were abandoned by the London Missionary Society in the 'sixties and
'seventies.

over, Dr. Philip's influence reached far beyond the range of his own Society. In 1829 he was invited both to Barmen and to Paris, and Barmen shortly afterwards began to send its quota of African missionaries, several sailing with Philip in 1829. But he was especially closely consulted by the Paris Society. His advice at least influenced the French missionaries in coming out to Africa at all. The first batch accompanied him to Africa in 1829, and he certainly determined their choice of stations, first in Bechuanaland, and shortly afterwards in the country of Moshesh. Philip's connection with the American Board of Missions, with headquarters at Boston, was almost equally close. From the early 'thirties he was in constant communication with Boston, and it was certainly by his advice that the Americans were brought to select Natal and Zululand, where their work has been both important and lasting. In the Natal troubles of the early 'forties he was in close correspondence both with Boston and with individual American missionaries in the troubled area. Even in the L.M.S. Records in London there are few reports from out-stations which have not either gone to Philip in duplicate, or passed through his hands *en route* to London. For example, in the crisis of 1835 Philip forwarded to London a series of letters bearing the dates 5, 11, 16, 28, 29 June; 4, 11, 14, 15 July from the frontier.

On the whole, Philip's views are sound and sensible. He had no illusions about missionaries 'with no qualification but their piety'. He knew only too well that both character and intellect were needed to fit men to bear even the loneliness of the missionary's life. In South Africa above all, especially on the frontier, where there was no magistrate or other Government representative, the difficulties arising from the contact of his coloured parishioners with the white colonists threw on any missionary an inevitable load of responsibility for the secular interests as well as for the spiritual welfare of his people. This is indeed sufficient reason for the 'political' activities of Philip himself and of so many of the greater South African missionaries. But Philip insisted too, both in season and out of season, on the need for sustained industry, and himself instituted experiments with hemp and cotton-seed at several stations, in the early days exchanging specimens with Colonel Cuyler of Uitenhage. As the responsible agent of his Society he discouraged the tendency to sink capital in buildings, which might have to be abandoned as Griquas and roving Bushmen moved on to pastures new, and in his estimate of the relative importance of stations he showed good judgment. In his concern for the barren and sparsely peopled north and north-west, he anticipated Cecil Rhodes in recognizing that in the direction of Bechuanaland lay, as he said, the 'Gate' to the interior of Africa.[1]

On an unusually thorough knowledge of South Africa he based what were essentially modern criticisms of the rough subsistence farming of the white colonists, and of the economic evils of trekking. At least as early as 1832 he had sensed the beginnings of what was to develop into the Great Trek. Already the over-expansion of the Colony was the cause of too low a standard of living, if not of poverty,—'since all are producers, and there are no consumers'. He may exaggerate the needs of the natives when he says of expansion towards the north:

Thus in thirty years the English Government has robbed the natives of Africa of a territory as large as was taken from them by the Dutch Government in 150 years, and on the same pretexts and by similar means.

But he is obviously right in principle when he continues:

All this extension of frontiers demands military strength to defend them. The opinion of military men is that if we continue to treat the Caffres as enemies 10,000 soldiers will not be sufficient to defend that Frontier. The expense of 20,000 men cannot be less than £1,200,000 expended on a colony not yielding more than £125,000 of revenue. . . . . British policy ought therefore to restrict the borders of the Colony, for . . . the colony is nearly all just farms and families. No villages are forming and the distant Boers, having no markets, never think of producing more than for their own consumption, and therefore they contribute nothing towards the colonial revenue.

The truth is that it was through Philip's effective championship of the freedom of the native races, in face of the persistent encroachments of white colonization, that the moral problem involved in the 'advance of Empire' in South Africa was forced to the front. If his views were sometimes extreme, his extremes may be the measure of those he had to fight. Philip more than any man compelled reluctant statesmen to face the fundamental issue of Emancipation, and to concede that the

[1] E.g., in a letter of 1847, Philip writes: 'I am sorry to say that Mr. Thomson has accepted a call to Grahamstown. Grahamstown is an important centre, but it is by no means of equal importance with Philippolis, the latter being the gate into the interior. Mr. Thomson 's removal (from Philippolis) is a public loss and one that may affect all our missions beyond the colony.'

coloured races were no longer to be regarded as slaves. A consideration of the development of the same problems since his death in 1851 leaves no possible doubt that, in a just view, John Philip must rank high among the Makers of South Africa.[1]

[1] For Philip's frontier policy see the Author's book *Bantu, Boer and Briton.*

Chapter IX

THE 1820 SETTLERS

WHILE the new missionary leader was getting his bearings, and before the position of the Hottentots received any further attention, the political situation at the Cape underwent a fundamental change by the arrival in 1820 of 4000 settlers of British origin. In itself this addition to its numbers was an epoch-making event in such a small community, and it was important also as bringing a new diversity into the homogeneity which had hitherto been a mark of its life and interests. There had already been some infiltration of discharged British soldiers and sailors,[1] but no influx calculated to make any real impression on the character of the settlement. The new Settlers, it is true, were concentrated by themselves in one small area on the Eastern Frontier, but their influence was generally felt, and at least till the Great Trek of 1836 they were in fairly close contact with the Dutch-speaking colonists.

From 1819, when the plans for a large immigration were maturing, the expected arrival of the Settlers aroused general interest. Boer farmers pitied the fate of the newcomers if they were to be settled in the 'drought-stricken' areas of the Great Fish River.[2] The Governor himself asked for all the advice he could get, from Dr. Philip among others. Newly returned from his first tour of the eastern districts in September 1819, Dr. Philip wrote:

Much must depend upon the character, disposition and capabilities of the Settlers. If they are chiefly from the agricultural

---

[1] *E.g.* nearly 800 in fifteen months ending 18 Dec. 1817. Cory, ii, p. 1, *note*.

[2] A letter shown me years ago by Sir G. E. Cory, and, if I remember rightly, in his possession.

districts, or from the Highlands of Scotland, it is likely they will bring with them sober and industrious habits, and the Emigration will be of service to the Colony; but if they are the refuse of our manufacturing towns, dissipated Mechanics whose political principles have been acquired in the Schools of Sedition, those connected with their settlement will have little pleasure in the undertaking. . . . Those who have been accustomed to work at one branch, where the division of labour is extreme, are the most helpless beings in the world; but agriculturists, carpenters, blacksmiths, with 'sober views', prepared for difficulties, with the intention of labouring with their hands, if it is only two-thirds of what a labouring man is obliged to do in England in the same time, may do well. . . . Settlers should be told not to expect the comforts of an English fireside, that tea and coffee and sugar and clothing are extremely scarce, that they must be content without luxuries they were in the habit of enjoying in England, and must learn to do many things for themselves. . . . For several years they will have to rely on herds and flocks rather than on agriculture.

Dr. Philip further advised that since there was likely to be a scarcity of water in the Zuurveld, this should be borne in mind in making a preliminary survey of the ground. The emigration, however, was very imperfectly planned and organized, being one of several sporadic schemes that preceded the more elaborate efforts of the Gibbon Wakefield school. Industrial changes and the economic unsettlement of the post-war period caused widespread poverty and distress in Great Britain, so that willing emigrants were available; at the same time, the chronic uncertainty of the position on the Cape frontier suggested the desirability of planting colonists there as a defence against the Kafirs; and the 1820 scheme was the result. A large proportion of the newcomers, therefore, were townsmen and industrialists rather than agriculturists. Their town-bred traditions, added to the natural difficulties of South African farming even for the country-bred among them, ensured that they soon had difficulties and grievances enough.

The local Government seems to have done its poor best, once the Settlers arrived, but took little of the more important preliminary advice. The Settlers were indeed carried direct to Algoa Bay, so that they might not 'waste their money' by landing in Cape Town; but there was little care exercised in the selection of Settlers, many of them being 'encouraged and assisted by Government in consequence of the great distress of the poor', regardless of their fitness for their new life; as one contemporary letter puts it: 'This sort of thing may be necessary to prevent revolution in England; and after all not so many will emigrate, and the Colonial Government will act honourably by those who do'. But in the matter of land—though the livelihood of the Settlers must of necessity depend largely on grazing, their allotments were too small, if not utterly inadequate—600 morgen [1] for parties of ten or twelve, or roughly 100 acres per adult, as against the 3000 or 4000 morgen farms normally allotted to a single Boer family. Two desperately bad seasons (drought being followed in October 1823 by devastating floods) made the continuance of Government and other help highly necessary. The price of 'colonial produce' (*i.e.* tea, sugar, coffee, and the like) was, according to letters, prohibitive, and even flour scarcely obtainable.

'The Radicals', wrote Dr. Philip to Mr. Hankey in 1820, 'soon began to murmur at their new situation. With no end to their claims and arrogance, they had their lands assigned to them and were left to ruminate upon their visionary schemes, and to talk of Cobbett and Hunt and Radicalism in English to the Boers and Hottentots who understand nothing but Dutch.'

Before long, therefore, many of the Settlers abandoned their holdings,[2] and went in search of new openings, a few of them to find salvation by traffic in ivory.[3] A great number naturally settled in Grahamstown, which soon grew to be something like a town, and a rival centre to Cape Town in a new phase of colonial development.

This is not to say, according to well-worn tradition, that the coming of the Settlers alone sufficiently accounts for the political developments of Lord Charles Somerset's second term of office as Governor, from 1821 to 1826.

Yet, if only because of the influx of individuals with some education and outlook, who have left a record of what was passing in their own minds, there was soon a visible widening of the interests of life at the Cape, and a new and more hopeful atmosphere. More immigration was contemplated; plans were devised for the introduction of workmen and children to make good the shortage of labour and to help to maintain the prohibition of slavery in the new district of Albany—not without recognition of the dangers that might beset children on isolated farms in a slave-owning community. In this, as in other respects, the humanitarians were before their time, not behind it, in urging a Government-aided 'white labour policy'.[4]

Dr. Thom, an Aberdonian, who broke with the London

[1] One morgen being just over two acres.
[2] By May 1823 'of the 1004 adults entitled to 100 acres each, only 438 remained upon the locations' (Cory, ii, p. 112).
[3] Cory, ii, p. 137.
[4] Sir Jahleel Brenton, from Surrey, to Dr. Philip, 9 Sept. 1822.

Missionary Society after 1817 and became minister of the Dutch
Church at Caledon, brought back with him in 1822 a useful
band of immigrants—teachers and ministers.   For the best
known of Dr. Thom's recruits, the Rev. Andrew Murray, the
way had been prepared.   As early as October 1820 an elder
brother, the Rev. John Murray of Aberdeen, wrote to Dr.
Philip that he was opposed to his brother 'going to such a
miserable place as Newfoundland', where an opening offered,
but welcoming the idea that 'you should procure for him the
Church to which you allude'.   And Dr. Philip, in reply, in
April 1821, wrote with enthusiasm of prospects in South
Africa:

[Cape Town is the vital centre, for health, social amenities, and
business,—Green Point being especially attractive, except for rents,
which are unduly high owing to the demands of East Indian visitors.
Port Elizabeth is the second best base in the Colony.   Especially on
the frontier a knowledge of Dutch is essential.   As for Andrew
Murray],—let him prepare to learn Dutch, live in my house with such
entertainment as I have for myself, or live in a Dutch family and
support himself by teaching till he is ready to accept a pastorate.   The
first people in the Colony have begged me to take their children and
would scarcely be denied, and have offered me any terms I might
have chosen to mention.

For the first time, indeed, there was much talk of education,
and some interest in general culture.   Pringle and Fairbairn,
two indefatigables, were prevented by the Governor from
pursuing their plans for a Literary and Scientific Society.   But
these aspirations bore fruit—in the first importation of fully-
equipped teachers, to meet the needs of new Settlers and of old
—the project of a magazine, in English and Dutch, to reach the
distant farmhouses—the effective demand for a newspaper—
and not long afterwards, the founding of the South African
College in 1829.   The last was the fulfilment of an 1821 hope
of Dr. Philip's.[1]   He was probably the first South African to
urge the desirability of training teachers and preachers in their
own country.[2]   All these things, with more secular demands
for the reform of the judicature, for safeguarding colonial

[1] ' I expect by-and-bye we shall be able to have a college here.'
Philip to J. Murray, April 1821.
[2] More fully, in a document ' for Sir J. Brenton and Mr. Wilberforce', with a covering letter to the London Missionary Society, dated
23rd March 1824, Philip urged the need for a college in South Africa
to serve both to train a ' native agency ' and for the religious and
educational needs of new white settlers.   Philip thought of South
Africa as a unit, for this document is inscribed ' A Defence of the
Hottentots '.

interests in the matter of depreciated currency, and generally for some more popular form of government, were undoubted signs that the scattered pioneers of the eighteenth century were slowly growing to be a real colonial community.

At first, however, the affairs of the Settlers themselves were pressing. In 1824 there was a violent dispute between the supporters of the 'Distressed Settlers' Fund', with head-quarters in Cape Town, and Dr. Philip as chairman, and those of an official and ineffective fund controlled by the Governor; a dispute in which, it has been said, the 'interference' of Dr. Philip, the future bugbear of the Colonists, 'was fraught with great good and proved a blessing to those in whose behalf he acted'.[1] A small bundle of letters preserved among Dr. Philip's papers [2] serves to prove that at this stage in the history of the Colony there was close co-operation and understanding between two groups of men who were a few years later ranged against each other in sharp hostility. On one side were Duncan Campbell, future Civil Commissioner of Albany, and Donald Moodie, holder of various offices (best known as compiler of an *Authentic Record*, designed to prove from the archives the mildness and justice of colonial dealings with the coloured races), together with J. C. Chase, Phillips, and other leaders of the Settlers; on the other, Pringle, Fairbairn, and especially Dr. Philip—the 'anti-colonial party' of the next decade.

Dr. Philip's activities as Chairman of the Distressed Settlers' Fund, together with a personal tour of investigation in the end of 1823, led him to write a long letter [3] on the 25th of January 1824, in which he reviews the points of the Settler problem:

1. Since the emigrants have expended all their capital they must have a new supply. Debits due to the government for rations should be remitted, diagrams and titles given them free of expense, and a loan bank formed to make advances secured on land and live-stock.

2. It being evident that the Settlers should in the first instance have had grazing farms, this defect should be remedied by increasing the size of their farms or giving them new areas out of the unappropriated lands of the colony.

3. To meet the labour shortage due to the breaking of their contracts by immigrant farm servants, Philip recommends the intro-

---

[1] Cory, ii, p. 415.

[2] A series, very intimate, from Duncan Campbell to T. Pringle, covering the years 1824 and 1825, with several from D. Moodie to Pringle or Philip, and from Biddulph and others to Dr. Philip as Chairman of the Settlers' Fund.

[3] Apparently to Major Pigot, but possibly intended for Pringle.

duction of 100 Hottentot families from the neighbouring districts. 'Even if the Boers should suffer partially by such a measure this is no reason why it should not be adopted. The claims of the emigrants should weigh as much as those of the Boers, and Hottentots should be allowed to bring their labour to the best market. The Boers have so many advantages over the Settlers, one Boer farm is as large as the ground allowed for sixty English families and they are allowed besides to keep slaves which the emigrants are not.'

4. The Hottentots should rent land, in villages under missionary supervision, until they can purchase it, this to serve as a relief for the overflow of applicants for admission to missionary institutions. The Hottentots moreover, with friendly Kafirs, should be placed as a buffer on the frontier.

5. The village of Bathurst should be re-established as a centre and market nearer the Settlers' locations than Grahamstown, with another village at Somerset Farm ; and trade between Colonists and Kafirs 'under certain restrictions' should be allowed and regulated by Government, since 'no evils arising from a fair trade can equal those that arise from an illicit trade. . . . I consider it highly impolitic to drive the Kafirs to desperation by depriving them of their cattle, by such illicit trade, or by encroachment on their grazing land. . . . Deprive a commercial people of their property, their ingenuity is still left and may be turned to advantage; deprive an agricultural people of the produce of their fields and they will continue to sow for themselves in the hope of obtaining some return; but if you deprive a pastoral people of their herds, you instantly convert them into banditti . . . they have no resources left, and they inevitably betake themselves to the thickets and attempt to live by plunder. In present circumstances everything but a display of weakness should be done to keep peace with the Caffres.'

6. Finally: 'I would advise the Government to select the local authorities of the district from among the Settlers. You have certainly as much talent, and perhaps as much honesty as is to be found in any other part of the Colony, and a measure of this nature would have a soothing tendency.'

The breadth of view displayed in this letter is remarkable. Opinions may differ as to the 'weakness' of the next ten years of frontier policy, if policy it was; but the wisdom and far-sightedness of Philip's advice was entirely lost on colonists and on Governors alike. Philip was in a detached and independent position. The concern of the Settlers was, perhaps excusably, with immediate practical details, and some of their leaders, it must be said, like the 'careerists' they were, showed great tenderness for their own personal interests.

The private letters of a group of friends, fellow-Scots, may be taken, out of their strict sequence, for the incidental light they throw on some of the personalities who were prominent in the next few years. Thomas Pringle, for example, poet, and Head of a 'Party' (i.e. of a group of Settlers), was a recognized and trusted champion of Settler interests. In

January 1822 he writes that by the precaution of early sowing he had '40 muids[1] of wheat, enough to go on with', most of his neighbours having none. Recognizing indeed that his relations, the members of his party, 'are more independent now than they had any prospect of in Scotland', he bethinks himself of the introduction he holds from Sir Walter Scott, welcomes the return from leave of Lord Charles Somerset, proposes to apply to him to see if there is any certain prospect of 'court favour', and, failing that, 'will endeavour to do something for myself, better if I can than merely existing in boorish rusticity here all my life'. There are debts to be paid (this same letter is endorsed 'unpaid'). In May of the same year 1822 he found himself still tied down by his efforts to get all his party located, and expects to be yet longer. New conditions had their interest for a poet; he mentions 'tigers every night', and how he

'rode through a herd of fifty elephants on the Khoonap'. . . . 'The alarming stories of Caffres were on slight foundations and nobody seems to apprehend any danger of another outbreak at this time. But the lions in our valley (near Bedford) are again disturbing us in the cold weather'; and of the first lion he actually saw he adds, 'Certainly he was a noble animal bounding over the bushes like a cat over a footstool'. . . . 'But,' for all this, and in short, 'I am for off'.

A few months later Mr. Pringle received as the small fruits of patronage an appointment in the Library in Cape Town, with a salary of £75 per annum. To eke out his living he was allowed to combine with this the work of carrying on an 'Academy', and, in addition, became immersed in the journalistic activities which brought him reputation as well as great trouble. In November 1822 he felt sufficiently confident to send for his friend and collaborator John Fairbairn, and not long afterwards the journalism of Pringle, Fairbairn, and Greig was lost in the dust of the first battle for the freedom of the Press at the Cape. To the Colony Pringle's services were of permanent value; to his own fortunes they contributed little. His Settler interests were the immediate occasion of some of his misfortunes. In May 1824 his article[2] on 'The Present State and Prospects of the English Emigrants' displeased the Governor. His later ventures were no great success, and by the middle of 1826 he had abandoned the country. His

---

[1] 1 muid or 'sack' = 3 bushels.
[2] The article was a temperate analysis on lines reminiscent of Dr. Philip's letter of January 1824 cited above.

patron, Sir Walter Scott, comments in his Journal for 23rd October 1826: [1]

Thomas Pringle has returned from the Cape and called in my absence. He might have done well there, could he have scoured his brain of politics, but he must needs publish a Whig journal at the Cape of Good Hope. He is a worthy creature, but conceited withal— *hinc illae lachrymae!*

In England, armed with some first-hand experience and with a recommendation from Dr. Philip to Mr. T. Fowell Buxton, he found unselfish occupation at the crisis of the anti-slavery movement, as Secretary to the Anti-Slavery Society, and in this employment he died, quite a young man, in 1834. Thomas Pringle at least served others better than himself.

One or two of the friends who were closely associated with Pringle in the days of struggle and adversity were rather more fortunate or successful in surviving the excitements of the middle 'twenties, when to be labelled a Radical was at once obnoxious to right-feeling people, and dangerous to a man's future prospects. When in February 1824 the newly appointed Crown Commissioners arrived in Grahamstown, bringing with them some hope of light and reform, Duncan Campbell at once began the task of keeping his friend Pringle, and the Press, posted in the news. He is highly pleased with his first copies of Pringle's paper, will occasionally communicate himself, and specially recommends as a likely and useful contributor 'a little Cockney of the name of Chase'. [2] The Governor is now the arch-enemy, and Campbell complains that the Commissioners are cautious in receiving

'communications respecting the highest power. There is no-one here but P . . . t and myself who will make a direct charge against *him*'.

Some ten days later he sent notes of the evidence he had given; 'the highest' (not specifically mentioned) had, it would appear, his obnoxious local representative, and Albany suffered much from being 'under the control of one individual', the Landdrost Rivers. (Campbell himself had been dismissed by the Governor in 1822 from a short-lived tenure of office as Special Heemraad.) In the Press crisis in May Campbell wrote again, approving of Pringle's action in closing down. Referring to the

[1] *Journal of Sir W. Scott*, Edinburgh, 1890, p. 282.

[2] D. Campbell to T. Pringle, 17 Feb. 1824. As to Chase, Fairbairn later took the hint and on the 9th of December 1825 tells Chase that his Journal, published in the *Commercial Advertiser*, is a valuable piece of work, 'too good to be lost in the columns of a newspaper'.

threatened banishment of the printer Greig, he contrasted India under 'its club of shopkeepers' with the 'unhappy lot of the Cape as a dependency of the British Crown'. He has now also sent forty pages of complaints 'against the highest', and is glad that written statements are taken, since 'if these are called for in the House of Commons they will tell their own tale'.

Even the Post Office fell under suspicion, and Campbell in June suggests that Pringle should in future address letters intended for him to one Macdonald, marking the envelope with a cross. By September it was a 'reign of terror'.

'*Not one* shopkeeper in town would allow the petition (for a public meeting) to lie at his house for signature.' As for the newspaper which had succeeded the *Advertiser*, 'I have seen No. 1 of Bridekirk's paper but I shall not touch it again. I do not think it will have much circulation here. *Wheelbarrow's* name—(a marginal note interprets, 'Wilberforce Bird')—is of itself enough to stamp its character.' [1]

From August onwards the use or abuse of the Settler Relief Funds was the subject of much correspondence. The Chairman, Dr. Philip, therefore, was much in the picture, receiving copious thanks for his championship of Settlers' interests, coupled with naive requests for 'advice'. Will the fund buy in a farm for B, to help him out of his present difficulties and enable him to undertake a profitable Government contract? One Adams, who had been in really serious difficulties, describes the total failure of his crops, the delay in getting his 'diagram,' and his losses of cattle by 'dog hyenas' (with no mention of Kafirs). He adds that his little girl Mary, who was threatened for childish malpractices with being 'sold', retorted that she did not mind: 'Dr. Philip would buy her'. And even more important people like Campbell and Moodie commonly sent messages by Pringle to tell Dr. Philip this and ask what he thinks of that—with obvious respect. Mr. Moodie writes to the Chairman direct, assuring him of his own and Mr. Bowker's support.

The trouble in Grahamstown [Moodie explains] has been that the lower classes have been too uppish; the chief malcontents were those who had so far prospered, were now anxious to better their social position, and accused the distributors of caring chiefly for the 'decayed gentry'.[2] The principle Mr. Moodie favoured was to

---

[1] D. Campbell to T. Pringle, 13.9.24.
[2] For Settler amenities:—Of the future Settlers' Editor, the cautious Moodie has an aside: 'Godlonton is a worthless black-guard, as a letter of his may show'.

recognize that all who had been on the land had suffered, but that most of those who had left the land had recovered; that the number of servants brought out or kept, social position, and amount of deposit money paid should qualify decisions on all claims made; and that all but the smallest sums should be given in loan. A post-script commissions Mrs. Philip (in Cape Town) to 'buy Mrs. Moodie a new lace bonnet'.

With it all, few of the Settlers showed much statesmanship or grasp of the difficulties or fundamental needs of the Colony as a whole. There is touchiness, rather than stout defence, on what seems to affect Settler interests; there is nice discrimination between the once 'comfortable' immigrants and mere artisans and servants; and even where they had an obviously good case, their self-assertion is tempered by extreme political caution. They must not run the risk of being charged with 'Radicalism'. Publicly they solemnly 'thank' the Land-drost Rivers for forwarding their requisition for a meeting; privately, Campbell complains as late as 7th December 1824 that the Landdrost is acting the van der Stel with a big contract for oat-hay, and that the Governor is coming to buy support by grants of titles.

Just at this point there is an atmospheric change. On the 16th of January 1825 Campbell writes in alarm that Pringle is sending Home his charges against the Governor; he had, it seems, been promised a 'billet' by Earl Bathurst, and does not 'want to be made use of by the Opposition' in the British Parliament. On the 22nd of January the unpopular Landdrost Rivers was transferred to Swellendam. On the 6th of February Campbell reports the arrival in Grahamstown of Lord Charles Somerset. He scoffs at the reception given him by the 'sycophants'; even Phillips and Moodie, 'the Radicals', were 'received in audience'; Campbell himself, being ill, has taken no part; but he intends to call. Then on the 8th of February Moodie writes to Dr. Philip, obviously in a hurry— he is 'dining with the Governor to-night'. Things are much brighter. Dundas's appointment as Landdrost has given general satisfaction, and the Settlers' Fund Committee, having waited on the Governor, decided that his attitude indicated a distinct change of manner and measures, and a willingness to meet their needs.

Everything possible therefore should be done towards conciliation.

Dr. Philip may make use of this letter in preparing the Report of the Settlers' Fund, but

Tell Pringle not to use my name in anything, and be equally cautious in anything you may say.

Mr. Moodie, in fact, has been offered the magistracy of the Kowie.[1]

This was very nearly the end of the quarrels between Somerset and his Settlers. Even Campbell, who found rest as a magistrate himself only in 1828, though he continued languidly hostile to the Governor, could whip up little excitement, and sent Pringle no news between February and August. The Commission of Inquiry and the Governor's visit had really done good; the speeding up of grants of land titles, the enlargement of land holdings, a popular Landdrost, even the appointment of the Governor's Council of Advice, had done much; a better season and 'the increasing prosperity of the people and settlement' still more.[2]   Major Pigot indeed remained 'staunch', but 'between ourselves, Donald Moodie has become mighty timid and shy since he has become a functionary'.[3]

And yet the troubles of Pringle and Fairbairn in Cape Town were far from ended,[4] and for anything the Settlers had done as an effective political force, the Colony was little nearer any radical reform of its governmental system.   Meanwhile the Dutch colonists, as a body, were quiet, and even deplored the news of Lord Charles Somerset's departure in laudatory addresses.[5]   On the other hand, individual Dutch leaders like the Rev. A. Faure, collaborator with Pringle in the *S.A. Magazine or Tijdschrift*, could write, as in September 1825, to Dr. Philip:

Your anticipations, as long as two years ago communicated to me, are verifying at present.   I have no doubt but a complete change will ere long take place in the political state of things.   It seems not yet decided whether our G—— will leave the Colony as yet, as he has received no official communication—but certain it is that he cannot remain much longer. . . . Colonel Bird is chosen as representative of the people of this Colony in the currency business. . . . About £1000 have been subscribed in three or four days to pay Bird's expenses. . . . All these transactions are paving the way for a representative system to which Mr. Baring alluded in the House of Commons. . . . Favour me with your observations which you think may be useful to the *Tijdschrift*.[6]

In other words, the Rev. Mr. Faure agreed with Campbell and Moodie in recognizing Dr. Philip as a leading champion

---

[1] D. Moodie to J. Philip, 8th and 26th Feb. 1825.
[2] Cory, ii, p. 179.   [3] Campbell to Pringle, October 1825.
[4] See Chapter XVI.   [5] Cory, ii, p. 320.
[6] Faure to Philip, 9 Sept. 1825.

of colonial interests; there was as yet no 'anti-colonial party'.
Philip himself was careful not to wound colonial susceptibilities;
'strictures' on slavery were sent to London in the name and
as the work of John Thomas, Esq., of Madras; he asks the
Directors of his Society to soften or omit anything in his own
references to the Hottentot question that may seem to reflect
on the character or the conduct of the colonists;[1] even Pringle
is 'warned' not to publish comments on the Edwards trial.

The Settlers were, however, but a small part of the South
African problem. So long as they were in serious trouble they
had Philip's stout support. It looks almost as if he may have
suffered from a complex in favour of the 'under dog'. But
now and at all times Philip's pre-occupation was with the
interests of the coloured people. The Settlers can hardly be
blamed if they were absorbed in their own task of reclaiming
a new district from barbarism—with little sympathy or attention to spare for the neighbouring barbarians,—the Bantu indeed
being dangerous and hostile neighbours. As it chanced, however, Settlers and coloured people alike (the Cape Hottentots)
suffered by their subjection to an irresponsible autocracy.
While the Settlers were fighting their Landdrost Rivers, the
missionary institutions were straitly controlled by regulations,
and by a *corvée* imposed and enforced at Theopolis by the
same Rivers, at Bethelsdorp by his neighbour Colonel Cuyler,
Landdrost of Uitenhage. In so far, therefore, as the Settlers
were 'under the control of one individual', and that one a
military functionary rather than one of themselves, Philip and
Campbell agreed in fighting for reform. But when a few years
later Settler interests and Settler prejudices stood in the way of
better conditions for the coloured races, Dr. Philip's quondam
allies found him as strenuous in opposition as he had been
zealous before in their defence. And even in the 'twenties
there were signs of the break that was bound to come. As
early as July 1822 Pringle writes:

> The Caffres will never be quiet unless either civilized or reduced
> into a state of vassalage like the Hottentots. Whether all the military

[1] Writing from Bethelsdorp on 9 July 1825 Philip indicated the
lines of an address he delivered at Pacaltsdorp. On the local authorities and farmers he urged that Hottentots 'were made of the same
material, by the same Divine Love', that they must therefore seek
the improvement of the Hottentots, but not be 'unreasonable in their
expectations'. The missionaries, he stressed, 'must remember
that the souls of the farmers were as precious in the sight of God as
the souls of those more immediately under their charge'.

power of the Colony could effect their subjugation or keep them in that state appears to me highly problematical. To civilize them is a task for missionaries, who must not be mere 'Government agents'. Government policy with regard to these and other frontier tribes is to me incomprehensible.

Duncan Campbell had different views. Following small thefts in January, Kafirs made three raids on Campbell's kraals near Grahamstown in October 1825, and what—even if only by significant chance—is the last of the series of letters from Campbell to Pringle, has these comments: He will have vengeance, and 'a commando to teach them'. He fumes at the 'absurd ideas prevailing' with regard to 'conciliation'. 'Powder and ball, by G—d, is the only means of civilizing them'. And in the margin, in Pringle's writing: 'How many commandos have gone into Caffreland and only rendered the Kafirs more barbarous?'

In 1828 'Powder and Ball' Campbell was the responsible magistrate for this frontier district of Albany. Little wonder that he and his sympathizers in Grahamstown broke utterly with a group who, though with sympathy to spare for the misfortunes of the handful of Settlers in the Eastern Province, were concerned also for the future welfare of the coloured races. At first glance the striking feature of the early 'twenties is the struggle of the white colonists for a modification of the autocracy of their government; and individually or collectively, the presence of the Settlers made some such struggle inevitable. For a while their affairs dominated the situation at the Cape, and the conspicuous events of the middle 'twenties have obscured even for the historians the greater significance of the almost underground developments that were soon to bring the Colour Question once again into the foreground. Though whole-heartedly with them, up to a point, Philip's real concern was wider than that of the Settlers; and the Governor, Somerset himself, seems to have deemed not a Settler but a missionary the most formidable of his many critics.

Chapter X

THE DEVELOPMENT OF THE HOTTENTOT QUESTION — EARLY ATTITUDE OF DR. PHILIP

THE London Missionary Deputation got to work in Cape Town early in 1819.

> Our reception (Dr. Philip writes) was everything that could be wished for. Lord Charles Somerset could well act the part of the finished courtier, and on this occasion he employed all his address. The Governor's hospitalities were followed by invitations to tables of the first men in office, and when we took our journey into the country (in April), we were handed over to the principal men in the districts through which we were to pass and who vied with each other in their attentions.

The start was, indeed, not quite so auspicious as this letter (written apparently some years later) would suggest. The first news that greeted them was of the secession of Dr. Thom and others from the Society. What was even more disturbing, Philip and Campbell were summoned to an interview with the Colonial Secretary, Colonel Bird, who,

> holding in his hands a paper, as if it had been the document itself, said with an air of great satisfaction—'I think it necessary to inform you that His Excellency the Governor has been empowered,' (presumably a discretionary power), 'by Lord Bathurst to put down all Missionary Institutions'.
>
> It could not (they replied), have been Lord Bathurst's intention, when we left London with his approbation, that such an order should be executed till we should have time to visit the stations and make our Report.

In spite of this, for nearly three years Philip's relations with the Government were cordial, even friendly. He certainly

did not begin with a stubborn resolve to plunge into controversy. The past troubles of the Society made him more
than cautious. Even though they had their differences, Philip
was most cordial with the Colonial Secretary, Colonel Bird.
'My dear Colonel', he writes in the middle of 1819, deprecat-
ing 'my dear Sir' as 'too formal to express the warmth of
my regard'. At one stage Philip was hinting that the Directors
might show their appreciation of Bird's services by the presentation of a 'piece of plate', and apparently this produced
from them at least 'a courteous letter of thanks'.[1] With
the acting Governor, Sir Rufane Donkin, Philip was for a
while on intimate terms—Miss Donkin being presented with
a 'token of esteem' late in 1820—and Philip himself writes
to a friend on 20th March 1821:

> I have a plate at the Governor's table every day, but seldom dine
> with him more than once a week, and I always prefer dining with him
> when he is alone. . . . He honours me with the appellation of
> friend. . . .

Personal relations being thus friendly, at first both Philip
and Campbell were disposed to accept not only official hos-
pitality, but also the current almost conventional criticisms of
the missionaries. It was almost as if official 'attentions' were
not without effect. Thanking Somerset for his early help,
they wrote assuring him that their instructions from their
Society inculcated 'respect' and 'cheerful compliance with
the reasonable demands of the civil authorities'. To Colonel
Bird a few weeks later Philip remarked that van der Kemp
himself, before his death, owned to having 'begun at the wrong
end'. With regard to Griquatown, originally Klaarwater.

> The Colonial Government may rest assured that every portion
> of our influence, and additional means to those hitherto employed,
> will be used to remove prejudice and to make the Griquas serviceable
> to the colony.

Even to Colonel Cuyler, Landdrost of Uitenhage—soon to be
almost a protagonist on the other side—Philip wrote urging the
removal of Bethelsdorp to a better site, since it is 'a pity it
should always remain the disgrace of our missionary exertions'.

---

[1] Happily there is evidence that some mutual regard survived
even the troubles of 1824, for there is an exchange of friendly sympathy
in 1825, Philip commiserating with Colonel Bird, now living in
forced retirement, and Bird in reply urging Philip not to be put off
his own line by the unconscionable delays of the visiting and investigat-
ing Crown Commissioners.

Towards the end of 1819, Philip and Campbell jointly made their full report to the Society. Their task, they think, is

to settle a wandering people in villages . . . to be Magistrate, Father, Master and Minister. . . . At the same time, in Africa the missionary is a person of social importance, on an easy footing with officers of the army and navy, and men in the first official stations under Government.

Their detailed suggestions for reform show that they were very far, as Philip said later, from 'seeking the quarrel'.

Dr. Philip, who hurried back from Bethelsdorp to Cape Town in September 1819, while Campbell lingered to go on tour in the far north, had his first serious disagreement with the Colonial Government over the refusal of the authorities to allow missionaries to proceed beyond the frontiers of the Colony, even to stations already established.[1] Before the deputation left England leaders of the Missionary Society reported how in an interview with Lord Bathurst, 'His Lordship dwelt on the danger arising from our outposts as rendezvous for bad people'. Bathurst himself wrote to the Governor on 22nd December:

Your Lordship will see no reason to object to permission being granted to some other members of their Society to proceed to the Colony, it being distinctly understood that they are in no case to proceed beyond the Frontier without Your Lordship's permission, and are again to return within the Colony on intimation from you to that effect.

The dispute about missions beyond the Colony was amicably ended. In the end of December Colonel Bird was adamant against giving Campbell and Moffat permission to do more than visit Lattakoo; they complained reasonably enough that they could not put things right till they had been to see what was wrong, but wanted also to leave Moffat in charge of the station. On 8th January they left Cape Town on their mere tour of inspection. Towards the middle of the year,[2] in

---

[1] Having made 'repeated applications' for permission to proceed to the North since January, on the 14th October 1817 Robert Moffat and James Kitchingman were at last allowed to go, not as they hoped to the Griqua-Bechuanaland frontier, but to the innocuous seclusion of Namaqualand.

On 13th January 1818 Colonel Bird refused the Wesleyans permission to found a mission among the Bushmen, being unwilling to 'break his rule prohibiting missions outside the colony'.

[2] 'For most urgent reasons of political necessity, Mr. Shaw was forbidden (24th January) to send missionaries to Namaqualand; and as late as 15th June Campbell wrote to ask if Moffat might remain at least at Griquatown till the Government ban on his settlement at Lattakoo was removed.'

spite of opposition from Colonel Bird, Donkin was prevailed upon by the importunacy of Dr. Philip to give way. The only surviving account of the closing episode was written many years later:

At his own request I dined and spent an evening with him (Donkin) alone, when the matter was the only subject of discussion. At eleven o'clock P.M. Sir Rufane rose from his seat, and, taking me by the hand, he said, ' I am satisfied, I shall write a note to Colonel Bird to-morrow morning recalling the order' (that which prevented missionaries going beyond the colonial boundaries).

Whatever the precise circumstances of the change of view, in the course of 1820 the Wesleyans reaped the benefit of Philip's resistance, and in May 1821 Robert Moffat returned to Lattakoo to begin his great fifty-year mission to the Bechuanas.

Now it was not that the Government officials had any objection to missions as such. With the best of intentions they themselves set about remedying, as they thought, the defects of the London Missions by providing missionaries under Government patronage. Towards the end of 1818 Mr. Brownlee was appointed to succeed Mr. Williams as 'Government' missionary to the Kafirs. Reporting the decision to Colonel Willshire on the frontier, Colonel Bird indicated that it was convenient for communication with the Kafirs to have a missionary at Gaika's Kraal.

His Excellency has more hopes of effecting a permanent change in the disposition of the body of the Caffres towards us by introducing moral and religious sentiments.[1]

About the same time, with some idea of a development of frontier trading, Bird was asking Mr. Baird, Deputy Landdrost of Beaufort West, and Mr. Taylor to recommend superintendents and instructors for a Government institution to be set on foot at 'Kookfontein'.[2] There were also official overtures to Mr. Moffat, and Dr. Philip, somewhat mystified, wrote an undated letter to England:

The Colonial Secretary and Governor are very anxious to get Mr. Moffat to join Brownlee as a Government missionary in Kaffraria. They have made him the most liberal offers and Colonel Bird has himself requested me upon the subject. It is quite a new thing and we are at some loss how to reject these applications. Colonel Bird says our object and his are the same, the Evangelization of the Caffres, and we oppose our own principles in refusing to let them have Moffat. There is something like a missionary spirit in the Secretary at present,

---

[1] Government Secretary to Col. Willshire, 25th February 1819.
[2] Bird to J. Baird, 4th December 1818.

but I confess I cannot help fearing that there is more of the spirit of the world than of the spirit of Christ in it.   It is obvious that he wishes to employ good men as missionaries among the Caffres and that he will provide for them in a manner sufficiently liberal, and allow them to do all they can for the conversion of the Caffres, and all is so far well; but I am apprehensive that they will be in danger of sinking into political agents, and of perhaps acting the politicians so far as to endanger their expulsion from the sphere of their labours.   [Dr. Philip then suggests sending 'a missionary or two, to be supplied to Government on these principles'.]   You have no other way of getting into Caffraria at present.   Before and since our arrival here the Colonial Governor had declared we should not send a missionary to Caffraria. . . . Mr. Campbell and myself were both decidedly of opinion that it would have been highly impolitic for us to have pressed the matter of allowing us to send missionaries to Caffraria under these circumstances.   When the Government begins to look for an excuse for retracting what has been said upon this subject will be our time to strike in.   But if we had had any chance of gaining Caffraria by entering into a dispute with the Colonial Government respecting it, we have no missionary at present to spare for that field, and it would have been a pity to have lost it in future by a dispute where, supposing us gainers, we had no means of improving our victory.

Dr. Philip not unnaturally took some time to get his bearings.   On his first tour in 1819 he had got little beyond Bethelsdorp—a Kafir War cutting short his time at Grahamstown and Theopolis.   Nor had he much time to check official or popular accounts by study of the papers of van der Kemp or others.   As late as December 1819, in a confidential report to explain the official distrust of missions, Philip himself expressed dissatisfaction with many of his missionaries, and dealt almost exclusively with questions of personal conduct.   His view then was that:

Had Read held the confidence of the Directors but four years longer, the whole would have been ruined.   After the ruin had become general he would have come Home—his representations would have been believed—the Government would have got the whole blame—the defence of Government would have come out, and disgrace and ruin would have been brought upon the cause of missions over the world.[1]

Campbell, it is true, thinks better of Read, but :

The ungodly world does not cry out against Morison and Milne as against Dr. van der Kemp and Read.   The world are accurate judges of character, and of the civilizing effect of missions.   Public support, once lost, cannot be recovered.

This is a hard saying on the lips of one whose life was a struggle with hostile colonial opinion, and whose memory is

[1] Confidential Report from Philip to R. Steven, a Director of the L.M.S., 20th December 1819.

anathema long after his death.[1] Dr. Philip, however, had reason to modify this early impression, and though slower than men like Read to condemn the normal attitude of the colonists to the coloured races, he was yet to take an even more uncompromising stand against its implications, which Read had sensed and in his own limited way attacked. Nor did Philip make the mistake of accepting the public opinion of one small colony as expressive of the moral judgement of the Christian world.

Even in these early days he was uneasy. One letter to the Directors, on the 8th January 1820, has an unexpected and at this time quite unusual outbreak.[2]

Colonel Bird still objects to our sending missionaries beyond the Colony. He is very polite and friendly—but I will not, I trust, compromise one particle of duty to please him or any man on earth. If he does not give way, I shall send you a memorial on the subject for Lord Bathurst. If his Lordship will not hear it, I trust you will publish it to the world and appeal to the tribunal of public opinion. . . . The General (Donkin, who is to act for Lord Charles Somerset) is very friendly and favourable, but can hardly make any alteration in the system of Government.

Brother Campbell, Brother Moffat and Mrs. Moffat leave this day for Lattakoo. Had the journey been delayed four months I might have joined them . . . but my presence is at present as necessary in Cape Town as yours in the Missionary Rooms. Brother Campbell will have a great deal to tell you which has not been committed to paper. I am almost persuaded that the fact of a conspiracy against our missions might be proved.

But the Lord reigns, and has delivered, and will deliver.

There was, of course, no 'conspiracy', but even then there were opposing and unreconciled views on how to treat the Natives. Dr. Philip was anxious to gain his ends by conciliation, and though, as on this occasion, he had grave doubts, for another year and more he had some reason to hope that a humanitarian view would prevail. The frontier question was settled in his favour. By the personal intervention of Colonel Bird he got a grant of land to establish a relief grazing station

---

[1] Latter-day critics of the tendencies of the native policy of the dominant party in South African political life are still sufficiently condemned if they can be called 'A New Philip Party'.

['Die Burger' and the 'South African Nation', article on the critics of the 'Colour Bar', May 1926.]

[2] As early as 28th September 1819, in reporting favours received from the authorities, he writes: 'All this is well . . . for my powers of doing good, but I am not without suspicions of their motives. Could the Government here make me its tool, it would gain the point it has been aiming at. . . . .'

for the Institution of Pacaltsdorp, at Dijsselsdorp on the Karoo. Though late in 1819, 'for urgent reasons', he was refused any addition to Theopolis, some six months later Sir Rufane Donkin made an important addition to the lands of this station, this time through the representations of 'our friend Colonel Cuyler'. Gradually, however—and in the end with something of a shock—he was to learn that official policy towards the coloured races was bound to be influenced by more than missionary interests and considerations. The missionaries' work was likely to thrive best in prosperous self-contained native communities; but there was a fundamental opposition between native rights on one hand and the colonists' interests on the other—colonial opinion being dominated by the insatiable demand for cheap native labour, as well as by a land-hunger which absorbed land regardless of native needs.

Government favour for missions was, in fact, likely to be whole-hearted only in proportion to their success in improving the relations of the Colony and colonists with the coloured races. The missionaries were expected to act, on occasion at least, almost as confidential Government agents. Mr. Williams, for example, who had died at his station at Gaika's Kraal, very near the later Fort Beaufort, was constantly giving offence to Colonel Cuyler of Uitenhage, by failing or refusing to act as a 'go-between'.[1] There was still more serious ground for disagreement. The official complaint was made against missionary institutions even within the Colony, as of Griquatown, that they tended, in Lord Bathurst's words, to become 'a rendezvous for bad people'. In other words, they were believed to accentuate, if not to cause, the chronic labour shortage; and this was the foundation of the hottest criticism they had to meet.

Had Dr. Philip studied, as he did later, the correspondence that passed between the Government and the missionaries about the suppression of certain Bushman stations early in 1818 he might have had more light on the original cause of the Government's disfavour and suspicion. The foundation of Hephzibah and Tooverberg for the benefit of the harassed Northern Bushmen seems to have been casual if not irregular.[2]

[1] MS. copy of Williams' Diary. Mr. Brownlee was told (Bird to Brownlee, 30th Dec. 1818; Cape Town Archives, vol. 'Consistories') that Williams was unsatisfactory because he was 'accountable to superiors far distant, and ignorant of the relations between the colonists and their neighbours'.

[2] On the 26th July 1814 Bird seems to have approved 'in principle', limiting the number of Hottentots on the station to ten. This letter—a copy—has no address.

Neither William Corner nor Erasmus Smit, later the teacher and pastor of the Voortrekkers, was a regularly ordained missionary. Nor were they well fitted for the singularly difficult task of civilizing the Bushmen. The Landdrost to whose lot it fell to deal especially with Smit was Andries Stockenstrom of Graaff-Reinet, whose views were to develop considerably as the years passed.[1] On the 30th May 1815, Stockenstrom reported to Colonel Bird that Smit himself had confessed the complete failure of his experiment and was negotiating for a return to the Colony; in October, however, Smit wrote to say he saw signs of progress and hoped to persevere. For his pains he was sharply reproved by Stockenstrom;[2] while praying Heaven to bless all endeavours towards the civilization of the Bushmen, the Landdrost complained that Smit had in his service more than the ten Hottentots, including men, women, and children, originally allowed to go to help him as interpreters. Further:

It appears plainly it was the intention of the Government that your instructions should be confined to the *wild* Bushmen without the limits of the Colony; and that those who had lived for a length of time among the farmers, accustomed to a more civilized mode of life, and consequently were in general accounted as Hottentots, would not be tolerated in that Institution. How very injurious such an Institution must be when the so-called *tame* Bushmen should leave their present mode of obtaining their support and abandon those persons to whom they are now so useful, who also give them what is necessary for their support and by that means convince them that civilized life is far superior to an uncivilized one! . . .

There is also injury to the Institution

because it is evident that it creates enmity betwixt you and the inhabitants of the Colony who will look with a jealous eye on your plan, and instead of assisting you, hinder the work as much as they can; and still you must acknowledge that you cannot be without assistance of the neighbouring farmers. Experience has taught it in the disobedient conduct of the Bastards, which arises out of a consciousness that they can escape the punishment of the law whenever they please. . . . Though tumult and sedition may be stifled for a

---

[1] As early as the 7th June 1820, the Rev. A. Faure quotes from a letter from Stockenstrom to Bird on Philip's memorandum on the Stations. 'Had the writer been in the Colony for a great number of years he could not have a better opinion on the subject. I agree with the statement because he seems to combine politics with the instruction of the heathen.' This, Mr. Faure hopes, may be favourable to Griquatown because of the importance of Stockenstrom's influence on frontier questions.

[2] Stockenstrom to Mr. Smit, 20th October 1815.

K

time, it will break out at last, with more violence than ever, where there is not a strong arm to quench the flame.

Two years later the correspondence was resumed.

Continual complaints (writes Stockenstrom on the 25th October 1817) are sent in respecting persons who have run away from their masters being kept at your Institution. . . . It is impossible that I can endure it any longer to see that my authority as well as that of the Governor are trodden under foot.

On representations being made by the Landdrost, Colonel Bird intervened, and on the 9th January 1818, wrote to Stockenstrom:

Since the missionary E. Smit still harbours several Bushmen from the service of the farmers, who are assembled at that place, and on account of having nothing to live on have returned to their old practice of stealing, I am commanded by His Excellency to request you to desire Mr. Smit to leave that place immediately and that you see that he complies with this order; at the same time to take care that he is not put to any inconvenience and that he does not suffer either in his person or goods. . . . It is His Excellency's wish if he can be useful in the Colony that due respect be paid to his wishes respecting his future abode.

This letter the Landdrost forwarded to Smit, with a remark that

your measures are a direct contradiction to the praiseworthy objects of the Missionary Society and . . . . expose our holy religion to the scoffs of turbulent and violent persons and to the contempt of the ignorant.

In reply to Smit's protests and appeals, Stockenstrom closed all discussion on the 17th March 1818:

This morning I received your letter of the 6th inst. still dated at the place which the Governor commanded you to leave. This last, as well as your letter of the 3rd and the 24th of February deserve no answer while His Excellency's determination was sent to you in such clear terms. It is only necessary to add here that I will not allow any person under my jurisdiction to trample under foot Government's commands without punishment; and I shall allow you as much time as I think proper and to see further how far you are determined to oppose me.[1]

He adds as one example the case of a Boer who has just paid a fine of Fifty Rix-Dollars for maltreating a Bushman:

by which you may see that every one who brings a well-founded charge instead of running away to you could have procured justice here; and by those means the evils complained of might have been

---

[1] MSS. copies of translations of correspondence on the Bushman Stations.

rooted out by degrees; instead of that your conduct has made the evil worse by creating irreconcilable hatred between the aborigines and the farmers.

Though Landdrost Stockenstrom, and the Governor behind him, expressed benevolence towards missions, and though they were, after a fashion, patient with Mr. Smit, and prepared to be considerate of his personal interests, the orders were peremptory and final enough. On the main issue they may have been right in judging that Tooverberg was very little of a success: yet four years was a short enough time for any missionary to make much impression on such difficult material as the Bushmen; and the reasons given for the suppression of these two stations betray the Government's very limited conception of the nature of its responsibilities. In his last sentence, indeed, Stockenstrom protested that the law was beginning to be of some effect in protecting the Bushmen from personal violence; but he makes no mention of remedial measures. For example, it was desirable to have a protector permanently settled among them to serve as a check on (what there is much evidence to suggest really did happen) the carrying off of Bushman children into farm 'service'.[1]

The history of the Bushman race is sufficient proof that effective protection of any kind was lacking; and the Government policy towards these two stations is a blank negative. In the absence of any Bushman 'reserve', an adequate missionary institution might have saved a remnant; and this was Mr. Smit's last plea, 'not deserving an answer'. His letter of the 3rd of February 1818 is not ill-constructed. He begs for one of four alternatives—(a) that Tooverberg be incorporated in the Colony and brought under Government control, (b) that 'Grootfontein' be provided as a substitute for Tooverberg,

[1] Rev. J. Campbell writes from the site of Tooverberg in 1820 suggesting that many Boers were glad to have the missionary station for the sake of the church. The real reason for wanting the station suppressed (a point he proposes to omit from his published journal) was really a 'dread in the minds of a certain description of Boer lest a nefarious slave-trade with Bushman children should be prevented'. This, he adds, to Dr. Philip, 'Between you and I'.

The traveller, George Thompson, also to Philip, July 1823, comments on the latest 'regulations' as a 'paper safeguard' for 'apprenticeship' of captured children, deplores the commandos against the Bushmen by whites and by Griquas, blames the whites as the real aggressors, and fears the 'annihilation' of the Bushmen. The best that can be said on this point is that children may sometimes have been carried off for humane reasons to save them from the danger of starvation; yet the alternative was virtual slavery.

(c) that admissions to the station be regulated by a strict permit system, or (d) that the station be kept intact for some one or two men more suitable than himself.

The chief concern of the Government, however, was to control runaway farm servants—with an underlying, if not a stated assumption, that farm service was a sufficient training in civilized living. Further, as in negotiations in 1819 and 1820 with Dr. Philip about Griquatown, an objection to Tooverberg was that it was beyond the Colony and out of control. The Bushman stations were both suppressed in 1818, their incorporation in the Colony, which was urged by Smit, being refused. The sequel has its own significance. In September 1820 the Rev. J. Campbell found the Bushmen's fountains in the possession of Boers; about 1825 the colonial boundary was quietly extended to recognize this effective occupation; and long before Erasmus Smit's further wanderings brought him back over the site of his old station in the capacity of minister to a party of Voortrekkers, Tooverberg had become the relatively important Dutch Church village of Colesberg.

Meantime a variant of this dispute was going on with regard to Griquatown. 'The missionary Anderson', wrote the Governor in reviewing the whole question,[1] 'has attracted to Griquatown some thousand of the class of Bastards who now range on the banks of the Orange River without order and without control'. Anderson, in fact, after years of wandering with these people in their nomadic life, had achieved the considerable feat of inducing some of them to settle down with him at Klaarwater, or Griquatown; but he had failed to act also as a recruiting sergeant. Since many of them were brought up in the Colony, and were fully capable of bearing arms, the Government in 1814 claimed their services and never forgave Anderson for failing to 'commandeer' them. A more serious allegation was that these nomads tended to live by plundering their neighbours. This charge, no doubt, had some substance, yet to hold the missionaries responsible was absurd. The very existence of these Griquas was proof that the Orange River was a 'natural rendezvous' for people wanting to escape the amenities of life as farm labourers within the Colony. It is clear also that, without their missionary, and still more before they were taught the rudiments of agriculture in village gardens, the Griquas must have been even less amenable to control. Some element of village life was a necessary stage in their civilization, but the Governor, in 1819, 'has told Dr.

[1] Cape Town Duplicate Despatches, vol. xi, 1818–23. No. 25.

Philip that Griquatown should be broke up'.[1]   Griquatown, in fact, unlike Tooverberg, remained—peacefully administered by Andries Waterboer; in 1822 (Philip opposing a missionary appointment), John Melville, a surveyor, was sent there as Government agent; and for some years there was trouble with other parties of Griquas who studiously avoided the restraints of village life, and showed little enthusiasm for being 'harboured' under the instruction and supervision of the missionaries.[2]

Within the Colony itself Dr. Philip presently began to realize that their potential usefulness as farm servants was the only reason for any attention that was paid to the Hottentots. Their own interests, moral or material, did not count.   The complaint against the mission stations was that they were attracting coloured persons to whose services the farmers assumed they were exclusively entitled.   In 1819, in his summing up of the need for strict 'control' of the missionaries, Lord Charles Somerset wrote to Lord Bathurst:

It clearly appeared that religion retrograded, and that useful class of labourers (Hottentot and Bastard) was subtracted from those occupations to which they were best suited, without benefit to themselves and with great detriment to the public.

The officials seem to have assumed that the Government had already done all that was necesssary, by its labour legislation, to safeguard the interests of the Hottentots as farm labourers.   But the fact that the basic law of 1809 had already had to be amended or supplemented twice over—in 1812 and again in 1819—might in itself have suggested a reasonable doubt of the efficacy of its measures.   For the rest, the Government evidently agreed with the colonists that farm service was all that could be expected or desired for the Hottentots; but in the absence of any practicable alternative, such service was forced service and virtual slavery.   Since the young, the aged, and the infirm could find homes on the farms only on sufferance, the 'institutions' were bound to become to some

[1] Cape Town Duplicate Despatches (*ibid.*).
[2] Cory, ii, p. 229.   Mr. Melville later joined the L.M.S.
The Namaqua chief, Afrikaner, who became a Christian and visited Cape Town, is reported to have given expression to his attitude in this matter: 'I have no objection to be under the British Government but I can never consent to lie in the neighbourhood of the farmers. Let Governor point me out a situation where I can live with my people at a distance from the Boers and I shall accompany you to that spot. I and my people are willing to serve the English Government but we are not willing to be slaves.'   Philip to Sir J. Brenton, May 1823.

extent Cities of Refuge.   The criticism levelled at the mission stations, therefore, provoked counter-criticism which went to the root of the matter.   If the Institutions, as the mission stations were called, were far from being satisfactory, much of the blame undoubtedly lay with the general conditions from which they sprang.   As soon as this became clear, the issue was joined, and a fight began to secure the status and the rights of the Hottentots throughout the Colony.

The opening up of this whole question was the result of an episode which occurred in 1821.   It arose out of that very intimacy of Dr. Philip with Sir Rufane Donkin, which, in itself, helped so long to keep the peace in spite of the disabilities both of the missions and of the Hottentots.   Having secured permission for missionaries to go beyond the Colony, Philip, in the middle of 1820, was almost jubilant, and inclined to rest on his oars:

Things had arrived at a dreadful crisis.   Had the deputation been delayed a few months longer the Hottentots would have been all dispersed and the stations converted into Government farms or bestowed on individuals. . . . Till lately I have had nothing but fighting with the Colonial Government.   I have at last gained the Governor and Deputy Colonial Secretary (*i.e.* Ellis) and Colonel Bird sees the labours of six years tumbling to the ground.   I am in possession of all the secrets of the Colonial Government, all that has been passing between the Cape and Lord Bathurst's office, and my intended publication will meet all the accusations which have been preferred against us at Home. . . . The object of the present work is to remove the prejudices at Home and to overthrow the dangerous and troublesome power of the Colonial Government.   I have hitherto gained my objects . . . it has required patience, address, and perseverance . . . but it is hard that our missions should be subject to the caprice of any new Government and Colonial Secretary that may be in office for the time being.   The blow aimed at our missions has been warded off but so long as the sword is suspended over our heads, we are in constant danger and at the mercy of accidents.

Such was Dr. Philip's vein on the 24th of May 1820—relieved of his first anxieties, but watchful,—concerned about the irresponsible autocracy of the Colonial Government, but apparently unconscious of any special problem of Hottentot rights or status. His impressions were to be published in a *Philosophical Review of Christian Missions*, with a concluding chapter on 'The General Influence of Missions in Improving the Colonists'!

As in 1812, it was James Read whose activities precipitated a crisis.   After various travels in the far North, some of them in Campbell's company, Read returned on the 20th January 1821 to Bethelsdorp, to be employed there and at Theopolis in the capacity of artisan or schoolmaster, but not again for many years as a missionary of the London Society. Almost immediately he began to find hard cases—instances of the harsh treatment of individual Hottentots by the local authorities— and on the 24th February reported some of them to Philip in Cape Town. The charges themselves matter little. If a Hottentot, capable of earning a good living for himself, was liable to be requisitioned for Government work for low pay or for none at all, without limit to the number of times he might so be called up, there was no doubt that the law was oppressive: whether it was three waggons he had, or only one, and even if every one else was liable to a similar *corvée*. It might have been wiser, in making official representations, to attack the general principles of the system, than to attempt to follow up particular cases in which the law appears to have been overstrained. Government departments are likely to have a detailed answer ready to prove the legality of a particular action, whereas if injustice exists, it often lies, as in this case, in the law itself and in the policy behind it.

In this instance Philip's action was careless and off-hand. Relying on his intimacy with Sir Rufane Donkin, who in April was going on a tour of inspection on the Eastern frontier, Philip wrote a very casual covering note,[1] and impulsively thrust upon the Governor a bundle of papers bearing upon Read's cases, as he was on the point of starting on his journey. From one later account it appears, quite plausibly, that Donkin

---

[1] This note is to be found in the Cape Town Archives, Vol. Missionary Complaints, 1821, and is dated 28th April. Philip's papers include a large mass of documents bearing on the dispute. Many of them are rough drafts, *e.g.* of a conversation with Donkin on the 24th July, and an unusual proportion are undated. Usually, perhaps in consequence of his experience in this case, there is no lack of duplicates of any later important communication made to Government; but the covering letter of 28th April does not exist, and so little was Philip prepared for a full-dress investigation that he seems to have forgotten that he wrote any letter at all and speaks of having put rough notes 'into the Governor's hand'. Sir Jahleel Brenton, a pious naval friend, intervened in an attempt to 'preserve harmony between the Colonial Government and the missions'; on the 5th August he reported to Philip a conversation with Donkin: 'I regretted that a letter from you had not accompanied the papers containing the complaint, expressing the view you took of them, viz. that you considered them as *only forming grounds for enquiry and not specific charges*. I am aware you did so express yourself—but regret the conversation was not embodied with the rest of the transaction.' He suggests therefore that a letter to this effect must now accompany the Reports to the Secretary of State and 'leave the matter at rest'.

pressed Philip to tell him what he could 'do for Missions' on his travels.

The misunderstanding which resulted is thus easily explained. Finding that Philip's papers at least cast a serious reflection upon the conduct of Government officials, Donkin quite rightly could not treat them as private. At Uitenhage or Bethelsdorp on the 17th May he examined Cuyler, Kitchingman (the new head of Bethelsdorp), and others, and was satisfied that Read's charges could not be proved. Next day he wrote to tell Philip the result, remarking, in a covering letter to Colonel Bird, on the difficulty of 'how to communicate the disagreeable intelligence to Dr. Philip. I have written telling him how grossly these fellows have deceived him'.[1]

Obviously Philip had not expected the Governor to do more than 'look into' the question. His casual action had been the cause of an official inquiry, and the local missionaries had had no warning or time to prepare their case. Yet, both in letters to Donkin and privately, at this time Philip seems to accept the verdict. Poor Read was soundly rated for the 'total failure of the investigation at Bethelsdorp'.[2]

I am sorry to tell you that I have been brought to much trouble by Read. He wrote paper after paper complaining of the horrid oppressions under which the Hottentots were groaning. I cautioned him, I dwelt on the consequences which might result to the cause in general should his statements prove incorrect, and he answered that he feared they were too true, that they could be too easily proved, and much in the same style. The Governor was in the interior two months ago. A public investigation took place. Read's charges could not be proved. The Governor, the Colonial and the local authorities, against whom the charges were exhibited, are indignant, and the consequences of his imprudent conduct have given me more anxiety and trouble (than everything put together before this). . . . I have pledged myself to the Colonial Government to visit the stations in September, when it is of course expected that I will investigate the business and do justice to the individuals who have been injured by Read's representations. It is probable that he had truth at the bottom but has ruined the business by his colouring and by incorrect details. . . . I know not what I shall do with him. . . . Few of the missionaries will be at a station where he is—and yet we cannot well cast him off. . . . Read is, I fear, the spoilt child of popularity. It is a dangerous thing for any man to emerge from obscurity into the eye of the world.[3]

---

[1] Cape Town: Missionary Complaints, 1821.

[2] In an undated letter Philip bids Read go and stay at Theopolis, as he cannot possibly be in the same neighbourhood as Colonel Cuyler, for—'If a man calls me a liar and a knave, and I ask his forgiveness, I accept those epithets!'

[3] Undated, probably July? to 'My dear, dear Sir.'

What especially distressed Dr. Philip was the breach in his good relations with the Acting Governor, who felt he had been reproached for a certain 'breach of trust':

'My heart bleeds and hand trembles' to contemplate a rupture, and for 'wounding the feelings of one to whom I am under so many obligations'. If 'arbitration' is not agreeable, 'let him soften his expressions regarding myself and the missionaries, and I am willing to give up Read and give Cuyler any satisfaction justice can require' for the sake of 'lasting oblivion'.

Yet it was not to be unconditional surrender. The depressed and humble Philip of this incident was even now the doughty fighter of later years.

If I am compelled to undertake a journey to England to defend the missions you must be aware that a number of collateral questions must be brought into the controversy. . . . But I wish to do everything to preserve peace.

This is in an undated draft to his friend Sir Jahleel Brenton, who did his best to heal the breach,[1] and comforted him:

Good has been done by the enquiry—abuses will be less frequent—the rights of the Hottentots are now clearly defined, and all that remains is to show your disapprobation of unsubstantiated charges being forwarded to you from persons under your direction.

On the 10th of September Donkin ended this correspondence, regretting, 'as Dr. Philip seems to do', that the papers had not been covered by a note suggesting 'privacy'. If that had been done Donkin would have asked for an 'official' statement. For the rest he renews his expressions of esteem, and is ready at any time to receive communications—official or private—provided that private communications do not concern the character of officials or of Government functionaries. On the 21st of September Dr. Philip wrote to London a letter full of domestic missionary details. He enlarged also on the spiritual benefits conferred on visiting Indian 'rulers' by his services in Cape Town, and for the last time mentions his papers 'for publication'. On the 24th of the same month he must fulfil his bargain with Brenton and the Governor and start for Bethelsdorp; if things are left like this, missionary repute must suffer; he must reinvestigate the case and feels 'depressed at the prospect'.

Very soon his spirits were to be revived. With Mrs. Philip for company he set out by way of Stellenbosch, stayed there with his friends the Faures, proceeding thence by 'Banghoek'

----

[1] P. 135, *note*, and letter of 5th August.

to Genadendal. At the Moravian station, though this is contrary to the accepted tradition, the Brethren were clearly in agreement with Read, and though Philip was hardly in the mood for more 'stories', they regaled him with instances of the hard and rough usage which resulted from the unsatisfactory legal status of the Hottentots. At Uitenhage his former friend Cuyler was 'not at home' when he called, and he proceeded to Bethelsdorp.

The results (he writes long afterwards) were triumphant.[1] I found in a corner of the missionary office what no one then at Bethelsdorp knew anything about—letters in the hand-writing of Colonel Cuyler containing the proofs of all the allegations except one. . . . I saw that I had in my hands not only the means of vindicating the calumniated missionaries—including James Read—but also the means of liberating the Hottentots from their cruel bondage, and in this opinion I was confirmed by the effects produced by the copy of it sent to the Colonial Office. The Colonial Secretary . . . after he had read the document[2] lost no time in waiting on me, and his first words were, 'You have got strong things against us at last'.

After his return to Cape Town on the 26th of December, Philip wrote comparatively little. His views were revolutionized, and he took some time to get his new perspective. So far as the question involved was only 'forced labour' the authorities had a case; and the Boer colonists themselves suffered their full share by 'responding to the many calls to go out on commando at their own expense, leaving their families unprotected and their farms and concerns neglected'.[3] For the Hottentots, however, there was a good deal more:

All Hottentots not in our Institutions at their commencement were in a state of hopeless bondage; we had no access to them to instruct them or preach to them without the permission of their masters— they could not travel half a mile to hear us preach without a written pass, without their being liable to be apprehended as vagabonds and subjected to severe punishments. The whole Hottentot nation, with the above exception, were *compelled to be in service* . . . any one of them being neither in service, nor in an Institution, might be had before a Field-Cornet by any Boer, then committed to the service

---

[1] In a 'Narrative', written about 1845 to supply material for a Life of Sir T. F. Buxton.

[2] The 'document' was the correspondence printed in the Appendix to Philip's *Researches*.—'Whatever doubt may be entertained as to statements in the body of that book, or as to the motives for which they were written—the actual letters which passed between the missionaries and local authorities are free from 'effect', and undoubtedly give the true state of the case'. (Cory, vol. ii, p. 414, *note*.) See also Cory, ii, pp. 413 and 414.

[3] Cory, vol. ii, p. 413.

of his apprehender, or to the Drostdy jail till he would go where he was *sent.* . . . His children were liable to be 'apprenticed'. . . .[1]

Dr. Philip now turned away from cases of individual hardship, and concentrated his attention on the general principles underlying them all. From now onwards the Hottentots were his first concern. In 1822 he obtained for them minor ameliorations and concessions:

The authorities now profess a willingness to treat; but I am much afraid that this change is merely to prevent me carrying the matter Home. . . . My business now is to be respectful to the Governor, the colony is against me. . . . If His Excellency refuse to comply with our reasonable request, all must go home and ultimately come before Parliament if nothing else will do. The Hottentots are acknowledged to be a free people . . . but labour is every day becoming scarcer, and the colonists are resolved to indemnify themselves for the loss of the slave trade by reducing the Hottentots to a condition of slavery the most shocking and oppressive.[2]

There is no more question of 'publication'. On the 15th of July 1822 he had written to Rev. George Burder:

I am very happy you approve of the manuscript papers transmitted to Mr. Durant for publication. They were compiled for the Society. I meant to give just views of our missionary labours in South Africa, and to obtain for our missions relief from the vexatious system with which we have been for some time distressed and counteracted. Since these papers were written my views are much enlarged, and I have come to the possession of facts of the greatest importance, as it respects the object proposed. Under these impressions I wrote to Mr. Durant, about six months ago, requesting him not to send my papers to the press, till I should write him authorizing him to do so. I sincerely hope my letter reached him in time to prevent their publication. I am at one object; the question is not with me about being an author, but in what way I can most certainly and effectually secure the emancipation of the poor Natives from their dreadful thraldom, the Missions from the oppressive system they are groaning under, and to give permanency to the cause of God in South Africa.

The trifling affair with Sir Rufane Donkin was the beginning of the long struggle to secure the rights and liberties of the Hottentots.

[1] *Journal of Philip's Tour,* 1832.
[2] To L.M.S., 13th September and 2nd October 1822, 'to be sent to Sir J. Brenton and especially to Mr. Wilberforce'.

Chapter XI

THE IMPORTANCE OF THE HOTTENTOT QUESTION—ORIGIN AND FUNCTION OF THE 'INSTITUTIONS'

THE status of the 'free' people of colour at the Cape could hardly have been worse than it was in 1822 when Dr. Philip took up their cause. The very name Hottentot is almost a byword of contempt; the Institutions, of some importance as the only places where Hottentots (some few thousands of them) had any chance of obtaining civilized instruction, were themselves insignificant. But it was in the effort to dispose of the Hottentots in the Colony that the issues of the modern colour problem first began to appear, and the difficulties that disturbed political harmony in those days remain; so that this old phase of the Hottentot question deserves particular attention.

Statistics of early South African population are very imperfect (the first scientific census in the old Cape Colony was made only in 1865). If available estimates may be accepted even as a rough guide, these so-called Hottentots were perhaps little more numerous than the white colonists. A low estimate of the numbers of the Hottentots is probably right, since, in those districts of the Union to-day, which made up the whole of the Cape Colony a century ago, the European and Coloured populations very nearly balance.[1] On this showing, after 1834, when the Hottentots and slaves were merged together as the

[1] If anything, there is a slight preponderance in favour of the Europeans, who are an absolute majority of the population in a considerable part of the West and South-west (see *e.g. Official Year Book*, No. VI. map).

'Cape Coloured' people, the combined class were, it would seem, only about twice as numerous as the whites.[1]

The details matter little, but the numerical proportion of the races is of cardinal importance. If, indeed, Hottentots and slaves together were to the Europeans only as two to one, the labour shortage, so much complained of, must really have been quite serious. But if on the other hand the Hottentot population is under-estimated, as seems probable, the old Hottentot question acquires new significance for the present day. Since the Bantu now outnumber the Europeans by little more than three to one, and since, inadequate though they be, their 'Reserves' provide for a considerable proportion of their population, the effective disproportion between white and black to-day is hardly greater than that between white and coloured a century ago, when practically all the coloured people were scattered among European masters. The problems to be solved in the present-day Union may be on a bigger scale, but they are inherently similar to those comparatively successfully dealt with in the old Cape Colony. There was perhaps one great difference, in the absence of the dominating fear that the white population would be 'swamped' by the coloured races. This dread has grown in intensity only in later years, as the component states of the modern Union have gradually absorbed more and more of the Bantu peoples, who proved far more formidable than the Hottentots, but who then lay beyond the borders. No fears were felt for the supremacy of the whites, nor for the survival of civilization itself.

The 'Hottentot' question of the 'twenties was vital because its solution was to determine the status of what was for some critical years the whole of the coloured population of British South Africa. The attitude shown by the colonists to the coloured races, in the days before the twentieth century fear of the numerical superiority of the backward races had become a distorting influence, is instructive in its simplicity. One

[1] Cory, iii, p. 11.
The Europeans are said to have outnumbered the slaves for the first time in 1810. About 1820, the slave population seems to have been over 30,000, and the Europeans about 40,000; a contemporary estimate of the Hottentots, who must have been difficult to count, puts their number at 28,000.

Understatement of the Hottentots seems likely, since those in outlying parts would tend to escape enumeration, and round about Cape Town some of them may have been counted with the Europeans.

See also Senator A. W. Roberts in *Transactions of Royal Society of South Africa*, vol. xiii, part iii.

leading characteristic was a profound belief in the efficacy, and
indeed in the necessity, of restrictions on people of colour.
'Passes', given or withheld by the 'master', to limit and
control their freedom of movement, were perhaps the keystone
of the arch in the system.   Measures for the betterment of the
coloured races must always be kept in strict subordination to
the supreme necessity for making their labour as cheap and
plentiful as possible for work on the farms.   There must also
be provisions against 'vagrancy' and 'vagabondage'; and
'apprentice' laws for the better 'control' of the children.
In all this there was little place for positive or constructive
plans.   The idea of any separate development of Native life
was undreamt of.   If only the Institutions which 'harboured'
them had been broken up, and the whole Hottentot population
dispersed among the farmers, the colonists would have rejoiced.
From the days of George Schmidt onwards, Christian missions
were suspect; for education of any kind was held to be inadvisable if not positively dangerous (as, of course, it is to mere
race ascendancy, the idea which still dominates the common
view of Native policy).   In principle, and even in details like
the belief in restrictive pass laws, the attitude of a hundred
years ago still lives, bound up with a new element, the fear of
preponderating numbers.   It may be doubted, in fact, whether
even to-day the disproportion between white and black in the
Union is much if any greater than it was in the 'twenties
between white and 'coloured' in the old Cape.   But in the
twentieth century, any plan of real reform is met with mountains
of obstruction from those whose notions of 'Colour' policy
are even yet summed up in the demand that the dark races
should be taught to 'know their place', and kept there.   That
'place' has never yet been defined, and, as commonly used,
the term can only mean something indistinguishable from the
old status of slavery.

In the eighteen twenties and thirties, these ideas, in crude
form, stood in the way of any attempt to arrive at a definition
of the legal status of the natives.   But though in the Cape there
was a legal victory for the reformers, the older theory and
practice survived in full vigour elsewhere.   Rather than submit
to the new order, those who most strongly cherished the older
ideas left the Colony altogether, and in the Boer Republics, for
two generations, carried on the older methods as a sufficient
rule of Native policy.   Nor in such a conservative atmosphere
was there any sensible modification of this outlook.   On the
contrary, recurrent misunderstandings with the British Govern-

ment rather confirmed the Republics in their own method of handling the Native population. The war of 1899–1902, which ended the separate life of the Republics, led directly or indirectly to the Union of 1910. But it also had the effect of re-uniting the Dutch-speaking South Africans of the Cape Colony with their brethren of the Republics, from whom they had been partly estranged. In this national reunion, it is the Boers of the Republics rather than of the Colony, who are regarded, even by old Cape colonists, as representing the continuous Afrikander tradition. The Voortrekkers are the national heroes *par excellence*, and it is almost forgotten that many of the most solid and efficient of the Afrikanders stayed behind and were proud to remain Cape Colonists.[1]

In the Union of to-day the old tradition of Native policy has taken a new lease of life. By the mistakes of the nineteenth century, perhaps above all by the utter chaos arising from a negative policy of restrictions, the Bantu problem is now far more difficult. The complaints of Bantu vagrancy and idleness, with plans to secure to farmers the 'control' of their squatters, are almost indistinguishable from those against the Hottentots of a century ago.[2] The Bantu are now to be politically and industrially segregated, and in some part separated from the Europeans. But, indirectly, the champions of a new-old view offer a triumphant testimony to the success of the full political and economic equality of the Cape policy, which, in spite of fears, has never threatened the leadership of the white race, nor produced the social equality which is so much dreaded. Like the ancient prophet, they bless what they came to curse; for they expressly recognize that the 'coloured' people—the old 'Hottentots'—have risen in a bare century from what they were in the days of vagrancy laws to the status of a civilized people.[3]

But while the fact of the rise of the Hottentots is accepted, its significance is forgotten. South Africa threatens in its

[1] Examination will show that, since Kruger, a considerable proportion of Dutch leaders, even in Union Cabinets, have been Western Province and Cape men. In the Transvaal itself, a great proportion of the good farms are held by newcomers from the South and West, and not a few of the direct descendants of the Trekkers are trekkers or frontiersmen still, or even 'Poor Whites'. Some old nicknames were obviously not given in admiration, and are clearly of Afrikander origin—*e.g.* the *tak haar* (*i.e.* with unkempt hair like branches (*tak*) of a tree) for the Transvaaler.

[2] Debates in session of 1926 on a Bill to amend the Transvaal Masters and Servants Act of 1880. The Bill sought to define 'squatters' as 'servants'.

[3] See especially 'Coloured Persons' Rights Bill', 1927.

blindness to turn its back on the ripest fruit of its own experience, and to seek to settle its more complex Bantu problem by methods subversive of all the experience gained in the smaller but essentially similar question of the disposal of the Hottentots.

In the days of the Company, the affairs of the coloured inhabitants received the minimum of attention, if only because slaves supplied all the labour that was required. Clearly there was little surplus labour. Used and misused as cheap and ineffective labour tends to be, not least by a race of masters accustomed to depend on slaves, an allowance of two coloured persons to one colonist was very low.[1] But it happened that just about the time that a State Government took control, the labour question became acute. Moreover the anomalies of the legal position of the Hottentots were forced on the attention, first of the British military authorities of the first Occupation, then of the Commissary de Mist, who in 1803 took charge in the name of the Batavian Republic and of the people of Holland.[2] A prolonged conflict arose, giving the illusion of a political and national division, in which colonists, mainly Dutch, took one side, and missionaries, most of them English, fought on the other. Yet the British Settlers were on the whole in sympathy with Dutch Boers, while Dutch officials, ministers, and missionaries often stood in support of the measures of a British Government. The truth is that there were grounds enough for dispute. The cardinal difficulty was to arrive at some definition of Native status, since, 'in spite of policies and governments, Native and white had come to live side by side in South Africa, and a *modus vivendi* had somehow to be found'.[3] At the very point when the new and foreign Government took control, the Hottentots indeed compelled attention. Only when their grievances threatened the public peace did they begin to be a concern of governments. In the disturbances of 1799 parties of Hottentots took the law into their own hands and rose in rebellion in alliance with the Kafirs of the Eastern Frontier—showing that it did not need the newly-arrived missionaries to make them conscious of their hardships.

[1] For example, there is usually said to be no 'need' either for 'segregation' or for 'Native Reserves' in the modern Free State, where the proportion of Natives is only three to one, and no more than 'necessary' to supply farm labour.

[2] See de Mist's *Report*, published by the Van Riebeeck Society, Cape Town, 1920.

[3] Miss M. L. Hodgson, 'The Hottentots, a Problem in Labour and Administration', in *S.A. Science Journal*, July 1924.

From this time onwards successive Governments showed a real anxiety to better Hottentot conditions and give them the protection of the law. General Dundas at once instituted careful inquiries, and the Report of the Fiscal van Ryneveld in 1801 [1] is perhaps the earliest document to throw light on the working and the deficiencies of the colonial system. He reported the fact that the Hottentots were self-consciously discontented, and even 'aimed at revenge', admitting also that the bias of the field-cornets and the imperfections of the mere machinery of Government in the remoter districts made the dispensation of elementary justice almost impossible. For remedy, he urged an increase of the official magistracy by the appointment of new whole-time deputy Landdrosts, and advised that Landdrosts should make periodical tours of their districts; he seems also to have been the first to suggest an annual commission or Circuit Court. On the other hand, his suggestions were carefully balanced, and reveal what was to be for many years the chief barrier to radical reform. While recognizing and emphasizing the disabilities of the coloured people, Fiscal van Ryneveld warned the Government that the farmers were likely to resent measures in any way weakening their control of their servants; he therefore advocated the introduction of a Pass system to serve as a check on vagrancy and desertion—thus giving a fillip to an idea that was by no means new. [2] General Dundas has at least the distinction of being the first to come to grips with what lay very near the heart of the problem, by the proclamation requiring the registration of all labour contracts between farmers and Hottentots, but the first British occupation was so short that it left little permanent impression.

The rule of the Batavian Republic also was too short-lived to make much difference, though de Mist and Janssens, like Dundas, showed clearly that they had an inkling of what was wrong, recognizing among other things that the Hottentots suffered from personal ill-usage, from payments in kind, which were usually inadequate, from wrongful personal detention, 'as if they belonged to the Boers', and from general insecurity of status, adding that 'these things drive them to robbery to obtain what is unjustly kept from them, and to desperation'. [3]

[1] Report to Dundas, *Records*, vol. viii, pp. 88 ff.
[2] Passes were suggested to Van Plettenberg by the Landdrost of Swellendam as early as 1774 as a means of distinguishing between 'free' Hottentots and runaway slaves.
[3] Janssens' Proclamation of the 10th May 1803.

L

Succeeding Governments were compelled to give the matter increasing attention, but from two conflicting motives; their anxiety to supply the farmers with labour was incompatible with their desire to protect the Hottentots. For example, Dundas's proclamation for the control of labour contracts was without effect; in a community widely scattered over a thinly populated country it was one thing to give orders, but quite another to see that orders were carried out. Even in 1806 there were but six drostdies, and the first regular inland post was instituted only about 1798.[1] Parties to a dispute therefore might be eight or ten days' journey from any drostdy, and there was no mobile police force to carry the law to the farms. To the end of the chapter the weakness of the administration was disastrous. Provisions calculated to force the Hottentots into service took full effect, while the softening clauses designed for their protection were evaded and neglected. Thus when the plan of Passes was adopted, it became, in spite of paper safeguards, the means of farther depressing the status of the Hottentots. It is possible that the same administrative weakness was responsible also for a failure to check abuses arising from the famous Emancipating Ordinance 50 of 1828. But the Government's honest efforts to protect the Hottentots were continually diverted by the exigencies of the farmers' demands for labour and for the discipline of their servants, on which, they believed, depended the entire economic development of the country.

It is important to bear in mind the close parallels between the position of the Hottentots a hundred years ago and that of the Bantu of the present day, but there is one respect in which the Hottentots were fully worse placed than were the Bantu (at least till the Land Act of 1913). The Hottentots were a purely nomadic people with no vestige of an agricultural tradition, and therefore with even less hold than the 'Kafirs' on any particular piece of land that might be regarded as their 'home'. In the course of more than a hundred and fifty years they had gradually been ousted by colonists, who had definite enough notions of personal property in land; and the Hottentots drifted, the great majority of them, into some kind of ill-defined economic dependence on colonial landowners. The country was so huge that there can be little doubt that on unappropriated

[1] The drostdies were Cape Town, Stellenbosch, Swellendam, Graaff-Reinet, Tulbagh, Uitenhage; the Batavian Government in creating the last two provided for subdivision into wards or field-cornetcies not greater in extent than could be ridden over in six hours.

Government lands, or even in the kloofs and secluded parts of the colonists' farms, many of them must have continued to live very much as of old, on roots and wild honey when cattle failed them. But when the abolition of the slave trade made their labour coveted by the farmers, such easy tolerance came to an end, and as a class they came to be complained of as 'idle vagrants'.[1] When this charge was laid against them it became apparent that in the eyes of the law they were vagrants indeed. Not only had they never acquired any effective title to remnants of their ancestral home, but it now appeared that, since in the eyes of the Company they were in the Colony, yet not of it, they were aliens in their own home, and were 'incapacitated by law from holding land'.[2]

On this fundamental disability there may be just the shadow of a doubt. Lord Charles Somerset, for example, seems to have denied it, explaining that owing to their practice of repairing when not in service to missionary institutions, 'application from them for land is very rare'.[3] The Crown Commissioners, on the other hand, expressed surprise that in spite of the terms of the proclamation of 1809, and since that date, 'the Hottentots have been considered as being incapacitated by law from holding land, and that with a few exceptions they have never held any'. On the whole this view rather than Lord Charles Somerset's is supported by the evidence. Sir John Cradock writes to Rev. J. Campbell about the grant of land for a station at Theopolis in 1814, and remarks on 'the legal difficulties of which you are well aware'.[4]

On the same grant, a year later, the Secretary to Government explains a certain delay to Rev. J. Read: 'Difficulties still occur as to the mode of making out a title, and to whom, as well as the general policy'.[5]

In 1831, in reporting to London a long dispute with Dr. Philip about an alleged encroachment by the Government of Lord Charles Somerset on this same station, Sir Lowry Cole had the temerity to base a refutation of Dr. Philip's claim on the ground that, till 1828, Hottentots had no right to property in land, adding that till 1826 even missionaries had no right to buy land.[6]

The Landdrost of Uitenhage could inform the Crown Com-

[1] See above, Chap. III.
[2] (Crown Commissioners) *Records*, xxxv, 312-313.
[3] *Records*, xix, 18.   [4] Letter of 10th Feb. 1814.
[5] Henry Alexander to Rev. J. Read, 11th August 1815.
[6] Cole to Goderich, 10th May 1831.

missioner of no instance of a Hottentot who possessed land, and was of opinion that if Hottentots were to hold land this 'would require alteration of the present system, especially while the distinction between the Burger class and the Hottentot people is so wide'.[1] The issue was definitely set at rest, with effect retrospective, only by the third section of Ordinance 50 of 1828.[2] But so long as the Hottentots were a race of pastoral nomads the question of land-ownership could hardly have been more than an academic one. They could not think in the formulæ and standards of 'civilized' society, of which the basis is the individual ownership of land. In a purely farming community, where even villages were scarce, land was the only avenue to real independence of status. But in eighteenth-century South Africa there was little or no attempt to impart to the Hottentots any of the blessings of civilization. Very few of them, therefore, were ever in a position to realize even the desirability of acquiring land of their own. Helpless as they were, they were swallowed up in a society whose social basis was a right from which to all intents they were debarred. This in itself had been sufficient disability to leave the Hottentots no practical alternative to serfdom.

In the early years of the nineteenth century, therefore, there was a considerable landless class. By no means all the Hottentots were in farm service; nor would the farmers have welcomed the non-effectives and natural dependants. The advent at this time of the missionaries suggested one way of dealing with some of the surplus. In the year 1801 Dr. van der Kemp had turned his attention from Kafirs to Hottentots, and for a time he struggled to gather together some sort of school and congregation at Graaff-Reinet. The Government was concerned about those Hottentots 'who were still roaming the country to the disturbance of law and order', and to this end 'it was decided to select a suitable site where a mission settlement or "Institution" could be established, and to invite Dr. van der Kemp to take charge'.[3] The site deemed in 1803 to be 'suitable' was a tract of land near Algoa Bay, and 'Bethelsdorp' thus had its beginning almost as a Government venture.

In the Eastern part of the country the Hottentots would

[1] *Records*, xxxv, cited by M. L. Hodgson.
[2] 'Whereas doubts have arisen as to the competency of Hottentots and other free persons of colour to purchase or possess land in this Colony; Be it therefore enacted . . . etc.'
[3] Du Plessis, *Christian Missions in South Africa*, p. 124 (see also Cory, i, 150).

seem to have been even more than normally dispersed and scattered, so that sites for mission stations had to be expressly chosen. In the Western Province, on the other hand, there must have been the relics of old tribes still concentrated in small groups. Thus the Moravians had already resumed their work among Hottentots surviving in Baviaan's Kloof, renamed Genadendal apparently by General Janssens, who was in sympathy with this new movement. As missionaries became more numerous, new institutions were formed, for the most part where there were the remnants of former tribes. The Moravians opened a new station at Groenekloof near Malmesbury, and in general gave so much satisfaction that about 1814 Lord Charles Somerset granted an addition of 3600 morgen to Genadendal. London stations were begun at 'Caledon Institution' or Zuurbraak, among the remnants of the tribe of the 'Attaquas', in 1811, and at Hooge Kraal or Pacaltsdorp near George, among the 'Outeniquas', in 1813.[1] Institutions were in fact the fashion, and in 1814 Sir John Cradock took a personal interest in selecting in Albany a site for the station known later as Theopolis. This seems to have been intended to relieve the pressure on Bethelsdorp,[2] and partly, as there is evidence to show, that the Hottentots might serve as an additional frontier defence against the Kafirs.

For all the Governor's doubts,[3] the process of founding or adding to the Institutions was almost continuous. In 1816 the Moravians made a fresh venture at Enon, not far from Uitenhage, and their experience, like that of the London Missionary Society, proved the greater difficulty of conditions in the East, for, unlike Genadendal, this seems to have been a totally unsuccessful venture. In 1819 Pacaltsdorp was granted a Karoo station, Dijsselsdorp, as an extension; shortly afterwards Theopolis got an additional Government grant of land, and even in 1822 Bethelsdorp once more was allowed to relieve its own necessities by contributing to the purchase of a farm on the Gamtoos River. This farm grew later to be an important Institution, called, after the Treasurer of the London Society, Hankey. The latest in time was again a Government venture,

[1] Du Plessis, p. 246.
[2] The missionaries Albrecht and Bartlett reported to J. Read, 10th December 1813, that they were to accompany the Governor 'to look out a place for Bethelsdorp'.
[3] The Governor wrote to the Rev. J. Campbell expressing a doubt as to whether the 'establishment of a missionary institution is going to bring sobriety and industry. This is not the general view of them.'

the Kat River Settlement of 1829, where the missionary came in as an afterthought.

All this indicates that the Institutions were an essential part of the life and system of the times. In spite of the hostile criticism they have evoked, they were designed to play an important part not merely in missionary but in official plans for the Hottentots. Without homes of some sort there must be 'vagrants', and without a degree of concentration there could be no possibility of instruction. There was also the ever-present fear that the Hottentots might join the Kafirs. Had the missionaries not undertaken the task, the Government would in all probability have been driven to invent some official substitute to check the growth of 'robber bands' in the North, or at least to provide poor relief for the utterly destitute. The comparatively settled life of the Bantu suggested that their tribes might be left where they were, with their old lands defined as 'reserves', such portion of them as was not given out as farms to colonists. For remnants of the Hottentots the Institutions were in some poor measure what the 'reserves' were later for the Bantu. Colonial hostility to these Institutions is largely due to failure to realize their necessity, and scarcely distinguishable from popular prejudices against modern native reserves.[1]

The missionaries did not have it all their own way with the Institutions. There was continual friction with the Government about their administration. First as to Bethelsdorp; Government foundation as it was, there is no contemporary missionary account of the circumstances that led to the choice of its site, but there is no doubt whatever that its unfavourable position was its greatest disability, and there is every reason to believe one fragment of evidence from a later anonymous 'Account of the Missions' in the Philip MSS.:

> Dr. van der Kemp on leaving Graaff-Reinet on return from Caffraria settled with his Hottentots at Botha's place which proved so unhealthy that on the advice of the Commander-in-Chief he retired for a short time to military quarters at Fort Frederick, Algoa Bay. When troops returned, Bethelsdorp was recommended to him *pro tempore*. After two years he applied to Government for a more suitable place, and one on the Zwartkops River was promised to him by

---

[1] For example, no 'necessity' is recognized for any provision at all of land for the occupation of the farm-labouring Natives of the High Veld. There is no such provision in the schedule even to the Natives' Land Act Amendment Bill of 1927. Yet without home bases of this sort, local Councils under the Act of 1920 are impossible, and even the provision of schools or churches a very great difficulty.

General Janssens.   Before he had time to take possession, the grant
was reassumed by the order of the Commissary de Mist.   Jackal's
Kraal on Plettenberg's Bay was the last place offered to van der Kemp,
but the extent of the ground offered was not enough for the increased
population.

Whatever the precise circumstances of its origin, its waterless, bush-covered area, even at its maximum of 6700 morgen,
could never have reproduced the success either of Genadendal,
of Pacaltsdorp, or even of Zuurbraak.[1]   The evidence of the
Rev. G. Barker, a sufficiently cautious witness,[2] is that:

On such a spot as Bethelsdorp, even the superior skill and industry
of Europeans would effect nothing in agriculture.[3]

Nor were casual visitor critics likely to receive a good
impression, since what fraction of garden land there is at
Bethelsdorp lies quite concealed from view in a small and
narrow kloof above the village.   It would seem to be true, as
was often alleged, that whoever was ultimately responsible for
assigning this site had the wisdom to calculate that such a
barren spot, while sufficing for the needs of Hottentots, could
not relieve too many of them from the necessity of eking out
a living by labour on the farms.   To some extent this nice
calculation was mistaken, for the Institution developed an
independence which gave continual offence both to colonists
and to local officials.[4]

Though Dr. Philip himself tended at times to get used
to the grievous disappointment of his hopes for Bethelsdorp,
and to cheer his own spirits by giving even a rosy tint to his
picture of the place, its history was one long struggle against
conditions highly unfavourable to the growth of a settled and

[1] Once Zuurbraak was rid of the incubus of its first missionary,
Seidenfaden (an incompetent, if not a man of gravely doubtful morals,
who was maintained in his office by Government against all that Philip
and the L.M.S. could do to secure his removal, from 1819 to 1826),
the Caledon Institution did creditably.
[2] Cited both by Cory, ii, 411, and by du Plessis, p. 430, as a critic
of the warlike Philip.
[3] Report by Barker to Government in 1830.
[4] The official view seemed to be that one prime function of the
education provided by the Institutions should be to train Hottentots
to be dispersed among the farms as servants; as early as 1809 Collins'
Report suggested that the local authorities should exercise a veto over
the admission of Hottentots to these places.   Colonel Cuyler's
'parting shot' to the missionary after a visit of the Circuit Court was:
'It would be better if the Hottentots were all with the Boers than
with you' (letter from Kitchingman, 18th November 1826).

civilized community.[1] The farm had no arable land, and as a grazing station alone could never have supported even a fraction of the population which occasionally, at its maximum, may have exceeded 2000.   Able-bodied inhabitants, therefore, were compelled to find other means of livelihood,—if not on the spot, by going out to work while still using the station as their base. Those more favoured individuals who throve sufficiently to acquire a waggon often made a fairly good, if irregular, living as 'transport riders'.   Others took advantage of the opportunities offered by their proximity to an infant seaport, Algoa Bay, to eke out an existence as lighter-men or tide-waiters. Bethelsdorp was also a convenient starting-point for the long trek into the interior, and missionaries and others repaired thither to make use of what is described as the 'best blacksmith's shop on the frontier', conducted by a Scotsman, with the help of Hottentot apprentices.   There were thus possibilities of a number of 'odd jobs'.   In addition, there were forests or bush in the neighbourhood offering a precarious livelihood for wood-cutters.   There is also a salt-pan of some little economic value, and though it is hardly mentioned in early letters, it still brings in some revenue.   If all else failed there were plentiful supplies of aloes.   In the early days aloes seem to have been of some market value, and later experience of 'Poor Whites' goes to show that a diet of 'prickly pears' may be a stand-by for people at a very low level of economic subsistence.   Most of these rather casual occupations involved long periods of absence from home, and constant interruption of the instruction of the missionaries.   In the long-run, ordinary farm-labour must still have been the most obvious means of earning a living.   But as it entailed more continuous work and no better pay, it was unpopular with the Hottentots.   Rather than accept the poor conditions offered them on the farms, they could at a pinch squat on the Institution and share a starvation ration with their fellows.

The general deductions drawn from the experience of Bethelsdorp hold good for all the Institutions.   In a country naturally hard and poor, the standards of these semi-barbarous nomads must have been extremely low to begin with ; and since the Institutions naturally included a high proportion of dependants and non-effectives, the presence of casual workers sharing the common stock of food must have reduced the average level of subsistence to an incredibly low minimum.

[1] Philip's MSS. almost *passim*; letters and reports from missionaries and visitors for thirty years.

Few, if any, of the Institutions could in any circumstances have been entirely self-supporting; some, indeed, like Genadendal and Pacaltsdorp, were comparatively well situated for the pursuit of agriculture; but if they had advantages of their own, they did not share others peculiar to Bethelsdorp, which was situated near a port, and near the starting-point of an important main road.[1] Their inhabitants, therefore, had little choice but to work on the farms, and habitually did so in large numbers ; these stations accordingly suffered rather less from criticism [2] than Bethelsdorp, which, miserably poor as it was, was more independent. The Institutions were, in fact, of distinct service to the farmers, providing them with a reserve of labour for the busy seasons,[3] and thus saving them the necessity of main-taining a larger staff of resident servants than they would ordinarily require. This, however, was taken for granted by the farmers (it was like the 'reserve' of casual labour in the slums and working-class quarters of large towns). Their grievance against the Institutions was that, in spite of their squalid poverty, some of their inhabitants preferred semi-starvation, with independence, to farm service without it.

The nomadic freedom of the Hottentots, however poor it may have been, was gone, and they had little motive for the unaccustomed manual labour which was the one thing now demanded of them, with the rigour of the law itself. Though many of the Hottentots preferred such poor chances as the Institutions offered, the charge that they 'flocked' to the Institutions is much exaggerated. Besides offering a modicum of freedom and security, the stations were the only village homes of this proletariat in the days before the growth of

[1] Philip claims that in 1822 (thanks to contracts for transport), while even Genadendal had to be relieved of its taxes and given 4000 lb. of rice and 15 muids of seed corn, Bethelsdorp not only paid its 2000 rix-dollars in taxation but contributed 5000 rix-dollars for the purchase of the farm at Hankey.

[2] Messrs. Jennings and J. H. Neethling on behalf of the Circuit of 1816 report with special approval on Hooge Kraal (Pacaltsdorp), where they found only *'n geringe getal* of male Hottentots at home, most of them being away in the service of the farmers. But even at Bethelsdorp a letter of the 27th January 1825, signed by W. Miller, Major, reports on 'the simple fact' that out of over 1800 people enrolled in the books, 'not more than 450 are *permanently resident at Bethelsdorp*. The remainder, of course, must be employed in the surrounding country'.

[3] In 1841, for example, certain building operations at Zuurbraak were entirely suspended about the end of September owing to the withdrawal of the labourers required for the sheep-shearing and for the 'sowing season' (Journal of Philip's Tour, 27th September 1841).

European towns had brought their regular accompaniment of slum 'locations'. Their freedom was after all only relative; there was constant friction with the local authorities about admission; once admitted, the inhabitants may have escaped some of the burden of Passes, but they had disabilities of their own—taxes like the 'Opgaaf', and especially a liability to forced service for public or Government work. Even so, the Institutions alone saved the Hottentots from absolute economic dependence on the farmers around them. A whole race having become a landless proletariat in a community that lived almost entirely by the land, they could not be otherwise than miserably poor. The wonder is how in spite of everything, by the patient labours of the missionaries, these Hottentots were already beginning to rise in the scale of civilization, to become the 'coloured' people of the next generation.[1]

In 1822 the Institutions were a characteristic feature of the social life of the country, and by giving them a centre of their own, tended to concentrate attention on the Hottentots as a class. The Institutions were, moreover, in close touch with the life and conditions on the farms, so that attention was drawn, not only to the plight of the Hottentots themselves, but to general questions of farm labour and service. It was, indeed, from his first-hand knowledge of the Institutions and their inhabitants that Dr. Philip conceived the necessity of attacking the whole question of Hottentot status in the Colony.

[1] W. Foster, a missionary teacher, reports to the L.M.S. on 22nd May 1826 that as 'the Gospel is not now a novelty', the Hottentots 'are in the position of a dissenting congregation in England, and normally profess Christianity'. Startling results, therefore, and conversions, cannot be looked for.

Chapter XII

THE STATUS OF THE HOTTENTOTS IN 1822
—LEGAL DISABILITIES AND THE LABOUR
QUESTION

IF the Company Government ignored the question of legal
status, its successors had soon embarked on the problem
of definition.   By 1822 a considerable body of law on the
subject had come into existence; but though the motives of
Dundas and Janssens, and later of Earl Caledon and others,
were respectable, their general policy was determined by their
anxiety to ensure to the farmers a supply of Hottentot labour,
and this proved, in practice, incompatible even with effective
protection of the persons of the Hottentots, and utterly destruc-
tive of anything approaching equality of legal status.   From
the very beginning there was this fatal conflict of motives.   In
1803, for example, General Janssens defined his aims; he
desired 'to encourage the free labour of Hottentots in hus-
bandry', rather than 'imported slaves who are dangerous and
degrading to morals';[1] a month earlier he emphasized the
necessity for personal security and justice:

If the Dutch Africans believe that their welfare is dear to me they
will do me justice.   But other human beings, the Hottentots, have
claims to protection and will have it next to the colonists.   They are
born free, and ought to be enabled to find liberty, safety and means
of subsistence on the soil which was originally theirs.   No private
person must dare to put them in chains or to chastise them; their
offences against others must be punished by the magistrates after
regular trial; and the magistrates must hear and do them justice when
they complain of offences against themselves. . . . . The most earnest
desire of the Commissary-General and myself is that they be not

---

[1] Janssens' Proclamation of 10th May 1803.

ill-treated . . . that there be no cruel punishment of voluntary servants . . . that contracts with them be *just, clear, and in writing*, and be observed with good faith.[1]

Especially when the supply of slaves ceased in 1807, it proved difficult to combine justice to the Hottentots with regulations designed first of all to secure their services as labourers.

Even in the eyes of the law, which should be colour-blind, the Hottentots were an inferior class. Their status in the courts illustrates the general attitude and the unreasonable demands made upon Hottentot servants. As a check on prevailing abuses, and to discourage masters from taking the law of the 'sjambok' into their own hands, the law of 1809 provided officially for 'domestic' discipline. On complaint against a Hottentot servant of *laziness* or *impertinence*—two highly characteristic South African offences—not the Land-drost merely, who was an official, but even the field-cornet, who was a farmer among farmers,[2] was given power to inflict corporal punishment *without the formality of a trial*. This was to throw a heavy burden on the independence and sense of responsibility of the field-cornet,[3] and that it should be part of a reforming measure throws considerable light on the prevailing conditions of service. At the same time the Hottentots' right to appeal for legal protection was somewhat qualified. When they complained of ill-treatment, or of breach of a labour contract, ordinary petty cases—those in-volving no question of 'life or limb'—were dealt with by the local Board of Landdrost and Heemraden. If the complaint was found to be justified, the farmer might be fined, there being no question of prison for the burgher. But the com-

---

[1] To the Landdrost of Swellendam, 10th April 1803 (quoted from a translated copy in Philip MSS.).

[2] . . . 'these people being all fellow-farmers, and consequently having but one and the same interest could not thus be impartial between farmer and Hottentot' (van Ryneveld to Dundas, 1801, *Records*, vol. iv).

[3] There is a well-authenticated story of Transvaal Republican days which shows both how faithfully the pre-1828 system was carried on by the Trekkers, and how in the best cases it might secure rough justice. An old field-cornet, respected by Europeans and loved by the Natives, once explained in confidential talk that when a Native was sent for such 'domestic' correction, he made it a rule to make full inquiry. If the Native was in the wrong he punished him. But if on inquiry he thought the farmer's complaint frivolous or unjust, he would bid the 'culprit go home *and tell his Baas he had had twenty-five cuts*'.

plainant—first no doubt for security and as a check on frivolous complaints—was liable to be detained in gaol till his case was heard; and then, as a further deterrent, if the charge failed, he was to be given 'such correction as the nature of the case shall require'. This extraordinary use of the *tronk* (prison) need not perhaps be taken too seriously. It was apparently a device to secure punctual attendance at court, and it may have guaranteed to the complainants regular meals of some sort. It was not even thought of as 'punishment'.[1] But added to the difficulties of Passes, and of proceeding at all against an employer, it was one more disability likely to induce Hottentots to suffer in silence, rather than make a possibly long and probably futile journey to the drostdy. And as for the *tronk*, used as it was to excess, it soon lost whatever efficacy it might have had, and came to be regarded by the coloured people with mere levity.[2]

The first systematic Hottentot law, proclaimed by Earl Caledon in 1809, did, however, mark one improvement of real importance in the legal status of the Hottentots. The field-cornets still had wide powers, but it was laid down that in the more serious cases, where charges were made of ill-treatment involving injury to 'life or limb', 'the fiscal or landdrost shall prosecute according to the common law in use in the Colony'. That such an obvious provision should require specific enactment, bears witness to the anomalies of their hitherto extra-legal position. Once this point was established, the way was open for the next step. The system of Circuit Courts, a suggestion made by Fiscal van Ryneveld to Dundas as early as 1801, was adopted in 1811. Though it was no easy matter to accustom the colonists to the innovation which laid them open to prosecution by, or on behalf of, mere Hottentots (see Chapter VII), the institution of Circuit Courts

---

[1] 'The landdrost may imprison and punish Hottentots at his discretion, whereas he cannot legally imprison and *much less punish* a burgher without a decree of the Court of Justice' (evidence of Landdrost of Uitenhage to Crown Commissioners, *C.C. Records*, xxxv, p. 313).

[2] To this day the cost of the South African prison system is excessive. The extreme poverty of the Hottentots, and later of the Natives, has made the general levying of fines for petty offences impracticable. The scale of fines, sometimes given as an option, runs too high, and out of all proportion to standards of earning.

For technical breaches of statutes, decent Natives, now as then, are herded together indiscriminately with criminals, so that gaols are often schools of vice, and undue familiarity with prison life has made criminals and bred contempt. Even in the best Native circles it carries with it little or no stigma to have served a term in prison.

helped to establish justice in more important cases on a sounder basis.

Where the laws in themselves were so far from perfect, the hope of reasonable protection for the coloured people now depended more than ever upon the efficiency of administration. In the best possible circumstances it is hard to measure the disadvantages of a backward Native who has to appear in a court of law, whether as plaintiff or complainant. He is deficient in, if not totally ignorant of, the language of the court's proceedings; even if he understands more than fragments from an interpreter, the atmosphere of a law-court must add to his natural embarrassment in the presence of masters who are still more conscious of their own superiority to this ragged unwashed, stammering mortal. This very feeling of superiority is a sore tax on the white man's impartiality and sense of justice in deciding for a coloured person against a white man. The conditions in those days were even more unfavourable than they are to-day, when Natives have learnt by more than a century of experience to value the protection of the law-courts. Then appeal to the law was a novelty; distances were far longer, and the Judges of High or Circuit Court necessarily dealt only with cases passed on by the Landdrosts, and followed only the main roads, never reaching the remote and outlying districts, where supervision was most necessary. The welfare of the Hottentots therefore would depend in the first instance on the nearest official, the field-cornet; and much definite evidence goes to show that the interests of these minor officials were so completely identified with those of their fellow-farmers that they were very unlikely to dispense impartial justice.[1]

It was, moreover, no easy matter for aggrieved Hottentots to get past the field-cornet, without whose authority they dared not so much as leave their own ward.[2] The field-cornet was in theory under the control of the Landdrost, but it was not yet usual for the Landdrost to make periodical tours of inspection in his far-flung district.[3] Moreover, the Hottentot

[1] Van Ryneveld, 1801, *Records*, vol. iv; Collins' Report, 1809, *Records*, vol. vii; Report of Circuit Commission, 1812, *Records*, vol. viii. Collins, for example, reports: 'These essential objects cannot, I fear, be perfectly secured until the Field-Cornets are placed upon a different footing. At present their position is not otherwise desirable than as it may afford them opportunities of favouring their friends or of oppressing their enemies.'

[2] Miss Hodgson, *in loc. cit.*, instances a 'secret' appeal of two slaves to the Circuit, reported in 1812.

[3] A partial remedy suggested by Collins, 1809.

laws of this time were so tentative that their effectiveness could only be tested by experience; but little of the experience gained by the field-cornets in their everyday work of administration was likely to be sympathetic, or of much use for the guidance of the Government at headquarters. There could be little consultation and deliberation about the operation of particular measures, and it is not too much to add that it would have been of little benefit to the Hottentots had such deliberation been guided by the opinions of the field-cornets.

The Landdrost, if he were a strong man, and disinterested, might afford a measure of protection, at least in his own immediate neighbourhood. There is occasional evidence of efficient action by the Landdrosts, of whom the Circuit Commissioners reported favourably in 1812, at the same time as they criticized the field-cornets.[1] During the visit of the Crown Commissioners in 1823–4 the Landdrost of Uitenhage

sentenced a field-commandant and a field-cornet to pay fines of 100 pounds each for the detention of Hottentots and their property beyond the terms of their contract.[2]

On the other hand, there is evidence that while the advent of the Commissioners put the local authorities on their mettle, at other times Landdrosts availed themselves of their legal hold over the persons of the Hottentots, which gave them what was in effect an extensive power of 'patronage'. In practice none could be admitted to the Institutions without the Landdrost's sanction, and Hottentots under his control he could assign as he saw fit, making their services available to his friends, or even keeping them for his own use.[3] On the whole, therefore, there was little to hope from sympathetic administration.

By 1822, however, colonial opinion had got used to the idea that on occasion white colonists might have to answer in court for wrongs committed against Hottentot servants. The Black Circuit and Slagter's Nek may have left a fatal legacy of bitterness behind them, but it was the price paid for a real

[1] Opinion of Circuit Commissioners, 1812, *Records*, vol. viii.
[2] Quoted by Miss Hodgson from Report of Crown Commissioners, *Records*, vol. xxxv.
(See below, p. 244). Philip in 1834 indicates that at least one field-cornet was suspended for putting in force the provisions of the Draft Vagrant Ordinance which never became law.
[3] This was Dr..Philip's perennial feud with Cuyler of Uitenhage. Evidence less open to the charge of bias may be cited from Report of Crown Commissioners, *Records*, vol. xxxv.

moral advance. It is difficult to trace how far, if at all, the Government was influenced by the agitation of the early missionaries in bringing ill - usage of Hottentots under the penalties of the common law. The authorities were bound by all their instincts and traditions to stand for the Rule of Law. But in seeking to establish this fundamental principle, the Government had always to reckon with the clamorous colonial demand for labour, and was itself honestly of opinion that the economic prosperity of the country depended upon the services of the Hottentots. All its laws therefore were two-edged. In making well-meant efforts for the legal protection of the Hottentots, they had at the same time, almost *pari passu*, been building up a host of provisions to drive them to service, and to keep them there. But the administration of these laws was in the first instance in the hands of the field-cornets, and in case of dispute it was a Hottentot's word against that of a white farmer. Dr. Philip sums up years later:

> The English Vagrant Laws are sure to be quoted by the supporters of vagrant laws in the colonies, but the cases are entirely different. In Europe the bondsman became strong, and broke his own bonds. In the colonies it took all the exertions of missionaries and philanthropists to secure freedom for the slaves. Generally I am correct in stating that the power is on the side of the oppressors, and the tide of colonial feeling is as much *against* freedom as the tide of English feeling is in favour of it.[1]

It was only after 1807 that the labour question became serious. The Company had left the country poor, and all but bankrupt. Succeeding Governments by a more liberal policy did something to put the Colony on a better economic basis. Any great European War tended to give a stimulus to trade at the Cape, an all-important station on the way to India. Cape Town itself was fully garrisoned, and was enjoying a period of unusual economic activity, creating by its influence a correspondingly greater demand for labour throughout the country. At this point, by the prohibition of the slave trade the ordinary labour supply was cut off at the source, and the Hottentots at once acquired a new importance as the obvious means of meeting the sudden deficiency. On the 1st of November 1809, acting on the full and careful report of a tour of investigation by Major Collins, Earl Caledon issued a Proclamation that has been rather too complacently described as the *Magna Carta* of the Hottentots. This, supplementing

---

[1] To James Cropper, Liverpool, a leading philanthropist, 26th May 1835.

Janssens' Proclamation of 1803, with important additions in 1812 and minor amendments in 1819 and 1823, was the basis of the law regulating the position of the Hottentots till 1828.

Lord Caledon's Proclamation of 1809 had the highest motives. Earlier laws had proved ineffective. In spite of Dundas's law, contracts were not registered; Hottentots were still poorly and irregularly paid, and preferred 'vagrancy' to farm service. It was considered desirable that they should enter the service of the farmers, and that, to put an end to vagrancy, they should have a 'fixed place of abode'. Hottentots and their dwellings therefore were to be registered, and (in 1812) a regular return sent in by the Landdrost to Head-quarters. Contracts of service were to be entered upon annually, in the presence of Landdrost or field-cornet, and drawn up *in triplio* for greater security. It was laid down also that wages must be duly paid; that no claims to personal service should lie against the servant in respect of debt; that payments in kind must be witnessed and registered; negatively, that no wines, brandy, etc., be considered as necessaries of life and no allowance made for their supply; and that debts due to the employer beyond the value of the servant's wages should be recoverable only by ordinary process of law.

The pivot of the whole system was the Pass Law. To check vagrancy it was laid down that no Hottentot should move about the country without a pass from the Landdrost or field-cornet.[1] Any Hottentot failing to produce this pass, which might or even should be demanded by any passing European, was liable to be apprehended as a 'vagrant', and dealt with by the local authorities, 'after due inquiry as they shall feel incumbent to do'. This meant that he would be contracted to some farmer wanting labour.

Further:

Since it appeared that farmers had 'no interest whatever in young Hottentots', many of whom, 'although free in name are more dependent and more to be pitied than slaves, for whose support even when old, crippled and incapable of service, their masters are obliged to provide,'[2]

in 1812 the Landdrosts were empowered to 'apprentice' Hottentot children, from their eighth year to the eighteenth,

[1] In practice probably he would need a 'pass' from his employer to leave the farm even to go to a field-cornet, without whose authority he could not leave the 'ward'; to move to another district might need the authority of the Landdrost.

[2] Report of First Circuit Commissioners, *Records*, vol. viii, p. 301.

M

to any farmers who had maintained them in their infancy. In the event of this master being considered unsuitable the Landdrost might assign the children to another, and in 1819 this provision was extended to cover the case of orphans, who might otherwise have been in danger of being detained without any protecting contract. 'Apprenticeship' of course implied servantship, but carried with it no responsibility requiring the master to give the child any instruction whatever.

The Hottentots of the 'Institutions' were in some ways privileged. They could not indeed go abroad without passes, but membership of an Institution saved them from being assigned, at the will of the Landdrost, to a farmer master, and their children from the provisions of the law of apprenticeship. On the other hand, they had disabilities of their own. They were subject in special degree to a *corvée*, or forced labour for Government purposes, military or other, which might or might not be reasonably paid for.[1] Even the patient Rev. George Barker fought strenuously with the Landdrost Rivers of Albany throughout the years 1822 and 1823, urging Dr. Philip to try to do something to stop the drain on the labour supply of Theopolis, where building operations were impeded by the heavy demands of the local authorities.[2] No doubt farm servants and the farmers themselves were liable to be called upon for military service, but the wives and children of Institution Hottentots, though largely dependent on wage-earning, were left without such maintenance as farmers were obliged to give the families of their servants, sometimes during long periods of absence like that entailed by service in the Kafir war of 1819.[3] In such cases the women inevitably 'contracted debts with the farmers on the faith that their husbands would serve them for those debts' on their return. Frequent calls for forced service were of course incompatible with sustained and continuous instruction; and the time of

---

[1] Cory, ii, p. 413, and Philip's *Researches*, Appendix.

[2] Barker to Philip, 14th March 1822. A long series of letters passing between Barker and Rivers is preserved, thanks to Dr. Philip's caution; he instructed his missionaries to act only on *written* instructions from the Landdrost, and to preserve the letters as evidence.

Barker's summary of grievances, in January 1824, when the Crown Commissioners had brought some amelioration, maintains that the men were not informed of any contract, that the six rix-dollars promised were not always paid, and that men were detained after the termination of the period of supposed contract.

[3] This instance is cited in evidence given to Crown Commissioners, *Records*, vol. xxxv. Even at this day I have heard of farmers who secure the services of Natives by paying their taxes for them.

the missionaries themselves was heavily entrenched upon by the burden of administrative work forced upon them. If they were not collecting the 'Opgaaf' or helping to take a 'census', they were kept writing passes and hunting out workers to send on Government service.[1]

A second peculiar disability of the Institution Hottentots was their liability to this 'Opgaaf' tax, of the nature of a 'tithe', escaped, of course, by mere servants. Though the land of Bethelsdorp was estimated at only one-eightieth part of the district, though the quality of its soil was admittedly poor, though none of it was owned by the Hottentots, and though, at least in the late 'thirties, their wages probably averaged about 6s. per month,[2] a statement for 1822 put the amount of the Bethelsdorp Opgaaf at eight and five-sixths rix-dollars a head, and the total between one-twelfth and one-fourteenth of that for the district.[3] Even if the details are open to question there is no doubt whatever that this tax in the eighteen-twenties operated in much the same way as that in the Transvaal a century later. Faithful to the old traditions, the tax on Transvaal native farm servants was for some time £1 per annum, fully more than the average monthly wage; but for semi-independent farm 'squatters', as an inducement to them to prefer farm service, the tax was double, being £2 instead of £1. The burden of taxation tended to force Hottentots into service.

In the long run, however, the position even of the Institution Hottentots was determined by the ordinary laws, since the right to retire to the Institution was subject to the veto of the Landrost, and closely circumscribed. It is difficult to arrive at a dispassionate judgment on the working of the laws. The missionaries, who were the most important critics of the administration, were often carried off into transports of anger by what may have been exceptional and individual hard cases. Gradually, leaders like Dr. Philip came to act on the sound advice tendered by a naval officer[4] against pursuing one such case. 'Our cause had better, if possible, rest on generals rather than on particulars.' Now, on general grounds, the Hottentots stood at a legal disadvantage, being subject to

[1] In 1825 Kitchingman complained that the 'Opgaaf' involved 'two months' work'. Edwards from Theopolis denied, December 1825, that he hindered the census-taking of the field-cornet.

[2] See note 5, p. 169.

[3] Memo., 'Strictures on Opgaaf Tax, certified by W. van Buchenroder', of Perseverance, Uitenhage. The rix-dollar was stabilized in 1826 at one shilling and sixpence.

[4] Capt. H. E. W. Owen, Port Elizabeth, 2nd July 1823.

summary procedure, to imprisonment for making any complaint at all, and to punishment almost 'by request' of their
masters; in points of detail, involving the interpretation and
application of the proclamations, they stood to suffer from the
antipathetic administration of farmer field-cornets.   In such
circumstances the individual cases of hardship cited by missionaries and others have a special significance.   The law governing
a subject race is to be judged by the hardships it sanctions
and countenances rather than by its verbal claim to counteract
abuses;   and the accumulated evidence of hard cases leaves
no doubt that the law which set out to secure to the Hottentots
a fixed place of abode, and to check vagrancy, worked to their
serious disadvantage.   The law of 1809, in words of a note
by Dr. Philip,

'made the first attempt to legislate for the benefit of the Hottentots,
stating in its preamble that the Hottentots must have some fixed place
of abode'.   This must appear 'very reasonable to a stranger', but
'I have never yet met with one colonist in South Africa acquainted
with the condition of the Hottentots or with the bearings of that part
of his Lordship's proclamation before I explained it to him'.

It was 'a matter of surprise' to the Crown Commissioners
that, in face of the words of this preamble, Hottentots 'should
have been considered as being incapacitated by law from holding
lands'.[1]   As John Fairbairn pointed out, however,[2] land-
ownership was the only foundation of 'property', as property
in its turn is 'the root of family life and of progress, and the
universal standard of respect'.   So it was that the Hottentots
had no real chance of progress.   Their 'fixed place of abode'
could not be land of their own, so that they were left to choose
between life on an Institution, where there were no prospects
of rising to real independence, an outlaw existence as vagrants,
and farm service on land belonging to colonists.   Thus with
no really practicable alternative to farm service, and with a
definitely inferior legal status, the Hottentots were left with
no bargaining power whatever and with little or no protection
against labour regulations, which operated in almost every
instance to depress them to the level of serfs.

First came the Pass Law.   Dr. Philip's summing up may
be given:

According to regulation they must be under contract.   The
contracts are annual, and when the contract has expired, if the

---

[1] *Records*, vol. xxxv.   See above, p. 147.
[2] To Philip, 20th July 1825.

Hottentot refuses to renew his engagement with his former master he demands a pass from him. This he shows to the neighbouring Landdrost or field-cornet, from whom he receives another pass permitting him to hire himself to another master. The time given him to find a master may be two weeks, one week, three days, one day or twelve hours, as it suits the caprice or may serve the interests of the local authority from whom it is received. If he finds a master in the time given he must come to this authority and enter into a new contract. If he does not find a master he must return within the time limited in the pass, or be liable to be seized and apprehended and punished as a vagabond. In both cases his services become the Patronage of the local authority from whom he received the pass.[1]

Now a Pass Law still has its stout supporters. A primitive and illiterate people torn out of their natural environment and allowed to wander at large in a civilized community may easily prove difficult to manage. For their own protection it may be an advantage that they should be easily identifiable by something in the nature of a passport, if only to enable any mishap to be reported to their friends, or to save them from wrongful arrest through mistaken identity. It is a very different matter when it delivers them bound to some petty local official, and ultimately to one who may be an unscrupulous employer; and Dr. Philip's criticisms are justified in important respects. The time allowed them, as in the Transvaal even yet, to go 'in search of work', might be utterly insufficient, especially in a country of huge distances. Except on the assumption, obviously unwarranted, that the demand for labour, and also the supply, are constant and equal in all districts, a pass law resting ultimately on the imperfectly controlled whim of the individual employer must operate to immobilize labour and to depress wages, since it adds to the natural difficulties of freedom of movement, and makes it harder for coloured people to carry their labour to the best market. In the republics, a pass law continued to restrict the Natives' movements, and from similar motives, even in 1913, squatters were 'encouraged' to become 'labour tenants' bound to do service for ninety days every year, which might in practice be spread over three hundred and sixty-five.[2] The colonists' dread of 'vagrancy', first roused in the days of the Hottentots, still operates to restrict the fluidity of the South African labour supply, and at the same time to keep Hottentot or Native standards low and depressed.

[1] Memo by Dr. Philip, apparently sent to L.M.S. to be submitted to T. Fowell Buxton, 23rd March 1824.
[2] Natives' Land Act 1913, confirming the definition given in a Taxation Act 1908.

But combined as passes were in those days with other provisions of the law, the total effect was not only depressing but oppressive. In theory contracts were limited to one year only, this being expressly designed to put some term to what tended to become long periods of almost indefinite servitude, and also to enable the Hottentots to secure better wages by having the power periodically to try a change of masters.[1]   In practice, however, the Hottentot was far from sure of getting a clear discharge at the end of his year. On one pretext or another, whether for food or clothing supplied, for animals lost or damaged while in the servant's care, for damage to waggons or other property, or even for medical attention or time lost through sickness,[2] the servant was liable to find himself presented with a bill for an amount exceeding all wages due, and obliged, before he could get his discharge pass, to serve his old master till his debts were paid off by his earnings. Administered as they were, the provisions of the 1809 law were almost powerless to protect the Hottentots from claims of service based on such accumulated debts, and the relevant clauses are repeated in the 50th Ordinance of 1828, in such detail as to throw some light on the prevailing practice. Since 'no liquor or tobacco shall be admitted as payment of money due for wages or in any manner charged in account against such (contracted) Hottentots',[3] it is not an unfair inference from masses of evidence in Reports from mission stations, that food, clothing, and probably loss and damage, were habitually so 'admitted' and 'charged'. The effect of the prevailing practice, if not of the provisions of the law, was to immobilize the Hottentots, and therefore to depress their standards, and weaken their hope of securing any real benefit from the actual scarcity of labour.[4]

The subsequent history of the labour contracts is also illuminating. In 1809 annual contracts were made normal for the express purpose of allowing Hottentots a more frequent change of masters. In 1828, 'to protect ignorant and unwary Hottentots', it was laid down that, except with the due formality of registration by the parties concerned, in the presence of

[1] Collins' Report, *Records*, vol. vii, p. 111.
[2] Circuit Commissioners' Report, 1813, cited by M. L. Hodgson, *loc. cit.*
[3] Ordinance 50 of 1828, par. v.
[4] In the 'twenties the labour shortage was particularly acute in Albany, where the Settlers were not allowed to keep slaves. Dr. Philip more than once (see Chapter IX above) urged the removal of Hottentots to Albany to better their own condition and to relieve this shortage.

properly constituted authority, contracts were to be regarded as renewable from month to month. The point of this drastic change is indicated by a Memo. from Pacaltsdorp in 1834:[1]

The Hottentots habitually work for the farmers *when required*, but on monthly terms, and not, as the farmers prefer, on yearly contract. Twelve months gives them inadequate protection; but on monthly terms they are free to leave masters who ill-treat or under-pay them, whereas, on the twelve-month basis, pay is less and the danger of loss greater.

The movement for Hottentot emancipation reached its height in 1828, but in later enactments there was a tightening up in favour of the master. (See below, Chapter XVII, p. 255). The result was that as early as 1841 the restriction which made verbal contracts valid for only one month was removed, with the stipulation that they might hold for 'not longer than one year', except for ex-slaves and 'apprenticed labourers', for whom a limit of three months was still provided. In 1856, when the farmers regained something like complete control in the newly-created Cape Parliament, save for the provision that contracts must be entered upon within one month of verbal agreement, the exception disappeared. Since that time the practice of giving Native or coloured farm servants the protection of formal written agreements has made little or no progress; and for farm service, verbal contracts, binding for twelve months, may be regarded as normal.

There was yet another law and practice which operated to some extent to immobilize the Hottentots, while seeking merely to 'control' them. Backward races are no exception to the rule that the age of adolescence is particularly difficult. Farmers must undoubtedly have had their troubles with high-spirited and mischievous children in their 'teens, *umfaans*, to use a common and convenient Bantu word. The first Circuit Commission added the pathetic touch, that most farmers 'are indifferent and evince little or no care for them',[2] and in 1812, accordingly, a new Proclamation sought to provide these young people with foster-parents by the method of 'apprenticeship'. Again the motive was respectable; though Colonel Collins in 1809 puts another complexion on the complaint that their keep was an expense to the farmers.

In distant parts of the colony the male Hottentot seldom receives more than 12 to 14 pounds which may be either in money, clothes or

---

[1] Memo. of Protest against proposed Vagrant Law.
[2] *Records*, vol. viii, p. 301.

cattle. The female obtains much less. A great deal is said by the inhabitants of the expense of maintaining the children of these people, but I think without justification, for a child can scarcely crawl before it is turned to some purpose.

Even in 1812 the claim that apprenticeship was justified by the support given by farmers to children in their nonage was upset by the provision that empowered the Landdrost to assign them to other farmers 'considered more satisfactory' than those on whose farm the children had grown to their eighth year.

The benefits of apprenticeship are not strikingly obvious. Though no doubt serious abuses were abnormal, there was no safeguard against their happening. For one thing, backward peoples are very vague about their ages, and the eighteen-year limit was by no means sure to give the apprentice his release. A far more serious possibility of abuse is described by Dr. Philip:

The Hottentots not on a missionary Institution, or who have their children residing at the place of a farmer, have no power to dispose of their children and no power to check such as assume this power in their manner of disposing of them. . . . At eight years of age the child is 'booked' and bound over to serve the farmer till eighteen years of age. . . . The father is now bound from affection to remain on any terms the farmer may prescribe to him. In the course of a year or two more, another child arrives at the age of eight years, and is apprenticed in the same manner, and so on in succession. The farmer treats the old people as he pleases, he has their children and they will not leave him. . . . If the farmer and Landdrost are not on the best footing, the authority of the Landdrost is paramount, he takes away the children and gives them to any one he pleases.[1]

Once more the effect of apprenticeship was to make the Hottentots a 'tied' labour force, with results similar to those of the parish 'settlement' provisions of the old English Poor Law.

Hedged about as the Hottentots were by so many restrictions on their freedom of contract, their wages were inevitably wretchedly low. Official complaints or any protection the law afforded were equally powerless to check the operations of this labour code. Even if the inference of low wages did not follow inevitably from the facts, the evidence is conclusive. Janssens and Collins have already been quoted. Colonel Bird, nearly

---

[1] Philip, reporting to England, 23rd March 1824. W. van Buchenroder from Perseverance, Uitenhage, 20th September 1821, gives details of one such case, and describes also how one van Rooyen bought an old decrepit slave, and then secured the apprenticeship of the slave's children by a free Hottentot woman.

ten years after Caledon's reforms, says much the same thing;[1]
and later still one of the Crown Commissioners wrote: 'The
Hottentots with few exceptions are known to be most inadequately remunerated for their service throughout the Colony'.[2]
The restrictions on truck in liquor merely confirmed farmers in
the practice of paying wages in food and clothing or cattle, or, it
might be, in goods of no intrinsic value.[3]   The Boers after all
were situated like the islanders of Skye, where Dr. Johnson
concluded that the cheapness of eggs was the measure of the
scarcity of pennies.   Their subsistence-farming had little need
or scope for cash transactions, and book debts and dealing in
kind met most of their own requirements.   The best hope for
the Hottentot labourer therefore was to be paid in stock.   As
three cows a year would be very good pay,[4] rapid accumulation
would not be easy; and the more stock he might have of his
own, the weaker were his powers of bargaining, since a servant
demanding grazing rights would not always be welcome to a new
master and dare not too easily leave the old employer lest his
stock perish on the *trek* involved in a removal.

To assess the money value of Hottentot wages is almost
impossible.   Shops were few and far between; purchases, if
he could afford any, reached the servant through the farmer,
and the servant was probably seldom out of some master's
debt, and, like the Boers themselves, rarely handled hard cash.[5]
The fact would seem to be that Hottentot wages were as low as
it was possible for adverse conditions to make them.   Even as
slaves they might have fared better.[6]   They were involved in a

---

[1] Bird refers to farmers who use unfair means to force a pro-
longation of the term of labour contracts.   'This it is that makes the
Hottentots so averse from entering into the service of the farmers;
the vigilance of the magistrates is the only means of counter-acting
this system should it prevail in the districts you are to superintend.'
Bird to J. Baird, Deputy Landdrost of Beaufort West.

[2] Colebrook to Earl Bathurst, cited by M. L. Hodgson, p. 618.

[3] Evidence of the Moravians, cited by M. L. Hodgson from *Records*,
vol. xxxv, p. 330.

[4] An instance from Pacaltsdorp, December 1823.

[5] An estimate based on returns from L.M.S. mission stations about
1840 gives the following monthly wage-rates: Cape Town and
Stellenbosch, 8s. to 12s.; Swellendam, 4s. 6d. to 8s.; George, 4s. 6d.
to 7s. 6d.; Uitenhage, average 6s.; Albany, average, 10s.

Since in the twentieth century native farm wages may be as low
as six shillings a month, with some food and possible limited grazing
or ploughing rights in addition, this may be approximately correct.

[6] W. von Buchenroder reports on the 24th December 1822 how
a responsible Hottentot left in charge of a farm was haled to the
'tronk' on a charge of stock theft, detained a fortnight without trial,

vicious circle. History had made them a vagrant landless race, and the law which sought to check this vagrancy failed to provide land, or any 'reserves' more adequate than the handful of farms called 'Institutions'. Passes, indeed, the principal check on vagrancy, did little but sanction forced labour; for in the last resort the Hottentot who refused to work for what he considered inadequate payment came under the pass law, and as a vagrant, was liable to be contracted by the local authorities to any one they pleased, on the farmer's own terms.[1] These terms in turn were so miserable that Hottentots continued to prefer the risk of vagrancy. 'The primary inducement to farmers to pay reasonable wages was lacking', and the conditions in every way highly unfavourable to progress. What was even more serious: 'the subordination of the freedom of the Hottentots to the economic interests of the white farmers was detrimental to both the moral and economic life of the community as a whole'.[2]

The colonists themselves, however, were perfectly satisfied with the system and had no desire for any reform calculated to relieve the pressure on the Hottentots. When in the end of 1821, as a result of the difference with Sir Rufane Donkin about Bethelsdorp (see Chapter X), Dr. Philip woke to a full realization of the unsatisfactory position of the Hottentots, the administration was undoubtedly weak and biassed, and the law itself profoundly unsatisfactory and unsound. He had ample justification for his criticisms.

---

and finally released. He was kept in a cell with two Hottentots who died of chest trouble and was himself infected. 'Had he been a slave, the property of a master, he would have been more carefully looked after.'

[1] Two typical letters may be cited from a Cradock series certified 'true copy', by Dr. Philip.

(a) To the inhabitant, H. Kruger. (Cradock, November 1, 1822.)

'Good friend, I have already sent you a letter to request your attendance at the Adjunct Drostdy to answer the complaint against you by your Hottentot Danster, on 28 Sept. last, and as yet I have heard nothing from you, I must inform you that if you do not come immediately to release him he must be hired to some other person.'

(b) To L. Pretorius, Brak River.

'In the name of the adjunct Landdrost I have to state that if you allow the Hottentot woman Tryn to go away, then to give her a pass, that she may take another master.'

[2] Miss M. L. Hodgson's conclusions in the detailed and valuable study frequently cited in this chapter.

Chapter *XIII*

NEW VIEWS ON THE COLOUR QUESTION—
THE BREWING OF A STORM

THERE is no doubt that Dr. Philip was the first South African of any importance to point the fact that the welfare of the coloured races is, not merely desirable in itself, but essential to the well-being of their white masters. A civilization which rests ultimately on a serf economy cannot endure, and modern students tend more and more to emphasize the disastrous effect of slavery upon ancient societies like Greece and Rome. No man so consistently as Philip struggled for the welfare of South Africa as an economic unit. His sympathy with the Settlers is obvious (see Chapter IX) and his criticism of the Boers was inspired above all by his fear of the economic consequences of the indefinite expansion of the Colony.

On this point, as on so much else, Dr. Philip's views have been seriously misrepresented, as if he and all his school were the theory-spinning champions of a crude and immediate equality between white and black. Philip, it is true, represents the extreme antithesis to those who believe in the inherent inferiority of the coloured races; but he was well aware that they stood in need of much guidance. If he sometimes tends to exaggerate the attainments of individual Hottentots—without such robust belief in their possibilities he could never have fought the long battle he did on their behalf. He may have believed that one or two generations of Christian teaching would suffice to make up the leeway of centuries and bring both Hottentots and Kafirs to the European level of civilization. But if in this he was the visionary, he was eminently the constructive thinker, and his letters show that even his 'visions' were as a rule in close relation to the immediate problem in hand. Some extracts from a long formal document, described as 'A Defence of the Hottentots'[1] may be taken as typical:

I hope the day will arrive when Hottentot institutions will be unknown in the Colony, and unnecessary, when the magical power of caste will be broken and all classes of the inhabitants blended into one community.

As an example of 'caste' he quotes that on a journey to Pacaltsdorp,

although we always had worship on the Sabbath we did not meet with more than three or four instances in which the farmers condescended to mingle with the Hottentots in our worship. We might as well expect to find Creoles at the table of a West India planter as to find farmers associating with Hottentots in religious worship.

To further the progress towards a united community,

the influence of our missions has procured for the Hottentots a milder treatment. It has bridled the temper of the master and bettered the condition of the slave. Institutions are therefore still an essential protection, till the Hottentots 'are treated with more consideration by the farmers', and to prevent them from 'falling back'. To this end, 'the use of any other means than such as are legitimized by the principles of civil liberty and good sense will seal the degradation of the whole colony'.

Arguing that for their loyalty in the early days of the British Occupation, when some of the frontier Boers were threatening rebellion,

'the poor Hottentots then, it is probable, for the first time enjoyed the smile of the colonial government', he continues : 'Since that period the political state of the Colony has undergone a great change. The colonial population are now in general cordial with the English Government. The result has been unfavourable to their interests, and institutions in particular have given rise to colonial hostility and to a feeling that the Hottentots are "property unjustly alienated from its rightful owners." . . . Where any class of people have been regarded as an inferior race, and when the interests of one colonist used to have more weight than the rights of four or five hundred Hottentots you cannot expect British ideas and feelings, and it is mortifying to observe how soon even British Settlers imbibe prejudices so flattering to their pride and so favourable to their imaginary interests.'

The document proceeds to illustrate the colonial attitude. Pacaltsdorp was an Institution in the District of George which,

[1] This document was sent to London with a covering letter dated 23/3/24, endorsed 'for Sir J. Brenton, and Mr. Wilberforce'. Dr. Philip's habit seems to have been to make use of notes written in the course of his tours; these extracts are probably from some earlier Journal.

doubtfully perhaps, Dr. Philip credits with 100,000 acres of arable land, and barely 100 acres under cultivation; but he was quite accurate in saying that in this well-watered area, with large farms, 'farmers can support their families with small exertion'.[1] Of Pacaltsdorp he writes:

Notwithstanding the improvement made upon this place and people in the course of a few years, and that each farmer in the neighbourhood has as much land for himself as is included in the whole of the Institution, and though the greater part of the farms around are in a state of nature, a plan was suggested to remove the Hottentots to George and give their houses and gardens and cultivated fields to a party of new Settlers! I must do His Excellency, the Acting Governor Sir Rufane Donkin, the credit to say that the plan was rejected the moment I had the opportunity of stating my sentiments upon the subject. . . . Disperse the Hottentots among the Farmers, leave them without asylums to which they can retreat, remove the Missionaries, who are the only link which connects them with the Government, they fall immediately into the hands of their old Masters, and South Africa would speedily retrograde, and all our visions vanish. . . . For the civil authorities of the country I have the highest respect. The Landdrosts of the different districts of the colony are Gentlemen, that would do credit to the first Magistracies in our English counties . . . but the farm houses are generally far from the Drostdy, and in sequestered situations and without the eyes of our Missionaries and the intervention of Missionary influence between the Hottentots and Farmers, the most active and humane magistrates would soon find their means inadequate to prevent the growth of oppression. . . . It is a hard case that the Hottentots should not only be prevented from purchasing or holding land in a Country which was once entirely their own, but that the small spots on which our Institutions are built should be grudged them. . . . I love my Country, I respect my Countrymen, I consider the Colonial Farmers as having been unjustly treated by the English Press. But I cannot sympathise with those gentlemen who would be pleased to see a hundred cottages demolished, and as many smiling gardens converted into a cornfield, to build a farm town, enlarge the territory and furnish effective labourers to a Man perhaps inferior in intellectual and moral qualities to many of the Individuals he has reduced to dependence and Slavery.

This last suggestion, that individual Hottentots might be superior to some colonists, for the time when it was written, is a startling hypothesis, and is an instance of Philip's 'extreme' views. It is, however, an isolated statement, and in fact goes no farther than to show his profound belief in the potential equality of the races.[2] Even in this context it must be taken

[1] See remarks on George in *S.A. Agrarian Problem*.
[2] I have found no specific reference to the question of mixed marriages. But as a result of the experience accumulated by the time of the 1817 'Synod', the marriage of missionaries with Hottentot women was officially distrusted, and little was heard of it after 1821.

along with his emphatic belief in the need to continue the Institutions as a protection for the weaker race, which, whatever it might show itself capable of becoming in happier conditions, was still in its nonage.   Nor is it reasonable to draw sweeping conclusions because on occasion Philip entertained or accepted invitations from his Hottentots, and habitually treated them with equal courtesy; before Andries Waterboer was allowed to accept an invitation to dine with Sir Benjamin D'Urban he was put through a course of training in manners at Mrs. Philip's own table.[1]   The truth is that Philip had thus early sensed what has become one of the most desperate practical difficulties of the colour question.   Both in quality and in attainment individual natives and coloured people now undoubtedly stand far above many Europeans, whose political, and other, privileges they are barred from sharing.   The arrogance shown by the 'Poor White' to a cultured Native is all the more bitter that, as some one has said, the colour of his skin may be the one quality left him to flatter his feeling of innate superiority.

The truth is that speculation and theory find little place in Dr. Philip's writing, and the over-emphasis laid on his belief in the equality of the races has entirely obscured the most striking characteristic of his work as a whole.   Though he may have believed that one or two generations would suffice to raise the coloured races to a level of equality with civilized Europeans, as members of a homogeneous society, his practical policy at every stage of his career was a passionate struggle to secure, first for the Hottentots, later for Griquas and Kafirs, land and homes of their own, with the opportunity to live and develop their own separate existence.   Individuals like 'friend Waterboer' and others, he regarded, even too confidently, as having already attained a degree of civilization; but so far from desiring a sudden and indiscriminate mixing of the races, Dr. Philip, it will be found, was the first and greatest 'segregationist'; his life was spent fighting to save the Hottentots from being 'dispersed among the farmers, without asylum to which they can retreat', and later, to save the Native races from 'extermination'.[2]   For the Bantu, at least, almost complete segregation might have been practicable, had such a policy been initiated in those early days; and the present confusion of black and white areas in South Africa is the antithesis rather than the outcome of what has been called 'the Philip policy'. The conciliatory policy (which had endured in a fashion for

[1] Mrs. Philip to Philip, November 1834.
[2] *I.e.* extrusion from their lands.   *Lat. terminus*, a boundary.

less than one generation) broke down; the Kafirs proved war-like and intractable, instead of amenable, and there were almost continuous wars from 1846 to 1853. In the violent revulsion of feeling that followed there was a throw-back in favour of repression, and a wholesale denunciation of Philip's policy as theoretical and unpractical.[1]

It is, in fact, the critics who are themselves the abstract theorists. Their view, now more popular than ever, is that which holds the definite and permanent inferiority of the dark races as an article of faith. If in untold centuries the Bantu have made no contribution to the common stock of civilization, nor evolved any distinctive culture of their own, their permanent inferiority, like that of the Hottentots, is held to be self-evident. But after all, the civilization of Western Europe itself is hardly a thousand years old, and 'industrial' civilization is a child of yesterday; there were strictures by early missionaries on our own ancestors,[2] and Bantu law or custom is remarkably like that of the early Teutons,[3] and final deductions are unwarranted. But even if the coloured races could be scientifically proved to be of an inferior stock, history has shown that they are capable of rising to something better that the state of the Hottentots in 1822. Their backwardness is precisely what makes these coloured races a 'problem'; as labourers they are less efficient; as competitors their low standards make them undercut the white workman's wages; as consumers they are still so poor and negligible as to be a drag on the prosperity of the whole country.[4] The weakness of the inferiority theory as the basis of a working policy is that it disastrously weakens the motive for raising coloured standards at all. It is now proposed to 'segregate' the races; but few are bold enough to suggest that agriculture and industries in South Africa should be deprived of their mass of coloured labourers, and for this class no real place is found in the 'separate development' of their own people.[5] If these necessary labourers are to be permanently

[1] Sir H. Smith wrote of the attempt to 'civilize' the Gaikas as 'an awful failure', and the Kafirs as 'perfidious, bloodthirsty and treacherous', to Earl Grey, 6th May, 1851, and 16th January 1852.
[2] E.g. Chapter III, p. 28, above.   [3] Cf. p. 31, above.
[4] In Herschel district investigation in 1925 showed the spending power of Native families to average about £1 per month.
[Articles in Cape Times, 12th April 1926 and days following, by W. M. Macmillan.]
[5] The farm native population, which may be nearly two millions, does not really fit into the scheme, e.g. of the 'Union Council Bill', 1927.

barred also from the political and even the economic privileges of the dominant whites, economic progress in South Africa will continue to rest on a basis of poorly paid and inefficient labour, which has so little stimulus to progress as to be little removed from serfdom. However desirable it may yet be to provide for the Natives as much separate and independent life as possible, in homogeneous communities of their own, it is but a lame and halting 'segregation' that shies at the real difficulty, and merely denies full scope to the human possibilities of millions of the native population who must still be employed by Europeans in European-owned areas. For after all, the crux of the matter is to maintain fitting relations between white and coloured people when and where they inevitably live and work together.

Dr. Philip was on far safer and stronger ground. He had a clear-sighted recognition of the permanent danger of just such a policy as this, with its emphasis on the provision of labour as a mere commodity. Again and again he returned to the theme that 'the short-sighted policy of the Government has never regarded the Hottentots as consumers', but solely as producers. The coloured people were mere tools designed by Providence to serve the farmers for the farmers' own interests; the colonists showed an utter disregard for the human interests of the labourers, and equal recklessness of the ultimate good of the community of which they were a part. In the document already cited in this chapter Philip enlarges in conclusion on how those responsible

never think of giving up present advantage for future gain, nor seem to have contemplated the aborigines of the colony as consumers, nor in any other light than as labourers and as furnishing a present accommodation to their masters.

For example, the Institutions were criticized for the inefficiency of their instruction. But the intermittent teaching was largely due to the dependence of the inhabitants on wage-earning, and to the calls which the Government made on their services. At the same time the Institutions were blamed for keeping Hottentots idle, though they were the only places where there was any hope of learning anything. Dr. Philip admitted that not all the blame was on the Government. At Theopolis he found the people scattered, and ordered them to rebuild the village, and live within reach of school and church.[1] Mr. Barker soon began the work of reconstruction. Yet as soon

[1] Letter to L.M.S., 31st January 1822.

as reforms were beginning to take effect in 1822, Dr. Philip found reason to complain:[1]

> Those who criticized the backwardness and lack of civilization at the Institutions before, are now alarmed and indignant at the improvements. They criticize the Institutions to destroy them. What the colonists want is an excuse to disperse the Hottentots among the farmers as servants.

With some justification he summarized the attitude of his opponents: 'an excess of civilization may spoil the Hottentots for the service of the Boers'.

The missionaries, so far as they were able, did a little to encourage the Hottentots to become 'consumers'. In 1821 the first shops were established at Bethelsdorp and Theopolis, by the direct encouragement of Dr. Philip, who in 1822 reported a turnover of 20,000 Rix-Dollars by the trader Kemp at Bethelsdorp (16,000 R.D.s of this in cash).[2] Years later, in 1845, he claimed two shops at Zuurbraak as 'evidence of progress not known in the previous one hundred and sixty years'. But the history of Albany is perhaps a better witness to the truth of Dr. Philip's criticism. It was only as trade with the independent Kafirs grew, that the Settlers began to surmount the worst of their initial difficulties.[3] The palmiest days of Grahamstown were in the two or three decades which followed. Doubtless much of its prosperity was fictitious, and some Grahamstown fortunes were of the nature of war 'profiteering'.[4] The fact that Grahamstown was the chief garrison town on a disturbed frontier, frequently involved in relatively costly wars, made this inevitable. Yet when the Kafir 'menace' was removed, and the worst of the 'thieving' which was supposed to make the agricultural development of the district almost impossible, stagnation set in.[5] The frontier trade was supposed to pass, with the railway, to King William's Town and East London; whereas it has since languished altogether, and examination would show the border towns to be in little better condition economically than Grahamstown. In spite of a teeming Native population in Bathurst, even in Albany, and

---

[1] Letter of 11th May, 1822.

[2] Report to L.M.S. for 1822.

[3] This is obviously the significance of events described in Cory ii, pp. 174 ff.

[4] Capt. Stretch makes definite allegations of profiteering in letters of January and February 1836 to Rev. J. Read in London.

[5] See, *e.g.*, my pamphlet, *Economic Conditions in a non-Industrial South African Town*, Grahamstown, 1915.

N

in all districts east of the Fish River,[1] the area conveniently described as the 'Cis-Kei' is economically among the most unhealthy in the Union. The Kafirs, whose trade as a free but savage people was the salvation of Grahamstown in the eighteen-twenties, are little but a drag on the prosperity of Cape Colony now that they have become a docile farm-labouring population, reduced to a condition of dependence not unlike that of the Hottentots a century ago.

In spite of Dr. Philip's correct diagnosis of the disease, and of the fight he began in 1822, when his eyes were first fully opened, South African policy has continued under the baneful influence of the 'short-sighted policy' which he denounced. Reform has been slow just because the farmers were so entirely satisfied with the law as it stood before 1828. Poor as it was in quality, labour was almost entirely under their own control. Even the Cape has done little that is constructive for the coloured races in its own borders; and so little did the Boer colonists desire a change that, after the Trek, they continued to carry out the essentials of the pre-1828 system in their own republics. The Native has, therefore, continued to be regarded as a labourer and 'producer' only.

But Philip's criticism came very near the root of the matter. A complete citizen is both producer and consumer. Aristotle long ago defined the slave as one who is not an end in himself, and therefore incomplete—a producer only, a mere 'animated tool'. In the struggle for the freedom of the Hottentots, the idea that thus dominated the minds of the old colonists had still to be reckoned with. Slavery as an institution died in the thirties, but the idea lives on that it has pleased God to call the larger part of mankind to learn and labour truly—not to get their own living, but to toil in the service of their betters.

It was, of course, some time before Dr. Philip's new vision of the Colour Question took definite shape or made much impression on the course of events at the Cape. The immediate effect was a sharpening of his complaints against local officials like Colonel Cuyler, whom at first he regarded as the prime cause of the troubles and disabilities of Bethelsdorp and other Institutions. By an almost imperceptible process he came to include the whole trend of colonial law and administration in the sweep of his condemnation; but till the crisis of 1824 his

---

[1] In 1925 a Commission was sitting to inquire into the development of the 'Hinterland' of Port Elizabeth. See figures in my pamphlet, *The Land, the Native, and Unemployment*, Johannesburg, 1924.

personal relations with the highest officials continued on the whole quite friendly. Even when it came to open war with Somerset,[1] the Governor was so unpopular with a large part of the colonial population that to be attacked by him was almost a guarantee of popularity, and it was not till after the publication of the *Researches* in 1828 that Dr. Philip came to be denounced as 'an enemy of the people'.

None the less, the last days of the year 1821 were a real turning-point in the history of the Cape Colony, as well as in the private life of Dr. Philip, who returned to Cape Town on the 26th December, armed with fresh and striking evidence of oppressions at Bethelsdorp. A few weeks earlier, on the 30th November, Lord Charles Somerset had returned to the Cape, and in relieving Sir Rufane Donkin, the acting Governor of 1820–21, embarked at once on a violent personal quarrel with his predecessor in office.[2] Lord Charles Somerset had ruled from 1814 to 1820, and his second term of office, which continued till March 1826, was destined to be momentous in Cape history. When the storms began to blow against Lord Charles, Dr. Philip commented on the unwisdom of such an unusually long term of office. When the Crown Commissioners were beginning to take evidence he wrote of how witnesses, like a certain farmer,

boasted of having painted the Governor black enough, and acquainted the Commissioners with his horse-jockey tricks. . . . I keep to my determination to avoid personalities, but I am of opinion that the Governor ought to have been quietly removed after five or six years of office. The people bear while there is a prospect of relief, and with a change of men expect a change of measures; but seeing no end to their sufferings they have burst through all restraints, and every mouth is open.[3]

Since opposition and criticism were likely, the quarrel with Donkin was an inauspicious start to Somerset's new term of office. Next year Sir Jahleel Brenton wrote from London:

I met Donkin in town this morning . . . with voluminous letters from the Cape. . . . I think the differences between the two Governors will be of great service to the Cape by bringing before the Secretary of State circumstances which would otherwise never have reached him.[4]

Donkin was, in fact, one of many thorns in the Governor's

[1] *E.g.* by the time of Somerset's despatch of 18th July 1824. [Below, Chap. XIV, p. 198].
[2] See Cory, vol. ii, p. 123.
[3] Philip to Sir J. Brenton, 27th August 1823.
[4] Brenton to Philip, 19th September 1823.

side, and though he was perhaps not very effective as a critic,[1] Somerset's precipitate quarrel with him may have been a sign of a growing tendency to arbitrariness in the disposition of the Governor. It was unfortunate, therefore, that about this time, the services of the notorious English Government agent, 'Oliver the Spy', seem to have become available in Cape Town.[2] How far Oliver was made use of is from the nature of his trade a matter of doubt;[3] it may be significant that in launching his first scurrilous attack on the leading missionaries, the Governor wrote:

> I would rejoice in an opportunity to expose Philip and Wright, but though I am aware of all they do by secret intelligence upon which I depend, I should if I were to bring their conduct forward disclose the only source of intelligence upon which I depend and which I consider of too much importance to the safety of my Government to give up.[4]

Dr. Philip's attention in 1822 continued at first to be given to questions directly concerning the mission stations under his control. A letter of January the 31st, reporting his investigations at Bethelsdorp,[5] contains one significant sign of his change of attitude. From the time of his first visit with Campbell in 1819, he had been negotiating to remove Bethelsdorp to a more favourable site. Numerous letters refer to negotiations for a transfer, hinting also that the colonists rejoiced at the prospect;[6] and even the Directors in London had given their consent to a change. No more was heard of this proposal.

[1] Sir Rufane Donkin, now an M.P., reappeared in 1836 as a critic of Philip and his friends on the Aborigines Select Committee. John Fairbairn then refers to him scathingly as 'an earthen vessel cracked by the Indian sun'.

[2] Oliver's position in England had become dangerous, and a letter from J. Mackintosh to Philip on the 10th April 1822, strengthens the evidence that he found asylum at the Cape. (J. L. and B. Hammond, *Skilled Labourer*, appendix). This letter runs, 'You have got Lord Charles again—at which I dare say you have no great cause to rejoice —and another valuable acquisition to your society in the person of OLIVER'.

[3] Cory, vol. ii, pp. 274 and 278.

[4] 'Secret and Confidential', Somerset to Bathurst, 18th July 1824 (Cape Town Duplicate Dispatches).

[5] To L.M.S., London, 31st January 1822.

[6] In a memo. of 1822 Philip writes: 'The people in (Uitenhage) district are almost wholly dependent on the services of the Hottentots, and flattered themselves that instead of depending on the Institution they would now have them in their power'. He continues that when Hankey was bought, and Bethelsdorp not sold, the farmers were 'enraged' and the Landdrost's 'interferences' correspondingly increased.

Now Philip decided that the Institution must remain. The surrounding country, he declared, was entirely dependent on Bethelsdorp for labour, and more particularly, the Institution was the only protection available for the Hottentots, who were alarmed at the prospect of its removal. He had provisionally arranged, therefore, for the purchase of a farm on the Gamtoos River (Hankey), to make an entirely new Institution. At the same time, along with regulations for their better government, he arranged for regular monthly reports to be sent from all stations to Cape Town; and whether or not this order was literally carried out, he was obviously well-informed about events in the interior.[1]

In the next few months Dr. Philip was particularly watchful of the local authorities. This was the period when even Mr. Barker was complaining of the effects of forced labour at Theopolis. In February and March there was a hint of trouble with the central Government, which evidently distrusted the missionaries. When the old Griqua missionary, Mr. Anderson, was appointed to Pacaltsdorp, Colonel Bird took occasion to point out that except at the London stations, Bethelsdorp and Theopolis (which had not formerly been Hottentot kraals), His Excellency expected that all appointments should be submitted to him for approval.[2] In the upshot Anderson's appointment stood, and the Government indicated that it had no intention of interfering with the Society's power to dismiss missionaries.[3]

There was dispute also about the question of admissions to the Institutions. Though no proclamation or definite law empowered Landdrosts to refuse to admit Hottentots, the local authorities relied and acted on the discretion left them by Sir John Cradock or earlier Governors:

Missionaries should be especially enjoined (wrote Sir John Cradock [4]) not to admit any persons into their societies without the

---

[1] Writing of this period in a later ' narrative ', Philip says: ' In reply (to complaints against Landdrosts) he told the missionaries to comply with none of the orders of the local authorities except such as were sent to them in writing. By this means the whole system of oppression which had been denied by the Governor was brought to light '.

[2] Colonial Secretary to Philip, 19th March 1822 (Cape Town Archives).

[3] Colonial Secretary to Philip, 22nd February 1822. This concession, however, does not seem to have sufficed to get rid of the unsatisfactory head of Zuurbraak, for Seidenfaden, first complained against in 1819, was made the subject of an 'Inquiry' ordered by the Governor on the 17th August 1820, but was dismissed by letter of Sir Richard Plaskett only on the 10th March 1825.

[4] To Rev. J. Campbell, Feb. 1814. [Printed in *Researches*, ii, p. 380.]

concurrence of the magistrate in writing, as laid down by former Governments. Without the performance of this indispensable condition there will be perpetual complaints and irritations.

The complaints and irritations, as things turned out, were not all suffered by the magistrates. It may have been quite sound that the authorities should have some effective control. But most of the local officials were unquestioning believers in the principles of the labour laws, which by themselves put most of the Hottentots under strait supervision; and rather than lose the power, as Dr. Philip put it, 'to dispose of their services (at the expiration of their labour contracts) once a year', some Landdrosts took unduly strong steps to put and keep Hottentots off the books of the Institutions. There was no redress against the arbitrary disposition shown in the following letter from Colonel Cuyler to Mr. Kitchingman of Bethelsdorp:

> You must excuse my giving any more Hottentots permission to join your Institution before I find those you already have can be made more useful to the community.[1]

Since the only alternatives the Hottentots had were an Institution, or service, such an attitude meant forced service.

Nor was the point ever finally set at rest, though at times there may have been a relaxation of control; the authorities were somewhat on their guard during the visit of the Crown Commissioners in 1824. Thus:

> In answer to an application from Col. Cuyler wishing to know whether he was to retain the power of preventing Hottentots from entering Bethelsdorp, His Lordship informed me that he had informed him that he had no such power, and that nothing but a contract could hinder any Hottentots who wished it to join the Institution. . . . This is one half the victory we at first contended for. But as an act of the Governor may be done to-day and undone to-morrow, I shall never think anything has been done for the Hottentots till their liberties are placed on the broad basis of Parliamentary enactments.[2]

On one point Philip seems to have gained a more immediate concession. When Cuyler put difficulties in the way of Hottentots of Bethelsdorp doing certain 'wood-cutting'[3] in Government forests, or seemed to adopt too high a hand in

[1] Quoted by Philip to Somerset, 25th July 1822 (Cape Town Archives, vol. 'Churches').

[2] Philip to L.M.S., 24th February 1824. In September 1824 the Landdrost of Albany complained that the Rev. Mr. Wright of Theopolis 'flouted' the authority of the field-cornet, and a minute by the Governor seems to warn the Landdrost to 'look out for the authority of the missionaries'.

[3] Philip to Colonial Secretary, 6th June 1822.

his treatment of some who were accused either of shooting game or of being in unlawful possession of firearms,[1] Dr. Philip went to headquarters:

> Since Colonel Cuyler refused to see me on my last journey, no alternative (was left) but the one now adopted of submitting all differences between the Landdrost and the conductor of the Institution to the decision of His Excellency.[2]

At last Colonel Bird seems to have felt that Philip's complaints may have had some substance, and

> to get.the business accommodated proposed that I should draft a few questions to be submitted to Colonel Cuyler that the Colonial Government might know the position. Till now (he continues) we have never had access to the papers transmitted by the Landdrosts to the Colonial Office, but for some reason the Colonial Secretary made an exception in these cases. . . . The local authorities could do what they pleased with Hottentot evidence and had it all their own way in tyrannizing over the missionaries (who) had no opportunity to reply to their reports. . . . Things are greatly altered in our favour at this time at the Colonial Office.[3]

There were very definite reasons for some 'change in our favour at this time'. On the 25th July 1822, a resolution of the House of Commons had approved in principle of the appointment of Crown Commissioners to inquire into the state not only of the civil government and legal administration of the Cape, but into the general conditions of the slave and Hottentot populations. In a supplementary motion it was Mr. Wilberforce who moved to

> recommend the state of the Hottentots to His Majesty's benevolent care, a race of men long misrepresented and vilified, who, however, have since abundantly proved that any efforts used for their moral improvement would not be employed in vain.[4]

The burden of his speech in support was to emphasize the futility of enslaving one part of the population while trying to liberate others. The origin of this Commission, whose Reports were to effect the first important changes in the political and administrative system of the Cape Colony, is a matter of interest; it is matter also of some doubt on which neither Hansard nor the correspondence of the Colonial Office throws much light.[5]

---

[1] Philip to Colonial Secretary, 8th August 1822, and other letters.
[2] Philip to Lord Charles Somerset, 25th July 1822.
[3] To L.M.S., 12th September 1822.
[4] Hansard, quoted in Theal's *Records* for July 1822.
[5] I am specially indebted to Mr. C. W. de Kiewiet, M.A., for search on this point at the Public Record Office.

That little of the pressure which led to the appointment of a Commission came from usual colonial channels is clear enough. The Settlers were newly arrived and far too preoccupied for organized political agitation.   The only hint of the need for investigation appears to be in a letter from Mr. H. Ellis, Under-Secretary at the Cape, who was moved by the unsatisfactory progress of the law-suits of Burnett, Hart and others [1] to urge the reform of the Cape judicature.[2]   There is evidence that in this instance it was from missionary sources that the first radical criticisms of the political system reached England, and that the wide scope of the inquiry, if not the very idea of an inquiry so important to Cape constitutional progress, was really due to the action of William Wilberforce, who acted on the representations of Dr. Philip.

While conducting his campaign of criticism against the local authorities Philip was also preparing a more formidable indictment; making use of offers of help from his friend Sir Jahleel Brenton, he sent to England the papers relating to the administration of Bethelsdorp with full and trenchant comments:

> Of what use is all this extension of the Colony if the Boers cannot render the lands of any value unless they can reduce the aboriginal inhabitants to the condition of slaves?   And even then, as there is no vent for agricultural products, and the market for grazing-farm products, or for obtaining products in return, is at a very great distance, they neither have an inducement to cultivate and improve their lands, nor can they provide even themselves but very scantily with the decencies and comforts of life.

He then turns to the central Government itself:

> The Colonial Government is in great measure a *military government*.   All the officials are military men, and were suddenly entrusted with the charge of an extensive civil and criminal Jurisdiction together with ecclesiastical authority, and the collection and disposal in some measure of the funds of their respective districts.   There is no check on their authority. . . . There is, moreover, no situation held by any individual in the Colony from which he is not removable at the pleasure of the Governor.
>
> The Press is exclusively a Government Press.   Lately it was announced that a printing press had reached Cape Town on one of the vessels and the authorities tried to stop its landing.   Finally they possessed themselves of it.
>
> The Governor, who is a Major-General, has the power of removing any of his judges at his will.   Members of the Court of Justice hold other lucrative situations under the Government.   For example, the President of the Court of Justice is also President of the Orphan

---

[1] Cory, vol. ii, chap. vi.
[2] Ellis to Goulburn, Theal's *Records* for December 1821.

Chamber. One member of the Court of Justice is also Auditor-General, another individual is a member of the Court of Justice, Receiver-General in the office of Land Revenue, and receives 2000 R.D.s from the proceeds of the Cape Paper.[1]

Referring to these and to his Bethelsdorp papers, intended for Brenton and Wilberforce, Philip remarks to Mr. Burder: [2]

You will not think me extravagant when I express to you my firm conviction that the papers in question (exposing the 'system') are of much greater importance to the cause of God and of humanity than all that has been done in South Africa by all the missions from their commencement till now. . . .

Then comes a note of caution:

I do not wish that anything actively should be done by them (e.g. Wilberforce) till I have done my utmost with the Colonial Government; but as I have no hope of doing anything effectual or permanent here I wish their minds to be prepared for what may be required in my attempt in Cape Town. The present system cannot go on longer.

The first fruits of Philip's agitation were of real importance. Years later Philip tells the first part of the story of the appeal to Wilberforce: 'Why does not Dr. Philip appeal to the Colonial Government?' Brenton was asked. 'My dear Mr. Wilberforce,' he replied, 'you are not aware of the state of things at the Cape. It is with the Government that the oppression rests.' 'Meet me to-morrow,' said Wilberforce, 'with Mr. Buxton and Dr. Lushington,' and . . . out of their labours and those resolutions arose the appointment of the Crown Commissioners.[3]

For these events there is (less dramatic) contemporary evidence:

FITCHAM, 1st Aug. 1822.

My dear Sir,

Your most kind and interesting letter reached me on board the Royal Sovereign yacht just as I was on the point of sailing for Antwerp with the Duke and Duchess of Clarence, and on my return I made an extract from it for Mr. Wilberforce (in confidence), stating it to be my firm conviction that nothing short of a Commission composed of disinterested and upright men being sent to our Colonies, and particularly to the Cape, would afford any prospect of effectual relief being bestowed upon the people of colour, or our black apprentices. I was delighted to hear from Mr. Wilberforce that such a measure was in contemplation for the West Indies, and to receive a request that I would meet him in London previous to his bringing forward his intended motion respecting the Cape.

---

[1] Memorandum on the Policy of the Colonial Government towards Hottentots, marked ' 1822 '.
[2] Philip to Burder, L.M.S., 13th September 1822.
[3] Philip to Mrs. Buxton, October 1834.

We met accordingly and had a very long conversation upon some interesting points. I have referred him to the missionary correspondence for the particular elucidation of some of them, particularly respecting Zwellendam, and the recent circumstance in Uitenhage. I also gave it as my opinion that no direct charge or complaint made against any of the Colonial authorities for a specific act of despotism can be attended with any good effect . . . they will be answered by an official document drawn up for the occasion, in which might will have right, and the question be banished from the House as litigious and frivolous; but if three men are sent who fear God, and who look to their own worldly interests less than to the sacred object put under their care, then we may have some hope of ultimate success. I am sanguine in the hope this will be the case, and I shall make a point of giving all the information in my power; I shall refer them for substantial evidence to you. . . . You will see by the papers how salutary are the resolutions moved by Mr. Wilberforce. . . . Indeed I am convinced the day is fast approaching when slavery will cease to exist, and pure Christianity will begin to be substituted for Mohammedanism. You are superior to any feeling of pride, but you must feel gratified in having been permitted to be instrumental in this great work.

I have, I hope, made a very deep impression upon the mind of Mr. Wilberforce and his friends as to the indispensable necessity of the cause of the Hottentots and black apprentices being taken up with a strong hand. The treatment your poor Hottentots have met with has been most barbarous; but I am convinced the fact itself will have a most salutary effect, as it will be a tangible case, and open the eyes of the public to the state of oppression they have so long suffered under. . . .

May the Colony in which you are placed bless your memory, and become by its prosperity a monument of the efficacy of consistent Christianity.—Yours most sincerely and affectionately,

J. A. W. BRENTON.

In reply to Philip's thanks, Brenton wrote on the 7th February 1823:

I found a fixed determination in the breasts of the great advocates for the lower classes to urge the attention of the legislature towards the wretched Hottentots, and have merely given them the information. . . . Mr. Wilberforce (he adds) has put your letter into the hands of Mr. Bigge. . . .

(Mr. Bigge being one of the Commissioners who was about to sail for the Cape.)

Brenton continued to have frequent communications with Mr. Wilberforce and 'had great hopes of the Commission, in spite of the very general interest in the Colony to conceal the truth from them'.[1]

From the time the Commission was announced till its arrival in July 1823, Dr. Philip was fully engaged in preparing masses of evidence to present in support of his case, confining

[1] Brenton to Philip, 7th February and 19th September 1823.

his own efforts to questions affecting Hottentots, Griquas, and Bushmen: but in his anxiety to do all he could to conciliate and 'stand on good terms with' his fellow-colonists, he left the cause of the slaves to 'J. Thomas, Esq. of Madras' and others:

You would instantly perceive by the perusal of the paper on the Court of Justice that nothing can be done for slaves, Hottentots, or indeed any of the aborigines of South Africa without a total change in the constitution of the Courts, and without the introduction of a new system of law.[1]

And again:

Every part of the present system must fall together. It cannot be mended; but I do not wish the Directors as a body to have anything to say on a subject not connected with missions. You will perceive that everything possible has been done by me to bring the Government to reason in order to avert this struggle. Nothing can now be of avail to save Africa but British statutes. I should be guilty of dereliction of duty if I quitted the subject till everything was done in my power to obtain emancipation for the wretched aborigines of South Africa.[2]

Philip's Directors, it would seem, were showing a little nervousness at his activities, for his criticism of the local authorities had grown imperceptibly into a 'struggle' with the Colonial Government itself. On the 11th May 1823, he had written to London:

In the midst of alarums I have the consolation that I did not seek the contest. I shunned it as long as possible. . . . I have no doubt that the papers I have sent Home and have in preparation will lead to the recall of the first authorities of the Colony and to a total change in its administration. . . . I know the Governor and Colonel Bird are dreadfully alarmed, and that they conceive me to be the origin of the evils coming upon them. . . . I confine my hostility, however, to the colonial system, without being personal against them, and if they had listened in time they might have kept their places, and the old system in a modified form. Now it is before the British Parliament.[3]

The prophecy was not far wrong. The next years were to see the first real political crisis in South African history. Philip's personal contest was soon merged in a struggle which was due to a general outburst of discontent through the whole Colony, and resulted in a total breakdown of the old colonial system as it was represented by Lord Charles Somerset.

[1] To the L.M.S., 11th May 1823.
[2] To the L.M.S., 27th June 1823.
[3] To the L.M.S., 11th May 1823, forwarding Memo. on Proclamations, on Courts of Justice, on Bushman Stations, and on Frontier Missions.

Chapter *XIV*

THE POLITICAL STRUGGLE WITH LORD CHARLES SOMERSET

THE mere sequence of events about 1824 is sufficiently well known.[1] It is tempting at first sight to accept without qualification the comment of a British officer,[2] who about 1824 suffered the 'tedium of fantastic idleness' in the capital of South Africa, and complained that racing, a 'south-easter', and the arrival of the mail were the only breaks in the monotony of existence for any one settled in Cape Town —'unless he chances to be a politician, a Cape party man; for here, as in most places, the feeling is virulent in proportion to its insignificance'. Yet the apparently meaningless clash of personalities in the episodes of this time really marks a signifi-cant stage in South African development. The thoroughly unsatisfactory political conditions of the Colony had brought the pent-up discontents of the colonists to bursting point, almost all classes being at one in feeling that the Somerset régime must be reformed. The Governor for his part did not fail to use the arbitrary powers he still possessed to make difficulties for his critics, so that only men with a good deal of assurance, perhaps only those who were somewhat thick-skinned, were prepared to face the social obloquy, if not the personal risks, of active opposition. The conditions and the atmosphere were such that an ex-convict, William Edwards, filled the rôle of a South African John Wilkes in exposing the abuses of the system, and the events of the time are only

---

[1] See Cory, ii, chaps. vi and vii.
[2] Cowper Rose, *Four Years in South Africa* (1824-29), quoted in the *Star*, 23/9/22.

intelligible as a manifestation of 'growing pains' in a community whose needs now demanded some more elastic and popular form of government. In the pre-occupation of the colonists with their own affairs, the question of coloured rights and wrongs sank for a time below the surface; but the part played by the leader of the 'humanitarians' in the fight with the Governor serves to show that 'colour' was none the less a strong undercurrent in the course of development.

The judicial system at the Cape stood in most obvious need of reform. Its defects were remarked upon as early as 1821 by Mr. Under-Secretary Ellis; and the judiciary, in particular, seems to have been in the mind of Mr. Wilmot Horton, when in the debate of July 1822 he announced the intention of the Government to appoint Commissioners of Inquiry. By 1823 the protracted and chaotic proceedings in the suits of Mr. Bishop Burnett had served to emphasize this weakness. The trouble was partly one of personnel; legal proficiency was not to be expected from judges who were elevated to the bench from the offices of wharf-masters, collectors of revenue, or land-surveyors.[1] But even had the qualifications of the judges been beyond cavil, there was some doubt about the law itself which it was their duty to administer, and the existing relations between judges and executive were altogether unsatisfactory. Thus it was not altogether extravagant for colonists to complain that there was 'no law in the Colony but the will of Lord Charles Somerset'.[2] The basic common law of the Colony was still Roman-Dutch; but in the absence of a well-organized legal system there was no sound tradition, and a dire possibility of conflict between laws and precedents drawn from Roman or from Roman-Dutch sources, possibly even from England, and certainly from the *Placaats* of the Dutch East Indian Government of Batavia; moreover, the Governor's power of making law by Proclamation was wide and indefinite.[3] None but a strong Bench could hope to evolve order out of such chaos.

[1] See Cory, ii, p. 299, *note 2*.

[2] From a draft among the Philip MSS., apparently drawn up when Philip and Fairbairn were in collaboration upon evidence to be submitted to the Commissioners—or to be sent to Brenton and Wilberforce in London.

[3] It was urged that Somerset's interest in Game Laws led him to admit circumstantial evidence in a Proclamation of 1822, thus setting aside the Roman-Dutch principle, which required two legal witnesses.

In February 1825, the Secretary of State saw fit to remind the Governor that, except in emergency, his legislative power was subordinate to, and subject to the approval of His Majesty in Council. Cory, ii, p. 317.

Much constructive work remained to be done in the lifetime of the late Lord de Villiers,[1] but till 1828 the judges were poorly qualified and weak, holding office only at the pleasure of the Governor, and liable to have their decisions reviewed on appeal by the Governor himself.   Somerset therefore had more absolute control of the machinery of the law than any of his Dutch predecessors.

For a time colonial discontents, legal and general, were kept in check by the hope of reform to come through the agency of the Crown Commissioners, who began their work in July 1823.   A few years later this hope was wearing thin:

It is obvious that the Commissioners are not sent out to inquire into particular grievances.   They are a piece of fudge—a trap for the true men. . . .   Mr. Canning said there was nothing in Lord Bathurst's office to warrant their proceeding immediately into an inquiry into Lord Charles's conduct.   You see how much we have been indebted to the Commissioners.   They have kept the matter from coming before Parliament for three solid years.[2]

In 1823, however, most of the malcontents were hopefully preparing their case for the Commission, and there was calm. The Governor and officials for their part seem to have been conciliatory in manner, or at least succeeded in giving this impression.   If Dr. Philip's attitude is to be taken as in any way typical, there was much marshalling of facts and opinions, and much drafting of 'memorials'.   Philip's interests were by no means confined to missionary or colour questions, but ranged over the general problems of government.   Obviously also he was in close touch with representative colonists, and availed himself on occasion of the help of distinguished visitors from India.   Thus in consultation with Philip, Sir Richard Ottley, 'one of H.M.'s Judges at Ceylon', drew up a paper[3] on the Cape Courts of Justice, with outlines of a plan, very much like that ultimately adopted.

In the first place a Crown Charter, though expensive, was held to be indispensable.   There must be a Supreme Court, with appeal only to King in Council.   Salaries must be adequate to secure the services on the bench of barristers of standing.   The Fiscal should be replaced by an Attorney-General.   The position of the Governor must be secure, but the judges must be protected against interference, and the Charter of Justice itself be inviolable by the Colonial Government.

---

[1] *Lord de Villiers and His Times*, by Prof. E. A. Walker.
[2] Fairbairn to D. Moodie, 25th September 1825.
[3] This document was sent to London under cover of a letter of 23rd September 1823.

In one important particular Sir Richard Ottley's advice unhappily was not followed; he favoured introduction of the jury system, but urged that it be not applied in cases (which have too often since seen a miscarriage of justice), where whites are accused of offences against blacks, or vice versa.

The Commissioners themselves seem to have been accessible. Dr. Philip in the latter half of 1823 was in constant touch, 'riding out to breakfast' with Mr. Bigge, exchanging specimens with Major Colebrooke, or providing their wives with Hottentot domestics, who had been trained at Bethelsdorp. On the 20th October Philip wrote to London:

From a late conversation with the Commissioners I think it is probable that ministers will be called upon to give us a new Court of Justice before the full Report of the Commissioners is sent home, and no time should be lost in endeavouring to have this settled on (sound) principles.

(He urges, therefore, that steps be taken to secure the appointment of Sir Richard Ottley, a 'pious man' and eminently suitable; adding sententiously: 'It is not enough to destroy a defective system without substituting a better'.)

Just at first, therefore, the Commissioners excited lively hopes of immediate, if not sweeping, reforms. Thus early in 1824 Dr. Philip had great encouragement and satisfaction from one of their preliminary actions. Towards the end of 1823 he had set off into the interior a little in advance of the Commissioners, to prepare his evidence on the Hottentot question, and to give them the benefit of a personally conducted tour of the Institutions. On the 1st of January 1824, Mr. Bigge wrote to the Superintendent of Bethelsdorp virtually inviting the Society to apply for more land for that station:

more especially as we anticipate a considerable augmentation of the numbers of the Hottentots when the present restrictions on their admission are removed.

Mr. Bigge's letter continues:

I am induced to make this suggestion more from a wish to complete the accommodation of the present numbers and to improve their condition by the accession of good or convenient pieces of land, than to (increase?) the accumulation of great numbers of Hottentots on the same spot, agreeing as I do with Dr. Philip that generally it will be found more advantageous to multiply the number of Institutions in the country, than to multiply the number of Hottentots in each place.

The hope thus aroused was doomed to be deferred.[1]

[1] In the sequel, the application which followed Mr. Bigge's hint led to considerable friction. So far from granting the request, the

For a time, however, even the Governor was friendly.   In September 1823, Dr. Philip was closely consulted about the problem of how to treat Bechuana refugees who fled into the Colony from the attack of the Mantatees.   There are several references to invitations to Newlands, Lord Somerset's country seat.   As late as 17th April 1824, Philip wrote to Sir J. Brenton of how Somerset now and 'for the last eight or nine months' has been

friendly, lately asked me to dine, and has only begun to learn the truth about the aborigines, and shows a disposition to grant requests made on behalf of the missions.

In the same month Somerset was in friendly correspondence with Philip about the desirability of urging the British annexation of Delagoa Bay as a check on the slave-trade.[1]

Just before this, however, the Governor had suffered a mortification: in face of the Colonial Office attitude he apparently had no sufficient excuse to prevent the launching of an unofficial, though hardly a 'free' press—the *South African Magazine*, and the *Commercial Advertiser*.   The first of these papers was the production of Rev. A. Faure, in partnership with Thomas Pringle, whom the Governor during the preliminary negotiations had described to Lord Bathurst as 'an arrant dissenter who[2] had scribbled' for a paper in

---

Governor seems to have given Bethelsdorp reason to fear rather an encroachment on desirable land in its neighbourhood.   During the troubles of July 1824, Dr. Philip drew up a memorial to be submitted to Lord Bathurst, and a rough draft has the following note in pencil, which suggests a continuation of close intimacy between Philip and the Commissioners: ' If Dr. Philip would merely explain that the memorial was addressed to the Governor in the first instance *at our suggestion*, and that as the evidence we obtained would enable us to bring the fair claims of the Institution before Lord Bathurst's consideration [some words illegible] to entreat that Lord Charles Somerset would not now accede to the (?) representations of Colonel Cuyler, it might answer his purpose better than attack on Lord Charles Somerset.'

Further evidence is furnished by a letter from Mr. R. W. Horton to Mr. Hankey of the L.M.S., dated Downing Street, 20th December 1824, to the effect that the Governor has been told to ' make no final grant of lands claimed by the inhabitants of Bethelsdorp until His Majesty's pleasure should be signified on the subject '.   In November 1825 Mr. Hankey reported to Philip that Lord Bathurst had at last ' decided in favour of Bethelsdorp in the land case '.   There was no word of compensation to the grantee, P. Marais, when London ordered restoration to Bethelsdorp.   [1] Cape Town Archives, vol. 388.

[2] Quoted, Cory, ii, p. 284.   Pringle was for a short time Editor of *Blackwood's Magazine*, but fell out with the publishers on politics and had to give it up.   (Scott's *Journal*, edn. 1890, p. 282, *note*.)

Edinburgh. The *Advertiser* was published by George Greig, with Pringle and his friend Fairbairn behind him. Before the country had fairly settled down to the novelty of having its own newspapers, public excitement was worked up to a high pitch in the first half of 1824 by a series of sensational trials: the failure of one Launcelot Cooke's action against the Collector of Customs, with whom he had some difference about the control of prize slaves; Cooke's prosecution for libel, in circumstances which made him appear a martyr, sacrificed to cover the mal-practices of this official; the association of the same Cooke with the ex-convict attorney William Edwards, and their ioint acquittal; the further trial of Edwards in April or May, marked by his unrestrained and scandalous reflections on the authorities, including the Fiscal, and even the Governor himself. Then came the curious episode of a libellous 'Placard' discovered posted on a tree on the *Heerengracht* on the morning of June the 1st, and the complication of the issue by the efforts to dis-cover a culprit; the attempted escape of Edwards and his trans-portation, with the subsequent prosecution of Captain Carnall for his share in the escapade; finally a sentence of imprison-ment and banishment passed upon Mr. Bishop Burnett, whose law-suits had for so long absorbed the time and energies of the law-courts, but whose escape in the end was connived at, so that he was able to carry his grievances with him to London.[1]

This unusual train of happenings naturally put a severe strain upon the political temper and sagacity both of the autocratic Government and of the fledgling Press. So much popular interest was aroused by the Edwards trial that no restricting 'prospectus', and no official 'conditions' ('the strict exclusion from the paper of all topics of political or personal controversy'[2]) could suffice to prevent difficulties and differ-ences between Press and Governor. In May 1824, accordingly, while the Edwards trial was proceeding, the Fiscal, resentful of hints already published, or fearful that more might follow, intervened. Sending for Greig, the printer of the *Commercial Advertiser*,[3] he warned him that it was only on condition of being strictly non-political that his publication was allowed; and demanded security for the observance of these terms.

---

[1] For a full account of all these happenings, see Cory, ii, ch. vi.
[2] Bathurst to Somerset, quoted, Cory, ii, p. 285.
[3] 'The truth is Mr. Greig was put down, not for anything he did or said, but from an apprehension that he would publish Edwards' trial' (Philip to L.M.S., 27th February 1825).

Greig, or Pringle and Fairbairn, who were behind him, there-upon suspended publication, but were none the less able to publish 'Facts connected with the stopping of the Press, and the censorship of the Fiscal'. The upshot was that on 8th May the Governor, on the advice of the Fiscal, issued a warrant 'to seal up all and every press or presses', ordering Greig 'to leave the Colony within one month from the date hereof'.

A few days later, on 13th May, the *South African Magazine* was in similar trouble, not, as it chanced, about the trials, but through the Governor's dislike of an apparently temperate and well-informed article by Pringle on 'The Present State and Prospects of the English Emigrants in South Africa'. On the 15th May, Pringle in his turn was sent for and warned; with Fairbairn, he retorted the next day by announcing the dis-continuance of the *Magazine* 'as inconsistent with our per-sonal safety', and incidentally, after a stormy interview with the Governor himself, on the 18th handed in his resignation of office as Librarian.[1] Within ten days, therefore, both these journals came to an end, and the Colony was reduced once more to dependence on the official *Cape Gazette*.

Now though the conjuncture of events may have been fortuitous, some outbreak was not unlikely owing to the severe restraint imposed by the system of government upon Cape society. That there was popular support for any newspaper showed that colonists were beginning to be aware of themselves as a community, and likely to demand some say in their own government; the countenance given to the uncontrolled extravagances of an adventurer like Edwards was a sign that there were sane citizens who felt that his assault upon the rulers of the country was not wholly without justification. At the same time, no doubt the colonists' leaders were difficult and even intemperate. Pringle was touchy, and in his inter-view with the Governor, almost insolent; Edwards was a 'bounder'; Philip must have appeared pompous and inter-fering, with a range far beyond the legitimate affairs of his own missions. But in the absence of any kind of popular and representative assembly, when even public meetings were strictly controlled and but grudgingly allowed, it was only through pushing individuals that grievances could find expres-sion at all. The test of a Governor, under such conditions, would have been his ability to tide the Colony over an inevitably difficult period of transition.

[1] See Cory, ii, pp. 285 ff.

For such a task (and this is in reality the main charge to be laid against him) Lord Charles was eminently unfitted. Born of the ducal House of Beaufort, confident in the support of the parliamentary borough interest of his family, he was the complete aristocrat: courtly, and, so long as he was not crossed, courteous. There is no reason to doubt that he was genuinely concerned for the interests of the Colony over which he ruled. When his departure was bruited in 1825, some at least of the Dutch colonists petitioned the King against the calumniation by ill-disposed persons of a Governor whose benevolent measures and upright conduct had done so much for the welfare of the country.[1] Like the gentleman he was, he did much for the permanent improvement of the breed of horses, and like the great Norman, he loved the chase and the high deer. But with all his estimable qualities he remained, to the end, of a thoroughly oligarchical temper, careful of the pickings of office for dependants like his undistinguished son,[2] with a full share of the limitations, and all the prejudices, of the Tories of the Reaction. It is little wonder therefore that his handling of popular discontents in 1824 was tactless and clumsy.

The crisis came, moreover, at an unfortunate moment in the history of his administration. For many years Somerset's Colonial Secretary and chief adviser was Colonel Bird, a man of some force and considerable experience. About this time the Governor seems to have tired of his secretary, whose Roman Catholic connection laid him open to attack. In a letter dated 13th March 1824, Earl Bathurst announced Bird's dismissal, and though his successor, Sir Richard Plaskett, took office only on the 31st of August, it seems likely that the news must have arrived about the height of the crisis, that it was not unexpected, that Bird's influence must have been at a low ebb, and that July and August may have been a period of virtual interregnum in the Colonial Secretary's office. Though in Philip's early years his opinion of Colonel Bird fluctuated considerably, he more than once spoke of him as the real ruler of the Colony; on 18th September 1823 he wrote: 'We gain nothing by the removal of Lord Charles Somerset, if Colonel Bird is left behind'. There is not much doubt, however, that Dr. Philip's maturer views were more correct.

[1] See Cory, ii, p. 320.
[2] Henry Somerset rose ultimately to be a Major-General, and did over twenty years of service on the Kafir frontier, in spite of glaring mistakes. See, *e.g.*, Cory, ii, p. 239, iii, 89.

In a paper dated July 1831, provoked by reading a pamphlet which Colonel Bird had published in 1827, he writes:

> Lord Bathurst's conduct against Colonel Bird was as silly as it was unjust.   Instead of befriending Lord Charles as he should have done, by restraining his violence and correcting his prejudices, and keeping him on terms with the only man who could have saved him (Colonel Bird), he joined him against that man, entered into his feelings and violence, cut him off from the Governor and used all his influence to run him down.   Col. Bird was the only man in the Colony who could have saved Lord Charles, and have continued to manage (?) his system of Government, and Colonel Bird was no sooner out of office than this began to appear.   As soon as Lord Charles got rid of Colonel Bird, he seemed like a boy let loose from school.   He jumped and frisked (?) about, playing all manner of foolish tricks, till he fell and brought down his patron, Lord Bathurst, with him.

Nothing short of some such removal of restraint can serve to explain the utter irresponsibility of a good many of the Governor's actions in the second half of 1824.   For a month or two he behaved like one who was *fey*.   In the virtual suppression of the two papers it may be true that he was not entirely to blame; but his subordinate, the Fiscal, was certainly tactless and unduly interfering.   In attempting to force an unpopular Landdrost on to the controlling body of the Settlers' Fund, and even printing a pamphlet in support of one party in a public controversy, the Governor became involved in a conflict in which public opinion among the still distressed settlers seems to have been solidly ranged against him.[1]   But in addition, not only was Greig summarily banished, but the ridiculous episode of the 'Placard', which was supposed to libel persons in high places, was made an occasion for a wholesale use of search warrants in a hopeless attempt to find a culprit. The 'Literary and Scientific Society' of Pringle and Fairbairn was strangled at its birth because of their connection with it, in spite of the countenance given by the Chief Justice, Sir John Truter, and other highly respectable citizens.   Not unnaturally also, Pringle, Philip, and others suffered some social ostracism, when it was made known that they were 'obnoxious' to Government House.[2]   In September Duncan Campbell

---

[1] See, *e.g.*, Cory, ii, p. 166.
[2] Dr. Philip writes (undated): ' My name has been handed about on a list of persons obnoxious to the Government, and on one occasion given to the Fiscal to occupy a place in a Search Warrant, with a view to get possession of my papers.   More than eight days ago, I was singled out and examined in the office of the Fiscal respecting an attempt to form a literary society, which contained upon its lists the

complained to Pringle from Grahamstown of the 'Reign of Terror' (his petition for a free Press had to be sent in with only forty names). It is true that, with Government countenance, one William Bridekirk was authorized to use Greig's printing material to make good the deficiency, and for a time continued to publish *The South African Chronicle and Mercantile Advertiser*; but this was 'to all intents a Government organ',[1] and did little to fill the gap.[2] There was really some justification for the view expressed by Philip and Fairbairn that the 'fixed policy' of the Governor was to

put down everything that indicated the slightest freedom of thought or action, and, after the principle of the Philosopher of Florence, to strike down everything and every person that might assume a character of independence.

His opposition 'to a Free Press, and especially to the missionaries, was not on personal but on political grounds', and because, in case of conflict, 'he dreaded the power of the L.M.S. and its Friends at Home'. Once the public opinion of the Colony had been wakened to self-expression, there was to be no rest for the Governor till the essential freedom of the Press had been vindicated, and absolute government somewhat restricted and modified by constitutional restraints.

In all this commotion Dr. Philip came in for special attention, and the Philip papers serve to throw light on some points that have been a little obscure. Dr. Philip's interests, not to say 'meddlings', were undoubtedly very wide; but his prominence in the controversies of this time, and the way he was singled out by Somerset for attack, are on the face of it surprising. Suddenly, and without warning, on the 18th of July Dr. Philip, who in March or April was dining at the Governor's table, and being consulted on questions of public importance, became almost the principal object of attack in

names of the Chief Justice, etc. . . . Yet I had proposed that His Excellency should be nominated as Patron of the Society!'

About the same time the Rev. A. Smith of Uitenhage proposed to found a 'society for the communication of religious and general instruction to all classes of people in the district'. On the 23rd of September 1824 Mr. P. G. Brink wrote on behalf of the Governor to Mr. Smith that 'as it is inconsistent with his duty to permit the establishment of an association which would not answer the end of its institution, His Excellency must decline to assent to the measure proposed at this moment'.

[1] Theal, i, p. 359.
[2] For a Grahamstown opinion, see Chapter IX, above, p. 117.

a 'Secret and Confidential' despatch, of more than eight
pages, in Somerset's own handwriting.[1]

> Earl Bathurst is informed that the Governor has sent a rebuke to
> the Court of Justice for permitting Edwards' outburst, but must avoid
> appearing to 'shake the Government by dividing it, and bringing the
> laws and authorities into contempt'.   For Edwards' attack on himself
> the real blame must rest on 'Philip—the *Reverend* as he styles himself
> —Pringle, Fairbairn and one Wright. . . . Philip was (my information
> gives me to understand) the real writer for that seditious Press. . . . I
> would rejoice in an opportunity to expose Philip and Wright; but
> though I am aware of all they do by secret intelligence, I should, if
> I were to bring their conduct forward, disclose my only source of
> intelligence upon which I depend. . . .[2]   It turns out that the sealed
> press was Philip's, and that Philip was in league with the Press.'

He gives the Moravian and Wesleyan missionaries a good
character, but he is violent in denunciation of 'Scotch Independents' who must be kept out of 'politics' . . . 'under
penalty of instant dismissal'.   A few months later, in October,
when indeed Dr. Philip had come into prominence as a leader
of the 'Settlers' against Somerset's protégé, the Landdrost
of Albany, the Governor began to denounce a 'conspiracy
against himself', adding: 'Philip should be removed'.[3]

Now there seemed to be some evidence against Philip, and
on the face of it, Somerset had a little justification for assuming
that he was in some way concerned.   To begin with, he was
a personal friend of Pringle and Fairbairn, the real editors of
the paper, and Greig, the printer, was sufficiently intimate
and respectful to send Philip the news from exile in London.[4]
Moreover, the press, or one of the presses, used by Greig to
produce the offending *Commercial Advertiser* was undoubtedly
the property of Philip or of the L.M.S.   The truth would
seem to be that Greig, unable to get a printing press in the
Colony, borrowed an old one from Philip, on condition of
repairing it for the Society.   From December to February,
when the newspaper began, Dr. Philip was away in the country.
In July, after Greig had left the Colony, Philip, with the rash-
ness of innocence, applied to the Government for the return

[1] Somerset to Bathurst, 'Secret and Confidential', 18th July
1824.   Cape Town Duplicate Despatches, vol. 12.
[2] See above, Chapter XIII, p. 180.   The quality of Somerset's
information is open to grave doubt, since he solemnly credits Philip
with £4000 a year, of which £3000 was for 'luxuries for himself'!
(Philip's salary, not at first a fixed sum, was apparently about £300.)
His pension from October 1850 was to be £200.
[3] Somerset to Bathurst, 'Confidential', 11th October 1824.
[4] Greig to Philip, 10th November 1824.

of the confiscated press, as the property of his Society, and was promptly met with a stiff demand for security against its use 'for political or personal controversy'.[1] From later correspondence it appears that the type used was Greig's own, and the press, as Philip agreed, worth no more than £18 or £20; also that the loan was very casually arranged. After some dispute, in which Greig claimed that the cost of repairs was greater than its value, in January 1826 he offered to take the press at a valuation. With regard to the conduct of the paper, however, Philip's only concern seems to have been to warn Greig at the time of the Edwards trial against publishing anything offensive to the Government. In June, though his sympathy was obvious, he seems to have declined to take any active part in support of the Memorial for a Free Press owing to his 'delicate situation', pleading in a letter to Pringle:

The manner in which I am circumstanced, standing, I may say, alone in the great question relating to the Aborigines of South Africa now pending, has induced me, finding that all my endeavours to prevent this crisis have failed, to abstain from uniting with either party, and made me now stand aloof from the present discussion.

In a later version he adds (to the L.M.S., 27th February 1825):

No sooner did the paper assume the slightest appearance of hostility to the Government than I interposed, and, had it not been for the madness of the Government itself, I should have saved them from all the odium and inconvenience of putting down a free press. Now the action will be published in England. . . .

Dr. Philip for his part, being obviously innocent, was at first frankly astonished at the virulence of the Governor's hostility to himself, some of it soon to be flagrantly personal. He cannot have suspected at the time it was written the tenor of the July despatch. On the contrary, the tone of his own letters is so friendly that there is no reason to suppose that he had his tongue in his cheek when, as late as the 25th of June, in applying for land for Bethelsdorp, he wrote that he 'desired to give His Excellency an opportunity of showing his good will to the L.M.S.'[2] Barely a month later, on the 29th of July, he was writing that he had Mr. Wilberforce Bird's authority for saying that Somerset hoped to get him identified with Greig, and, if possible, entrapped as guilty of libel, in order 'to destroy my influence by having me described as a " convict "

[1] Correspondence in Cape Town Archives, July and August 1824.
[2] A minute on the Cape Town Archives copy of this letter notes that the matter is ' postponed '.

bound for Botany Bay'.   Soon, indeed, he had ample justification for a remark, repeated in several letters, that 'Lord Charles
Somerset has drawn the sword and thrown away the scabbard';
and so far as he could, by representations to the visiting Commissioners, and by preparing his case for an appeal to London,
he took up the challenge, urging his Society to send all his
papers to Lord Bathurst, extenuating nothing.   Both Somerset
and Philip, however, were really under a misapprehension; and
some of their conflict was mutual misunderstanding.   The
Governor's wrath was due to his firm conviction that Dr. Philip
was the real power behind the Press, and primarily responsible
for the unpopularity of his administration.   Philip, on the
other hand, was only very indirectly concerned with the establishment of either of the newspapers.   Attacked as he was,
therefore, he quite mistakenly drew the conclusion that the
attack upon himself was but part of a 'conspiracy' against the
missions under his control—the missions, as such, being probably a matter of sublime ind .erence to Lord Charles Somerset.

A year later, when the storm had partly subsided, Philip
wrote to the Directors thanking them for calling his attention
to a 'disrespectful remark' in one of his letters to the Governor.
He pleads in extenuation his 'arduous work', and that correspondence, necessitated by his difficulties with the Government,
frequently kept him in his study 'till one and two in the morning', with Mrs. Philip as his only adviser.   He might, he said,
have 'paid the missionaries to do nothing, and so gained
popularity; the only alternatives were to take them all back to
England, or to fight as he had done'.   The real cause of conflict,
he considered, was '——'s determination to resist any improvement in the condition of the Hottentots, and if possible to put
an end to our missions'.[1]   This exaggerated idea of a conspiracy became, in fact, an obsession; and if Dr. Philip in these
years turned 'politician', it was apprehension caused by
Somerset's action that drove him to it.   For the moment the
Colony was with him.   With an eye for big issues he wrote:

My struggle has at last merged in a general question respecting the
aborigines; but it did not commence here; and now that the Colonial
Government has brought it to this crisis, the missions and the rights
of the people must stand or fall together.   I wish the Missionary
Rooms may understand the question in this light.   It is this fear that
urges upon me the necessity of visiting England.[2]

---

[1] Letters of 4th May and 23rd May 1825.
[2] Philip to his friend the Rev. T. Durant, from Bethelsdorp, 1st
July 1825.

Two episodes of this personal conflict have been dragged from the obscurity they deserved, and should be restored to their proper setting in the Somerset *imbroglio*.[1]

By the time of the Governor's despatch[2] to Earl Bathurst it was known to His Excellency that in 1815 Philip was involved in a dispute about the qualifications of a candidate for the charge of the Scots Church in London Wall. Philip no doubt had a little 'burnt his fingers'. Having given some sort of support to a certain Mr. Rennie, he later qualified his testimonial, and when challenged, offered a rather lame explanation of his reasons for a change of mind. Now, though, by proclamation of June 11, 1824, the Governor had imposed severe restrictions on printing of a 'political or personal nature', in October there appeared, 'printed at the Government Press', certain 'Extracts from a Statement on the Late Divisions at the Scots Church, London Wall'. The Governor's despatch of October 11 says expressly that it was printed for the purpose of exposing 'Philip's sense of honour'. Examination of this precious pamphlet[3] suggests comments. The original professed to be a statement of 'All the Facts', by the Rev. A. Barclay, A.M.: the Cape Government pamphlet consists of pp. 73-113 and 154-162, (a total of 48 pages) out of the 162 of the original. But even these pages suffice to show that Philip's name was involved only in one incident in a violent congregational dispute. The illiterate spelling, which was the subject of such ridicule, is obviously in part due to his copyist, though the style may also suggest over-hasty action, without due consideration or consultation. As an Independent, he was ill-advised to seem to interfere in the affairs of a congregation of the Scottish Established Church. On the other hand, the 'statement of facts' itself is obviously *ex parte*: Mr. Rennie was an ambitious youth, anxious to push his candidature by means of support from one who evidently stood well in the North of Scotland; and Philip in his change of attitude may have come to suspect him of 'climbing'. This seems in fact to have been the opinion of the elders of the Church, and the 'Divisions' at London Wall were primarily a sharp dispute between the Kirk Session and a congregational Committee.

In his desperate anxiety to discredit Philip's character by any and every means that offered, Lord Charles Somerset stooped officially to rake this petty squabble out of the forgotten past. A second episode had better have remained in oblivion.

Towards the end of the year, Messrs. A. Murray of Graaff-Reinet, and Smith of Uitenhage, were in Cape Town for the first Synod of the Dutch Reformed Church, and called on Dr. Philip. The conversation naturally turned on the state of the Hottentots, and Dr. Philip soon after seems to have mentioned the talk to the Crown Commissioners,

---

[1] Cory, ii, pp. 404 ff., on *The Case of the Scots Church in London Wall*; and pp. 416-17, on the Rev. Andrew Murray.

[2] On 18th July 1824 (Cape Town Duplicate Despatches) Somerset calls Bathurst's attention to the original London Wall pamphlet.

[3] Kindly lent me by Mr. J. G. Gubbins of Ottoshoop.

and to have suggested that they might take the evidence of Mr. Murray. As Landdrost of Mr. Murray's district, Stockenstrom's name came into the discussion, and in the electric atmosphere of Cape Town it soon got about, and came to the ears of the Governor, that Philip had traduced the Landdrost, or at least made Mr. Murray appear to do so. The result was that after Mr. Murray and his companion had left Cape Town, the Governor, according to Pringle, 'scented an opportunity for assailing the indomitable Dr. Philip',[1] and sent post haste to recall Mr. Murray from the Brak River, and Mr. Smith all the way from Uitenhage, to Cape Town. He then questioned Mr. Murray, and instructed him to write a full account of the conversation, Mr. Smith to vouch for the accuracy of this report, which does not appear to have been in any way epoch-making. Justifiably annoyed at this sequel to a visit of courtesy, Mr. Murray gave Dr. Philip short shrift, refused or made no attempt to get any explanation, and closed discussion with the curt and crushing note, unearthed long after, out of its real context, for the sole purpose of throwing discredit on Dr. Philip. The incident may show at most a certain indiscretion on Philip's part in retailing even to the Commissioners a private conversation which was so liable to involve another in controversy. But however pardonably, Mr. Murray's note too bears on the face of it marks of unconsidered haste: 'Being just on the eve of leaving Town', it begins. Happily the episode was soon closed; as it should have remained, but that three honoured names were involved in its unearthing. Captain Stockenstrom, who was supposed to have been calumniated, apparently did not think so himself; and it was while living as a guest in the Landdrost's house at Graaff-Reinet that, in the following August, Dr. Philip called on Mr. Murray and effected a lasting reconciliation.[2] Once more the real offender was the Governor, whose childish vendetta against his critics led him into the pettiness of recalling the two ministers to Cape Town on such a futile errand.

Finally, on 27th January 1825, the Governor forwarded with his despatch to London what purported to be a *Biographical Sketch of John Philip*, 'formerly a journeyman weaver, now head of a Missionary Society at the Cape, and calling himself *Doctor* Philip'.[3] This introductory sentence, in itself, shows what an extraordinary document this was to have found a place in the despatches of any serious and responsible Governor. Nor was Somerset discreetly silent about his plans. It came to Philip's ears that it was a favourite subject of bets at Government House that in a few months he would be obliged to return home; and on the 10th of February, a fortnight after

---

[1] Pringle to Stockenstrom, 17th December 1824.

[2] 'Mr. & Mrs. Murray have just left after returning our call.' *Journal* of Philip's tour, 8th August 1825, which refers to a (missing) letter to Mr. Faure for a full account of this reconciliation. Casual references in later letters show that Murray and Philip were on calling terms as a matter of course.

[3] 'Moodie Papers', Cape Town Archives, vol. 699.

this despatch was written, Dr. Samuel Bailey, head of the Somerset Hospital, wrote to him that he had it

from a source in which I have the greatest confidence that it is the intention of this Government to request that Lord Bathurst will interest himself with the Directors for your immediate removal from this Colony. . . . (Such is) that dread and alarm which all iniquitous rulers have of being under the eye and observation of honest and honourable men possessing that weight and influence you have so justly acquired and maintained in this colony.

By this time, however, the Cape Governor had shot his bolt. On Earl Bathurst's doorstep in London, Sir Rufane Donkin, the champions of the Settlers, Greig the printer, as well as Bishop Burnett and Captain Carnall, were shouting against him; even the *Times* directed some of its thunder against 'this borough Governor',[1] and Bathurst was little likely, for the beautiful eyes of Lord Charles Somerset, to incur still more criticism from the leaders of Exeter Hall, who were already pressing the rights of the Hottentots. It was rather Somerset's own position that was now precarious. In Grahamstown, indeed, he showed more discretion (see Chapter IX), and helped to bring the Settlers to a better frame of mind. In March and April he turned at last to consider the removal of the missionary Seidenfaden, who had so long made ruin of the Zuurbraak Institution; and in the lull, Dr. Philip set out in May on a long tour of the stations, to arm himself for the battle in England to get

the aborigines put upon the same footing as Europeans with respect to law and privilege, since short of this, laws made in England will be evaded in this Colony, and everything respecting them will soon return to the old condition.

Thus the principles of the 50th Ordinance were already shaping themselves in his conversation; as was the plan of the *Researches*.

I see it my duty on my return from the interior to visit England. In that case I shall lay before Lord Bathurst numerous and large documents, and, if that fails, shall instantly and on my own responsibility lay the whole before the British public.[2]

Then, early in May, the first Legislative Council was sworn in; and though its composition was entirely official and its power insignificant, this was the first check on the Governor's

___
[1] *Times*, 3rd November 1824.
[2] 29th May 1825.

absolutism.[1] As for Somerset's personal position, in the end
of June Dr. Bailey wrote from London that he had it from
Mr. Brougham that 'the thing is done':

'I (Brougham) have this morning received a private communication from Mr. Canning that he is recalled, and that Mr. Canning has
given a pledge that Lord Charles have *permission to return to this
country*.' . . . Moreover, the *Gazette* of yesterday morning announces
the appointment of Major-General Bourke to be Lieut.-Governor of
the Eastern districts in South Africa, though why Ministers still
persist in this humbugging system I cannot make out, when everybody
must know that this General is sent out to relieve Lord Charles for
the time being: in fact it is well known in certain quarters that he was
absolutely recalled five months ago, and remained on the recall list
for four days; but for the interference of the Duke of Beaufort he
would now have been in England. . . . If I am not very much misinformed, Lord Bathurst will do everything in his power to quash
the inquiry of the Commissioners, not perhaps from an overstock of
affection for Lord Charles, but for fear of the public knowing that he
has suppressed for many months information which, in justice, he
ought to have acted upon, but which he neglected under apprehension
of losing the Beaufort interest.

Substantially Dr. Bailey's gossip was accurate, and he was
right in laying stress on the 'Beaufort Interest'. Though his
'leave of absence' was decreed in June 1825, and unofficially
known at the Cape in September,[2] Somerset did not leave the
Cape till March 1826; and even then he continued 'on leave'
till 1827, not despairing of return. It seems to have been only
the political changes at Home, the fall of Bathurst with Lord
Liverpool, and the succession of Canning's more liberal
administration, with some continued pressure from his critics,
that eventually forced his resignation.[3] The loose talk of

---

[1] 'The reason for the Council is said to be that it may interfere
between the Governor and the people, but our wiseacres cannot say
whether a shield is intended, and whether that shield is to protect the
people, the governed, or the Governor' (Philip to Bailey, 6th May
1825).

[2] *E.g.*, Faure to Philip, chap. ix, p. 119.

[3] The Philip MSS. contain several pages of political gossip on
questions arising from Lord Charles Somerset's return to England;
e.g., in a letter of July 1831: 'Pringle was invited by Mr. Rogers, the
poet, to breakfast with him one morning. He could not go that
morning, and on meeting with Mr. Rogers next day, Mr. Rogers said:
"I am sorry that you were not with us yesterday. We had your old
friend Mr. Wilmot Horton with us. In the course of conversation
I asked him if, among the changes which were taking place, we were
to have Lord Bathurst and himself back again at the Colonial Office.
Mr. Horton, starting to his feet, exclaimed with great vehemence:
'No! that d—d *Times* has turned us out of office and will keep us
out of office'." The paragraph in the *Times* to which he referred

impeachment came, indeed, to nothing; his powers as Governor were so wide that he probably did nothing technically illegal. But Governors have been dismissed for less than his incompetence, and it seems incredible that responsible persons in Downing Street should have contemplated the possibility of sending him back—even to carry on as before; it was still more inauspicious for the ushering in of changes which were now inevitable; and only the power and influence of Somerset's family connection constrained Ministers to contemplate even the possibility of reappointing him to his post as Governor of the Cape.

Meantime the fight for the Press continued at the Cape, and John Fairbairn emerged as the protagonist of freedom. Tempers were still on edge. In August 1825 Greig returned from London with Lord Bathurst's permission to resume publication of the *Commercial Advertiser*, provided he adhered to the terms of his original prospectus. Fairbairn seems to have been the editor and principal partner in the enterprise,[1] and he at once embarked on a somewhat truculent correspondence with the Crown Commissioners. Reviewing the history of the Press dispute, he wrote:

'I could not at once admit the *idea* of a Government jealous of such an undertaking, or of so obscure an individual as myself,' adding cryptically, 'I had read Machiavelli, but did not believe in him'. He also complained that originally he 'would express himself freely as a matter of course (*e.g.*, on Settlers' troubles), thinking that

---

was a series of strictures on the Government of Lord Charles Somerset, and they were all of them furnished by Mr. Pringle.'

Dr. Philip clearly and carefully avoided all entanglement with Somerset's mere political critics, and confined his efforts, as in the *Researches*, to championing the cause of the 'Aborigines'. Contemporary letters are incomplete, but he seems to have made it clear in interviews with Mr. James Stephen and others at the Colonial Office that he considered Somerset an important part of the 'oppressive' system. His maturest views were summarized in a document of about 1845, as follows:

'The line of policy (Somerset) pursued toward the English Settlers, his conduct toward Sir Rufane Donkin, his quarrel with Colonel Bird, his bearing toward the Crown Commissioners of Inquiry, and his persecution of Mr. Pringle, involved him in difficulties out of which his friends could not extricate him . . . and he had to come Home to answer the charges against him.'

[1] Greig is to publish what Fairbairn sends him, or Fairbairn 'will get another printer'. Correspondence with the Commissioners is to be sent to 'Brougham or Hume, or both', and Pringle will see the importance of keeping this branch of business in our own hands (Fairbairn to Pringle, 29th September 1825).

the Government would welcome the truth; but that a year or so later he would do so expecting Government hostility and opposition '.[1]

To forbid the journal to deal with matters concerning the Governor was impossible, since the Governor 'dabbled with everything'; even in Lord Bathurst's opinion 'the endangering the peace and safety of the Colony' was the only ground for interference on the part of the Governor. The Commissioners for their part showed such caution, defending, for example, the suppression of the Literary and Scientific Society on the ground that such a Society, run by the Press people, was inadvisable at that juncture, when opinion was excited, that Fairbairn concluded that the inquiry was 'a piece of fudge', that they had no intention of inquiring into particular grievances:

I am determined to try the question respecting the liberty of the Press here. If it turns out that we are not free, I mean to propose immediately a Petition to the House of Commons on the subject, including a severe censure on the policy of Lord Bathurst.[2]

Meantime in private Fairbairn used still more unmeasured terms. To D. Moodie he wrote on the 25th of September:

Greig was not the lad to make too good a bargain with such crafty carles as Lord Bathurst and the Attorney-General. That noble Earl has now in writing identified himself with Lord Charles' views respecting newspapers, having bound Greig over to his old Prospectus, and directed him to get a licence from the Governor and Council.

For doubt of the secrecy of the Post Office, the Governor's name is usually given as 'our old Philosopher'—or in Scots, 'The Muckle Sumph'!—but here he continues:

Horton said he could not imagine that Lord Charles Somerset had anything but the good of the Colony at heart. . . . I have nothing to do with his heart. It may be in the right place . . . only let him keep off his hands and his ill-scraped tongue.

Referring to the Commissioner's plea that the Governor's attitude to the Press was justified by the state of excitement in the Colony, he maintains that 'the agitation was really the work of the martyred Governor about that infamous placard'. Stressing the need for 'witnesses in duplicate' in any representations they might make, he concludes:

Under a reign of terror, falsehood saps from coward to coward, till

---

[1] Fairbairn to His Majesty's Commissioners, 25th August 1825.
[2] Letters of 26th and 29th September 1825 to the Commissioners, and Fairbairn to Pringle, 7th October 1825.

Truth is not only driven to the bottom of her own well, but buried there under a heap of stones.[1]

Fairbairn, moreover, was concerned for the welfare of the country.   The tragedy about that

consummation of earthly ills—the Government of Lord Charles Somerset in South Africa—is the poverty, dependence and local situation of the people.   They are dispersed over an immense and almost pathless country.   The men in office who should form a sort of aristocracy are liable to be deprived, almost of their daily bread, at the caprice of one man whom neither they nor their fathers chose to rule over them, and the whole people have been plundered or led to ruin by a rapacious and wrong-headed Government.[2]

But though, by December, Somerset's fate was sealed, the troubles of Cape journalists were not ended, and on 14th January 1826 Fairbairn's *New Organ* was suspended by the Governor, on the old grounds of failure to adhere to the terms of Greig's Prospectus; in April his action in suppressing the paper was confirmed by Earl Bathurst.   At the end of the year, indeed, Earl Bathurst himself intervened to order the cancellation of Greig's licence for the offence of reproducing from the *Times* an article which reflected on the doings of Lord Charles Somerset; on 10th May 1827 this order took effect, and a second time the *Commercial Advertiser* had to close down.[3]   It was, therefore, not only the personality of Lord Charles Somerset, but the whole system and structure of the Cape Government that was incompatible with any real freedom of the Press.   This time Fairbairn himself carried his appeal to Downing Street, and after delays due to political changes in England, was able, in July 1828, to return with guarantees which set the Press free from the direct control of Governor and Council.

These events at the Cape are not to be judged without some reference to the situation in Great Britain.   Lord Charles Somerset, with little originality of his own, was, like his immediate superior, Earl Bathurst, bound by the conventions of his class, thoroughly steeped, as it was at that time, in the fears and prejudices of the Tory Reaction.   It was only when the anti-Jacobin panic of the war era had somewhat subsided that there was any hope of the rise to power in Great Britain

[1] Fairbairn to Pringle, 7th October 1825.
[2] Fairbairn to Pringle, 21st October 1825.
[3] The Acting Governor, indeed, combined with liberal sentiments a belief that 'some efficient control of the Press here is without doubt necessary'. (Cory, ii, p. 332.)

of a younger generation, who might be prepared to recognize that, even in a new British Colony, it might be safer and more expedient to meet than to repress popular demands like that for a free Press.   On a very small scale, with much that was inevitably petty and factious, the manifestations of popular discontent at the Cape were the local expression of the British movement which culminated in the Reform Act of 1832. The coming of the Albany Settlers, some of whom no doubt had been active supporters of the British Reform Movement, does not sufficiently explain the growth of political activity at the Cape; Grahamstown indeed was rather ineffective in its political protests. Except that Pringle was originally a Settler, even the demand for a free Press, probably the most effective popular movement, the very epitome as it was of the prevailing discontents, owed very little to the Settlers. The collaboration with Pringle of the Rev. A. Faure, in their bi-lingual *Magazine*, together with the little-noticed emergence in 1824 of a regularly constituted Synod of the Dutch Reformed Church, and a few years later the establishment of a wholly Dutch newspaper, *De Zuid Afrikaan*, may be signs that the Dutch also were coming to share in the development of the Cape as a real community.

For all its significance, however, the mere Press Ordinance of 1828 could not by itself have been of much avail; for not only was administration of the law wholly in the hands of the Executive Government, and the judges nominees of the Governor, but its interpretation lay ultimately with an Appeal Court presided over by the Governor himself. The really important constitutional innovation was not the Press Law, still less the merely advisory Council established in 1825, but the Charter of Justice, which took effect on 1st January 1828. Following on the lines sketched by Sir Richard Ottley in 1823 (see above, p. 190), the Charter took the laws out of the hands of the Governor and placed them under the impartial control of an independent Bench. If, in future, the Press, by its criticisms, seemed to endanger the peace and safety of the Colony, it might be subject to prosecution in the ordinary courts, but not to arbitrary suppression by order of the Governor. Later Governors had direct legislative as well as executive powers, but the judicature at least was now independent.

Some of the incidental changes of 1828 are open to criticism. The new stress on the use of English in the Courts was probably inevitable—efficient Dutch-speaking recruits to the legal service being hardly obtainable in the requisite numbers—but it was rashly done. (At the time, however, it was accepted with little expressed criticism,[1] and its importance has been anachronistically magnified in the twentieth century.) Again, the total abolition of the Boards of Heemraden was unfortunate, as snapping the only shadow of a link between the people themselves and the machinery that governed them. But the reforms of 1828 also came to a sudden full stop. Apart from the strengthening of the Council after 1834, by adding to it a body of unofficial members, there was, for more than twenty years, no further change in the constitutional position of the Central Government, and no approach to the 'representative institutions', confidently prognosticated in September 1825 as the outcome of the struggle.[2]

A common failure to recognize the significance of this abrupt stop arises from the habit of reading the history of South Africa through the eyes of the dominant colonists, as if the coloured races hardly affected the political situation. Now such constitutional progress as was effected in 1828 was due to the clear findings of the Crown Commissioners in a Report presented in September 1826, and acted upon comparatively promptly by Lord Bathurst's successor in office. It is no unwarranted exaggeration that no single individual did more than Dr. Philip, the champion of the coloured races, to bring about this initial development of colonial freedom. Even if he was not directly instrumental, through Mr. Wilberforce, in inducing Downing Street to initiate a full inquiry, his evidence on the working of the whole system of Government, and possibly also his personal share in the events of 1824 (the details of which he constantly kept before them),[3] clearly made a considerable impression on the Commissioners.

But about 1828 the hitherto latent divisions in colonial society became evident. A fierce controversy followed the enactment of Ordinance No. 50, for the liberation of 'Hottentots and other free persons of colour'. Dr. Philip and John Fairbairn, effective leaders of a united Colony in the contest with Governor Somerset, were now thrown into violent opposition to their former followers, and were for many years denounced as the 'Anti-Colonial Party'. The agitation against 'Vagrancy', which seemed to threaten the Hottentot

[1] The language question hardly figures among Trekker grievances, e.g. in Bird's *Annals of Natal*.
[2] Faure to Philip, quoted above, Chapter IX, p. 119.
[3] The Philip MSS., Correspondence with the Commissioners, 1823–25; also their Reports, e.g. in Theal's *Records*, xxxv.

P

legislation of 1828, was followed by a series of events arising from contact with the formidable Bantu race; and the distractions of Kafir Wars, and of the Great Trek, with the subsidiary complications of the Native Treaty States, completely dominated the domestic problems of the European Colonists till 1848. It was only then that parties came together again to protest against the proposal to make the Cape a convict station; then once more John Fairbairn, with the equally unpopular Andries Stockenstrom, emerged as the Cape leaders in a now formidable demand for a Parliamentary constitution. But until this reconciliation took place, the constitutional progress of the Cape Colony, which made so notable a beginning in 1828, had to wait full twenty years on the settlement of affairs for the coloured peoples, while controversy raged between the 'Colonial Party' on the one side and the agitators for a more liberal Native policy on the other.

Chapter XV

COLOUR ONCE MORE—THE EMANCIPATION OF THE HOTTENTOTS—ORDINANCE NO. 50

THIS often cited Ordinance No. 50, 'for improving the condition of the Hottentots and other free persons of colour at the Cape of Good Hope, and for consolidating and amending the Laws affecting those Persons', was promulgated by the Lieutenant-Governor, General Bourke, on the 17th July 1828. Not only as an epoch in the history of the coloured people, but for its reactions on the affairs and politics of the European colonists, this measure is of first-rate social importance.

So far as mere legislation could upset established social customs and over-ride the hard facts of economic helplessness, the position of the Hottentots was revolutionized. At one fell swoop all existing Proclamations like those of 1809 and 1812 (Chapters XI and XII above) were repealed. The important second clause, though its effect in equalizing the races has been exaggerated, swept away the law of Passes, the liability to summary correction, and any special obligations of forced labour, other than those that were the common duty of all citizens.[1] Clause 3 finally laid at rest the doubts that had

---

[1] The language of this clause is almost reminiscent of Magna Carta itself:

'And whereas by usage and custom of this Colony, Hottentots and other free persons of colour have been subjected to certain restraints as to their residence, mode of life, and employment, and to certain compulsory services to which others of His Majesty's subjects are not liable: Be it therefore enacted, that from and after the passing of this Ordinance, no Hottentot or other free person of colour, lawfully residing in this Colony, shall be subject to any compulsory service to which other of His Majesty's subjects therein are

arisen as to 'the competence of Hottentots and other free Persons of colour to purchase or possess land in this Colony'. Clause 4, on the ground that it was expedient to 'protect ignorant and unwary . . . persons aforesaid from the effects of improvident contracts for service', established a rule that oral contracts (the vast majority) should hold only from month to month; while Clause 5 limited even written contracts to twelve months, and required them to be registered by both parties together before a competent authority. Added to these innovations there were the old provisions in restraint of truck in liquor or tobacco, and clauses protecting servants against the detention of their goods or cattle. Various penalties were prescribed, and special provisions added to protect 'Prize' Negroes. In cases of dispute, wages were to be fixed by 'the Judge or Magistrate', the jurisdiction of the lesser officials being restricted to cases involving less than 20s. Later clauses drastically reformed, without abolishing, the laws of 'apprenticeship', requiring the wife to execute her own contract, and each of the children to be separately specified in any contract purporting to bind him. Children might be bound, boys till their eighteenth year, girls till sixteen, but for not more than seven years in all, and not in any case after the expiration of the parents' contract. There was to be no claim to the services of the children

'under colour of (their) having been fed or clothed by their employer . . . or under any other pretence whatever'; moreover, 'it shall and may be lawful for any contracting Hottentot to keep his or her children on the premises of the employer without contracting them', and, particularly, 'it shall not be lawful for the employer to claim the labour or services of such uncontracted children, by reason of their residence thereon'.

Thus all the major counts in the missionary indictment of the old system came under review, and the legal disability to hold land, the pass system, summary imprisonment, forced labour and apprenticeship (see Chapter XII) were either reformed or abolished. The Ordinance did not, however, as is still sometimes supposed, place the Hottentots upon a footing of absolute equality with the white colonists; the very wording of the law gives it special application only to 'Hottentots and

not liable, nor to any hindrance, molestation, fine, imprisonment, or punishment of any kind whatsoever, under the pretence that such person has been guilty of vagrancy or any other offence, unless after trial in due course of law; any custom or usage to the contrary in anywise notwithstanding.'

other free persons of colour'; the detailed regulation of conditions of service was expressly class legislation; and even the reformed system of 'apprenticeship' would have been a shock to the colonists, who complained of 'equality', had it been in any way applied to their own children.   For the rest, though formally repealed in 1842, the 50th Ordinance was actually reincorporated in later measures and remains the unmistakable basis of the Masters and Servants Laws that are in force both in the Cape and (1880) in the Transvaal to this day.   But great are the healing powers of use and wont.   Ordinance 50 was perhaps more liberal in a few details; but its successors went farther and enacted one law for masters and servants, irrespective of colour; and the measures that remain on the Statute Book are now even clung to with tenacity, by conservative legislators, as the accepted model for the regulation of relations with coloured servants.[1]

The general significance of the law of 1828, and even its precise origins,[2] have been somewhat obscured by the clouds of prejudice it raised at the time of its enactment.   The actual sequence of events is clear.   The Commissioner-General, Captain Stockenstrom, made suggestions for reform in a Memorandum submitted to General Bourke about April 1828; this secured the Governor's approval; the law was drafted by Judge Burton, and promulgated on the 17th July following.   It is absurd to suggest, though Philip had been in England for two years, that the Ordinance was entirely uninfluenced by the previous agitation and the criticisms directed by him against the very practices that were now reformed. Stockenstrom's views were those of a just and practical colonist, and could not be called sentimental; he laughs at the idea that 'whites have no business here'; he would be equally severe with robbers, be they black or white, holding that

the Natives would get no benefit either if we run away, or stay and have our throats cut, but they might benefit if we (justly) defend 'our own'.[3]

From 1819 onwards he and Philip met occasionally, or corresponded; in 1825 they 'talked it over' and 'agreed';[4] so

[1] Again cf. debates on Masters and Servants Law Amendment Bill, in Union Parliament, 1926, a measure designed to apply the law of 1880 to Native 'squatters' as to servants.

[2] Cory, ii, p. 371, *note*.   See also *note* on p. 232, below.

[3] Stockenstrom's *Autobiography* for 1826, vol. i, p. 243.

[4] 'The Landdrost here and I agree remarkably well on the subject of the aborigines' (Philip, from Graaff-Reinet, 2nd August 1825).

that there is good reason to believe that, even before he left for England, early in 1826, Captain Stockenstrom, the sponsor of the law of 1828, had reached some common basis with Dr. Philip. In 1832 Stockenstrom expressed a desire that they might 'continue to work together' for 'equal justice', and paid tribute to Philip's 'laudable zeal' for 'the weaker'.[1]

As a newcomer, General Bourke, the other principal in the case, was likely to act on the advice of men like the Commissioner-General. But before he came to the country, the heads of the London Missionary Society had forewarned him of the need for reform of the Hottentot laws. Before going out to relieve Lord Charles Somerset, General Bourke wrote to the L.M.S.:

> Though not a member of the Society I am extremely anxious for the improvement of the Hottentots, and without inquiry into the particular notions of Christianity inculcated, I shall, wherever it may be in my power, afford assistance to those missionaries who labour to raise the unhappy natives in the scale of civilized beings.[2]

This non-committal letter is enough to show at least a preliminary awareness of a Hottentot question, and indicates a direct link between Philip's criticisms in 1825 and the reforming measure of 1828. General Bourke's despatch of 22nd July 1828, forwarding the finished Ordinance to Mr. Huskisson, throws a little light on the interval between 1826 and 1828:

> The necessity for such a measure has been apparent to me from a very early period after my arrival. . . . I abstained from bringing my own measure until it was likely that none was to emanate from them, . . .

—that is to say, he waited in the hope of guidance from the Report of the Commissioners, 'whose attention it had engaged'.

Meantime Dr. Philip's activities were transferred to London, and were not without some bearing on the event. His own

---

Further, on 3rd November 1825, Stockenstrom wrote familiarly to Philip, noting with reference to a difference with Mr. Melville about Griqua and Bushman claims to Philippolis that it 'would be a pity if people who agree in general should fall out about trifles'. Philip at the same time wrote to the Directors rejoicing that he now had 'a few fellow-workers in a good cause'.

[1] Stockenstrom to Philip, October 1832.

[2] Reported to Dr. Philip on 4th November 1825 by Mr. Hankey, Treasurer of the L.M.S., and independently by R. Steven, a Director.

account is summarized in several documents,[1] obviously based on contemporary letters, a few of which survive:

Immediately on my arrival in London I received a note from Sir John Cam Hobhouse, stating that, having heard I had come home to impeach Lord Charles Somerset, he and some friends were ready to assist me, if I would come forward with an impeachment. To this note I replied that he must have been misinformed with respect to my object in coming to England; that I had come Home on a question involving the interests of the Hottentot people—that I had nothing to do with Lord Charles, futher than he might be implicated in that question as Governor of the Colony—that I certainly would have no part in any impeachment that might be brought forward against him: but that I should be greatly obliged to Sir John and to his friends if any would help me on my public question. To the above reply I received no answer. I found many at that time, who for party purposes, were willing to assist me in an impeachment of his Lordship, but took no interest in the deliverance of a people from the most cruel slavery, or in the salvation of the Missions.

After describing how, unexpectedly, he met Somerset's brother-in-law, the Hon. F. Calthorpe, at dinner, and was able to reassure the Beaufort family about his designs against the ex-Governor, he continues:

My first reception at the Board of Directors of the L.M.S. was gratifying: but I soon began to find that my labours were not known, nor was the object for which I had come home duly appreciated. I had the mortification to find that few of my friends understood me, that a great portion of the religious public thought I had stepped out of my sphere and had committed the deadly sin of having meddled with politics, and I found very little sympathy with my object in returning to England—nor were those impressions removed till the publication of my *Researches*. . . . Then (indeed) . . . I was congratulated on having written a book that was at first regarded as of an entirely political character, without having allowed myself to interfere with politics at all.

Meantime his own Directors were either difficult to move, or when they moved, ineffective:

I soon found that I should have a great deal to do before I could receive the co-operation I had anticipated. After the first greetings were over, I was told by an influential man that Lord Bathurst was opposed to my views—that the Directors could not enter into a contest with Government—that I must yield the point and drop the matter. In short I found that the Board was perfectly ignorant of the

---

[1] The quotations which follow are drawn from several long statements, drafted probably in 1845, when Dr. Philip supplied material that might be used by the compilers of a life of Sir T. Fowell Buxton. Several drafts survive, and the originals were in 1851 handed over by Sir E. Buxton to the care of the L.M.S.

question. A proposal was then made that I should inform the Board
as to what I had been doing in Africa, and I received the motion with
very different ideas from those that prompted it.   The next Monday
I furnished a document that occupied three hours in reading, pre-
senting my labours under a new aspect to most of those who heard it.
The members who were afraid of offending Lord Bathurst, finding
that they had lost ground, then proposed that I should draw up a
memorial to Lord Bathurst to read at the meeting of the Board on the
following Monday.   The memorial occupied about the same time in
reading as the former document.   On a proposal being made that I
should send it to Lord Bathurst in my own name, I instantly replied:
    'No! if I am not introduced at the Porch, Lord Bathurst shall
never see me enter the Colonial Office by a Postern.'
    A committee of eight was then appointed. . . . After three days,
John Dyer, Esq., as chairman of the Committee, gave in its report,
and I shall never forget the manner in which that noble-minded man
delivered his sentiments on that occasion.   Addressing the Chairman
of the Board he spoke as follows:
    'Sir, it is our unanimous opinion that the Memorial requires no
alteration and that it should be adopted by the Board and transmitted
to Lord Bathurst in the name of the Directors of the London Missionary Society.   It is known that I have been in the service of the
British Government from my boyhood; that I have for many years
had a liberal salary from the Government and that, though in receipt
of a liberal salary, I have laid up no money; but were I assured that
I should lose my office to-morrow for the opinion I am about to give,
I should say, it is the duty of the Board to send the Memorial to Lord
Bathurst.'
    From the triumphant manner in which the motion of the Com-
mittee was carried my mind was relieved on this point.   The Memorial
was transmitted to the Colonial Secretary after some delay; he replied,
by stating that he had not received all the reports of the Crown
Commissioners of Inquiry, and till then he must decline giving an
opinion on the subject of the Memorial.   This was postponing the
matter *sine die*, but it was nothing more than I expected from his
Lordship.
    The Directors had done all they could at that time.   It seemed
fruitless, but a great step had been gained, and I had Messrs. Buxton
and Wilberforce and Dr. Lushington to consult with, and to keep the
question before the Government.
    The changes taking place in the Colonial Office retarded for some
time the progress of the question.   I found few of his Majesty's
Ministers who understood the question or cared about it.   Mr.
Huskisson was an exception.   I found he did not require to ask me
a single question for his own information, unless I except the words:
    'Tell me in one sentence what you want for the Hottentots?'
My reply was: 'I require nothing for the Hottentots, but the power
of bringing their labour to a fair market.'   'That', he immediately
added, 'is all that you require.   It includes everything else.'
    I had put the whole affair into his hands and, had he continued in
office, Government would have done all that was required.   But his
misunderstanding with the Duke of Wellington and his secession from
the office speedily followed.   From the interviews I had with other
men in office, I had no hope from Government.

From the very outset, Dr. Philip cut himself off completely from any merely personal attack on Lord Charles Somerset, and hammered at general principles.

The statement to Mr. Huskisson is characteristic of the directness with which Dr. Philip conducted his campaign for Hottentot emancipation. On the eve of success, in a letter to Mr. Buxton, whom he coached persistently, he repeated, with a significant addition, that 'all that is wanted for the Hottentots, more correctly for the natives of South Africa, is liberty to bring their labour to the best market'.[1] In the first instance, he had secured even Mr. Buxton's active support with some difficulty. At first Buxton had urged that he was too fully absorbed by the West Indian slave question to concern himself with anything else, and suggested that Dr. Philip appeal to Sir R. Wilson. But in the December of 1826 Philip carried his papers with him to Buxton's house near Cromer, and very soon convinced him that the questions of Slave and Hottentot were closely related:

If they aim at the abolition of slavery, is it to put freed slaves in the position of 'free' Hottentots?[2]

Soon the Buxton-Philip alliance was cemented.[3] Throughout the session of 1827 the two men worked together, but in the face of distractions caused by great political changes they made no real progress.

The Clapham Sect with whom Dr. Philip was now associated were expert propagandists, and it was apparently on the suggestion of Zacchary Macaulay that at last he carried out his resolve to make his 'appeal to the British public':

Public engagements I could not get rid of made this an anxious undertaking; but I had made up my mind to get through with it. I devoted two days in the week to it. My plan was this—I read over and digested my papers, and then dictated to an amanuensis. I went to the Press as soon as I had a few sheets and I kept it at work till the book was finished.

The *Researches*, thus hastily thrown together, were published in April 1828, and Philip soon realized that the book was

[1] Philip to T. F. Buxton, 1st July 1828, a letter which was really an outline for a speech in support of Buxton's motion in the House on the 15th July.
[2] Philip to Buxton, 4th May 1827.
[3] Relations became still more intimate a little later. A significant letter from Mrs. Buxton to Dr. Philip is dated August 1828: 'I was vexed that we never met you in London this year. I hope another time you will remember *we are at home* when you call upon my husband.'

likely to reach only those already prepared to be converted: he himself tells of how Brougham received two copies, neither of which he seems to have read.[1] The 'elect', however, were now armed for decisive action and gave notice of motion in the House of Commons:

It was agreed that Mr. Buxton should bring forward the motion, whilst Sir James Mackintosh, Charles Grant, Esq. (afterwards Lord Glenelg), Dr. Lushington and Mr. Huskisson were expected to support it. In the meantime two copies of the *Researches* had found their way to the Colonial Office in Downing Street. Mr. Buxton was immediately sent for. At the office he found Sir George Murray with a copy open before him. Sir George informed Mr. Buxton that he had sent for him to ascertain whether he would not postpone his motion for six months. 'Not an hour, Sir George. On Tuesday next at 7 o'clock I shall bring forward my motion.' 'You are not an Opposition man,' said Sir George. 'You take and you give; and if you promise to have no speeches on the subject I will allow you and Dr. Philip to draw up your motion. We shall make it a Cabinet question, and it will get through the House by acclamation.'

As Sir George Murray required an answer next evening, Dr. Philip was sent for post haste from Colchester, and was informed by Mr. Buxton:

You can do as you please. Our speeches are all cut and dry. They will sell two or three editions of your *Researches*, but we all think you should accept the offer. The *Researches* have done their work and you may leave them to find their way without our assistance.

Dr. Philip, of course, agreed, and on the 15th of July 1828—two days before the promulgation of the 50th Ordinance at the distant Cape—the House resolved, without opposition, to ask for the publication of the Commissioners' Reports, as well as of the evidence given them by Dr. Philip and by the L.M.S.; more particularly, they begged His Majesty that

directions be given for effectually securing to all the natives of South Africa the same freedom and protection as are enjoyed by other free persons residing at the Cape, whether they be English or Dutch.[2]

In the end, therefore, the laws affecting the Hottentots were recognized, almost simultaneously, by the responsible authorities in both countries, as constituting too glaring a scandal to be permitted to continue. Sir George Murray's instructions to the Governor, consequent on the Resolution of the Commons,

[1] Letter of 1st July 1828. It is interesting that T. B. Macaulay was asked to review the *Researches*, but unfortunately did not do so.
[2] *Hansard*, Parliamentary Debates, new series, April to July 1828; and Sir George Murray to Sir Lowry Cole, despatch of 3rd August 1828.

were, as it happened, unnecessary; but Dr. Philip was now responsible for one very definite and important contribution to the settlement of this issue. At once he began to press for an Order in Council to put the motion of 15th July into operative effect. Before he had made further progress a copy of the newly enacted 50th Ordinance reached him from Downing Street, with a request to give his opinion, and indicate how far this satisfied his demands. After consulting Dr. Lushington and others, he replied that he

disliked a separate legislation; that it was invidious, and liable to be abused in the hands of Magistrates and Judges; that if the people were to have equal rights he saw no necessity for more than one Code of Laws; but that, if Ministers insisted, he might receive it as an additional protection to the Hottentots, and not in any instance to be construed as subversive of any of the Just Rights belonging to them in common with the white inhabitants of the Colony.

Asked again by Ministers if he was now satisfied, he replied that

there was nothing wanted but the Seal of the King in Council, without which Ministers must be aware that it would be of no value in the Colony, as it might otherwise be set aside by new enactments and leave us where we were.

This suggestion was at first opposed on the ground of the alarm it might cause to the West Indian interest. Dr. Philip, however, persisted in his demand. Whether or not Ministers paid much heed to his threat of deluging the House with petitions from all over Great Britain, they gave way; on 15th January 1829 the Ordinance was ratified, with an additional clause which put it out of the power of the Governor and the Council of the Cape to amend or repeal the 50th Ordinance without the express sanction of H.M. Government.[1]

Events soon proved the wisdom of securing this additional safeguard for the newly won freedom of the Hottentots. When Dr. Philip returned to the Cape in September 1829 he found that the new law was strongly resented. He himself, once almost a popular leader,[2] was becoming the object of ever increasing hostility for his share in securing its enactment, and for the opinions expressed in the *Researches*. General Bourke's short tenure of office was over, and though Stockenstrom had induced the new Governor, Sir Lowry Cole, to provide the Hottentots

[1] At Mr. Buxton's instigation, in April 1829 an Order in Council applied the principles of Ordinance 50 to the free coloured inhabitants of the Crown Colony of Trinidad.
[2] As late as 1832 an occasional letter in the *Grahamstown Journal* reminded critics of Philip's earlier services to the Settlers.

with one new outlet on the frontier, in the Kat River Settlement, the conditions were by no means favourable for the experiments in social reconstruction which were essential as a complement to the changed legal position of the Hottentots. By Philip's own account, Sir Lowry Cole, Judge Menzies and others were highly incensed by the Order in Council; at the same time there were ominous signs that some colonists had heard rumours of 'many hard things said and written' by Philip in England 'against the Africanders'.[1] In a private and confidential letter of 5th January 1830 to Buxton, Philip indicated that Cole had refused to see him. The situation caused him uneasiness, and James Clark, writing from the Orange River on 22nd September 1828, had shown that the missionaries were looking to him to keep an eye on the administration:

I wonder that Mr. Miles (the acting Superintendent) any longer confines his labours merely to the stations, without having regard to the slavery or freedom of the people at these stations. It is necessary that you return to see your measures carried into effect.[2]

Now the condition of the Hottentots was so deplorably backward (Chapters XI and XII above) that, with the best possible administration, their sudden emancipation from a state of barbaric serfdom was bound to be attended by peculiar difficulties. The abolition of the pass system in the first place, with the consequent reaction from long habituation to virtually forced labour, gave the Hottentots a measure of freedom that was very liable to abuse by a people who had even now little scope or motive for ambition. The passing of a single piece of legislation was no more capable then than it would be for the Bantu to-day, of reforming social and economic conditions that are radically bad; and one serious defect of the 50th Ordinance was that, apart from such relief as was given by the establishment of the Kat River Settlement in 1829, it was accompanied by no grants of land; nor was there any other provision to provide the Hottentots scattered throughout the Colony with any fresh means of subsistence. Many of them might well be disposed merely to exist, squatting wherever they might, and at times turning 'vagrant'. The rough

[1] Rev. J. Kitchingman to Philip (Paarl, 26th October 1829), a very early instance of the use of a term famous later in the forms *Afrikander* and *Afrikaner*.

[2] Mr. Miles was either ignorant of, or unaccountably ignored, the promise made in 1826 of land for Theopolis. Nothing happened about it till after Philip's return in 1829 (see p. 226).

and ready control hitherto exercised by their white masters
being weakened, an almost impossible burden was thrown on
to the feeble shoulders of the local authorities, who were neither
sufficiently numerous, nor equipped with adequate machinery
(such as police or even prisons), to cope with any additional
administrative work. Under the circumstances, though there
seem to be no impressive figures of increased crime among
the Hottentots (the grievance was indeed that crime went
undetected and unpunished), the very general complaints of
increased vagrancy no doubt had some justification. Almost
as certainly, however, the prevalence of crime and vagrancy
after 1828 has been exaggerated.[1] Even were this not so, the
fact that the Cape police system was too weak to control the

---

[1] Dr. Philip's condensed account, written after a tour of the
Eastern districts with Mr. Fairbairn between 4th January and 2nd
June 1830, is as follows:

On my arrival in Cape Town (September 1829) I found the country
full of alarm. It was asserted in numerous letters and in all the pro-
slavery Journals that the Hottentots had all left their masters, that the
country was full of banditti; that they were living by robbing their
former masters, and that the farmers and their families were trembling
for their lives. . . . To allay the panic of the people the Governor
had intimated publicly that something must be done, and had solicited
several individuals to furnish him with suggestions for the construction of a new system of Vagrant Acts.

I believed that the Reports on the subject must have been much
exaggerated, but I could not believe that there was not something in
them. To ascertain the extent of the evil and the necessity for the
Vagrant Acts to protect the white colonists, in company with J. Fairbairn, Esq., I left Cape Town to visit the scene of the alleged disorders. In Cape Town we were told this dreadful vendetta was to
be found at Hottentots Holland. At Hottentots Holland, it was at
Swellendam. At Swellendam, it was at George. At George, in the
Long Kloof. In the Long Kloof, it was at Port Elizabeth—at Uitenhage—at Bethelsdorp. At these places we found it had removed—
to the Bushman's River. At Bushman's River it was at Grahamstown,
and at Grahamstown we were referred to the ravines in the neighbourhood of the town. Here we found a number of Hottentots living in
the bushes; we examined them, we ascertained that they comprised
all the servile population of the town, that all (that could labour) were
employed by the people of the town, and could give a most satisfactory
account of their means of subsistence. When we had finished our
inquiries we were obliged to listen to some of their complaints. Mr.
Fairbairn, without my knowledge, summoned those who had injured
them before the sitting Magistrate, and half a dozen of their employers
were compelled to pay them what had been iniquitously withheld from
them; and, by a curious coincidence, among those who were condemned for injustice to the Hottentots were some of the inhabitants
of Grahamstown who had taken the most active part in promoting the
panic that has been described.

situation does not affect the main principle, that the old Hottentot Code was radically bad, and was justly abolished by Ordinance No. 50.

The situation eminently called for constructive thought and action. It was not enough to have abolished the old restrictions. It was probably a misfortune that a new Governor, who had less direct interest in making the reform a success, came into office before the Ordinance had fairly begun to take effect.[1] The prosperity of the 'better-class' Hottentots at Stockenstrom's new Settlement on the Kat River was hampered by those of the 'vagrants', who 'sturdily refused' to give up their practice of 'hanging on',[2] for the simple reason that there was no other obvious place for them to go to. Had mutual suspicions been less acute, an effort might have been made to find a basis for a progressive policy. Some at least of the colonists were prepared to be reasonable. Thus, shortly after Philip's return to Africa, a Frontiersman wrote, seemingly from Grahamstown, of Mr. Fairbairn's expected visit with Dr. Philip:[3]

I hope Fairbairn will not fail us. He will find many anxious to know him personally, in spite of Hottentot divisions. A well-digested Vagrant Act will set all to rights and we shall all be friends again. But there is positively not so much difference between us; *no-one* wishes the old system (I speak of our countrymen). The arguments are (in conversation): the Ordinance was too sudden. It led the Hottentot astray. He did not know his bounds and he could not be legally checked because the Ordinance contained a clause contradictory to the Vagrant Law in existence, and he ran riot. I wish Dr. Philip was up. I have some ideas on the subject of *domicile* which I noticed to Judge B——, and which will obviate the necessity of their living in the Bush *near Towns*, by giving them an erf on a small scale and making them porters, etc. etc.

And Dr. Philip, for his part, critical as he was of colonial demands, and distrustful of their complaints, was by no means

[1] Cole's tone in a letter of 28th January 1829 to the missionary Robson of Uitenhage is far from conciliatory: 'The cause of those people would be better served by their confiding in the favourable disposition of Government (than by) pretensions instilled into their minds by sincere but indiscreet friends' (Cape Town Ecclesiastical Letter Book, 1829).

[2] Cory, ii, p. 391. It is not mentioned that the best of the Kat River Settlers were drawn from the L.M.S. stations Bethelsdorp and Theopolis.

[3] Fragment of a letter in Philip manuscripts, addressed to 'Mr. Greig, Publisher, Cape Town', bearing date stamp 19th November 1829. Last page and signature are missing. It was presumably given by Greig to Philip, whom it concerned.

wholly negative in his attitude.   In 'Notes on a Journey into the Interior', under date 18th January 1830, after 'dining and spending the afternoon and evening with Mr. and Mrs. B. Moodie, near Swellendam', he wrote:

Mr. Moodie takes a great interest in the improvement of the Colony and our conversation turned upon the 50th Ordinance.

Arguing that only the act of the King in Council 'prevented colonial hostility from upsetting the Ordinance', Philip goes on:

Finding that there was no possibility of succeeding in getting it wholly cancelled, they now become clamorous for a Vagrant Act, and finding that this could not be done in reference to the Hottentots alone without authority from home, they have now proposed in Albany that such an Act should be passed by the Governor and Council embracing all classes of the inhabitants. . . . Reasoning with Mr. Moodie on this subject, I (argued) that the statements made were exaggerated . . . that in one or two places the people may have assembled in greater numbers, since they were freed from their cruel bondage, and that in those places more thefts had been committed . . . but vague and contradictory assertions (all the 'proofs' offered in reply to any challenge) are insufficient evidence of the truth of these allegations . . . and it remains to be proved that the aggregate of crime over the whole Colony has increased since their liberties were granted them.

To 'secure their property' the supporters of this comprehensive Vagrant Law 'are acting against their interests, and the interests of the Colony at large, in proposing to surrender their civil rights'.

If it is necessary, their property should be rendered more secure against such depredations.   The method to be adopted is simple. Let them surrender a part of their property to increase the number of their prisons, magistrates, constables and cattle herds, and not wantonly throw away those civil rights, on which the future prosperity of the Colony must depend, in such a way as to give no additional protection. . . . If the penalties against stealing a sheep are insufficient, let them be increased; if the Dutch law, requiring two witnesses to substantiate the fact is not convenient (?), let circumstantial evidence be admitted in its stead.   This alteration was made in the law by Lord Charles Somerset in reference to game, and the preservation of sheep is certainly of much greater importance to the interests of the Colony than is the former.

Dr. Philip was very ready to believe that 'the complaints were a mere pretext'.   But he sensed rightly that the desire to control the labour of the Hottentots was the dominant idea in the agitation against 'vagrancy'.

'The real object', he maintained, 'was to have the Hottentots again in the farmers' power on what terms they might please to hold them.

. . . Arbitrary control, when indulged, becomes one of the strongest passions in the human mind and the last species of authority which men are disposed to part with.'

For the rest, he argued that passes and corporal punishment would not solve the problem, and would do nothing to check the 'thieving propensities' of any Hottentot disposed to steal; that it would not be long till they would want to revert to the old system, and then the persons of the Hottentots would 'again fall into the hands of the magistrate, to be disposed of by him at his pleasure'.

So far, however, as the colonists had a just grievance, not to be remedied by better wages and better conditions, he was prepared to accept even a 'Vagrant Act' if it was accompanied by a 'Poor Law Settlement' for the helpless and indigent.[1] He also proposed more 'prisons, magistrates and constables'. He may have underestimated the expense and difficulty of making this provision; but all rational discussion of ways and means was soon lost in another almost typical dust-storm of South African politics. Interest was diverted from the main issue by the 'red-herring' of a personal attack on Dr. Philip for his *Researches*. The show of 'public feeling' and the 'great interest' aroused [2] by the trial drove him into a posture of defence, and into blank denial of abuses.[3] For two years he was immersed in factitious disputes, which finally passed over into a concentrated struggle to safeguard the reform that was gained by the 50th Ordinance against the forces of reaction.

There is a mass of documents bearing on the libel action of 1830, but to retail the story would only be to give the episode

[1] Philip makes this point again to Buxton, 30th May 1834. Even the Editor of the *Grahamstown Journal* warns his readers that rates for poor relief would be a burden if a vagrant law was to be enforced (1st November 1832). Yet a week later, in the issue of 8th November, he had the hardihood to argue that 'the Hottentot now has equal rights', and 'the *Colony for his home*'.

[2] Cory, ii, pp. 418-420.

[3] Dr. Philip's attitude was hardened by his own experiences on tour in 1830. A gang of thieves grew very bold in Grahamstown and increased the demand for restrictions on the Hottentots; in the end the culprits were found to be not Hottentots, but men of the 55th Regiment. His own Hottentots were driven off one night when they had outspanned on a Settler's ground; this person, probably a crank, if not 'broken-down', was known as 'Philosopher Bennett', and wanted 'to show the Hottentots that this was now a civilized country'!

Philip's comment is that 'in Albany a *civilized* Hottentot is content to work without wages, or for any trifle, without complaining'.

a significance it never deserved. Soon after Philip's return, Mr. Mackay, Deputy Landdrost of Somerset East, took action, alleging that in the *Researches* (i, pp. 353 ff.) he was libellously said to have abused his official position by a vindictive sentence on a Hottentot in his own employment, and by contracting to himself for three years, at only 15 R.D.s per annum, two Hottentot families who could have earned very much more had they been left free to dispose of their own services. Whether or not, as Dr. Philip, or his friends, privately alleged, Mr. Mackay was instigated by others to press the matter, he seems to have refused any composition out of court. Undoubtedly also Mackay had the overwhelming sympathy of the Colony when he took proceedings,[1] and the case dragged on for three months to keep the excitement alive. Philip's 'exception', to the effect that the alleged libel was published in England, and the case therefore one for the English Courts to settle, was overruled; and on the 16th of July 1830 the three judges agreed in giving judgement for plaintiff for £200 of damages, and costs that were taxed at some £900. He would have had difficulty in footing this heavy bill himself; but friends in London, and especially in Manchester, stood by him strongly, and in the course of a year subscribed more than enough to save him from entrenching, as he certainly began to do, on his own and Mrs. Philip's small invested capital. Whether in the end the penalty was exorbitant, or nothing more than a libel merited, trial and verdict alike are of significance at all, only as incidents in the struggle to secure Hottentot rights and legal status. Philip's *Researches* were an attack on a vicious system; and just as he carefully refrained, in England, from joining in the personal attack on Lord Charles Somerset, so, in his book, charges against individuals were clearly subordinate to its main purpose. The exposure of the abuses that were possible under the law, as it stood,[2] led him to cite

[1] Sir George Cory, ii, p. 420, exaggerates the importance both of Dr. Philip and of the Cape when he suggests that had the defendant had his way and got the case heard in London, 'the state of feeling in England' would have been unfavourable to Mackay. But if public feeling was liable to distort justice in this case, it was Philip, tried in the excited atmosphere of Cape Colony, that was likely to suffer.

[2] Mr. Henry Cloete, the well-known Cape advocate, wrote to Dr. Philip on 1st October 1830: 'Not only were the damages exorbitant, but while your publication avowedly professed merely to impugn a system, and not to attack private individuals, the plaintiff proved himself at the trial that he had been guilty of a very gross violation of his instructions and authority as a Landdrost'.

Q

particular instances, and, it may be, details that were open to question. But the result of his exposure of abuses was that the system, which made such happenings possible as those alleged against Mackay, was definitely overthrown. In 1835 he was able to decline the offer of James Cropper, a Liverpool philanthropist, to contribute to the cost of a second edition of the *Researches*; he had no desire, he wrote, to reopen old sores, since the immediate purpose of the book had been accomplished, with the support of the Colonial Government of 1828, as well as of the paramount Downing Street.

While the libel case was going on, Dr. Philip became involved in a long and troublesome controversy with the Colonial Secretary, Colonel Bell, about the affairs of Theopolis. The dispute dated back to 1825, when Dr. Philip had alleged some encroachment on the original land of the Institution; at the same time he asserted the prescriptive right of Theopolis to a certain strip of land three or four miles wide lying between the station and the sea, and asked for it to be definitely granted to the Institution, whose claim, he asserted, was prior to that of certain white colonists who coveted the same piece. The question of encroachment lapsed, but the Directors of the L.M.S. shortly afterwards made an appeal to Earl Bathurst for a grant of this strip, and in November 1826 obtained assurances from Downing Street that the request would be granted.[1]

In the *Researches* in 1828, Dr. Philip reasserted this claim, again with allegations of encroachment, but nothing further happened till 26th January 1829, when the Directors renewed their application to have the promise of 1826 carried out;on 4th March 1830, Hottentot ex-soldiers at Theopolis petitioned the Governor, Sir Lowry Cole, in the same sense. At last, only on 30th April 1830, Colonel Bell wrote to Dr. Philip, not with a view to carrying out his instructions, but to ask him for detailed information about the extent of land, when it was granted, and the date of the 'resumption', thus re-opening a tedious dispute four years after Downing Street, like

---

[1] The original letter from R. W. Hay to Hankey, Treasurer of the L.M.S., dated 4th November 1826, runs:

'Directions will be given to the Lieut.-Governor of the Cape to grant the land in question to Theopolis, or as much of it, with access to the sea, as that officer may deem fit to limit, and *without restriction of the right of the Society to purchase land*, but subject to the (usual) quit-rent.'

the Crown Commissioners,[1] whose Report was published in 1830, was satisfied that Theopolis had a case, and had ordered the extension to be 'granted'. This was the line of least resistance, for his predecessors in office had put Colonel Bell in a difficulty. Though there must have been reason to know that appeal had been made to Earl Bathurst, and that the matter was *sub judice*, the Colonial Government had, in September 1826, made a grant of the land in question to a certain Mr. Bovey and to one Sergeant Grant, and could not now grant it afresh to Theopolis. The facts are tiresome, and a little obscure, but they have been dragged from blessed oblivion[2] to emphasize the iniquity of Dr. Philip.

There were many predisposing causes for disputes like that about Theopolis: early land surveys were not very exact; land registration was careless;[3] Hottentot occupation was superficial and their cultivation rough; fences were not; and land was so cheap, and the population so sparse, that no one took any serious notice, when, as at Theopolis, the Hottentots spread beyond their original bounds.[4] Though the farmers' own titles were secure enough in practice, they probably would not have stood inspection by expert surveyors. In March 1817 a Proclamation by Lord Charles Somerset, by the promise of effective title as a reward for cultivation, seems to have encouraged expansion; nor is there any reason to doubt that in the same year Somerset gave the missionary Albrecht the assurance that the lands between Theopolis and the sea were 'just as useful to the station as they were, for no person beside could occupy them',—(for want of water).[5] The Hottentots were in the habit

[1] Report of Crown Commissioners, 28th January 1830. See Theal's *Records*, xxxv, pp. 45-47.

[2] Cory, ii, pp. 421 ff., and chart.

[3] H. Alexander, Colonial Secretary, on 11th August 1815, to J. Read, acknowledged the 'diagram which has arrived' of land lately granted to be 'held in the same manner you have occupied Bethelsdorp'. Theopolis was originally looked upon as a grant 'for Bethelsdorp', the phrase used by Mr. Albrecht in reporting to Read at the very beginning, in December 1813. Alexander's letter, on the face of it, and by Read's testimony, can only refer to Theopolis; but no such diagram was afterwards forthcoming, and Colonel Bell evaded the challenge to produce this document by alleging that the letter referred to Bethelsdorp, and not to Theopolis.

[4] The sea-board was always coveted, and from the beginning the grant was vague. The Rev. J. Albrecht, who accompanied Sir John Cradock on the original tour of investigation, obviously delighted, reported to James Read in December 1813, that the Governor was granting them all the land, 'na Lombards, *en na de zee*'.

[5] Reported in a letter of 7/6/30 by his colleague Barker.

of using this land for lime-burning, for access to sea-fishing, and, if Barker may be trusted, for some cultivation—in such a way as to increase the vagueness about the exact boundaries of the station. No need for a definite grant of title arose till the middle 'twenties, when the coming of the British Settlers created a new demand for land in the neighbourhood, and made it necessary for land holdings to be more carefully examined and defined. Unfortunately for Theopolis, when it came to loaves and fishes, the interests of 'returned soldiers' were likely to take precedence of those of Dr. Philip or of the Hottentots.

As for Dr. Philip's 'untruths',[1] on the first main count, there is strong ground for suspicion that if in 1825 there was no actual encroachment on the land about the Institution itself, it was effectually prevented only by Philip's active intervention.[2] In the second place, it is said, 'far from being deprived of any of the original grant, an *addition* of nearly 2000 *morgen* was made to it'.[3] It seems to be agreed that in 1820 Sir Rufane Donkin added 2000 morgen, making the total 5000, and that there was further 'addition' in 1825 or 1826. This addition was refused by the L.M.S. on the grounds that the grant was conditional, and precluded the right to acquire any more land for the Institution;[4] the land in question, moreover, was described on the chart (reproduced by Sir George Cory) as 'deep ravines and bad rocky ground'. The Landdrost of Albany himself seemed to defend this 'addition', on the express plea that the land was 'high and perfectly without water', and therefore 'useless and unacceptable to any other'.[5] On the other hand, the part denied them, between the village and the sea, included more open rolling grass land; and to this, by prescription and

[1] The alleged publication of a ' garbled ' version of the Theopolis chart needs no comment. Some marks, such as the incriminated ' dotted lines ', were necessary to explain any departure from the lines of the original grant.
[2] The first hint of trouble is in a letter from the Rev. Mr. Brownlee, a reliable witness, who reported to Dr. Philip from the Chumie, on 28th March 1825, that he ' heard that Theopolis grounds, including the Long Fountain, had been taken away'. Brownlee's information may have been only frontier gossip, but gossip arose because rival claimants to land in the neighbourhood were then pressing; and later in the year the land was actually re-surveyed, and the ' Long Foun- tain ', first ' left out by oversight ', was this time definitely included in Theopolis. Letter from the Government Surveyor, Knobel, to Colonial Secretary, 5/9/30.
[3] Cory, ii, p. 422.
[4] See terms of Hay's letter to Hankey, Nov. 1826, page 226, *note* 1, promising a grant ' without restriction ' of this sort.
[5] Dundas to Sir R. Plasket, 5th December 1825.

use, the Hottentots of Theopolis, with barely two average Boer farms for five or six hundred people, had as reasonable a claim as any potential white settler. It is, therefore, incorrect to state that, in terms of the Downing Street letter of November 1826, and 'long before Dr. Philip published his book',[1] Theopolis was in possession of this 'coveted tract'. Colonel Bell himself protested 'three times over',[2] that the first he heard of Lord Bathurst's decision was only on 30th October 1829. Three years earlier, in September 1826, his predecessors in office had tied his hands by making grants of the land in question to Bovey and Grant aforesaid. Mr. Bovey seems to have been an adventurer with friends at court, who never made any attempt to occupy his land, or do more than make a profitable ' deal ' of it; and Dr. Philip

had to choose between breaking up the Institution, and purchasing (for £250) the land given in 1826 to Mr. Bovey;[3]

at the same time he appealed to the Directors to raise another £200 to buy what had been given to Mr. Grant.

The truth is that the original boundaries of Theopolis were obviously indefinite; and when greater accuracy became necessary, owing to the increase of the white population, prescriptive claims on behalf of the Hottentots were ignored. In the end no satisfactory settlement was arrived at. In May 1831, Sir Lowry Cole received fresh orders from Lord Goderich to grant this land to the L.M.S., and was asked why he had not acted sooner. As early as 20th January 1831, Colonel Bell had told Philip that the discrepancies in the story necessitated appeal to London for further instructions; and on 10th May Cole wrote a despatch, which refuted at length the claim of Theopolis, urging that till 1828 Hottentots had had no legal right to property in land at all (which was surely a good reason for granting land to the Institutions). Cole made the most of Philip's admission of some inaccuracy with regard to the chart published in the *Researches*, and informed Lord Goderich that the land claimed for Theopolis had been *ten* years in the possession of white settlers. (This was a manifest exaggeration; Bovey's grant certainly dated only from 1826.)[4]

[1] Cory, ii, p. 423.
[2] *E.g.* to Philip, 2nd February 1831.
[3] Philip's summing up report to L.M.S. on 11th December 1831.
[4] Cole to Goderich, 10th May 1831. The Governor ended with an attack on Dr. Philip for claiming a large share of the credit for Ordinance 50, for vaunting himself as the ' sole champion ' of the Hottentots, for his ' interference ' and ' influence ', which tend against

This was virtually the end of a dispute that dragged on for a very long time, with the passing to and fro of masses of letters and documents, with a good deal of publicity and personal abuse of Philip.[1] The Directors, 'after repeated and careful consideration', threw up the sponge.[2] Perhaps they were wise. They considered that actual danger to the station was removed, and that a mere claim for compensation had little prospect of success. They even favoured encouraging the Hottentots to buy land for themselves, rather than look for a 'present from yourself'; but they also directed Philip to take steps to secure diagrams and titles for all the stations, to prevent any more occurrences of this kind.

The years 1830 to 1832 were indeed among the most discouraging in Dr. Philip's career. Though friends in England stood by him stoutly after his conviction for libel, the case gave him a good many months of private worry and anxiety. Following hard on the libel action, the Theopolis dispute seemed to throw further discredit in colonial eyes on Philip's truthfulness; and on the other hand, since his own conscience was quite clear in the matter, Philip was confirmed in a belief in the determined hostility both of the Colonial Government and of public opinion. In the end of it he neither gained his point, nor secured any public vindication of his own character or conduct; while these land troubles, and the migration of many of the better residents to the more favourably situated Kat River Settlement, ushered in a period of steady decline in the prosperity of Theopolis itself. In addition, Philip seems to have had friction with the office in London about the conduct of the domestic affairs of the L.M.S. His energies were so much absorbed in the details of administration that he somewhat lost touch with the development of Hottentot affairs, so

---

authority, disturbing the Hottentots and preventing their further improvement—for example, by a vagrant law designed to teach them to 'settle', and 'acquire fixed property in the usual way'. This statement conveys what from this point became the almost generally accepted view, both of Dr. Philip and of the Hottentot problem.

[1] Philip complained that the Government must have been privy to an account that appeared in the hostile paper, *De Zuid Afrikaan*, in December 1830. On the other hand, some of the relevant documents he alleged to be missing entirely, and it was only in December 1835 that Fairbairn, in the *Commercial Advertiser*, published material which did any justice to Philip's side in the dispute, for the benefit of any who were still interested.

[2] Rev. W. Ellis to Philip, 13th September 1833.

much as to imagine that all was settled.[1] Even his letters became less interesting, until after September 1832, when a six months' tour of the Kafir frontier and Griqualand revived his energies and directed his thoughts to new difficulties that were coming into being in the East and North.

When these new questions became pressing, or even in 1833 when there was a recrudescence of the demand for Hottentot Vagrant Laws, the chasm that divided Philip from the great majority of the colonists was deep and wide;[2] an unfortunate state of feeling to exist on the eve of the most critical period in South African history. With slavery doomed in 1833, the Colour question was before the country, but there was little hope now of concerted action. Colonial opinion did not disguise its hostility to Philip and Fairbairn and all their works. In its early years the *Commercial Advertiser* had had the field of journalism all to itself. But while these two leaders were away on the frontier, in 1830, a rival and hostile weekly paper, *De Zuid Afrikaan*, made its appearance in Cape Town. In Grahamstown, moreover, Fairbairn's action in proceeding against exploiters of Hottentot labour was little calculated to restore the popularity of one who had been 'the idol of Cape

[1] ' You will perhaps be surprised to hear that I have not, since my return to this Colony in 1829, had occasion to be once in the Colonial Office on those matters which were formerly of weekly occurrence.' Philip to Stockenstrom, 13th January 1833.

[2] In a rather unusually personal letter, Dr. Philip showed himself conscious of his changed status in the Colony:

' On my first journey beyond the limits of the Colony I recollect with what lingering feelings I left the last farm house within the pale of civil government, and the sense of loneliness and insecurity which took possession of my mind the first nights I endeavoured to compose my mind to rest in a country without the protection of law and government. I had now no dependence but on the Providence which the Patriarchs had for their protection. . . . I saw nothing now before me but privations and dangers, and looking back to the country I was leaving I more than once said to myself, "What a blessing it is to be under civil government". (This was in 1825.)'

' Allow me now to make the contrast. . . . When it was heard that I was to visit the Interior in 1832 letters appeared in *De Zuid Afrikaan* daring me to set foot in the country and threatening me. . . . When I proceeded on my journey I took care previously to be as independent as possible. I had oxen from the mission stations, and I took provisions on my waggon. I crossed the Orange River at the same place I had crossed it on my first journey and I encamped for the night at the same place, and when I had got among uncivilized men, I felt thankful to God. I was in a state of security. In my journey through the Colony my waggon was once set fire to in Albany by one of the Settlers,' . . . and he goes on to give other instances of rough usage in the Colony.

society', and the 'Father of a Free Press'. In the 'Journal' of his tour, in the first part of 1830, Dr. Philip reported that Grahamstown 'threatened' Fairbairn with an opposition journal; and in 1831 the *Grahamstown Journal* began its long career. Now it was all to the good that Grahamstown was progressive enough to support its own newspaper, and that there should be room in Cape Town for two journals. But in the time and manner of their appearance, the new papers were a sign of internal divisions which now rent a society that had stood together in the troubles of 1824, and by its unity secured both the right to a free Press, and the first steps towards constitutional government. For years to come the *Commercial Advertiser* on one side, *De Zuid Afrikaan* and the *Grahamstown Journal* on the other, were constantly at each other's throats. The liberal principles of legal equality that triumphed in Ordinance 50 had yet to go through the fire.

NOTE.—(See p. 213). From the proofs of Professor E. A. Walker's History of South Africa, I learn that Stockenstrom's Report on Hottentot conditions was the result of orders sent to General Bourke by Mr. Huskisson. Dr. Philip's action, therefore, would seem to have contributed directly to the Ordinance of 1828, and he had reason to be pleased (p. 216) with his interview with Mr. Huskisson.

Chapter XVI

REACTION—THE DRAFT VAGRANT LAW OF 1834—THE GREAT TREK

BY Ordinance 50 'Free Persons of Colour' were released from the older laws that placed their labour and their persons very much at the disposal of farmers and of local officials; but they were still an economically dependent and backward community. Their very helplessness made their comparative freedom a difficulty to themselves and a grave responsibility to the Colonial Government. When a few years later the Emancipation Act was passed, the Government was faced with the prospect of a similar fundamental change in the status of the slaves (the remaining half of the coloured population of the Cape Colony) which created a new situation. As in the days before 1828, there were the same two conflicting and almost irreconcilable motives for action; on the one hand, farmers, who were almost the whole Colony, were clamorous for more labour (not even for more efficient labour), and complained that the removal of restraints had turned the Hottentots into vagabonds; on the other, the policy which triumphed in 1828 seemed to commit the Government to plans which must make it possible for numbers of the coloured people to rise to be something better than common, if not servile, labourers. The second and longer view was upheld chiefly by the missionaries, with whom the colonists were now at daggers drawn; and even had there been more common ground and sympathy between these two parties, the rise of the Hottentots in the scale of civilization could not have evolved except in the course of generations.

The Governor, Sir Lowry Cole, and Colonel Wade, who acted for some months before January 1834, were men of no great vision, whose weight naturally came down on the side of the practical men who were anxious to deal with the situation of the moment, and, like so many after them, they emphasized the merely negative aspect of the problem. Very early Sir Lowry Cole stated his own view:

Unhappily the very act which rescued the Hottentots from oppression made no provision for that wholesome degree of restraint by which a great proportion of them can alone be induced or made to labour for their maintenance and cease to be a scourge upon their neighbours.[1]

The Emancipation Act of 1833 made Colonel Wade return to the subject: in December 1833 he wrote of the scarcity of labour, and of the need for a Vagrant Act, agreeing that wide spaces would make it difficult to enforce, but urging that the difficulties were 'not insurmountable'. Next month, January 1834, he was more definite, issuing a Circular, and reporting to the Secretary of State, to the effect that:

The Proprietors may further rest satisfied that long before the period of the expiration of the Apprenticeship arrives, other laws will be enacted having in like manner for their objects the prevention or punishment of Vagrancy after that period, and for securing a sufficiency of labourers to the Colony by compelling not only the liberated apprentices to earn an honest livelihood, but all others who, being capable of doing so, may be inclined to lead an idle and vagabondizing life.

Now that the Hottentots were 'liberated', and slavery being almost at an end, the first necessity, according to Cole and Wade, was to make sure of the labour supply, and apparently to make the new status of these people as much like the old as conditions would permit. In the spirit of Colonel Wade's Circular of January, on 7th May 1834 the draft of an Ordinance on Vagrancy was laid before the Legislative Council, now presided over by Sir Benjamin D'Urban.

The first clause of this measure [2] provided that

every Field Commandant, Field Cornet or Provisional Field Cornet may, and is hereby required to apprehend all (such) persons found within his jurisdiction, (as) he may reasonably suspect of having no honest means of subsistence—or who cannot give a satisfactory account of themselves—and bring them before any Magistrate or Justice of the Peace for examination.

Certain safeguards were laid down: individuals with

[1] Cole to Goderich, 10th May 1831.
[2] See *Commercial Advertiser* of 9th August 1834, *Grahamstown Journal* of 25th September 1834, and *Cape Gazette*.

property valued at 100 Rix-dollars, or with 10 cattle or 100 goats, were presumed to have reasonable means of subsistence (this being no very low standard for a people whose grazing must almost of necessity be on a white farmer's land); further, provided that travellers who may be charged 'shall prove' their means of subsistence, they may be allowed to proceed to their destination, *e.g.* to the office of J.P. or Magistrate.   On the other hand, the characteristic definition of 'persons wilfully idle' lays it down expressly (see also Chapter III above):

> That the searching for and digging for roots or fruits, the natural produce of the earth, or wild honey; or the searching for, taking and killing any game, or any other wild animal . . . on any ground not being the property of the person so doing, (or) . . . not having previously obtained permission . . . shall not be deemed to be in lawful employment by which any person can honestly earn the means of subsistence.[1]

Any coloured persons who failed to circumvent these fairly stringent provisions, or alternatively, to accept employment on such very poor terms as they could get, were liable, at the discretion of the magistrate or J.P., to be set to employment on the public roads until they should find security for good behaviour, until 'some responsible person shall take them into employment', or until they themselves enter into such.

Such a draft, had it become law, was well calculated to satisfy even the crudest demands of the white colonists.   It at once reopened the case which Dr. Philip had argued, largely in private, with Government officials before 1828; this time the discussion was public, and Philip and his views were more than suspect to the promoters of the new Ordinance.   At once masses of evidence and of protest poured in from L.M.S. mission stations.   Dr. Philip himself collected more on a journey to the frontier between August and December of 1834, and poured out in the columns of the *Commercial Advertiser*, and upon the Governor himself, an uncertain number of long memorials of close argument and protest.[2]   At the Kat River there was one

---

[1] To this day, in the ' prickly pear ' belt, and other very poor districts of the South-West Cape, a good many 'coloured people' still depend very largely on the 'natural produce of the earth' for food.   With the still less developed agriculture of those days, this definition must have been a true picture of the normal and traditional life of a large proportion of the population, and since wages were exceedingly low, and the land a white monopoly, the only alternative would be such remains as were given them of the meat that was the staple food of the farmers themselves.

[2] I cannot entirely disentangle the dates of these memorials and letters—a great mass of papers with a good many repetitions.   There

almost famous Protest Meeting,[1] the whole heated discussion being conducted in the full glare of publicity.

The missionaries' case for the coloured people, then as later, was slow of acceptance by the man in the street. It was not 'practical politics'. The object of the missionaries was to foster the growth of a civilized community out of a scattered proletariat of backward Hottentots and half-breeds:

'In England', Philip wrote in an undated journal, 'you have your magistrates, your police, public opinion, a national standard of morals, usages, and customs, and regular employment in which people have been trained up from infancy, which constitutes the framework of civilization. The value of (all this) in connection with religion is not known in England, because none living have known the want of it; but it is different in a country like this where all this has to be erected, and where there is everything to impede the progress of the missionary in this work, and scarcely anything separate from his own resources to aid him in it.'

Not many of the missionaries themselves had all the qualities necessary to manage the 'temporal concerns of an Institution'.

Few of them (Dr. Philip wrote again from Theopolis in January 1824) have the turn of mind to govern others. . . . It takes a rare combination of qualities to fit a man for conducting the process of civilization till it arrive at that point where it can be left to the operation of the various institutions which distinguish a civilized country, and are sufficient to preserve it from degenerating.

More than once he quotes, or adapts: 'The missionary for India must be a learned man; for Africa, a philosopher'.

The missionary stands to the Africans as a teacher of civilization, as much as of religion. The service they seek to render to Africa, by the success of which they will be judged, is that rendered to Western Europe by the Church of the Middle Ages. The task in Africa is if possible still more difficult. It is not that the African races have not even the slender cultural achievements of the early English or French. But on the whole in the Middle Ages, not only in the great days of Charlemagne, Church and State worked together to evolve civilized order out of feudal chaos. Hildebrand and his successors, it is true, fought against the chief temporal ruler of the day, but the Church by that time had great material resources of its own, and the contest was by no means unequal.

---

were two main letters to the Governor, in May and in November, but also numerous references in semi-private letters to the Governor from the frontier.

[1] Cory, iii, pp. 50, 51.

But in the Cape of the 'thirties, as in modern Africa, the missionary representatives of civilization among the primitive peoples have had to contend with the active or passive hostility of a very strong section of European society, with the result that sympathetic Governments, which would fain accept the doctrine of trusteeship for the backward races, have often found their power of effective action paralysed and thwarted.   The missionary task of the modern Church, in face of 'civilized' opposition, is like that which was met in the earliest days by the Christian Church in the Roman Empire.

Almost instinctively the missionaries in 1834 felt that the Vagrant Law was a betrayal of the essential principles of civilized policy.   In their handling of the practical details of the situation around them, they were perhaps less clear-sighted and helpful; but the narrow self-interest of the colonists, and their physical dread of the immediate dangers of Hottentot 'vagrancy', made any constructive policy hopeless.   Philip and Fairbairn and their school saw the need to plant the roots of the coloured people in the soil.   The Ordinance itself suggested the granting of land to Hottentot applicants who had cattle or other property in stock; but this was to put the cart before the horse, since a Hottentot arrested for 'vagrancy' would probably lose such cattle as he had before the Government had taken the necessary steps to provide him with grazing.   For already the Government was faced with the difficulty that white farmers were actually leaving the Colony,[1] because their own grazing lands were insufficient; and Fairbairn wrote to Philip on 29th August 1834 warning him against the 'blind' of offers of land, since 'all are to come under the Vagrant Law'.

It is not desirable (Fairbairn continued, not irrelevantly) that all should hold land even if it could be found for them. . . . Of what use is land to a man who has no property to work it?

But constructive measures had little place in the discussion. The missionaries were forced into a defensive position.   The new Ordinance was almost unmitigated reaction, and it was all they could do to save what they had gained for the Hottentots in 1828, and for the slaves about to be emancipated by the Act of 1833.   The Draft Law was calculated, Philip at once protested, 'to place the whole of the people once more in the power of the local authorities of the country', an experiment that had already been tried and found wanting because of the

[1] Cory, ii, pp. 460 ff.   Also correspondence of Philip and D'Urban, June–July 1834.

bias and the uncontrolled position of the field-cornet (Chapters XI and XII above). The *Commercial Advertiser* was severe in its criticism.[1] The local authority was '*required*' to apprehend those 'who cannot give a (to him) satisfactory account of themselves', and bring them, it may be, before a Justice of the Peace—'even one who has no assessor, clerk, or *record* . . . and in many cases no pen and ink, or no skill to use them'—and this with no remedy whatever against the vexation and expense of wrongful arrest. The plea that Hottentots were without legal restraint was disingenuous; the police force may have been inadequate, but if Hottentots broke the law, they were both more readily convicted and more severely punished than white colonists; and the defence that the Vagrant Act applied to white and black alike was said to be like a law that purported 'to prohibit Natives of the interior as well as those at the coast from fishing in the sea'.[2]

Many relevant criticisms reached Dr. Philip from the out-stations. Mr. Helm of Zuurbraak had ample justification for stressing the unduly low wages of coloured persons; the average, he maintained, was not more than 4s. 6d. a month; wages being so low, many Hottentots live in freedom, not because they are averse to service, but because they can support their families better. Other missionaries agreed, or added, that to force the so-called vagrants into farm service by the intervention of the authorities would tend only to keep wages disastrously low, if not to reduce them still further. Mr. Kitchingman of Bethelsdorp, Mr. Anderson, now of Pacaltsdorp, and Mr. Melville (formerly Government agent in Griquatown, now of Hankey), men of considerable experience, remark upon the Hottentot dread of being forced back into a 'contract for life'. Rather than be at the mercy of farmers and field-cornets, Hottentots really did 'crowd' for a few months to seek the shelter of the Institutions. On 13th June 1834, Mr. Kitchingman reported that in 1833 the number on the roll of Bethelsdorp was only 1204; now it was 1887 (and in October, 2300); Pacaltsdorp in August reported an influx of 450. It was as true then, as it is in the Transvaal in the twentieth century, that though a few may go short of labour, farmers will tolerate on their land only those coloured people likely to be of service to themselves; but the more natives there are, the less the demand for such service, and since the coloured people are still so communally minded that they will share

[1] 9th August 1834.
[2] Philip's Memo. to Governor in November 1834.

almost their last crumb with their fellows, there tends to be a ruinous pressure of 'squatters' on what land is available either, as then, in 'Institutions', or to-day on Native 'Reserves'.

Therefore (said Mr. Kitchingman) let these people have but some remnants of the land still in the hands of the Government and there will be no need for such laws.

Even the cautious Mr. Barker of Theopolis was as strongly opposed as any of his colleagues to what he denounced as 'class' legislation. He pointed the moral of the beneficent effect of the foundation of the Kat River Settlement in reducing 'vagrancy' in Albany, and, without giving his own numbers, makes the same point as his colleagues, that the threatened law was already having the effect of driving Hottentots out of the labour market on to the lands of the Institutions. Moreover, the Petition Mr. Barker forwarded from Theopolis emphasized in picturesque language that Settlers wanted the Vagrant Law

to save themselves the trouble of keeping, if it were only an old woman, to protect their cattle and sheep from jackals, wolves and tigers, whose sins have often been laid on the backs of Hottentots and Kafirs, *memorialists not excepted!*

The missionaries were agreed, and were justified in believing, that the Vagrant Law by itself (it was all that was offered) would be worse than the disease of which the colonists were complaining, and that the Hottentots who had now known a short period of comparative freedom, would, as Mr. Kitchingman put it, 'take to the mountains', rather than return to their 'former servitude'. It remained for James Read again to diagnose an evil which escaped even Dr. Philip's notice. The preference of the Hottentots for daily or monthly, rather than for yearly contracts, with their small recompense on the farms, (a 'wretched hut' for home, and the 'dead or very thin sheep of the flock' for food,) was already responsible for a 'superabundance of labour in the towns'. Even at that early date, the Hottentots, so lately a tribe of nomads, were drifting, to become slum dwellers on the fringes of South African *dorps* and towns.

At the Kat River a few of the more solid Settlers, members of the congregation of the Government missionary, Mr. Thomson, seemed disposed even to welcome a law directed against vagrants and squatters, of whom the Kat River, like the other Institutions, doubtless suffered an influx. Among the Hottentots of the far more numerous L.M.S. section, however, the excitement caused by the threatened Vagrant Law was so intense as to attract particular attention, not so much at the time as in the light of subsequent events.[1] The proximity of the Kat River to the Kafir frontier gave special importance to any serious unrest at this station; and it has been said, on utterly inadequate evidence, that it was here that the Kafir War of 1835 was hatched.[2] When South African opinion demands some peculiarly irritating anti-Native measure, and the coloured people concerned show signs of resentment, it commonly blames the critics of the proposal, rather than the proposal itself. In this instance, the hostility of the Hottentots to an ill-designed and oppressive Vagrant Law possibly gave some of the Kafir chiefs occasion to think they could rely on Hottentot support in an attack upon the Colony. In that case, the missionaries and others who succeeded, in the end, in saving the Colony from itself, and prevented the enactment of this law, may also have saved it from the horrors of a joint attack by Kafirs and Hottentots; for when war broke out in the end of the year, the Hottentots, both at the Kat River and throughout the Colony, were entirely loyal; the services they rendered to the authorities were more than formally acknowledged by Colonel Harry Smith and many

[1] On 18th September 1834, in its first account of the August Missionary Meeting at Kat River, the *Grahamstown Journal* does not mention Kafirs as concerned in what was a Hottentot protest against the Vagrant Law. Only on 13th February 1835 a correspondent, calling himself 'An English Settler', writes of how the Kafir chiefs were impressed by that meeting. The disaster of the Kafir War was likely to favour the growth of a legend about the intimacy between discontented Hottentots and Kafirs.

[2] Cory, iii, pp. 47 ff.
Sir George Cory speaks of a 'conspiracy', and of 'sedition' in the Kat River Settlement. His sense of humour might have saved him from laying undue stress on flimsy evidence. The doughty 'conspirator', Dirk by name, failed to distract the attention of the soldiers of Fort Willshire, and so to give Maqomo's warriors the chance of a surprise attack, by setting fire to a trader's store 'just *outside*' the walls, because he 'could not get the key of the fort'.
Tyali's evidence (p. 50, *note*) was: 'The Hottentots induced us to go to war; they assured us we could beat the English.' . . . It is hard to imagine a more characteristic example of Hottentot speech, and 'leg-pulling'. It was very like them to say to the Kafir malcontents: '*Julle kan mos makelik die Engelse op-neuk*, etc. etc.'.
As for Tyali's account of Dr. Philip's words, 'I shall *speak* in the Governor's ear'—the chiefs may possibly have gathered from him that 'I *have* the ear of the Governor', as he certainly says in some of his letters, and as indeed, in 1834, he had. (See Appendix.)

others, and even occasional deserters seem to have been few and far between.

The fortunes of the Kat River Settlement are, however, significant and of more positive interest in connection with Hottentot 'vagrancy'. The pioneers of the Settlement were the pick of the older population of Bethelsdorp and Theopolis; [1] they enjoyed for a while the inestimable benefit of virgin soil in a comparatively fertile and well-watered district; in its early prime the station was less overcrowded and retarded by 'squatters', and many eye - witnesses [2] write in almost unstinted praise of the beneficent effects of this almost solitary opportunity for Hottentots to acquire 'a stake in the country'.

But on the Kat River, as on other coloured settlements and potentially fertile Native Reserves all over South Africa, these early hopes were blasted. So long as even the best of 'Reserves' are mere islands, set in the midst of a sea of farm labourers who have no prospects—left to their own poor farming devices, and carefully screeened from the benefits of the public expenditure devoted to Agricultural Departments, roads, or railways—all of them must suffer a similar fate. They are inevitably swamped by 'squatters' from the neighbouring districts, and dragged down to the level of the socially derelict, farm-labouring population around them. 'Vagrancy' was the natural outlet in a miserably poor country for a starving landless class, like the Hottentots of 1834. Measures like the Vagrant Law, designed to make them obedient serfs, and to drive them bound into the service of scattered farmers, must also debar them from the benefits of schools or even of churches. A scattered farm population cannot easily be provided with schools; and even their churches must depend for their

---

[1] Dr. Theal's account is that 'the settlement was intended to draw away some of the people from the London Missionary Society's stations, which were regarded by the Government as politically dangerous institutions'.—Dr. Philip at that time had not returned from England, and it is clear that the Hottentots themselves, finding that no missionary was provided, 'called' their own first minister or missionary, Mr. James Read, who was known to them, and popular, after ten years in an 'unofficial capacity' at Bethelsdorp. Dr. Philip acknowledged that Mr. Read had sufficiently atoned for misdemeanour, and shown 'repentance', and agreed to his reinstatement as a servant of the L.M.S. Thereupon, in the hope of preventing 'interference by Dr. Philip', the Governor sent them Mr. Thomson 'at the public expense'.

[2] Cory, ii, pp. 389 ff. These included Col. Wade and Mr. R. Godlonton.

R

existence on the goodwill of some more liberal landlord. This disability of the coloured population remains a bar to the progress of the whole country; landlessness makes low-grade workers and vagrants; vagrants are driven into underpaid service; underpaid servants make for bad and inefficient farming; and bad farming intensifies the general poverty. Thus the projected legislation of 1834 was no remedy for the disease in South African society. The Kat River, at its short-lived best, suggests that the Hottentots were not incapable of becoming useful citizens, and that sufficiently extensive and sustained efforts to establish model coloured communities might have done something towards solving the problem.

The farmers of 1834 were pioneers, struggling to open up a new and difficult country, and their short-sightedness deserves sympathy rather than censure. They did not plead, like their successors of the twentieth century, an overwhelming fear that their children's bread would be taken out of their mouths by unfair Native competition, nor that census figures showed that White Civilization was about to be 'swamped' by a 'rising tide of colour'. Hottentots and slaves did not together more than twice outnumber the Europeans. In a military sense they were as harmless neighbours as they were helpless—unless, indeed (as might have chanced had the farmers had their way with the Vagrant Law) the Colony chose to drive discontented Hottentots into the arms of the warlike Kafirs of 1835. Colour consciousness, indeed, entered comparatively little into this early quarrel.

But neither had colonists then the later dream of South Africa's 'great future'. The missionaries stood almost alone in having some vision of a better state of society, and in their attempt to view the problems of the country as a whole. Dr. Philip emphasized how disastrous it was

that the present state of things among the farmers should remain stationary, that their kitchens should swarm with men, women and children in a state of Nature, that their children should grow up without any other companions than naked children brought up in ignorance and slavery, that they should have no work done but by people they are obliged to superintend with a sjambok in their hands, and that the cultivation of their ground should never extend beyond what is barely sufficient to feed their wives and daughters and their wretched dependants. . . . Would it not (he asks) be more desirable to see an estate cultivated by a respectable peasantry, paying rent for every acre of it, than to see it in its present unproductive condition?[1]

[1] Memorandum against Vagrant Law, November 1834.

The Vagrant Law was a commonplace attempt of re-
actionary, or merely ignorant, employers to get State sanction
for a policy that would secure a plentiful supply of cheap,
subservient, and exploitable labour.   And most 'native policy'
to this day persists in the old fallacy of contemplating the
coloured people as producers only, never as consumers, nor
even as potentially effective citizens.

The weight of argument against the Draft Law of 1834 was
decisive, and in this instance the State took its stand against
the wishes of a colonial majority.   The votes of the unofficial
members sufficed to carry the measure through the Legislative
Council.   The Governor, however, who was not on the best
of terms with its sponsor, Colonel Wade, was uneasy, and
reserved the law for His Majesty's sanction; and the official
members of Council minuted the reasons for the votes they
cast against it.   It was a law designed, they said, only against
the aboriginals, who had been deprived of their means of
natural subsistence, with no adequate compensation in land;
who had received no systematic instruction in better ways of
living, and no education; they ought not, therefore, to be
punished for continuing to live their own life, unless or until
they were given a decent alternative.   The law was 'vexatious' and 'inhuman' (for example, in its probable effect
on the children of convicted vagrants), and, because of the
insufficiency of magistrates and prisons, it would prove
impossibly expensive in administration.[1]
Armed with these opinions from responsible officials at
the Cape, and agreeing with Mr. Buxton (who was 'kept
informed' by Dr. Philip) that the Draft was 'an insidious
document',[2] Lord Aberdeen confirmed Sir Benjamin D'Urban's
action and disallowed the measure.   In a despatch of 11th
March 1835 he gave his reasons—that the existing law was
sufficient to deal with active crime, that the Draft was in
conflict with the provisions of Ordinance 50, specially entrenched as that measure was against amendment, that it was
not drawn 'to cover the avowed design of the authors', and
that it was at variance with the principles of personal freedom.
By this action His Majesty's Government definitely committed
itself to upholding the legal equality laid down by Ordinance 50
of 1828.   But a very strong section of colonial opinion abomin-

[1] *Grahamstown Journal*, 2nd October 1834.
[2] So Dr. Philip was told in a letter from Miss Anna Gurney,
Buxton's niece and secretary, on 7th December 1834.

ated and repudiated this line of policy, and were set rather on that of 1834. So much did it agree with their views of what was right that several of them immediately took action on the mere Draft—field-cornets finding it hard to believe that the introduction of the Vagrant Law in the Council, and its passing by a majority, did not give it the immediate force of law. A memorial from Pacaltsdorp in August 1834 gave the names of four field-cornets of George, and copies of the 'Permits' or 'Passes' they issued between 14th May and 11th August to Hottentots on that station, contrary to Ordinance 50. Dr. Philip reported from George on 23rd August,[1] that one P. Meiring told the Hottentots of the 'grazing place' belonging to Pacaltsdorp, that they could not move without passes, and informed those in the service of farmers that they must now enter into formal contracts. Other cases, involving real hardship, must undoubtedly have occurred. Thus in July 1835 Captain Stretch informed Fairbairn[2] that in Beaufort, 'some six months since', an armed patrol brought in thirty Hottentots, 'with as many cattle' as ordinary Boers would have, because they 'were loitering about in the waste lands of the Nieuwveld and would not work for farmers'. The field cornet thought the Vagrant Law was 'passed', but was warned by the magistrate that he might prove liable to damages for wrongful arrest. From the Kat River came definite reports of the arrival of Hottentots, similarly expelled from 'waste lands', who had lost many of their cattle in an enforced *trek*. Nor is there any reason to doubt the evidence of Dr. Philip that Sir Benjamin D'Urban was constrained to make an example of such offenders, by Proclamation in the *Gazette*, removing some of them from the roll of field-cornets. Thus the decision of Downing Street against the Draft Law was in itself of momentous importance; but the suspension of field-cornets was calculated to bring home to the farmers the significance of the decision, and caused the resentment and sense of personal injury that predisposed so many of the Boers to leave the Colony. Of such stuff Trekkers were made.

The Great Trek was, indeed, the almost inevitable sequel to the irritations of twenty years, beginning with the application of the Rule of Law to the offences of masters against servants after 1809, continuing in the slave regulations, and culminating in Ordinance 50, in the Emancipation Act, and in the refusal to go back on the principles of 1828. It may be

---

[1] Letter to Sir Edward Ryan, Chief Justice of Bengal.
[2] Letter in possession of J. G. Gubbins, Esq.

that it was the Kafir frontier policy of 1836 that converted a steady stream of emigration into a torrent, but this was almost evidently occasion rather than root cause. The grievances on which all the spokesmen of the Voortrekkers are at one [1] are those which have to do with slave regulations and emancipation, vagrancy and 'unchecked vagabondage'. The significance of Retief's complaint—the classic statement of Trekker griev-ances—must be read in its context: [2] first come three sections of his manifesto, protesting against the prevalence of vagrancy, against slave regulations, and against losses by emancipation and by 'the continual system of plunder endured from Caffres and *other coloured classes*':

We complain of the unjustifiable odium cast upon us by interested and dishonest persons under the cloak of religion, to the exclusion of all evidence in our favour; and we can foresee as the result of this prejudice nothing but the total ruin of the country. . . .

'We are resolved', he sums up, 'wherever we go that we will uphold the just principles of liberty; but whilst we will take care that no one shall be held in a state of slavery it is our determination to maintain such regulations as may suppress crime *and preserve proper relations between master and servant.*'

Never was there a more curiously phrased declaration of liberty. It is the business of the State to 'suppress crime', and nothing could be more significant or more conclusive as to the determination of the masters to be sole judges of what constitutes either crime or 'proper' relations with their servants. The safeguarding of the rights of the natives against their masters, and the attempt to fix the terms on which the colonists might look for the protection of the State, which included a majority of servants—that was a different matter. As for 'dishonesty' and 'interestedness', the missionaries had nothing whatever to gain for themselves. Their claim that the arbitrator in all cases should be not the master but the Law was manifestly just. Unfortunately the division of opinion was so deep that there was no basis for compromise or co-operation in the framing of just laws. The farmers set their face against any legislation but that of their own way of think-ing, and left the country rather than submit even to com-promise their opinions. It was perhaps natural and inevitable that they should approach the problem from the point of view

[1] All those quoted, *e.g.* in Bird's *Annals of Natal*; Piet Uys, quoted in *Theal's Sketches*; Retief and others in the *Grahamstown Journal*, and in Eybers' *Documents*.
[2] See Eybers, p. 144.

of slave-owners, the essence of slavery being, as it has been said, that 'the slave is regarded not as an end in himself but as a means to the well-being of his master', and that he stands therefore 'outside the laws which regulate the relations between one citizen and another'.[1]   Even to-day the damnation of slavery is a matter very often rather of lip service than of profound conviction, and ninety years ago the new attitude to the coloured races was likely to be vigorously contested.   So 'the unjustifiable odium', of which Retief complained, arose almost from the very idea that the Hottentot should be regarded as a free person, or that relations with natives should be regulated by any law but that of the doubtless quite honest goodwill of the farmers, who were divinely appointed to be their masters.

[1] L. Curtis, *Commonwealth of Nations*, p. 172.

Chapter XVII

THE BIRTH OF CAPE POLITICAL FREEDOM

IF Slagter's Nek marked the first phase of the missionary fight with the idea of slavery, the disallowance of the Vagrant Law of 1834 was the second; and the Great Trek of so many of the frontier farmers from the still imperfectly developed Cape was the great disaster of South African history. It is said in glorification of its heroes that the Trek was the means of opening up the interior of Africa. But the civilizing work of the Trek was prematurely and superficially done. The butter was spread too thin. Till the rather artificial prosperity that began with the opening of the Diamond Fields after 1869, and of the Rand Goldfields some two decades later, the 'development' of the country, with no solid base to build upon, was but an intensification of eighteenth-century backwardness. Even the Eastern Province suffered fatally from the loss of its none too dense population; and no reverential regard for the heroism of the pioneers can make the history of the early republics, that became the Transvaal, other than a sorry story of petty internal dissensions and of state bankruptcy. Economically there was little or no production for export, and no adequate transport to make production possible, with the result that the mass of the people learned not merely to do without luxuries, but to accept a standard of living that was altogether too low for civilized well-being. Socially, the dispersal of the population defeated for generations the power of poverty-stricken governments to overtake the need for schools; and this educational disability, with the economic backwardness of the country, inevitably produced the 'Poor White'. Above all, in the realm of politics, the Great Trek destroyed South African unity, the Cape going one way, the Republics and Natal

247

following different courses of their own. Almost at the time that Abraham Lincoln was fighting a civil war to maintain the American Union on a basis of freedom, in South Africa what had been one state was rent into four separate parts, the hope of federal or even of confederate union was destroyed, and at least two of its four components were left to establish themselves with constitutions which expressly denied civil rights to people of colour. In the United States repression is driven to follow indirect if not illegal methods. But in South Africa, where actual slavery ceased long ago, and political unity was restored in 1910, measures openly designed to give people of colour, as such, not merely a separate, but a definitely subordinate status, are still generally accepted, like articles of a creed. At a heavy cost to the social and economic well-being of the country, the Die-hards of Colour Policy went into exile rather than accept the humane implications of Emancipation. The Cape Colony, including a large proportion of the Dutch population, gradually adjusted itself to the decisions of 1828 and of 1833, and developed as a liberal state. But the liberal view enjoyed only a limited triumph; it never spread beyond the Cape, and the Union of South Africa to-day, like the old Cape of the 'thirties, has to take up the conflict against a belief in repression that is now more formidable for being entrenched by custom and rooted in a blinding fear.

The 'differential development' of the Cape Colony took form during the 'thirties and 'forties; but events beyond the frontiers have, by their almost epic appeal, diverted attention from very significant developments of policy in the Mother Colony itself. United for a time, Settlers and Philanthropists, with the Dutch on the whole a neutral or consenting party, had obtained by the Charter of Justice the first effective limitation of the hitherto irresponsible autocracy of the Governor. But in the early 'thirties, for the reasons assigned, the Settlers, and still more emphatically the stalwart frontiersmen, fell out violently with Philanthropists like Philip and Fairbairn, who in the struggle of the 'twenties had proved themselves by far the most effective of the colonial politicians. The advance towards constitutional self-government was stayed. The weight of the "Philip Party" was more and more definitely thrown against vesting the control of the Colony, with its coloured population, in the hands of a Parliament of white colonists. Obviously, a handful of whites could not lightly be entrusted with full responsibility for the political control of a great mass of unfree, or only partially free, coloured people—

who were also their own servants.   The West Indian Legislatures had even then a more than doubtful record, and with the
emancipation struggle fresh in men's minds, self-government
on the West Indian model was not lightly to be given to the
Cape.[1]   In 1830, therefore, when a Cape petition asking for
Parliamentary Government was presented in the House of
Commons, Sir George Murray definitely took a stand against
the request,[2] on the ground that while His Majesty's Government was responsible for the welfare of both white and black,
the potential white voters were a handful of the population, and
the coloured people were as yet unfit to share their privileges;
consequently the grant of Parliamentary institutions to the
Cape was for the present impossible.   This decision in itself
widened the breach between Philanthropists and colonists,
English as well as Dutch.   As one colonist wrote:

But for the *Researches*, little doubt we should have had a Legislative
Assembly, and some legal and constitutional check on the amount
of our taxation, and the manner of our expenditure . . . as becomes
our improved state of society.[3]

The wrangle about the Vagrant Law completed the schism.
As late as 1834 Fairbairn still favoured a Cape Parliament;
but at a meeting in Cape Town about September of that year,
on account of his unpopular views on the Hottentot question,
and in spite of his former services, he was refused election to
the committee of an Association formed to press for Parliamentary Government.   In October Mrs. Philip reported to her
husband, who was away on the frontier:

Fairbairn has just been in, and authorizes you to tell A. Stoffles
that he is quite of his opinion now about a Legislative Assembly, and
that he will not advocate the measure any more till the Hottentots
and people of colour are fit to take their places in it along with the
white population.   But he wishes them to make haste, as he is still
anxious that such an Assembly should be introduced.

The defection of Fairbairn was probably enough in itself
to postpone the Assembly for a good many years; for the boon
was not likely to be thrust upon a Colony that was sharply
divided about the desirability of having any Parliament at all.
Sporadically, petitions continued to reach London, but there

---

[1] The experiment broke down completely in Jamaica in the
'sixties.   It was resurrected, with doubtful success, in Natal in the
'nineties, and its ghost shows signs of vigorous life to-day in Kenya
and elsewhere.

[2] Hansard.   Quoted also in Eybers' *Documents*, p. 30.

[3] 'A. B.' in the *Grahamstown Journal*, 24th February 1832.

could be no development till there was a more stable settlement of the affairs of the coloured races within the Colony; and this was not yet. For a few months in 1835 the Kafir War seemed to endanger the very existence of a large part of the Colony, and even when the danger had passed, events on and beyond the frontier monopolized colonial attention. The Die-hards had now withdrawn from the Colony altogether. The result was that, for some years, the bulk of those who remained behind, whether from indifference, or from lack of conspicuously able leaders, or for very weariness of faction, paid little attention to the domestic proceedings of the Government; the Philanthropists themselves were absorbed in their own affairs and in watching the doings of the Die-hard Trekkers beyond the borders.

Philip's correspondence after 1838 shows that he had his own personal difficulties. In consequence partly of the unpopularity he incurred by his attitude during the Kafir War, and partly because he was a person of public importance, he had his full share of the troubles attendant on a pastorate.[1] There was, for example, constant friction about the supply of substitutes during his long absences from Cape Town on tour in the interior, and there were threats in his congregation of secession. He had to mediate between certain of his missionaries (Read and Calderwood) who fell out about colour questions. Of personal quarrels he had one in particular with Robert Moffat, who wished to transfer some of the authority in the North to a Northern District Committee—where he himself would be the big man,—the upshot of the quarrel being that on 26th June 1843 Philip tendered his resignation at the Cape, and prepared to return to England. But at this point the Treaty States and the disposal of the Boers, Griquas, and Basutos beyond the Orange River, assumed pressing importance in the affairs of the country ; on these questions Philip had concentrated most of his attention after his return from England in 1838. They had even taken him in 1842 on a great eleven months tour of the interior, so that in the Cape his influence was not as vital as it had been. The London Missionary Society itself was in

[1] Philip was not only Superintendent of the L.M.S. missions, but 'pastor' of 'Union Chapel', a somewhat exacting Independent European congregation.

A frank letter from one Mr. Merrington in April 1839 complained that Dr. Philip was 'aloof from those of low degree', absorbed in 'high things', and showed a marked preference for the company of 'rank and talent'. His preaching also was criticised as difficult, 'and to children and servants almost unintelligible'.

difficulties; in South Africa there was little new blood, and by 1845 a proportion of the active missionaries, including Read, Anderson, and Dr. Philip himself, were over seventy.[1] In England times were hard and funds were very short, so that English support was enfeebled. In 1845 also, after years in virtual retirement, his ally, Fowell Buxton, died; and in July of the same year, by the accident which caused the loss of his able son William and his eleven-year-old grandson, 'Johnny' Fairbairn, Dr. Philip himself was rather suddenly stricken with the infirmities of old age.

The result of it all was that events in the Colony itself moved very quietly. Not altogether unwarrantably, the missionaries, after their earlier struggles, rested on their oars, believing that the contest for the rights of the Hottentots had been settled in their favour.[2] Ordinance 50 was indeed now a closed issue. 'No liberal-minded man,' wrote the leader writer of the *Grahamstown Journal* on 11th August 1836, 'condemned the Act itself; it was admitted to be founded on benevolence and justice, but it was due to the mass of the people that proper checks should have been provided. . . .' A new attitude begins to show itself. On 19th January 1837 the editor described the Hottentots as, in effect, 'colonists', professing the same religion, (rather startlingly) ' often related by marriage ', and now 'inseparably blended', even if they are landless. A year later (18th March 1838) the editor returned to the theme, remarking that so great is the European mixture that he 'does not know a *pure* Hottentot within the Colony'. Rather too previously, thereupon, there was talk of allowing these new fellow-colonists to acquire land with 'title-deeds' that were said [3] to be (mischievously) 'withheld' by the London Missionary Society. It was highly probable that, since there were Hottentot land-holders who could not 'sell up and depart', they went 'hunting instead on the Bontebok Flats' (over the mountains to the North), or even 'stealing from' and 'worrying ' their neighbours. But later experience has abundantly justified the hesitation of the L.M.S. in this

[1] Philip reported in 1845 that the ages of six of them totalled 430 years, and ' something must be done '.

[2] In a fragment of 1840 or 1841, for example, Dr. Philip wrote: ' Sir George Napier has been two and a half years Governor of this Colony, and during the whole of that period I have never had occasion to bring before him any one case in connection with the Hottentots. Such is the difference between a people under the protection of the law and the same people without any law to protect them.'

[3] *Grahamstown Journal*, 9th September 1837.

instance. The difference between European and coloured
standards was so immense that to put coloured men on land,
and then to allow them to sell freely to whom they chose,
would have been the speediest possible way of breaking up the
'Institutions' for good and all. And the evidence of the files
of the *Grahamstown Journal* suggests that there were Europeans
who must have been fully aware that 'titles' would inevitably
have led to the absorption of the Kat River by white colonists.
Sir Benjamin D'Urban also flirted with the idea of 'titles'. He
had 'long ago contemplated settling the Hottentots on locations' in order to 'fix them on plots of ground', and give them
an 'interest in the soil'.[1]   The *Commercial Advertiser* was
suspicious and Lord Glenelg discouraging, preferring rather
to encourage the Hottentots to become 'free labourers'.[2]
Stockenstrom's Hottentot plantations on the (rather arid)
banks of the Fish River were a failure,[3] and with this experiment all attempt to give Hottentots the hope of rising
to economic independence was allowed to lapse. It is still
commonly forgotten that low-grade labour makes low-grade
employers; and in a country where, at best, economic and
social conditions made the masters themselves but poor and
unprogressive, the constant disregard for the interests and
improvement of the labourers has reacted disastrously on the
whites themselves. Constructive reform was left to chance.

Just about 1837, however, there were other reasons for a
visible decline in the interest bestowed upon the Hottentots,
even as a potential labour supply. Some years before 1835 the
Chaka wars had had the effect of unsettling the Bantu and
causing the break-up and dispersal of many tribes. Even in
the 'twenties Bechuana refugees began to filter into Cape farm
service. But the Kafir War of 1835 greatly intensified this
unsettlement. A large tribe who had earlier been scattered
among the Kafirs, virtually as slaves, seized the opportunity of
obtaining British protection in return for services rendered to
the authorities during the war. The Governor even took these
'Fingoes', as the Kafirs called them, under his own special
care, and assigned them land in the neighbourhood of Fort

[1] D'Urban's Circular to Civil Commissioners, 5th February, and
despatches to Glenelg, 19th August and 20th November 1837.
[2] Glenelg to Napier, 9th November, 1837.
[3] Mrs. Philip visited several of these hamlets in November 1838,
and even then found little that was encouraging. They seem to have
been abandoned soon after.

Peddie, between the Fish and Keiskama Rivers; there indeed their position seems to have been a constant source of annoyance to the Kafirs or 'Amaxosa', who doubtless regarded them as 'traitors', and resented having these refugees settled (with Kafir cattle,) on their own (Kafir) land. It was, however, hardly a sufficiently large or fertile area to support all the refugees, and groups of them passed over the Fish River into the Colony proper, at least as far west as Uitenhage. From this time, therefore, much stray evidence goes to show that Kafir refugees of one sort or another, principally Fingoes, were increasingly absorbed in employment on the farms. As early as 1837 a Report from Bethelsdorp complained, not only of poor crops and high prices, but that

there has not been the same demand for labourers as formerly, a great number of Fingoes having come into the Colony, who are employed at lower wages than those usually given to Hottentots. These circumstances have been assigned by the inhabitants as reasons for so little being done to make better houses this year and to improve the Institution.

Correspondents in the *Grahamstown Journal* from time to time abused their fellow-farmers for encouraging the recruiting of Kafir labour, and Government agents in Kafirland pointed out that the farmers had themselves to thank for the prevalence of a new class of Kafir 'vagrants'. Categorically, in 1839, a Report from Theopolis cited the case of a neighbouring farmer who habitually refused to pay more than 1s. a day for harvesters (the demand and the price being of course seasonal only), instead of the normal 1s. 6d., because he could get all the Fingoes he needed for the lower price. Dr. Philip on one occasion seems to have commended the Fingoes to the Hottentots of Bethelsdorp for their greater frugality—rather unkind comfort for a people whose sufficiently low standard of wages was being 'under-cut' by one still lower. Evidently, even if wages were reduced, the old labour shortage on the Eastern frontier was sensibly relieved by the coming of the Fingoes and other natives,[1] and labour has continued to be an unduly cheap commodity in those areas unto this day.

[1] The official diaries of T. Shepstone, Stretch, and other agents in Kafirland make frequent mention of passes given to natives for 'reasonable purposes'. Shepstone on 15th November 1845 reported a 'usual application' for thirty Fingoes to help with crops in Lower Albany. But there is no reason to suppose that all the labour recruits were Fingoes. On 28th January 1846 the *Grahamstown Journal* remarked on the increase of population in Albany and estimated that 'six or seven thousand' had been absorbed 'in the last

The unsettlement on the Kafir frontier, and this coming and going of 'foreigners' in search of work, caused the authorities to take action for the control of native immigrants by enacting a law 'for the more effectual prevention of crimes against life and property within the Colony'. Ordinance No. 2 of 1837, promulgated on 21st June, gave the local officials considerably increased powers; it sanctioned the use of force, and admitted in extreme cases a plea of 'justifiable homicide', if force proved necessary to effect the arrest of any person charged with crime; in effect this was a measure for the prevention of 'criminal' vagrancy, but the crime to be prevented no longer included, as in the Draft Law of 1834, living by roots or by killing game, but only such clearly defined offences as murder, homicide, rape, robbery, assault, arson, and cattle-stealing. With modifications, the Ordinance re-introduced some of the old provisions of the Pass Law, requiring 'foreigners' who entered or moved about in the Colony to carry passes, on pain of being returned to the service of their master, or of being assigned, with their own consent, to the service of some 'creditable inhabitants'; failing either alternative, they were to be removed beyond the limits of the Colony. But it was bound to take more than paper laws to undo the harrying effects of the war of 1835, and of the wars among the Bantu themselves; and it is necessary to bear in mind the general uprooting of tribes (together with the 'sins of wolves and jackals' complained of by Theopolis in 1834), in judging the unrest after 1836, and the charges of 'theft' levelled indiscriminately against 'the Kafirs'.[1] The *Grahamstown Journal*, indeed, in announcing the measure of 1837, seemed to recognize that, even with these increased powers, effective administration would be hampered by the absence of police, the insufficient number of magistrates, and the inadequacy of prisons.[2] But at least the letter of the law, and above all the supply of labour, were now more adequate to colonial demands, and the long-vexed 'Hottentot' question ceased to attract public attention or interest. The further definition of Hottentot status was left to the almost unnoticed

---

ten years'. On 21st February the paper remarked on the inconvenience of relying on the labours of 'Kafirs who fly on the first rumour of war'. In May it reminded its readers of the unparalleled 'increase' that followed the last war.—Possibly increased dependence on sheepfarming helped to relieve the shortage of labour at this time.

[1] Cory, iv, *passim*.

[2] 6th July 1837. The *Journal* mentions that at Somerset gaol there were only 'three diminutive Hottentots' to guard over sixty prisoners.

action of the responsible officials; the Colony, for the most part, silently acquiescing in whatever was done.

In this comparative calm, Sir George Napier, who relieved Sir Benjamin D'Urban in January 1838, began at once to consider the situation. The effect of Ordinance 50 had now been tested by ten years' experience in administration. Amendments might reasonably suggest themselves, especially now that the number of 'free' persons of colour was to be permanently augmented; it was proposed to abandon the system of 'apprenticeship', that had been designed in 1833 for the more recently emancipated slaves, partly owing to the anomalous position of the liberated apprentices.[1] While the Governor recognized that the Hottentots had reason to dislike long-term contracts, he also thought they needed stricter control, and unlike Stockenstrom (whose criticisms of a Vagrant Law he forwarded to London), he was at first inclined to regard a further stiffening up of the laws against vagrancy as necessary and desirable. In the end he was wiser and brought forward a more general measure, for the revision and consolidation of existing laws for the protection of the labouring classes, and for defining the respective rights and duties of masters and servants.[2] On the whole (see also Chapter XII) this Ordinance tightened up the provisions of 1828 in favour of the masters; while contemplating monthly or even weekly contracts of service, it now provided that oral contracts might in some circumstances be binding for twelve months; and since unlettered servants instinctively distrust written bonds, and masters tended to prefer merely spoken agreements, this plan was possibly more to the liking of both parties than the law of 1828, which restricted oral contracts to one month only. Written and attested agreements were now compulsory only for contracts of more than twelve months, with an upper limit of *three* years (extended by Act 15 of 1856 to *five* years). Further clauses which deal with the conditions governing contracts, with apprenticeship, offences and penalties, made little notable departure from the law of 1828, but did not go quite so far in stiffening the law as the Amending Act of 1856, which was framed when the farmers had more direct influence on law-making by their votes in the

[1] To carry out the term of indentures might have the effect either of separating parents from their children, or of making virtual serfs of free parents who were unwilling to be parted from apprenticed children (Napier to Secretary of State, 22nd June 1838).

[2] Ordinance No. 1. of 1841, confirmed by London, in accordance with the special safeguards against amendment of No. 50 of 1828, in August 1842.

new Cape Parliament.[1]   Compared with Ordinance No. 50, the law of 1842 was marked chiefly by a more rigid definition of the duties of servants, with appropriate penalties for neglect, refusal to work, desertion, damage to property, violence, insolence, and insubordination; there was more consideration for the inevitable difficulty of enforcing civil penalties or exacting compensation from penniless servants, and the stress was now laid, less on the necessity for safeguarding the freedom of servants, and more on giving a reasonable definition of their actual status.   If only from the necessarily disadvantageous position of a servant who takes proceedings against a master, the scales may be somewhat weighted in the master's favour; but the 1856 statute, as it still stands, gives servants a fair measure of the protection of the law-courts against the wrongful acts of employers.

Special legislation for the protection of servants was indeed less necessary owing to the general terms in which the new 'Masters and Servants' Ordinance was framed.   The really essential innovation of 1842 has often been missed, probably just because it was so quietly done that it attracted little or no comment.[2]   We are left to infer that Ordinance No. 50 was so mistaken that it was deliberately annulled.   What happened was that, to the satisfaction of the 'friends of the Hottentots', Sir George Napier advisedly dropped anything like the much criticised second clause[3] on the express ground that it was undesirable to continue to brand the free coloured people as an inferior class by a special law like Ordinance No. 50.[4] Some three years later Lord Stanley made inquiries about the 'practical effect' of the new Ordinance, and was told that the

[1] As examples of changes in 1856: the age limit for apprenticed males was extended from 16 to 18 years.   The penalty for unlawful detention of apprentices was changed from ' 20s.' to 'not more than 20s. nor less than 5s. '.   In 1842 non-resident servants were exempted from removing with their masters to a distance of more than two miles; resident servants could not be compelled to move more than ten miles. In 1856 it is added that servants may not legally refuse to go on a journey (*e.g.* with cattle) if so ordered by the master.

In 1856 a provision of 1842 which allowed a servant damages in a sum three times that of any illegal deduction from wages is dropped altogether.

[2] Dr. Theal leaves the impression that the Hottentot question merely lapsed.   Sir George Cory hastens to add a footnote of relief to his first mention of Ordinance No. 50.   'It was repealed, August 27, 1842' (ii, p. 370).   Repealed it was; but its work was done, and its principles established.

[3] Cory, ii, p. 370, and above, Chapter XVII, p. 211, and *note*.

[4] Napier to Russell, 30th January 1841

Council concurred with the Governor in describing it as 'well fitted' to its object, and further, that 'it is not complained against'.[1] The effect of repealing the Ordinance was actually to place the coloured population of the Colony on a footing of complete legal equality with Europeans, and to give them at last the full protection of the ordinary law of the land. The Cape Colony ceased to know any legal distinction between 'white' and 'coloured'.

So far as the Cape Colony was concerned, this legal equality paved the way for further progress towards the 'representative institutions' which many desired. The period of internal peace which resulted, after 1836, from the easing of the labour shortage, and even more (unfortunately) from the withdrawal of the extremists who had gone on *trek*, was marked, in spite of external excitement enough, by a number of important preparatory developments. The mistake of snapping the last link between government and governed, by the abolition in 1828 of the local Boards of *Heemraden*, was gradually rectified. After 1836, by an Ordinance of that year, Municipal Boards were authorized; and Municipal Government actually 'broke out' in Beaufort West in the following January. In 1843 there were the beginnings of a central Road Board, with local District Road Boards, as well as advisory School Committees; and though none of these had wide powers, they were all useful as tending to promote in colonists the habit of association for public purposes. Its Divisional Council system (1855) helps to make the Cape politically still the soundest part of the Union. It was about 1845, in the light of these developments, that Dr. Philip wrote with some complacency:

The white colonists of South Africa were often told, while the struggle for the oppressed aborigines was going on, that the tyranny of which they complained as exercised over them by those above them was the price they paid for the power they enjoyed of tyrannizing over the coloured classes. Fortunately for themselves, they failed in their efforts to perpetuate the slavery of their oppressed bondsmen, and the Cape Reign of Terror, as Pringle called it, has been exchanged . . . for a state in which 'they shall sit every one under his own vine and under his own fig-tree, and none shall make them afraid'.

Meantime, on the introduction of the new Masters and Servants Ordinance, Sir George Napier had expressed the opinion that a legislative assembly would be valuable, as a means of educating public opinion, and of somewhat lessening

[1] Sir P. Maitland on 17th October 1845, replying to Stanley's despatch of 24th November 1844.

S

the excessive reliance of the colonists in all matters on the initiative of the Government. Lord Stanley [1] was disposed to agree in principle, but expressed fear of the difficulties that might still arise from racial divisions, and of the danger, especially, that a Parliament in practice might mean 'the rule of a dominant caste'.

It remained to reassure Downing Street on this point, and, first, the colonists themselves must reach some basis of agreement. Fairbairn, who was the leader of a section of colonial opinion chiefly represented in Cape Town,[2] had broken with the party of self-government in 1834, and on this occasion Dr. Philip wrote:

> I should as soon think of recommending the British Constitution as a model of Government to the Kafir Chiefs, as a Legislative Assembly in the present state of this colony. . . . I have long seen that if ever this Colony is to be made fit for an assembly, the schoolmaster must do among its inhabitants more than has been done. . . . The alphabet must come before Montesquieu and Locke.

Fairbairn, however, probably never quite abandoned hope. About 1836 his own *Commercial Advertiser* had been nearly ruined by the unpopularity of his views on the Kafir question. Between 1836 and 1838 he was in almost weekly touch with Sir Andries Stockenstrom,[3] and he had reason to know also, from the unhappy personal experience of the Lieutenant-Governor of the Eastern Province, the power of hostile public opinion, even without any representative assembly. Fairbairn's suggestion, therefore, was to make treaties of alliance with leading Kafir chiefs; let the Governor be 'unhampered in *foreign* (*i.e.* frontier) affairs by any sort of Colonial Council, and arm him with a strong military force to protect (Native) allies'.[4] He, too, was thinking of something like 'territorial

---

[1] Cf. Lord Stanley's reply to this despatch, 15th April 1842.
[2] See above, Chapter XVII, p. 249.
Of Fairbairn's defection in October 1834 Mrs. Philip reported that when Fairbairn's candidature for the Representative Assembly Committee was defeated, one Prince 'thereupon publicly recanted all he had said in favour of an assembly, for he saw that they were not fit for it'.
Unfortunately the cleavage tended to be between English and Dutch, for Mrs. Philip added that Fairbairn learned by this experience that 'the English must make common cause with the coloured race'.
[3] This is evident from perusal of a remarkable series of letters which passed between Fairbairn and Stockenstrom, and are now in the possession of J. G. Gubbins, Esq.
[4] Fairbairn to Philip, 28th March 1836, and more fully in an undated document, probably of 1838.

segregation'. If only the new Kafir complications were kept
at a distance there was no reason why the Cape should not be
left to manage its own domestic internal affairs through its
own Parliament.

Though hardly in the way Fairbairn hoped, it was, in the
end, in isolation from the rest of South Africa that the Cape
Colony was to attain parliamentary government. In 1847 a
large number of Bantu, for the first time, became British
subjects,[1] but till 1865 they remained a separate administrative
unit as British Kaffraria. In 1848 Sir Harry Smith took a
plunge and annexed another separate province, the 'Orange
River Sovereignty'. Natal had by this time come into existence with a Lieutenant-Governor of its own, while, like the
colonists of Natal, the handful of Boers scattered beyond the
Vaal River were too distant and still too insignificant to be
of much account. It was in these circumstances, while there
were still hardly any but the original Hottentots and former
slaves among the coloured subjects of the Cape, that the final
steps were taken.

In 1848 Earl Grey's proposals for a colonial Parliament
were being seriously canvassed,[2] as appears from a despatch
of the Governor, who sought to assure Downing Street that
the rights of the coloured people were secure. Consulted
by the Governor, the Attorney-General advocated a parliament
with a low electoral qualification, so that the suffrage might be
kept 'within the reach of the more intelligent and industrious
men of colour'. He wished it made clear that nothing
depended in this free country on the 'accident of colour';
and he did not fear 'vagrant laws of undue stringency', owing
to the 'protection' afforded in the last resort by the royal
power of veto.[3] Assurances were the more necessary, for there
was a faint recrudescence at this time of the old 'vagrancy'
agitation; petitions poured in from country districts, protesting that a proposed new Militia Law might create a shortage
of labour, or even, by the withdrawal of able-bodied men, give

[1] Apart, that is, from a few thousand Fingoes absorbed at the time
of the 1835 war, and the abortive annexation of the 'Province of
Queen Adelaide' in the same year.
[2] 'Natal has too many lawyers, the Cape too much legislation.
The Colony has been brought to the brink of ruin by absolute vacuity
at one time, and witless meddling mediocrity at another. Let us look
for, and labour to bring about, a more natural order of society.'
Fairbairn to Dr. Philip at Hankey, 2nd March 1848.
[3] Governor to Secretary of State, *Duplicate Despatches*, 17th March
1848.

rise to a state of insecurity.[1] In face of this outcry, Judge
Menzies, whose attitude seems to have mellowed since the
time of Ordinance 50, would have a 'fundamental' clause
requiring the Governor to withhold his assent to any law which
sought to impose special disabilities on people of colour; he
would also have the Masters and Servants Law 'embodied,
as at present,' in an Order in Council, which the colonial
legislature could not repeal or alter.[2] There were, however,
signals of alarm once more from the Kat River, which distrusted
the formation of a Political League, and was suspicious of a
new move for a Vagrant Law, 'both of which inspire the entire
native population with fear and a want of confidence as to
their rights and liberty'.[3]

Suddenly Downing Street itself supplied an issue, calculated
to bring all sections in the Colony together, and to unite them
as they had never been since 1824. According to a despatch
of August 1848 the Cape w·s to be made a Penal Settlement.
Following hard on this ⸱.nouncement, and others supplementary to it, in September 1849 the *Neptune* arrived with
the first load of convicts; and immediately the Colony was
in the uproar of the 'Anti-Convict Agitation'.[4] The unanimity
was striking, and 'philanthropists' were as determined in
their resistance as any of the old colonists. In October and
November 1849 Durant Philip wrote repeatedly to Fairbairn,
sending him signatures, and even funds, collected from the
'Hottentots' of Hankey. Old Dr. Philip joined the Rev. J.
Freeman, a visiting Director of the L.M.S., in a 'Memorial'
(pretty certainly the last of his long series) which protested
against the danger of introducing convicts among a population
of backward coloured people.

[1] The Memorial from Koeberg corn farmers (quite near Cape
Town) is typical. It suggested selling up missionary institution lands
to finance itinerant preachers. None, it says, will object to missionaries preaching on their farms 'if it be done with a due regard to
propriety' (the masters once more to be sole judges of the 'propriety').
Significantly also it wanted to increase the power of the J.P. in master
and servant cases.

This memorial has one note that is more familiar in the twentieth
century. Koeberg blamed 'landowners in corn districts who hire
out land to persons of colour'. On the other hand, by the evidence
of Mr. J. Montagu, the Colonial Secretary, colour prejudice was so
little pronounced that a Malay was elected as a 'Ward-master' in
Cape Town; but he did not sit.

[2] Enclosure in despatch of 17th March 1848.

[3] James Read (jun.) to Dr. Philip, from Kat River, 19th September
1848. Mr. Read feared 'another San Domingo'.

[4] See Theal, iii, pp. 68 ff.

This is the first occasion in which the Dutch and English inhabitants have coalesced in opposition to Government,

wrote the Governor in warning (January 1850).

Now Earl Grey was on occasion a stubborn man. His plan of increasing the population of the Cape by means of convicts was perfectly well-intentioned, and he was loth to abandon it. In November 1849, however, he gave way, and in February 1850 orders arrived to send the *Neptune* on to Van Diemen's Land. But, unlike Lord Bathurst in 1824, Grey was also the great advocate of experiments in colonial self-government, and, faced by the united opposition of the Cape Colonists, he had reason to believe that they were not ill-fitted for a greater degree of responsibility in the management of their own affairs. He was compelled to abandon the plans for a new Penal Settlement, but the Constitution was now safe, and the further delay was apparently fortuitous, and due largely to the upheaval of the great Kafir War which began in 1850. By Letters Patent of 1850, the Governor and Council of the Cape of Good Hope were empowered, subject, of course, to His Majesty's approval, to make a draft of their own future bi-cameral parliamentary Constitution; and the initiative passed to the Colony. In September of the same year John Fairbairn and Andries Stockenstrom (almost equally unpopular members of the 'anti-colonial' party of less than twelve years earlier), were on their way to England as the chosen spokesmen of the Colony. They were commissioned to press for the acceptance of the draft constitution, if possible without amendment. In London they had the full support of the missionary spokesman; Mr. Freeman, indeed, on his return from South Africa, was emphatic about the depressing effect on the commandos engaged in the Kafir war both of the 'Convict Affair' and of delay in granting a Constitution. 'No colonist is admitted to power and influence', and the result was a 'sense of degradation'; to increase a colonial sense of 'responsibility', he urged that the grant of the Cape Constitution be hastened, with a proviso only that the franchise be as 'wide' as possible, to 'include' and 'secure the consent of the coloured races'.[1]

Except, perhaps, for the low franchise qualification, the Constitution which came into effect in July 1853 was in essentials the colonial draft.[2] In spite of its elective Upper House,

[1] J. Freeman, *The Kafir War of 1851*; pamphlet in collection of J. G. Gubbins, Esq.

[2] Constitution Ordinance, originally drafted by Governor and Council of Cape of Good Hope—as authorized by Letters Patent on

it hardly deserves to be called 'unusually liberal';[1] it provided
only for 'representative', not for 'responsible' government.
But this was as much the choice of the colonists themselves
as the result of the veto of His Majesty's Government. In
1872, with strong encouragement from London, but in the face
of stout opposition from stalwarts in the Eastern Province, it
was an Act of the Cape Parliament[2] itself that carried the
reform a stage further. Henceforth, ministers were no longer
mere officials and nominees of the Governor, but men chosen
by and responsible to the legislature.

Finally, much of the significance of the new Constitution
lies in the spirit in which it was accepted. The legal equality
of black and white, though no doubt a condition without which
it would never have been sanctioned by Downing Street, did
not have to be forcibly and immediately imposed from without.
It was accepted by all parties in the Colony, and never challenged
till our own day. The active opposition had gone North. A
contemporary letter gives the true statement of the case;[3] writing of the mission of Fairbairn and Stockenstrom it proceeds:

They are out to pray for a constitution which shall ensure their
right position to all citizens of this colony in respect of each other
and of the rule of the country—a constitution based on principles
which forbid class government or class legislation, and which has for
this reason evidently met with support and countenance in England.

When in 1850 John Fairbairn set out on this second political
mission to England, his prospects of success were very different
from what they had been a quarter of a century earlier when he
fought his stormy battle for the Freedom of the Press. He
at once bethought him of the man to whom so much of the
change was due, the veteran leader in so many fights for freedom—now retired and very near his end;[4] and Fairbairn, who
could write a good letter, expressed himself as follows:

> St. Helena, on Board
> the *Madagascar*,
> *November 7, 1850.*
>
> My dear Dr. Philip,
> This expedition became so suddenly necessary that I had no

23rd May of thirteenth year of Queen Victoria—amended and confirmed by Order in Council 11th March 1853.
  [1] Theal, iii, p. 132.
  [2] Act No. 1 of 1872 (text in Eybers' *Documents*, p. 63).
  [3] A fragment, dated 3rd May 1851, in the possession of J. G.
Gubbins, Esq. From internal evidence it would seem to be by a
friend of the Fairbairn family, possibly Judge Watermeyer.
  [4] Dr. Philip finally gave over to the Rev. W. Thomson from
1st October 1850. He died in the following August.

opportunity of consulting you on its objects or the best manner of obtaining them, which I would gladly have done; but I feel assured that generally you will agree with me in the course that has been adopted. I never was more clear about anything in my life. The Colony has in part become self-governing, and some form of government is immediately required for the establishment of authority and the preservation of order. It is most dangerous for such a community to remain long under an administration which no one even professes to respect. I can see many dangers in such circumstances, but there are probably many and much greater dangers which no one can see, though they may be close at hand. Should disunion spring up among the different classes, and delay will almost certainly cause it, the Colony would plunge headlong into ruin. Deeply impressed with this, I have resolved to decline all discussion on the constitution which the people have now accepted as a beginning. It is to be considered as passed, and only submitted to the Queen for a formal sanction. It may not be the best that could be contrived, but it will restore confidence and place improvement in better hands than those of secretaries and clerks either at the Cape or in London. All this in substance is the natural result of your labours, and of those who have had the privilege of working with you for the last quarter of a century. Political liberty and legal equality were the final objects with all; and these are substantially gained. It will now be the perpetual work of all classes to break oppression and injustice in the details of future administration. This will be comparatively easy when they have the Institutions and Laws on their side, instead of being against them, as they were when you first began the great work in Southern Africa.

Ever faithfully yours,

JOHN FAIRBAIRN.[1]

No doubt a political appeal to the Colonial Office under Earl Bathurst in the 'twenties was one thing, and appeal to Earl Grey and the Liberals of the 'fifties quite another. But the more he believed in self-government, the more any responsible Minister must have hesitated to confer the boon of a Parliament on a handful of white settlers, who stood in relation to a subservient coloured population as the Cape colonists stood to the Hottentots before 1828. As Fairbairn foresaw, there were dangers ahead. But the legal equality of 1842 had paved the way for potential political equality, and for a Constitution which did not so much as mention colour and knew no 'Colour Bar'. Looking back over the events of these years, history must recognize that the two great landmarks along the road

---

[1] A curious feature of old family relationships is that this son-in-law, in innumerable letters, was always 'Fairbairn', the parents-in-law in return being 'Dr.' and 'Mrs. Philip'. Miss Buxton is once at least addressed by Dr. Philip as 'My much valued Correspondent'.

that led to full parliamentary government are the liberation of the Hottentots by Ordinance 50 of 1828, and the Emancipation Act of 1833. By 1853, though thorny social and economic difficulties remained, the internal colour problem of the Cape Colony had ceased to be a question of politics.

Chapter *XVIII*

FROM 'HOTTENTOT' TO 'EURAFRICAN'

THE political status of the coloured people was now defined, but their place and progress in economic society
were by no means assured. Economically, indeed, they
were in an exceedingly unfavourable condition. Long before this
time direct pressure had deprived the Hottentots of grazing land,
and therefore also of cattle, and had made them an easy prey
to diseases like smallpox; the indirect pressure of the labour
laws completed the process that changed a race of primitive
nomads into a band of serfs, existing on the verge of starvation.
Before 1828 the so-called 'Hottentots' had probably made
little or no advance; what capacity they had for improvement
was never put to the test of opportunity. A few years later
there were some signs of progress: the early success of the Kat
River Settlement; the achievement in 1844, under supervision,
of such a feat as the irrigation tunnel, which diverted the
Gamtoos River, and made a potential garden of the Institution
at Hankey; and even the authenticated fact that by 1845
Zuurbraak could support two shops.[1] Such experiments, and
doubtless also the example of individuals and families, were
some evidence that more progress was made in less than twenty
years than in nearly two centuries preceding. But in the mid-
nineteenth century there were few of the original strain of
Hottentots left in the Colony. The emancipation of the slaves
(who were originally imported Africans or Malays,) and the
establishment of legal equality, tended to merge any separate
groups, whether of Hottentots or of 'other free persons of

[1] Report for 1845, confirmed in 1849 by the testimony of a prosperous neighbouring farmer, Mr. Ben. Moodie. (Evidence to
Commission on Masters and Servants Law.)

colour', into a composite mass — almost all of them equally resourceless and landless—and later history was left to deal with 'the Coloured People'.[1]

The composition of this mass of 'coloured' people is of some interest and importance. The colonists of South Africa, especially the Dutch people, are marked by a strong race pride which has prevented wholesale miscegenation, though it appears that the colour prejudice was far less strongly felt in earlier days. Even in the early nineteenth century, the so-called 'Griquas',[2] as well as a proportion, at least, of the Kat River Hottentots,[3] were rather indiscriminately known as 'Bastards'. The writer in the Grahamstown Journal, already quoted (Chapter XVII, p. 251), is not the only witness in this decade who had never seen a pure Hottentot within the Colony. Even then, as later, many of the 'coloured' people might be a mixture of Hottentot, Malay, negro slave, and even 'Kafir',[4] without white admixture, but the common use of the term 'Bastard' is in itself some evidence that there was considerable miscegenation even when the total white population of the country little exceeded 30,000. That the largest single strain in the 'Coloured People' was probably Hottentot is indicated by the colloquial Afrikaans, which still applies the abbreviated word, Hot'nots; modern statisticians tell the rest of the tale in classifying them as 'Eurafricans'. The contempt of colonists and of colonial historians, and their conviction of the worthlessness of the 'Hottentots', (not incompatible with a strong desire to command their services as labourers,) were no more the outcome of a scientific study of ethnology than the modern assumption that the Coloured People are inherently superior to the pure-blooded Bantu. The undoubted general superiority of many Coloured People is probably due, not so much to the admixture of European blood, as to the immeasurable advantage

[1] In the common speech of South Africa the term 'Native' is reserved for the Bantu, and tends even to be spelt with a capital N. Some half a million people of many varying shades, the descendants of Hottentots, Malays, negro slaves, and many others, with a strong admixture of European blood, are comprehensively spoken of as 'the Coloured People'.

[2] According to J. Melville, missionary, and Government Agent at Griquatown in 1823, the total in his scattered district was about 3000. In 1842 there were said by the Rev. P. Wright to be about 4800 in the immediate neighbourhood of Griquatown.

[3] Cory, iii, pp. 248, 149. Also J. Boshof, on Dr. Philip's 'Bastards' (Bird's Annals of Natal, i, 505).

[4] The Bantu seem to have contributed comparatively little to the 'Coloured People'.

given them by their habitual use of the Dutch language, and often their proficiency in English, and, in fact, to their longer contact with European civilization.

In the middle of the nineteenth century the affairs of the Coloured People, as they had now become, ceased to be of any pressing public importance. The political rights of 1853 satisfied the coloured people themselves, and left them not only without any sense of grievance, but loyal and contented. Though their interests have habitually been neglected,[1] from this time they themselves have never been actively repressed, and have never even made a separate political party. It is no mean achievement that the Cape has thus retained the devoted loyalty of its coloured citizens, gradually absorbing a fair but by no means even a large number of them into its electorate. But they were utterly destitute of organization. With no centres of common life, and too much divided to be conscious of common interests, they were for many years almost negligible as a political factor. Their very insignificance, now that they were free, saved them from such direct pressure as is now rapidly breaking down the historical lines of cleavage between Xosa and Fingo and Zulu and Basuto—giving a philological term like 'Bantu' something of the connotation of nationality. As a political experiment the Constitution of 1853 has been abundantly justified. Had not this Constitution rested on principles which gave the coloured people security and potential equality, the Cape could not so early have been entrusted with political responsibility; and the fact that the coloured people have political rights has helped to prevent this trust from being abused.

But the very success of the experiment was won at a price in economic well-being. The coloured people have remained a community of poor and backward dependants, a drag, as such a class must be, on the welfare of the whole. The violence of the controversies which preceded 'Hottentot' liberation caused a reaction, in which the adjustment of their economic conditions to their revolutionized political standing was neglected and forgotten. Even their contentment is testimony chiefly to the beneficent effects of a freedom that allowed at any rate the abler or more fortunate individuals

[1] Perhaps even sorely 'neglected' when predominantly Bantu districts came to be incorporated in the Colony. The old Kaffraria was still being administered in 1924 under an Act of 1884; urgently needed amendments were merely crowded out of consideration by the preoccupation of Parliament with the affairs of its own white members.

among them to rise to a competence. The great mass of them were still a poor servant class, and were left to find their own level.

The very fact that there were signs of progress encouraged this neglect. Tendencies clearly discernible in the 'forties went all unchecked, and though constructive reform must have been difficult at best, after about 1851 concerted efforts for their advancement languished altogether. Even the 'Institutions' ceased to function as centres of Hottentot life; and the successors of the 'Hottentots' were left to become hangers-on and slum-dwellers about the fringes of European civilization. Whereas the worst features of poverty and degradation in the old-established countries of Europe are a by-product of the industrial upheaval of the last two centuries, the Cape was launched as a self-governing community hampered by a ready-made landless proletariat.

One effect of the liberation of 1828 must have been to accelerate the drift of coloured people to the towns and villages, where life was more interesting, and where also, as James Read pointed out, (above, p. 239) the conditions of employment were at least less unfavourable than on the farms. The burden of missionary letters is of the 'growing importance of work in the *drostdies*', rather than, as formerly, in the 'Institutions'. But in the villages, after 1836, control passed into the hands of local municipalities, whose coloured labourers might have had more to hope from the beneficent administration of enlightened magistrates than from being handed over to the tender mercies of their lords and masters. For example, in 1836, a Mr. van der Riet, the Magistrate of Uitenhage, took steps to provide applicants from Hankey with sites in the Uitenhage 'location'; plots were to be a quarter or half an acre of *good* land, and title was to be given, free of expense, on fulfilment of the conditions, which required the land to be fenced, and a 'decent' house erected, within three years.[1] Not only is little more heard of any such experiments; but eight years later the municipal authorities of the same Uitenhage seem to have found this location site unnecessarily good. The complaints and letters of the Rev. W. Elliott, a resident missionary, show that in 1844 both Hottentots and Fingoes were removed to a new and inferior and waterless site at a more convenient distance from the town. Graaff-Reinet distinguished itself about the same time by a

[1] Letter to Mr. Melville, Hankey. The house was to be of brick or other suitable material, plastered and whitened, with 90 square feet of floor space, and at least one six-paned window.

regulation designed to prohibit any individual not possessed of property to the value of £200 from keeping more than two head of cattle on the town commonage. Graaff-Reinet had its excuse; its rainfall is uncertain, and any common grazing land in South Africa tends to be disastrously over-stocked and 'eaten off'. But its solution of the difficulty was grossly unfair to the poorest inhabitants, who were of course the coloured people. It was more particularly hard because in the absence of banks, with the scarcity even of currency, the general custom of the country people even yet is to put savings into 'stock' (*i.e.* cattle).[1] The guiding principle of such municipal councils was undoubtedly the old desire to make the coloured people serviceable as 'producers only'.

The spread of local government institutions was therefore no unmixed blessing. The Coloured People were of course too weak to do anything for themselves, and the central government was never seriously driven to concern itself for their interests. In the mid-nineteenth century many new villages sprang up on sites chosen for the erection of a Dutch church. The Kerkraad, ('Kirk Session') having acquired some farm, normally paid for it by dividing it up into building lots, or *erven*, which they sold for the erection of 'Sunday houses' for the use of farmers coming in, especially to *Nachtmaal*. Church and 'Sunday houses' normally attracted permanent residents and shops, and grew into regular 'dorps', with of course a retinue of coloured servants. The poor prospects for the Coloured People may be illustrated from Colesberg, which had grown up on the site of the ill-fated Bushman Station, Tooverberg. The London Mission Station in the village reported a membership, in 1844, of about four hundred, and Mr. Atkinson, who was in charge, in excusing the smallness of an annual missionary collection of only £35, explained that his people could neither make a garden nor keep cattle unless they could afford to hire an *erf* from the church. Nor, he added, could they even build a hut or house except, by favour, on their masters' property, and then with no security of tenure.

[1] A letter of comment from the Rev. W. Elliott asks pertinently: 'If the favoured possessors of £200 had themselves always been affected by the limitations now proposed, what would their position have been'? In Uitenhage also, it would appear, the cattle owned especially by the Fingoes were a reason for wanting to force them to move. On farms, to this day, even landless white squatters, like coloured people, tend to be moved on if they acquire cattle of their own, and probably lose any they have accumulated by the enforced *trek*.

But whatever the practice was in Colesberg, on the whole even the hiring of *erven* to coloured men was discouraged—certainly the hiring of what are called *water-erven* (those carrying a right to use the irrigation furrows of the township). The normal outcome was that squalid locations, destitute of even a pretence of civilized amenity, sprang up somewhere on the outskirts. The one rendezvous for the coloured inhabitants was the 'canteen', which purveyed cheap spirits. Mr. Read had reason to complain that whereas the Kat River Settlement, with the consent of the inhabitants, refused to allow a canteen, the twenty-mile distant European village of Fort Beaufort was 'the most dissipated place in the Colony, with three canteens before the war (1846), now fourteen or sixteen'. The municipal administration of Coloured and Native locations is on the whole a sorry story.[1]

Now this urban difficulty has only been accentuated by the peculiar South African accident of Colour. Fundamentally it is the familiar, though baffling enough, economic problem of poverty, with its normal accompaniment, the growth of slums. The problem was less baffling perhaps than it is to reconcile in any way the interests of present-day Kensington and Poplar. It is comparatively easy in the light of experience to look back and see how necessary it had been from the beginning to take precautions against municipal maladministration and neglect. But the question first arose at a time when the London Missionary Society, whose missionaries were most directly concerned, had already borne the burden and heat of the fight for coloured rights. Dr. Philip, absorbed by the difficulties arising out of the Trek, was an old man. The funds of the Society were low (the age was indeed the *Hungry 'Forties*), and the very shortage, both of funds and of men, gave rise to a certain rivalry between the claims and interests of

---

[1] It is impracticable here to detail evidence of my own researches into some aspects of this question. Some facts relating to Grahamstown were submitted in evidence to the Union Local Government Commission, 1916; others were published in pamphlet, *The Place of Local Government in South Africa* (Johannesburg, 1917). I have met with a coloured death-rate of 67 (the average rate for Europeans being 12 or 14); an *average* 'location' infantile death-rate of 333 per 1000 over a period of twelve years; for single years 429 and more. In spite of figures like these, Municipal Councils have been known to make locations a means of relieving the general ratepayer, levying rates on coloured people, and spending practically nothing on their location. The Natives' Urban Areas Act, passed only in 1923, has at last taken power to the central Government to compel municipalities to provide decent living conditions for the coloured inhabitants.

'drostdies', and of 'Institutions', of Town against Country. Yet this was a most critical stage in the history of the Coloured People, demanding a degree of united thought and action that at this period was strangely lacking. The growth of 'towns', or even of villages, was a new phenomenon. They were bound to have their quota of coloured workers; but the urban missionaries, though insisting on the importance of their own 'work', hardly showed sufficient realization of the difficulty, under the prevailing conditions, of making the villages satisfactory bases of work for the maintenance and development of coloured civilization. Rural centres like the Institutions (the 'last relics of Hottentot land between Cape Town and Colesberg', as one of the Reads said of them) were to be preferred, if possible, both as educational and training centres, and to give some of the people an interest in and a hold on the land.

Things were far from well with the Institutions. Originally, as Dr. Philip had always emphasized, they had been the means of weaning the Hottentots from a wandering nomadic life.

When Dr. van der Kemp and I commenced our labours in 1801 (wrote old James Read in a discussion in 1848) we found the whole nation in the most degraded and miserable condition, *without lands, without liberty* (slaves), *without property, without knowledge, without clothing,* except the sheep-skin, *without education, without religion.*

Even the later Kat River was heavily handicapped. Like the others, it was one of 'the only asylums for the destitute and infirm', therefore of the nature of a 'Poor Law Institution', and therefore also, almost of necessity full of non-effectives and 'idlers'. Though the Settlement had now about five thousand inhabitants, its founders (some hundreds, from Bethelsdorp and elsewhere) started their work with '*nothing*',— and this in spite of the modern South African dogma, that 'capital' is indispensable to successful South African farming. To this Dr. Philip had given early expression: [1]

I have found out that it will not do to set up for a gentleman farmer in South Africa without the fortune of a gentleman.

The Institutions could make little headway against such tremendous handicaps. Some stations, like Zuurbraak and Pacaltsdorp, were said to be overcrowded, though the over-crowding was relative only to the small area, since the population even of the larger station was little more than eleven hundred.

[1] *Journal of Tour of 1841–42.*

On the other hand the population of Bethelsdorp was in decline. Its people partly made a living from its own salt-pan, and even then it was a 'coloured' suburb of Port Elizabeth, nine miles away. Theopolis was in decline, seriously named for total abandonment in a letter of 1846; and the Kat River, with difficulties of its own, was badly shattered by losses in the Kafir Wars of 1846 and 1847. In all parts, moreover, as with Poor Whites later, the best prospect for the people was in rather casual occupations like 'transport-riding', for by the time political freedom was secured for the Coloured People financial stringency was so acute as to prevent the L.M.S. from promoting the works of development sorely needed on the Institutions.[1] With the greatest possible skill, however, and ample

[1] The energy and engineering skill of Dr. Philip's son, William, with the help of about £500 in subscriptions from Cape Town and elsewhere, made use of the labours of the Hottentots to such good purpose as to achieve the notable success of bringing Hankey under water. The accidental death by drowning of the author of this scheme, in 1845, was probably an irreparable blow to the fortunes of the station; his account of the end of the work follows:

HANKEY,
August 16th, 1844.

MY DEAR MOTHER,

I am sure you will be most happy to hear of the conclusion of our work. I cannot but think that your joy in Church Square will only be inferior to our own. On Tuesday night, the 13th inst., about one or two o'clock in the morning, I was startled out of a restless sleep, the only sort of sleep I had enjoyed for some nights previously, by a shot fired off at my bedroom window. I knew the signal, and started up: ' The tunnel is through!' I looked out and saw the messenger from the rock still running with a flaming brand towards the village and our house, and screaming as he ran; some in the village had seen the signal at the mountain, and heard the firing before he arrived. It is impossible to describe the state of the village a few minutes after; in every direction was heard shouting, hallooing, yelling, screaming, while these serenades were constantly broken by shots fired off from the houses. If you can imagine all the jackals, wolves, baboons, men, women, and children gathered together in mingled war, you will have some idea of the noise. Some thought the Caffers were in the village, when the flash from a gun fell upon their half-awakened eyeballs, and ducked under the bedclothes again: the bell was ringing, fires were blazing, and lighted brands seemed as if they had got legs and were traversing the place in every direction. Bands of children had in the meantime collected all the old iron and tin scuttles out of the houses, and were accompanying the local concert with rough music and shrill screams. I wisely went to bed again thinking to snatch a little sleep before the morning. It was in vain, the noises continued, our house was surrounded, and the kitchen filled, principally with women who were all sobbing; one burst into my bedroom with a loud yell, and coming to my bedside caught hold of my hand: ' What a

financial resources, it must have been difficult to convert half a dozen ordinary sized farms into thriving centres of civilization for any considerable population.

An observant but anonymous missionary commented on the situation in 1848; first with regard to the people:

I have not seen a pure Hottentot since I have been in the colony; some are scarcely distinguishable from white men, others by connection with the slaves or Kafirs, have darkened their skins, but I cannot say deteriorated their character, as almost any remove from the pure Hottentot must be an improvement. These people have acquired most of the habits of the European colonists among whom they are resident . . . they eat, they clothe, they cultivate, they build in the same manner. . . . In all things that the eye can see and the

---

great work, and the Lord has spared us to see it through!' She could not say any more, but went sobbing out of the room. I ordered the servants to make coffee for them, but scarcely any of them stopped to partake of it, they ran about from one house to another, and many went off to the tunnel before it was daylight. All this enthusiasm was quite spontaneous. I had no conception of the extent of feeling on the subject, and can only account for this extreme degree of it by the previous extreme of unbelief. The measurements have all proved much more accurate than I had reason to expect. Considering that I had only a sextant to perform them with, the galleries ran into one another in a right line, and the floors were also on nearly the same level at point of meeting, the waterside being four or five inches higher than the other, so that my first essay in practical engineering has been successful. I could only wish now, to make my contentment perfect, that my father and yourself should see it, and I think all the anxiety which you as well as myself have endured would be fully compensated. I had a little mason work to do on the river side, but go to put the water through to-day. I shall now throw all remaining work upon the people; we may therefore conclude that our expenses are ended with this week. These will be about £500 altogether.

As I think now of starting from here for Cape Town in the first week of September, I shall not make any fixed regulation with regard to disposal of lands, etc. till I can communicate with my father. It strikes me the place must now support itself.

Evening: I have been to bring the water through. We only opened half the channel for it, but the stream was irresistible; it was a small *river*, and would have turned the largest mill in the country, the bed of the river is at least twenty feet above the level of the ground to be irrigated. It is I have no doubt the very finest position for the erection of mill machinery in the Colony, and if a capitalist would rent the water power, and employ some hundred hands, it would be an object as great as the irrigation of land, but not to speak of manufactories, I have no doubt that for flour mill, saw mill, etc., you could rent the water power for £100 per annum, and it would be a pity to let waste such a source of profit to the Institution.

Your affectionate son,
WILLIAM PHILIP.

T

hand handle, they are quick and retentive; having once seen an ox, a goat or a horse they will pick it out of a thousand; but if there is a mental junction in any work, a reflective process necessary to connect parts that are *see-able*, if a why or a wherefore intervenes, you must not grudge a little time and trouble in the repetition of your instructions. . . . They are awake to a *present* interest, and to a *right*, but are deficient in forethought, seldom requiring to be preached to from the text, 'Take no thought for the morrow'. That precept applies to a civilized people. What might serve for to-morrow's food is eaten up to-day, and if a stranger comes to partake of the family meal, he not improbably gets for his share the greatest part of to-day's and to-morrow's food also. They are hospitable to an excess, . . . [it seems an acknowledged principle in explaining the crowding of Institutions, as of modern native 'reserves', with 'squatters'.]

Turning to the Institutions, the letter continues:

We have a people located on a farm where there exists in general no foreign influence but that of the missionary. The land is not their own, but they have the privilege to graze it in any part, while whatever of the soil can be irrigated is divided among the residents in plots of little more than *half an acre*, affording food during a fruitful year for a family, for about *three months*. During the rest of the year they must seek food where they can, and generally hire themselves out as farm servants, sometimes transporting their whole family to the farms, more frequently leaving their families on the station while they bring in at the end of week, or month, the fruits of their labour in food; this is usually about as much as a man can carry twenty or thirty miles on his back, not, as you will readily see, too much for ever so small a family to live upon for a week or a month. 4s. 6d. are often their wages for a month, very seldom more than 10s. . . .[1] Can there be a rapid improvement in a people thus situated? When the cravings of hunger are to be satisfied by veld roots and berries for a great part of the year . . . is it a wonder that the Hottentot on our stations retains much of his original indolence . . . when he does not possess a single motive to industry? . . . And yet the astonishing thing to me is that this People, so situated, are *no longer* Savages,—they are decent in their persons, well dressed, cleanly in their houses. We appear, if I contemplate our stations, to have taken the surest and quickest plan to injure and destroy this people; for we have located on a spot where twenty families could not live, two hundred or more perhaps, who might otherwise by being distributed among the farmers have had abundance of wholesome food and many of the comforts of life.

But, in another light, there is . . . the counter-acting principle. 'Man shall not live by bread alone'; for in spite of the disabilities of the people of the Institution they must be acknowledged a more civilized, virtuous and respectable class than those of their nation either resident in the towns or among the Farmers. . . . Could the means of subsistence be supplied on these (Institution) farms, everything might then be accomplished. . . . But to preach the gospel to a people unsettled and deprived of the common necessaries of life,

[1] Rev. D. J. Helm, Zuurbraak, 1848, vouches for offers of wages of only 1s. 6d. a month, and explains the preference shown for casual daily employment at a rate of about 1s. a day.

embittered by the past, and anxious for the future, was to persuade to its acceptance at a most unfavourable time and to contend against a most unfair advantage.

The letter concludes on a note that might apply even to the conditions of the twentieth century:

Hence our effort to teach these people trades: but in a thinly scattered country like this, where almost everyone is his own smith and carpenter, where is the demand for such tradesmen? Hence the attempt to establish a woollen cloth manufactory; but the evident impossibility of taking that leap over the middle age of a nation's civilization, and turning a pastoral race into a manufacturing population will sufficiently explain the failure of this scheme. The only practicable and legitimate means of subsistence open to any large class of people in such a country as this, where the markets are over-stocked with every foreign article, is agriculture and the grazing of cattle.

For reasons like those expressed in this letter, the Rev. W. Elliott, in the latter part of 1848, urged on the L.M.S. an attempt to secure the approval of the Government for a plan of granting the tenants on the Institutions a definite *individual title* to their plots of land. (Since many of the stations were still held vaguely 'of the Government', official sanction was needed to effect any change.) The Victorian Age had begun, even for the missionary guides of the 'Hottentots,' [1] and, in the next half century, in many parts of South Africa, disastrous mistakes were due to an over-confident belief that the principles of an individualist political economy were applicable even to a backward people only beginning to emerge from barbarism. The experience of that half century has made it obvious enough to-day, as it was not then, that the backward races cannot hold land by individual title, in free and open competition with more advanced Europeans.[2] The principle of 'reserves' evolved only gradually in later years. Mr. Elliott's aim was sound enough—to make the Coloured People more self-reliant, to give some of them a definite interest in their land, and to reduce the evil of squatting on the stations. For one short moment his

---

[1] 'They have now reached a point of civilization beyond which it is extremely difficult to raise them. . . . In one respect they may still rise, and that is by the *acquisition of more property*.' These were the early impressions of the Rev. T. Durant Philip in 1845, when he succeeded his brother William at Hankey.

[2] 'Griqualand East', granted to Adam Kok after 1869, and by him divided up among his 'burghers', is now almost wholly European-owned; the older Griqualand, now part of the Orange Free State, is entirely so. In what was once British Kaffraria, land held on 'Native Title' is very largely owned by Europeans. Among many other instances, see facts for Hankey and Zuurbraak cited below, pp. 285-6.

proposals roused Dr. Philip, who seized at once on the weak spot, though with some of the impatience of a frail old man:

> Among other things that Elliott proposes as remedies, the giving of the people lands, to be transferable, as their own etc. etc., seems to be the panacea. We have not time to go into that subject at present, but a little reflection is sufficient to teach us that the scheme he proposes would be the ruin of our Institutions. Canteen keepers would in a short time be the chief proprietors of the villages, a Government Agent would be absolutely necessary, a Field Cornet or something of the kind; and a missionary and a Government of that kind would not go together. Elliott and others appear to forget that the great object of our Institutions is of a Religious character. . . .[1]

One reason for Dr. Philip's curtness was that at this time public criticism of the stations by a missionary was ardently welcomed by less friendly and sympathetic critics.[2] There seems to have been talk once more of 'breaking up the Institutions', and even of a 'Vagrant Act'.[3] In the following February, a Commission, presided over by a magistrate, Mr. le Sueur, reported highly unfavourably on Zuurbraak to a Committee of Council appointed to consider the Masters and Servants Law. Control was loose, education was poor, numbers uncertain, and emphasis was laid once more on 'numbers thus withdrawn from agricultural labour'. With a complete lack of constructive sympathy, the Commission merely denounced. It seems to have 'forwarded without remark' a statement in reply to its criticisms prepared by the missionary, Mr. Helm, together with a memorandum in support of Mr. Helm by Mr. Benjamin Moodie, a neighbouring farmer, who had also been a J.P.[4] Mr. Moodie's statement is valuable, first as the testimony of a substantial farmer, with more than twenty-five years' experience, to the steady improvement of the Hottentots of his neighbourhood, and to the increasingly beneficial effects of milder laws. In the second place, Mr. Moodie made some obviously necessary amendments to Mr. Elliott's suggestion of 'individual title':

> If the objection (that free title would lead to alienation of land and the break-up of the Institutions) is of weight enough to justify

---

[1] A very short note to Durant Philip, 30th October 1848, written apparently to Dr. Philip's dictation.

[2] What was intended to be a private letter of Elliott's was published in *Evangelical Christendom* about September 1848.

[3] Cf. Read's letter from Kat River, above, Chapter XVII, p. 260.

[4] MSS. Copy of Commissioners' Report to Council, dated 26th February, with statements by Messrs. Helm and Moodie, dated 25th May 1849.

the exclusion of the capital which whites would bring along with them, it may be obviated by making the grants of land inalienable except to persons of the same race, or making the Missionary Society trustees, whose consent should be necessary to the transfer. . . . My own conviction is that every *desirable* purpose would be accomplished by a condition in the grant, that one person could only hold one original share of the land.

There was perhaps some faint hope that, with intelligent leadership, a constructive policy might be evolved. But Dr. Philip could do no more than collect evidence from the stations, and what little he wrote shows that he was mainly concerned to defend the Institutions from being 'broken up'.[1] Yet his latest views were not incompatible with constructive reform. The Institutions, he held, were indispensable, as 'the only means of concentrating the population for church and school'; and since scattered farms or village slums were the only alternatives, he was clearly right to cling to the Institutions as the potential centres of coloured civilization. In the second place, Dr. Philip's assistants, like Mr. Helm, had learnt from his teaching to emphasize the value of such bases as Zuurbraak as potential *reservoirs* of labour. It was beneficial even to the farmers to be able to draw on the services of labourers from the Institutions at times of stress, like harvest or shearing; failing such colonies, farmers must retain a larger permanent staff than was necessary except at the busy seasons, and, therefore (as happens notoriously with 'labour tenants', under the laws of the modern Transvaal) keep this redundant staff both under-paid and under-employed. South Africans who freely criticize the 'idlers', whether on old Institutions or on modern 'reserves', give far too little attention to the waste and the poverty caused by their own farmers who still demand Pass Laws, and conditions of 90-day 'labour tenancy', which have the effect of creating a large class of 'tied' labourers. The services of these labourers, then as now, being incompletely

---

[1] Dr. Philip's latest memorandum on the Institutions was written without reference to Elliott's suggestions, certainly later than the 1842 tour, and probably arising out of that of 1845. Its theme, significantly, was the impossibility of relieving the Society from the *expense* of maintaining them—so little was the Society able to think of spending money on their economic development.

Probably the latest of all the letters in Dr. Philip's own handwriting is a pathetic little quarter sheet to Miss Wills, in a thin quavering hand, dated '5th February' (1849 or possibly 1850). He speaks of 'the old struggle under a new form' . . . 'to bring the people back to slavery by putting down our Institutions' . . . 'This has been a life of conflicts with me. . . . May this be my last!'

278 THE CAPE COLOUR QUESTION

utilized, can only be inadequately paid. There is no possible doubt, on the evidence, that the Institutions actually furnished farmers with reserves of labour at the busy seasons — just as Native 'Reserves' to-day, unlike the farms with 'tied' squatters, are the only 'reservoir' of labourers for mines, industries, sugar-estates, and at a pinch, even for High Veld maize farmers.[1] Dr. Philip, with almost unrivalled knowledge of the country, saw clearly that even such poor homes as were furnished by the Institutions had an economic function; as a 'refuge' they afforded the Hottentots some vestige of a base from which to bargain and stand out against unduly bad conditions of service. At worst, as many of them did, they could 'squat' with their fellows at the Institutions.[2]

These principles were by no means irreconcilable with a reform on the lines hinted at by Mr. Elliott, and more fully sketched by Mr. Moodie. 'Squatting' is but a poor resort; if habitual, it must depress the general economic standard, since it is a drain on the slender resources of those who entertain the squatters. Measures to raise the standard of living at the existing Institutions, thus justifying their enlargement, might have been the means of strengthening the Coloured People; by increasing the general prosperity, it might ultimately not only lessen the dependence of most of them on starvation wages, but, by stopping the supply at the source, it might also have begun, at the right time and the right place, the painful process of forcing South African farmers away from their incurable habit of depending on low-grade labour. Carefully planned reform of the Institutions would not have been too late in 1848 to set South Africa on the lines of the policy associated long afterwards with the name of Booker Washington, the

---

[1] I know of Transvaal farmers who wilfully tie up labour by calling up *different* squatters on one day a week, on pain of ejection if they fail to appear. This prevents them from hiring themselves elsewhere, and is designed to keep as many as possible available for occasional 'rush' seasons.

[2] At a further remove, the position of the landless Hottentots was not wholly unlike that of some of the peasants dispossessed by the 'Agrarian Revolution' in sixteenth-century Europe. Of these Mr. R. H. Tawney writes that, 'being normally themselves the sons of peasants, with the prospect of stepping into a holding of their own, or at worst, the chance of squatting on the waste (they) were often in a strong position *vis-a-vis* their employers' (*Religion and the Rise of Capitalism*, p. 151).

The Hottentots were not in a 'strong' position, but they, and still more the present-day Bantu, would have been completely helpless but for this penultimate resort of 'squatting'.

reformer of negro policy in the Southern States.   The Coloured People in South Africa had even then no destiny except to develop as part of the economic system of Cape Colony; but an effort might have saved them from being a mere proletariat. Dr. Philip at least, for all his hope that they might ultimately be incorporated in the ordinary life of the Colony, did his utmost to preserve for them a separate existence of their own. He alone came near evolving a hopeful practical policy, both for the Coloured People within, and for the Natives who were then beyond the Colony.   His policy was that these backward people should be firmly fixed in homes and on lands of their own.   With a secure home base, they might well have provided all that was needed in the way of a reserve of labour, without being wholly and utterly dependent on their chances of wage-earning alone; and modern South Africa might have escaped the clogging of its prosperity and the complication of its social life by the dispersal through its farms, towns, and *dorps* alike, of a great mass of landless and homeless, poorly equipped, and helpless unskilled labourers.

Yet the years that saw the attainment of political freedom in the Cape Colony, and the dawning of hopes of a constructive social policy, were followed hard by events that decided the issue and relegated the Coloured People to mere proletarianism. The Kafir war that began in 1846 was quiescent for nearly three years, and then broke out again with extended fury from 1850 to 1853. Both Kafirland and, in 1852, Basutoland, were involved; and Downing Street, in impatience, or despair, so far as the Interior was concerned, abandoned the attempt to control the situation as a whole, and recognized the separate existence of the Transvaal (1852) and of the Orange Free State (1854). Within the Colony there was one minor episode which was to prove disastrous for the future of the Coloured People.   In the war of 1851 discontented 'Hottentots' at Theopolis, and on the Kat River, threw in their lot with the Kafirs and entered into rebellion.

For 'Hottentots' in any numbers to join the Kafirs against Europeans was in itself a startling and almost unprecedented development.   In 1835, in spite of tradition, the truth is that they fought solidly against the Kafirs, not with them; [1] and there is very little doubt that the participation of Institution Hottentots in hostile acts of war, as in the lamentable outbreak of 1851, lost nothing in colonial telling.   Theopolis by this

[1] Above, Chapter XVI, p. 240.

time was clearly in a parlous state; for years it had been in charge of an aged or infirm missionary, and in 1850, after the death of Mr. Sass, it had none at all;[1] its 'buildings' were neglected and its numbers insignificant. The upshot of the war was that Theopolis ceased to exist. Ten years later the lands came up for disposal, after a perfunctory inquiry by a Select Committee of Parliament. His own evidence in 1861 suggests that Sir Walter Currie, as officer in charge in 1851, handled the inhabitants with so little tact as almost to drive them into the 'careless' attitude he first complained of; and in the end, his evidence is by no means convincing that the station was destroyed, as he alleged, by its own people. But because the causes and circumstances of the 'Rebellion' were never adequately investigated, and because no war losses compensation was ever paid, the London Missionary Society took no steps to reoccupy or restore the Institution.[2] The Kat River Settlement in some fashion survived; but in spite of the efforts and services of a 'Loyal Burgher Association', and of a Cape Corps of about one thousand men, which proved that the rebellion was far from general,[3] it was thrown into ruin and confusion.

The outbreak was obviously a reckless and unconsidered protest against unsatisfactory conditions by people who had only too little to lose. The one Theopolis family specially commended for loyalty was that of Moses Jacobs, a comparatively substantial 'deacon'. 'My opinion', wrote Mr. J. Rose Innes on 30th May 1851, 'is that the Kat River Settlement had not entirely recovered from the war of 1846–47 when

[1] 'Taylor is unwilling to leave Theopolis lest anyone succeed where he failed.' Dr. Philip to L.M.S., December 1844 (or 1845).

[2] Report of the Select Committee on the Theopolis Lands (Cape Town, A 5, 1861). The Committee recommended that the site be granted, to be disposed of for the benefit of the Albany General Hospital, Grahamstown. They ignored an amazing claim by Mr. T. H. Bowker, M.L.A., who filed a petition claiming that he was entitled to compensation for his services to Sir George Cathcart and to the country, in the Kafir war: 'I said to (Cathcart) he might give the Theopolis land, about 14,000 acres, valued at about £5000. He said it was a good deal. I rejoined that if the Governor only gave me a trifle, it would leave me just where it found me, and would not put me in the position I ought to be in.'

[3] The 'Cape Corps' served under General Somerset. A return claiming the authority of the Rev. W. R. Thomson classified 818 Settlers as 'loyal', and 266 'rebels', the latter mostly, but not all, 'non-erf-holders', i.e. 'squatters'. Quoted by Rev. J. Read in *The Kat River Settlement in 1851*. Cape Town, 1852 (A. S. Robertson).

that of 1850 commenced.'[1]   A score of Mr. Read's letters [2] indicate that the whole station was devastated, and he himself, and many of his people, were refugees under cover of the fort at Eland's Post (Seymour), throughout those war years (1846–1847) when the loyalty of the Hottentots was unimpeachable. In February 1847, Read sent Fairbairn a memorandum on the grievances and hardships of the people;[3] the Hottentots, who had served, shared the grievances freely expressed by the European burghers; and even for direct war losses there was little if any adequate compensation.[4]   On the contrary, there were difficulties about the exaction of quit-rent for the grant of land made to a troublesome person called Hermanus; and, doubtful character though Hermanus may have been, Mr. Freeman pointed out, with some relevance, that the amount to be exacted from him and his followers, some £100 or £150, would have been only £7 for a single European farm of similar size.   Further, the administration was far from sympathetic. Two local officials in succession, Messrs. Biddulph and Bowker, had to be superseded before ever the war began—'too late', says Mr. Freeman.[5]   An even earlier example is only too characteristic of the clumsy way in which the feelings of 'Hottentots' were rough-handled.   In papers dated '1845', 'H. Hudson' (for Col. Hare) replied to a Kat River petition asking for easier terms than were offered to coloured applicants for land at Blinkwater:

> Blinkwater was never intended as a refuge for hordes of idlers, but for an industrious population, from amongst whom the worthless and sluggard will be ruthlessly weeded.

The Hottentots asked for bread and were given a stone. Though their grievances were real, if they asked for redress, they were liable to be dismissed, as they were by Mr. Hudson, with such terms as 'worthless' and 'sluggard', or as political 'agitators'; if European sympathizers took up their case they were 'sowers of sedition'.

But neither before 1850, nor later, was there any official

---

[1] Quoted in Read's *Kat River Settlement*.
[2] Philip MSS.   [3] MSS. of J. G. Gubbins, Esq.
[4] Cory, iv, cc. ix and x; cf. esp. p. 467.
[5] Freeman, *Kafir War of 1851*. By courtesy of J. G. Gubbins, Esq., I had access to an interesting copy of this pamphlet, annotated by Mr. Robert Godlonton, editor of *Grahamstown Journal*. The only comment Mr. Godlonton can make on the Hermanus quit-rent is unconvincing: 'At any rate *all* the Kat River had previously been taken from the Kafirs and given to the Hottentots '.

attempt to examine their alleged grievances and remove the causes of possible sedition. The tradition was established (I met it alive more than seventy years later among old white residents on the Kat River) that the seditious teaching of the missionaries Read, father and son, was sufficient to account for all that happened. Now, letters from the Kat River show that before the outbreak there undoubtedly was 'political' excitement—not without reason. A fair number of the 'Hottentots' could and did read, not only the friendly *Commercial Advertiser*, but the highly provocative *Grahamstown Journal*. A good many more were in the habit of doing 'transport-riding' that took them across the Katberg and the Stormberg to the Orange River, and beyond, where they got 'news', of sorts, of the contemporary doings of the Trekkers. As pupils of the missionaries, they were now in the second generation; but being flesh and blood, and no doubt unstable and excitable, they had enough of the older generation among them to be thoroughly alarmed by renewed threats against 'vagrancy', and fearful of a return to the bad old days of only twenty years earlier. The prospect of being ruled by a Parliament of 'Settlers' undoubtedly alarmed them. At the same time, the flouting of Government authority by the Trekkers set them a bad example. The war in Natal in 1842, the defiance of Andries Pretorius, the campaign of Boomplaats in 1848, led some of the Hottentots to comment: 'How cheap is rebellion nowadays!' It was not the missionary, but the colonial attitude which was 'unsettling', and when at the end of 1850 the Kafirs took the field, there were enough of these unfortunate Hottentots, who had nothing to lose, to try the chances of rebellion.

The day had now fairly come for all the old enemies of the 'Institutions'. The comment of the *Grahamstown Journal*, 15th March 1851, shows more than the sudden heat of war-time panic and excitement:

'On the Eastern frontier a contest between stern justice and mistaken philanthropy has been raging upwards of thirty years' . . . the Home Government and the British people being 'influenced by certain powerful, presumably religious associations' . . . There has 'never been so important a crisis as is now at hand, and each party, finding it bears very much the aspect of a death-struggle, is preparing its weapons accordingly. The voice of every Colonist must be loud in demanding that every Institution where a number of the coloured races are, or can be drawn together, shall be broken up, and restricted from reassembling. If we destroy, or prevent the building of the nest, we shall not be liable to invasions of the brood.'

From the blighting influence of the taint of rebellion the 'Institutions' never even began to recover; and the London Missionary Society, no longer strong with the driving force and statesmanlike genius of the mind and personality of Philip, abandoned all thought of comprehensive efforts to achieve a social policy, and was content to function as one of many merely evangelizing agencies. In the 'sixties the L.M.S. plunged into a policy of abandonment. Their Cape congregations must prepare to stand on their own feet, and release the Society, its men and its resources, for 'pioneer' work in 'heathen fields' beyond.[1] Its policy was one of deliberate withdrawal, and from the 'seventies onwards its responsibilities were confined to Hankey and to Bechuanaland, ultimately to Kuruman alone.

Through the London Missionary Society, in spite sometimes of the Society's own officials, Dr. Philip was the principal means of vindicating and gaining acceptance for the enlightened principles which underlie the advance towards political and social freedom in the Cape Colony before 1853, and have guided its coloured and Native policy to this day. The effectiveness of Dr. Philip's work contrasts with the later, almost tragic, futility of his own Society in the same Colony, where, as a factor in the social life of the Coloured People, it ceased to count. Yet we are told that Dr. Philip by his activities as a politician ruined all; that, at any rate, by the 'violence' of his advocacy, he aroused 'unnecessary' antagonism. Bowing before the storm of obloquy, his own successors feared to be 'branded as political',[2] and blush and apologize even yet for their great forerunner. But the overthrow of slavery, and especially the changed status which this involved for coloured people generally, demanded sacrifices from the colonists which were hard for them to meet. Rather than bow to the new demands, they went out into the wilderness. It was likely that opposition would be fierce against the man who seemed to them the embodiment of the ideas that robbed them of their homes. The obloquy that attaches to Dr. Philip is the lot of men who attain great ends. The charge of imprudence made even by the kindest of his critics is of a piece with the heresy that religion is for Sundays and holidays. For Christian missionaries, set in the midst of any backward people, like the

[1] See Lovett's *History of the L.M.S.*, vol. ii.
[2] The Rev. R. Niven's phrase in 1852 when he failed to rouse any of the mission authorities in London to make official representations about the Kafir war.

Churchmen teachers of our own fathers in the Middle Ages, must be the responsible representatives of civilization and culture in the widest sense. This is a truly political though not a partisan function; and it is a function that cannot be fulfilled by eschewing politics. To disregard questions affecting the social welfare and economic security of their people is to doom their work as teachers of religion to sterility. Efforts to fulfil a 'purely' religious function may be completely overwhelmed by the social and economic facts that are thought to be 'outside the proper sphere of missions'.

In South Africa the heat that Dr. Philip's activities had engendered was followed by a long reaction after his death, in which the fear of taking any political stand, however necessary it might seem, has acted on the missionary societies like a creeping paralysis. Considerations affecting the economic standing and welfare of the Coloured Peoples (and Natives) have been regarded as political, and *taboo*. For a long time this attitude fitted well, and disastrously, with the prevailing economic theory of the age. The L.M.S. was driven to abandonment of its stations, partly by its own financial straits, but it was also justified in its action by the perfectly orthodox principles of *laissez-faire*. In 1872, for example, in promoting the 'Missionary Institutions Bill', with the necessary Government approval and support, Rev. T. Durant Philip was the principal spokesman. He explained that the L.M.S. favoured plans for giving grants of land on the stations, with 'individual title'. Forgetting his father's warning, which was backed and repeated now by a well-disposed colonist, Mr. T. D. Barry, M.L.A., he even went so far as to express himself in favour of encouraging an admixture of white erf-holders 'for the betterment of the Hottentots'.[1] 'Whereas', says the Preamble to the Act of 1873, 'it is desirable that connection in secular matters between the said society and the said inhabitants should cease'—that is, because by 1853 the political status of the Coloured People was secure,—they were now thought fit to take their places in society as good, respectable mid-Victorian individualists.

The economic results were in the long run disastrous. Except in countries like France, with a long peasant tradition, 'small-holdings' are notoriously difficult and disappointing, attractive though they be, in the abstract, to reformers. What tradition the 'Hottentots' had was not good, and the

[1] Report of Select Committee on Missionary Institutions Bill, Cape Town, 1872.

usual difficulties of debt and credit were enhanced for them by the presence of more advanced European neighbours—by their standards almost 'capitalists'. Moreover, the most elementary ideas of 'passing transfer', and the technicalities of Western Land Laws, were beyond their comprehension.

Two outstanding examples of the consequences may suffice. So chaotic did conditions become on the Kat River that it was difficult to know from whom to collect quit-rents, though these often amounted to no more than 1s. 9d. or 2s. It was hardly possible even to know on whom to fix the liability for cleaning the common irrigation furrows. About 1905 'we agitated' (so a European in the district told me), and one Adendorf, the Member for the Division, succeeded in piloting through Parliament a reform measure known as the *Boedel Erven* Act No. 38 of 1905). The *Boedel* (estate) *Erf* belongs to the 'estate' of the original grantee. The Act, that is, deals with holdings, *erven*, 'jointly' owned by an indefinite and possibly indefinable number of 'Hottentot' peasants. The object was to facilitate sub-division and transfer (with a lower limit of 300 square roods for sub-divided units), in fact, to return to effective 'individual title'. The upshot, however, was that the legal costs of effecting transfer proved to be beyond the means of the mass of the tenants, and swamped them with more debt. There was no restrictive clause to safeguard the original design of making the Settlement a Coloured 'Reserve'. Within twenty years, the nineteen or more villages of Coloured People, which survived from the old days of the plantation, were reduced to about three. In 1922 'Philipton' survived as an 'Independent' Church community, too poor to maintain a regular 'minister'; but 'Readsdale', with 'Wilberforce', 'Buxton', 'Fairbairn' and other village settlements which had survived, with names that indicated their origin in the exciting 'thirties, were for the most part European farms, in a more and more predominantly European-owned district, still known as 'Stockenstrom'.

The fate of Hankey was similar. Of the land originally held by the L.M.S., in trust for its coloured people,

small lots were sold at various times, and in 1924 the remainder was transferred by the Society to the Municipal Council of Hankey. . . . The ground appears to have been subdivided into building and agricultural lots, most of which are held by Europeans, some of whom own as many as twenty-two of the latter, averaging about half a morgen each. The Census for 1921[1] (290 Europeans and 833 Coloured

---

[1] In 1904 there were 146 and 1444 respectively.

persons) 'shows that the coloured population still predominates, although the greater portion of the agricultural land is owned by whites.'—[Yet in 1822 Bethelsdorp helped to pay for Hankey].

It appears that, in 1926, 78 Europeans held 277 agricultural holdings officially valued at £23,105, while 55 Coloured Persons and Natives held only 79 agricultural holdings valued at £4843. On the other hand, 89 Europeans held 407 building lots valued at £32,068, while 147 Coloured People or Natives held 198 building lots valued at £4742.[1]

Others reap where William Philip and his Hottentots watered, and the educational establishment that began to grow on the promising irrigated farm settlement has been removed, to make a new start in the neighbouring town of Uitenhage.

So much for 'individual title' as a panacea for the economic ills of a backward community of Coloured People. The difficulties no doubt were overwhelming; and since the older Institutions so dismally failed as 'reserves', it was impossible to extend them or add to their number. The social results of the policy of 'abandonment' were therefore no less disastrous, for when the Institutions failed, only the slums remained. There were no centres of any kind for the Coloured People, nor had they any outside organization like the Church to bind them together. In the early days, it will be remembered, the L.M.S. had its congregations and mission stations in almost every possible centre of 'Hottentot' life. The Society was also definitely 'Independent' or 'Congregational' in its ideas of Church government, and when it finally withdrew from South Africa it did so piecemeal, leaving each tiny community to stand on its own feet, with no vestige of a national Church organization. When Dr. Philip was 'Superintendent', his personality gave the Society in South Africa many of the advantages of almost episcopal unity of aim. But in his later years, even Philip's own control was considerably weakened by the impatience of strong Independents like Robert Moffat; and when all these units were left to themselves, the construction they were likely to put on the word 'Independent' did not necessarily bear much relation to the great traditions of 'historic Independency'. The great majority in fact were too weak to

---

[1] For these recent facts and figures I am indebted to C. Duk, Esq., magistrate of Humansdorp, and through him to Dr. J. J. Coulton of Humansdorp and to the Town Clerk of Hankey. The magistrate remarks also that the large commonage is ' badly infested with jointed cactus' (being visibly ruined by poverty, neglect, and incompetent control).

survive at all, and were either taken over or superseded by some more strongly organized Communion.[1]

From the nature of the case there was never anything like a distinct 'Coloured' national consciousness or pride of race. There is not even now any effective educational institution to provide for the Coloured People, as Lovedale, or its neighbouring Fort Hare (an incipient University), now does for the Natives. Even the ministry appears to find relatively few coloured recruits for work among their own people. Independency did its work. The ministers of an Established Church could with difficulty have fought as Independents did against a hostile public, and against a Government that was often more than indifferent to their ends. But Independency could hardly furnish a tradition, or give national cohesion against such odds as faced the successors of the 'Hottentots'. With no home base of their own, they have no social standing in the European life around them, but are helplessly suspended between white and black, and can only 'think' white. Many of the missionaries who know them best tell how even their girls are exposed to abnormal temptation by the well-established tradition among them that, though European barriers are rigid against even a taint of colour, a child of white parentage is rather an honour than a social disgrace. The coloured people are in the end a predominantly urban community of low-grade labourers. The old hostility to separate Hottentot institutions has been avenged, for it has worked itself out to make the Coloured People irrevocably a part of the European community.

Such measure of freedom as they have enjoyed is, however, justified by its fruits. The Coloured People have no political grievance, are proud of their rights, and, in spite of all disabilities, not only survive, but are definitely making upward progress. With every generation that passes, the new term, 'Eurafrican', becomes more and more an accurate description of a people who to-day number something more than half a million of the population of the Union. That more than 90 per cent of them still belong to the old Cape Colony is proof of their direct lineage from the old Hottentots or slaves, who are now slowly emerging from the urban slums to take their place in the economic and political life of the bigger South

[1] For example, the Magistrate of Swellendam has informed me that at Zuurbraak, where there is still a Coloured population of about 1500, 'the L.M.S. does not exist, the English and Dutch Missions being at work there'.

African society. Divorced long since from the land, they have
been forced into industrial occupations where many of them
have attained a 'respectable' position, making life harder for
Europeans by their competition, even in the skilled trades.
Yet the Europeans now accept them as a part of their system.
All recent restrictive legislation, designed for the 'segregation'
of the Natives, classes the 'Eurafricans' with the Europeans.
Perhaps only by the magic influence of the 'Cape Coloured'
parliamentary vote, it begins to be said that, since the
Europeans are in a special degree responsible for the lighter
hue of their skins, they must look to their privileges and well-
being. They are still complication enough of a sufficiently
diverse society. But because the Eurafricans belong mostly to
the Cape Colony, even the Northern provinces show a disposition to accept them at last as an inevitable part of the South
African whole. Their 'problem' is in a measure 'solved'.
So John Philip's work was not in vain; and while he sleeps on
in peace in a rather lonely grave over against the fire-blackened
ruins of the old Mission House at Hankey, South Africa may
yet be brought to make amends for the grievous wrong it has
done his memory.

The history of the development of the Hottentot into the
'Eurafrican' is of enormous social significance. To-day it
is the far more numerous 'Bantu' who are being uprooted
from the land and driven into the slums, to a life of crime and
vagrancy, which mark the first stages of the modern process
of 'industrialization'. Even while the descendants of the
'Hottentots' are being legally recognized as a 'civilized' people,
the old restrictions, and new, are being urged, in much the same
terms, as a cure for the 'lazy thieving vagabondage' of the
Natives; as if similar measures had not been tried, and failed,
in the eighteen-thirties. There is the old pathetic faith in the
efficacy of a Pass Law, and in new and more oppressive restrictions like a 'Colour Bar'.

If by general agreement the 'Eurafricans', with all their
manifest weaknesses, rank to-day as a civilized people, this is
the result not of the policy of restrictions, but of the measure of
freedom allowed them. The forces of civilization are triumph-
ing, at a cost, even over generations of slum life. Too little is
known of the process that has made the Eurafrican what he is.
It may still be possible to save the Bantu—and South Africa—
from the worst penalties of the slum stage in development; they
have their own race-pride, their own educational establishments, and they still have some homes on the land. But the

process is already too far advanced to prevent the Native peoples from proceeding towards some sort of European civilization. They may be helped; or like the Hottentots, they may be hindered, and by the heaping up of restrictions, driven from their peasant life, into conditions that must incidentally encourage race-mixture, and depressed into still greater dependence and social degradation.

'Our feet are', in truth, 'on the edge of an abyss.'[1] Politically, its European people are now in almost complete control of South African destinies, and the danger is that they look only to the well-being of the white people. But white South Africa must carry its child races along with it on the way of progress. There can be no vision of a 'Civilization' that will rest on a base of serfdom, and live. The policy for the future is to be judged according as it stands by those principles of Freedom which have been tried in some measure, and have not been found wanting.

[1]Words spoken to the Author in 1926 by General J. C. Smuts.

U

APPENDIX TO CHAPTER VIII

THE story of the Bantu peoples lies outside the scope of this book, but the traditional condemnation of Dr. Philip for the part he played in events connected with the Kafir War of 1835 calls for comment.

In the first place, his ' unwarrantable interference' (Cory, iii, p. 52) is alleged to have inflamed the Kafirs with so acute a sense of grievance as to drive them 'to attempt to regain by violence' some of the land they had lately lost. 'Peace', of a sort, had indeed followed the war of 1819; but not only was the 'paramountcy' of the chief Gaika very largely of Governor Somerset's making, and unacknowledged by the tribes generally; but in addition, the 1819 boundary itself was very ill-defined. In the prevailing uncertainty, it happened, on the one hand, that by an unexplained process the 'neutral' belt of 1819 had before 1834 become the 'Ceded Territory'; on the other, that the chief Maqomo was alternately admitted to and (finally in 1833) expelled from land about the Kat River. Partly, at least, in consequence of this chaos, cattle-lifting on one side and 'reprisals' on the other kept the Kafir frontier in a chronic state of unrest and alarm. At this point, thanks it may be to representations made by Fowell Buxton at Dr. Philip's instigation, Sir Benjamin D'Urban came out as Governor in January 1834 with definite orders to establish a more satisfactory frontier system. On the 20th of March the Governor wrote formally acknowledging a Memorial by Philip (whose suggestions were substantially acted upon in D'Urban's administration of Kafirland in the following year). But it was not till the 31st of May that the Governor summoned him to an interview, since 'the time is now come for me to take into my serious consideration the whole of the frontier system'. For the next few months D'Urban and Philip were in close and constant touch (though with such parade of secrecy that the facts have never yet come to light). In August, with the Governor's express sanction, Philip set out for the frontier to interview the chiefs and to prepare the way for the Governor, who was to follow in person to initiate a 'new system' by direct negotiation. While Philip was on the frontier in September and October things were even abnormally peaceful. Mrs. Philip, at whose house Lady D'Urban was a constant caller, wrote almost weekly to assure him that the Governor was about to start for the interior. Sir Benjamin, however, procrastinated, and in November Dr. Philip began his return journey to Cape Town. Thereupon, in November and December, instead of the looked-for pacific visit from the Governor, the Kafirs received unusually severe chastisement from a 'commando' under Colonel Somerset (notwithstanding the fact that 'the total amount of ammunition in the Government magazine was at its lowest ebb'—Cory, iii, p. 64). For the Kafirs to retaliate by invading the Colony was not surprising. Now Philip's consistent contention was, not that the Kafirs never stole cattle, but that there was no attempt at administrative control of an inherently difficult frontier situation, and his attempt to strengthen the civil administration was clearly frustrated by the precipitate action of Colonel Somerset, and by the incurable dilatoriness of Sir Benjamin D'Urban.

Secondly, till May at least Philip's letters were sufficiently restrained, and urged the Hottentots to do their duty for the defence of the Colony, deploring the 'mad folly of the poor Kafirs', and expressing complete confidence in the Governor. Then came D'Urban's May Proclamation, decreeing that the guilty chiefs be 'expelled for ever' from the newly annexed 'Province of Queen Adelaide'. Philip at once saw that such a settlement was not only impolitic, but in a military sense impracticable. In 1835, and in evidence before the Select Committee of 1836, as both earlier and later with regard to the Griquas, he urged the desirability of taking *administrative* control of the backward races and extending 'British institutions' even as far as Delagoa Bay. With greater prescience than any contemporary he saw the consequences likely to result from any serious encroachment on Native lands. D'Urban himself was soon fain to admit the impossibility of the policy of expulsion. His final settlement in September was a complete *volte-face*, for he accepted the chiefs as British subjects, with lands inside the new Province. But weak or muddled as he was, the Governor failed to emphasize his radical change of policy, and the famous Glenelg despatch of December 1835 was a commentary on the earlier May policy. Glenelg clearly left the Governor a certain discretion, while insisting on fuller information and answers to definite questions. D'Urban's reply was embodied in a portentous despatch *dated* 6th June 1836, but sent off only on 8th January 1837.   He failed to take the obvious means to secure a modification of Glenelg's first judgment.   Glenelg, for his part, in spite of the evidence laid before him by Fowell Buxton and the L.M.S., missed Philip's main point.   Considerations of expense made him incline to total abandonment rather than to the shouldering of the responsibilities of administration.   Meantime D'Urban, who was excusably rattled by Glenelg's first criticisms, took further umbrage at the appointment of Stockenström as Lieutenant-Governor, and plunged into precipitate withdrawal. Even Sir George Cory's evidence (iii, 326) justifies the deduction that the touchy incompetence and the unconscionable delays of the Governor himself were mainly responsible for the issue.

This view is borne out by Dr. Philip's attitude to the annexation of 'British Kafiraria' in 1847.   This was entirely in accordance with the views he had sponsored eleven years before.   Unhappily there was no one with Philip's clear vision to prevent the degeneration of 'Kaffraria' into the chaotic and congested 'Cis-Kei' described in my pamphlet *Land, Native, and Unemployment* (1924).

Index

Circuit Courts, 6, 40, 157; 'Black Circuit', 89-91, 159

Cis-Kei, 178

Clapham Sect, 58, 61 *n*., 217

Clark, James, 220

Cloete, Henry, 225 *n*.

Cole, Sir Lowry, 74, 96 *n*., 147, 219-20, 222, 226, 229 and *n*., 233-4

Colesberg, 269-70. See also *Tooverberg*

Collins Report 1809, 160, 167

Colonization, in South Africa, 11-14, 23-4; and Economic Imperialism, 11, 13; and the Dutch East India Company, 14-16, 19, 35, 84-6, 144; geographical influences upon, 15-19

'Colour Bar' Act 1926, 4, 288

Colour Question, world-wide bearing of, 10-11; traditional South African attitude to, 4, 24, 81-2, 126-8, 141-144, 150, 156 *n*., 163, 165, 167-9, 209, 236-7, 240-3, 288-9; influence of missionaries on development of, 37-8, 65-7, 87-8, 210, 247-9, 263-4; implications of Emancipation for, 81-2, 233; Dr. Philip's general attitude to, 171-4, 236-7,

278-9; Dr. Philip's views and his S. African critics, 174-8; policy dominated by economic considerations, 11, 176-8, 233, 270; missionary attitude towards, 236-7, 239, 245, 250; and legal equality in the Cape, 256-7, 264; present position in S. Africa, 4-5, 288-9

Columbia University, 99 and *n*.

Commercial Advertiser, 7, 61 *n*., 207, 231-2, 235, 252, 282. See also *Press*

Commissioners of Inquiry, Crown, 116-17, 123, 183-187; work of, 190-2; Press dispute with, 205-6; reforms of, 209, 214, 218

Constitution, see *Parliamentary Government*

Cory, Sir George E., 9, 96, 109 *n*.

Cradock, Sir John, 28, 147, 181

Cropper, James, 61 *n*., 226

Currency disorders, 40

Currie, Sir Walter, 280

Cuyler, Colonel, 106, 123, 128, 136, 138, 178, 182-3

Delagoa Bay, 192

de Mist, Commissary, 37, 144-145